AN EASTERN ORTHODOX VIEW OF PASCAL

MARY EFROSINI GREGORY

Light & Life Publishing Company
P.O. Box 26421
Minneapolis, Minnesota 55426-0421

An Eastern Orthodox View of Pascal
Mary Efrosini Gregory
Copyright © 2008

Cover Image Source: http://www.thocp.net/biographies/pascal_blaise.html

All rights reserved. No part of this book may be reproduced, stored in a retrieval system, or transmitted in any form or by any means, electronic, mechanical, photocopying, recording, or otherwise without the written permission of Light & Life Publishing Company.

ISBN 1-933654-15-5

Library of Congress Control Number: 2008926424

This book is dedicated to our Lord and Savior Jesus Christ.
He did so much for us,
I would like to do something to honor Him.

This study will provide the fragment numbers of Pascal's *Thoughts* (*Pensées*) according to the Brunschvicg, Lafuma, and Sellier numbering systems. Unless otherwise indicated, the English translation that appears in the body of this text will be that of W.F. Trotter, Brunschvicg numbering system (New York: P.F. Collier & Son, 1910). Biblical references will be according to the King James Version, unless otherwise indicated.

Table of Contents

Introduction 6

Christ's Fulfillment of Prophecy Proves His Divinity .. 48

Table of Messianic Prophecies Fulfilled in Christ 93

Christ's Miracles Prove His Divinity 115

The Holy Trinity in the Old Testament 180

Typology 196

Predestination vs. Free Will 214

Conclusion 279

Bibliography 285

Introduction

And in order that this agreement might not be taken

for an effect of chance,

it was necessary that this should be foretold.[1]
—Blaise Pascal, *Thoughts*

    Skeptics have asked throughout the ages and they still do today, "Is there any scientific, mathematical, empirical proof that God exists?" The objective of this study is to demonstrate that the answer is a resounding, "Yes," and that Blaise Pascal does provide evidence to answer this question. Pascal's genius resides in his ability to prove the existence of God using probability theory as a tool: because he was a brilliant scientist and mathematician, he was able to demonstrate that the fulfillment of hundreds of Messianic prophecies in the person of one man, Jesus Christ, the historicity of miracles, the unity of the OT and New (ie: evidence of the Holy Trinity in the OT and types), all fall outside the realm of statistical probability and that therefore, they provide clear evidence of the Will of God. The first five chapters of this study will examine in detail these proofs based on probability theory. We believe that Pascal's evidence does substantiate the thesis that God exists.

    However, Pascal's personal brand of theology, Jansenism, based on Augustine, is erroneous in its tenet that God predestines people to believe or disbelieve and that they have no free will in the matter. His Augustinian belief system holds that God chooses to impart irresistible efficacious grace to some, but not to others: those who receive it, believe and are saved, while those who do not, remain in unbelief and are damned. This tenet, as Pierre Force points out in *The Hermeneutical Problem in Pascal's Writing* (*Le Problème herméneutique chez Pascal*), leads to a vicious cycle out of which there is no escape: a person believes (receives grace) by reading the Bible, but he needs God's gift of grace in order to understand Scripture.[2] For this reason, the last chapter of this study will offer an alternative to the Augustinians' flawed theology: this alternative, which sets forth a logical plan for God's redemption based on the original texts of Hebrew and Greek Scriptures, comes from a different tradition, one generally unfamiliar to Western Christianity, and which was foreign to Pascal: that of the Eastern

Orthodox Church. Hence, the title of this book. The Augustinians' doctrine of the election of the damned was based on a Latin mistranslation of the Greek verse of Rom 5:12 and this error will be examined in detail.

Pascal was a mathematical and scientific prodigy and also a man of devout faith who had had a personal encounter with the Living God one night. Combining the two great loves of his life, God and mathematics, he set out to provide evidence that in any court of law, would prove beyond the shadow of a doubt, that God exists, that He is one God comprised of three distinct persons, the Father, the Son, and the Holy Spirit, and that He sent His only beloved Son, Jesus, to suffer and die for the redemption of man.

Pascal believed that faith is a gift of God: the Christian apologist can employ reason to appeal to the skeptic's mind, but only God can put conviction in his heart. Therefore, he used the logic of probability theory to appeal to the skeptic's mind and entice him to open up a Bible and search Scripture for the plethora of Messianic prophecies that it contains. His goal was to intrigue the unbeliever to the point where he would begin to compare the Old Testament with the New, look for the fulfillment of prophecies in Jesus Christ and find them, and see the unity of the OT with the New; then he would pray that God would plant the seed of faith in the skeptic's heart.

The Man of Science

Pascal understood logic and reason more than most men did: he was an especially gifted scientist and mathematician. He attempted his first treatise on acoustics as soon as he could write; by age 12, he proved Euclid's theorems by himself and also composed a treatise on the communication of sounds; by age 16 he wrote a significant work on the geometry of conical sections, the *Essay on Conics* (*Essai pour les coniques*), which included his famous theorem on hexagons (called Pascal's Theorem or the Mystic Hexagram). Between the ages of 19-21 he invented a calculator to help his father, who was the chief tax officer in Normandy's capital city, Rouen, with his job computing taxes. His calculator, called the "Pascaline," was a long narrow box containing eight cylinders (each bearing printed numbers zero to nine), wheels, and gears. Eight movable dials added sums of a maximum of eight figures. When the wheel in the units column moved ten notches, the dial in the tens column moved one notch; when the dial in the tens column

Introduction

moved ten notches, the dial in the hundreds column moved one notch, and so on. The machine both added and subtracted. In addition, Pascal's legacy includes experiments he conducted that prove the existence of vacuum, contrary to Aristotle's belief that nature does not tolerate vacuums; he proved that there is a vacuum above the atmosphere; he produced important theorems on projective geometry; he discovered the principle that is the basis of the hydraulic press, called Pascal's Law of Pressure. Pascal's Law states that when there is an increase in pressure at any point in a confined liquid, there is an increase equal at every other point in the container (in other words, that incompressible fluid transmits pressure). In addition, he corresponded with Pierre Fermat and together they laid down the foundations of probability theory; he was able to advise gamblers how to win at games of chance; he devised Pascal's Triangle (used in algebra and in probability where it is applied to find combinations); he produced a work on the cycloid (the curve traced by a point on the circumference or radius of a circle rolling along a straight line); he devised a primitive version of the roulette wheel, as a result of his attempt to create a perpetual motion machine (*perpetuum mobile*); he invented the wristwatch-he tied his pocket watch to his wrist with a piece of string and transformed it into a wristwatch. His contributions to science have been recognized in the naming of the unit of atmospheric pressure and a computer language after him. The pascal (Pa) is the unit of atmospheric pressure that is the force of one newton acting on a surface area of one square meter. Pascal, the computer language, is named after him in honor of his invention of the calculator: in 1972 computer scientist Nicklaus Wirth insisted that his new computer language not be spelled in capitals, as are other computer languages, but rather, "Pascal," in honor of the inventor of the calculator.

In addition, during the last year of his life, in 1662, Pascal devised the first mass transit system. Acknowledging that only those with wealth could afford to own horses and buggies for traveling around Paris, Pascal set out to meet the needs of the poor. He and his associates formed a company that owned several horse-drawn carriages. The plan was that for a modest fee, they would transport many passengers in these public conveyances along a set route throughout the day; all profits would be donated to charity. Hence, Pascal used his genius to help humanity right up until he died.

Witness to Miracles

However, there was another side of this man of scientific and mathematical genius: he was a devout Christian and mystic whose life was transformed by a spiritual encounter with God and numerous miracles that he had witnessed at the Cistercian abbey of Port Royal. Pascal did not merely believe in the existence of God: he was sure of it. He was privileged to have witnessed several miracles with his own eyes, first hand, just as the apostles had done during Christ's 3 ½ year ministry and again after His Resurrection. There were at least eighty miracles that were said to have occurred at Port Royal.

The spiritual encounter with God occurred on November 23, 1654. Pascal underwent a conversion during what he called a night of fire that last two hours, from 10:30 PM until 12:30 AM. During this time his soul experienced God as fire. He recorded on parchment the spiritual ecstasy that he experienced. This text, called "The Memorial," reads in part, "Fire. 'God of Abraham, God of Isaac, God of Jacob,' not of philosophers and scholars. Certainty, certainty, heartfelt, joy, peace. God of Jesus Christ. God of Jesus Christ. *My God and your God*…'O righteous Father, the world has not known thee, but I have known thee.' Joy, joy, joy, tears of joy."[3]

Pascal was so deeply impacted by this "night of fire," he resolved to renounce his greatest loves in life, mathematics and physics, and to put aside all of the scientific and mathematical discoveries that he had made in order to embrace the life of the mystic. He resolved to carry out the Great Commission in his own way, using the gifts that God had given him: he set out to write a book about his faith, one that would prove, once and for all, that of all the religions in the world, Christianity alone is the one true religion. His new objective in life was to persuade skeptics that God does indeed exist, that He had announced through the Jewish prophets that He would come to earth through the line of David, and that the New Testament contains the fulfillment of these prophecies. Unfortunately, Pascal was sickly most of his life and he died at age 39; his book was never completed, but remained as a sequence of fragments.

There was another great event that occurred in Pascal's life, a miracle that further concretized his deep Christian conviction. This miracle is related by his sister, Gilberte Périer, in her biography of her brother, *The Life of Mr.*

Introduction

Pascal (*La Vie de M. Pascal*). In her work, Gilberte recounts the miracle of her daughter's cure of a serious debilitating disease. Her little girl was not only Pascal's niece, but also his goddaughter. Gilberte's daughter had suffered from a lachrymal fistula that had grown so rapidly in 3½ years, pus oozed out of not only the girl's eye, but from her nose and mouth, as well. The finest surgeons in Paris judged the growth to be incurable. However, on March 24, 1656, she was miraculously cured the moment a Holy Thorn from the Crown of Thorns worn by Christ was held against her eye. This miracle was declared to be authentic not only by everyone who had seen the girl before and after the cure, but it was also attested to by the best doctors and the most accomplished surgeons of France, and was officially declared to be a miracle by the Archbishop of Paris in 1656.[4]

Gilberte says that her brother was so deeply moved by God's mercy on his niece, that it was as if he had been cured himself. His joy was so great, he wanted to proclaim the Christian faith to all the world and refute the principles and false reasoning of atheists. Having witnessed this miracle, Pascal resolved to study the works of unbelievers with great care so that he could find errors in their logic and convince them of the truth.[5] He also made a seal depicting a crown of thorns from which emanate rays of light. Beneath was the motto "Scio cui credidi" ("I know whom I have believed") (2 Tim 1:12). He sewed this seal to his clothing and wore it the rest of his life.

The Miracle of the Holy Thorn, that Blaise had personally witnessed, provided even more proof that everything in the New Testament was true: the gates of death have been rendered powerless through Christ's sacrifice and, as He promised, He went ahead to prepare a place in Heaven for those who believe in Him. God was a personal God who was involved in human affairs, not the God of philosophers, who was hypothesized to have set the universe in motion and then remain uninvolved. Now he had physical proof that God existed and he wanted to tell the world. Blaise also felt the conviction in his heart that the miracle was a sign of God's election of not only himself, but of the entire Jansenist community. He extrapolated that he, who embraced predestination, must have found favor with God, and he had the duty to illuminate the hierarchy of the Catholic Church through his writing. During the course of this study Pascal's heretical views and false assumptions about double predestination will be examined in detail and it will be demonstrated that his notion of the election of the damned is antithetical to statements that Christ, Himself, made about his intentions and purpose on earth.

In the months following the miraculous cure of Marguerite Périer, the number of miracles attributed to the Holy Thorn at Port Royal increased to 14, and then to 80. These miracles caused Pascal to reflect on their significance. Pascal carefully examined the miracles in the Old and New Testaments and extrapolated that a causality exists between miracles and religious truth. In *Thoughts* (*Pensées*), he argues that one of the purposes of miracles, since the time of the apostles, has been to differentiate true doctrine from false. The Jansenists of the Port Royal community regarded the numerous miracles of the Holy Thorn as proof that God approved of their doctrine of irresistible efficacious grace and that He was on their side in their dispute with the King, the Pope, and the Jesuits regarding predestination.

The question arises as to how the Cistercian abbey of Port Royal had come to acquire a Holy Thorn from the Crown of Thorns worn by Christ during the Crucifixion. The abbey also claimed to have obtained a piece of the True Cross. There is enough information in history books to indicate that it is, indeed, quite possible that the abbey had obtained a true Holy Thorn.

Three of the four gospel writers, Matthew, Mark, and John, testify that the Roman soldiers had placed the Crown of Thorns on Christ's head. John recalls:

> Then Pilate therefore took Jesus, and scourged him. And the soldiers plaited a crown of thorns, and put it on his head, and they put on him a purple robe, And said, Hail, King of the Jews! and they smote him with their hands. Pilate therefore went forth again, and saith unto them, Behold, I bring him forth to you, that ye may know that I find no fault in him. Then came Jesus forth, wearing the crown of thorns, and the purple robe. And Pilate saith unto them, Behold the man!"[6]

Introduction

The fact that Christ wore a Crown of Thorns is highly symbolic. Gen 3:18 says, "thorns also and thistles shall it bring forth to thee." God spoke this to Adam immediately after his disobedience when He cursed the ground. Thereafter, thorns in the Bible came to symbolize sin. Christ, who was the perfect sacrifice, bore the sins of the world although He, Himself, was without sin. Hence, the Crown of Thorns, worn by Christ, symbolizes humanity's sin that Christ bore.

Textual evidence indicates that after the Crucifixion, the Crown of Thorns was kept in a safe place in Jerusalem, where it was venerated until the 9th century. The *Catholic Encyclopedia* advises:

> ...our Saviour's Crown of Thorns is mentioned by three Evangelists and is often alluded to by the early Christian Fathers, such as Clement of Alexandria, Origen, and others... St. Paulinus of Nola, writing after 409, refers to "the thorns with which Our Saviour was crowned" as relics held in honour along with the Cross to which He was nailed and the pillar at which He was scourged (Ep. ad Macar. in Migne, P.L., LXI, 407). Cassiodorus (c. 570), when commenting on Ps. lxxxvi, speaks of the Crown of Thorns among the other relics which are the glory of the earthly Jerusalem. "There," he says, "we may behold the thorny crown, which was only set upon the head of Our Redeemer in order that all the thorns of the world might be gathered together and broken" (Migne, P.L., LXX, 621)...the "Breviarus" and the "Itinerary" of Antoninus of Piacenza, both of the sixth century, clearly state that the Crown of Thorns was at that period shown in the church upon Mount Sion (Geyer, Itinera Hierosolymitana, 154 and 174). From these fragments of evidence and others of later date-the "Pilgrimage" of the monk Bernard shows that the relic was still at Mount Sion in 870-it is certain that what purported to be the Crown of Thorns was venerated at Jerusalem for several hundred years.
>
> If we may adopt the conclusion of M. de Mély, the whole Crown was only transferred to Byzantium about 1063, although it seems that smaller portions must have been

presented to the Eastern emperors at an earlier date. In any case Justinian, who died in 565, is stated to have given a thorn to St. Germanus, Bishop of Paris, which was long preserved at Saint-Germain-des Prés, while the empress Irene, in 798 or 802, sent Charlemagne several thorns which were deposited by him at Aachen. Eight of these are known to have been there at the consecration of the basilica of Aachen by Pope Leo III, and the subsequent history of several of them can be traced without difficulty. Four were given to Saint-Corneille of Compiègne in 877 by Charles the Bald. One was sent by Hugh the Great to the Anglo-Saxon King Athelstan in 927 on the occasion of certain marriage negotiations, and eventually found its way to Malmesbury Abbey. Another was presented to a Spanish princess about 1160, and again another was taken to Andechs in Germany in the Year 1200.

In 1238 Baldwin II, the Latin Emperor of Constantinople, anxious to obtain support for his tottering empire, offered the Crown of Thorns to St. Louis, King of France. It was then actually in the hands of the Venetians as security for a heavy loan, but it was redeemed and conveyed to Paris where St. Louis built the Sainte-Chapelle (completed in 1248) for its reception. There the great relic remained until the Revolution, when, after finding a home for a while in the Bibliothèque Nationale, it was eventually restored to the Church and was deposited in the Cathedral of Notre-Dame in 1806. Ninety years later (in 1896) a magnificent new reliquary of rock crystal was made for it, covered for two-thirds of its circumference with a silver case splendidly wrought and jeweled.[7]

Hence, it is quite possible that Port Royal really did come into possession of a true Holy Thorn. It is also plausible that the thorn that the abbey had acquired was not one from the Crown of Thorns, but rather, one that had touched an original Holy Thorn. In any event, the 80 or so cures that had occurred through it bolstered the faith of the people residing in the Port Royal community and all those who heard of them. The miracles also

Introduction

caused people to believe that the Jansenists, who embraced predestination, had found favor with God.

Reason vs. the Heart

Pascal wrote his Christian apology working on the premise that reason does not need to be the enemy of the heart: it could be a conduit leading straight to it. Recognizing this to be a fact, he declares, "Faith is different from proof; the one is human, the other is a gift of God…It is this faith that God Himself puts into the heart, of which the proof is often the instrument."[8] Hence, Pascal held that proof can be an instrument that leads to faith. The task, then, for the apologist, who can hope to do only the best that a human can do, is to offer the skeptic proof and pray that God will use it as an instrument by which He implants the seed of faith in the skeptic's heart.

Pascal also believed that it is God who implants reason into the mind. Therefore, when the apologist tries to appeal to the skeptic's reason, he is hoping to be the instrument by which God's will is done. Pascal observes, "The conduct of God, who disposes all things kindly, is to put religion into the mind by reason, and into the heart by grace."[9] Here God does things in a gentle way and Pascal urges the Christian apologist, who wants to do God's will and bring people to faith, to do it with gentleness and with respect, not by force, threats or fear: "But to will to put it into the mind and heart by force and threats is not to put religion there, but terror."[10] He states that God is the one who "puts religion into the mind by reason" and "into the heart by grace." Pascal advocates ministering to the whole person: to the rational part and to the intuitive part. Again, since God imparts the gift of faith, the most that the apologist can do is appeal to the mind.

Pascal establishes that thought is the source of dignity. Man is weak and vulnerable in hostile nature; he is merely a reed, but a thinking reed. This ability to think is what makes man a noble creature. Man is nobler than the universe, because even though a drop of water could kill a man, the universe would be ignorant of it because it (the universe) is inanimate. Therefore, even though the universe is expansive and has the power of death, it is mindless and without consciousness, and hence, not as noble as man.[11] Here Pascal is taking a jab at Spinoza's pantheism: the universe is not conscious, it is inanimate and insensate; pantheism is a false religion. Therefore, as small and powerless as man is, he is superior to the universe. This is because God created man in His image and gave him consciousness and reason.

Man's nobility lies in his ability to think. This is Pascal's eulogy to reason and to the faculties of the mind: "All our dignity consists, then, in thought. By it we must elevate ourselves, and not by space and time which we cannot fill. Let us endeavour, then, to think well; this is the principle of morality."[12]

The Goal of this study

This study has two objectives. First, it will examine Pascal's use of probability theory to prove that the fulfillment of hundreds of Messianic prophecies in the person of one man, Jesus Christ, the historicity of miracles, and the unity between the OT and New (ie: textual evidence of the Holy Trinity in the OT and typology), clearly fall outside the realm of random chance and therefore, are proofs of Christ and of the existence of Divine Will. Secondly, this study will expose the heresies inherent in Pascal's notion of double predestination and provide a thoroughly reasonable alternative to understanding Scripture, one that provides a blueprint not only of God's plan for man's redemption from sin, but also for his theosis (divinization), as taught by the Eastern Orthodox Church and substantiated by Holy Scripture.

This work will be divided into six chapters. The first five will address Pascal's key proofs that Christianity is the one true religion on earth; the last, chapter 6, will shine a halogen lamp on Pascal's notion of the election of the damned and uncover the lies and heresies inherent therein. The court of arbitration will be the teachings of the Orthodox Church, which has remained untouched by the schisms of the West and whose scholars explain why the election of the damned is antithetical to Scripture as well as to statements that Christ Himself made about His intention and purpose on earth. These chapters will be entitled:

1. Christ's Fulfillment of Prophecy Proves His Divinity
2. Table of Messianic Prophecies Fulfilled in Christ
3. Christ's Miracles Prove His Divinity

Introduction

4. The Holy Trinity in the Old Testament
5. Typology
6. Predestination vs. Free Will

Taken together, these six chapters will illustrate Pascal's use of reason and logic to offer reality-based evidence of God's existence and of Christ's divinity based on probability theory, the historicity of miracles, and the agreement of both Testaments; this study will also examine his heresies and provide an eminently reasonable alternative to Jansenism based on Orthodoxy and the original Hebrew and Greek texts of Holy Scripture.

Overview

Pascal recognized that the three greatest proofs of Christ's Messianic identity are His fulfillment of hundreds of biblical prophecies, miracles (those that He performed as well as those that have continued throughout the centuries), and the unity of the OT and New. Chapter 1 ("Christ's Fulfillment of Prophecy Proves His Divinity") examines Pascal's use of probability theory as a polemical tool to refute the argument of atheists that everything in the universe is the result of random chance. Pascal demonstrates that the fact that one man fulfilled hundreds of Messianic prophecies lies outside the realm of statistical probability and provides rational, mathematical proof that the will of an Intelligent Being is at work.

First, God announces in advance that He will establish a new covenant, one that surpasses the old one in its intent and purpose: the objective of this new covenant will be to inscribe the law in people's hearts, ensure that the whole world will know the One True God, and forgive people their sins: "Behold, the days come, saith the LORD, that I will make a new covenant with the house of Israel, and with the house of Judah: Not according to the covenant that I made with their fathers in the day that I took them by the hand to bring them out of the land of Egypt...But this shall be the covenant that I will make with the house of Israel; After those days, saith the LORD, I will put my law in their inward parts, and write it in their hearts; and will be their God, and they shall be my people. And they shall teach no more every man his neighbour, and every man his brother, saying Know the LORD: for they shall all know me, from the least of them unto the greatest of them, saith the LORD: for I will forgive their iniquity, and I will remember their sin no more" (Jer 31:31-34). The key concepts here are that God will establish a new covenant ("I will make a new covenant"), that sins will be forgiven forever ("I will forgive their iniquity, and I will remember their sin no more"), that this time, the Law will be inscribed in people's minds and hearts, in their conscience ("I will put my law in their inward parts, and write it in their hearts"), and that paganism will end and the whole world will worship the One True God: ("And they shall teach no more every man his neighbour, and every man his brothers, saying, Know the LORD: for they shall all know me, from the least of them unto the greatest of them").

The prophet Isaiah explains that the Messiah will restore the God-man relationship that existed before Adam disobeyed by bearing the sins of His people: "But he was wounded for our transgressions, he was bruised for our iniquities…with his stripes we are healed" (Is 53:5). In fact, Isaiah states seven times in one chapter (53) that the reason that the Messiah will suffer is because He will bear the sins of others so that they may be forgiven vicariously through His punishment: "Surely he hath borne our griefs, and carried our sorrows" (Is 53:4); "But he was wounded for our transgressions, he was bruised for our iniquities: the chastisement of our peace was upon him; and with his stripes we are healed" (Is 53:5); "All we like sheep have gone astray; we have turned every one to his own way; and the LORD hath laid on him the iniquity of us all" (Is 53:6); "for the transgression of my people was he stricken" (Is 53:8); "when thou shalt make his soul an offering for sin, he shall see his seed, he shall prolong his days, and the pleasure of the LORD shall prosper in his hand" (Is 53:10); "by his knowledge shall my righteous servant justify many; for he shall bear their iniquities" (Is 53:11); "he bare the sin of many, and made intercession for the transgressors" (Is 53:12). Furthermore, Isaiah provides an analogy with the sacrifice of the lamb during Yom Kippur: "He was oppressed, and he was afflicted, yet he opened not his mouth: he is brought as a lamb to the slaughter, and as a sheep before her shearers is dumb, so he openeth not his mouth." Christ, who was without sin, was the perfect sacrifice and His sacrifice was foreshadowed by the sacrifice of the red heifer in Num 19. The red heifer was a unique sacrifice, unlike any other, one that was special and

Introduction

set apart from the rest. For example, it had to have been red and must never have had a yoke placed on it.

Moreover, we find that biblical prophecies are striking in the depth of their detail of Christ's Crucifixion. For example, "I am poured out like water, and all my bones are out of joint: my heart is like wax; it is melted in the midst of my bowels" (Ps 22:14) provides is a high definition laser print of a man whose lungs have collapsed. During crucifixion, the arms, which support the weight of the body, are stretched upward; respiratory muscles become paralyzed; the lungs collapse; the victim undergoes gradual suffocation. The biological precision of the description, uttered by David centuries before the fact, is too significant to ignore. In addition, this prophecy is articulated from the point of view of someone who is elevated on a cross and is looking down at those who have pierced him: "they look up and stare upon me" (Ps 22:17).

There are two OT verses that specify that the Messiah would be pierced: "For dogs have compassed me: the assembly of the wicked have inclosed me: they pierced my hands and my feet" (Ps 22:16); "and they shall look upon me whom they have pierced, and they shall mourn for him, as one mourneth for his only son" (Zech 12:10).

There are hundreds of more prophecies that Christ fulfilled. Among them are that the Messiah would be born in Bethlehem, would be preceded by a messenger, enter Jerusalem on a donkey, be betrayed by a friend, be sold for thirty pieces of silver, that this blood money would be thrown to the potter in God's house, that He would be silent before His accusers, crucified as a thief, that He would rise from the dead on the third day, that He would be a light to the Gentiles, and that He would be exalted among the heathen.

Pascal had a formidable command of the Bible and cites a vast wealth of prophecies that Jesus fulfilled. Pascal the rationalist reminds the reader on several occasions that the fulfillment of so many prophecies by one person is not the result of random chance, but rather, the will of God: "And what crowns all this is prediction, so that it should not be said that it is chance which has done it";[13] "And in order that this agreement might not be taken for an effect of chance, it was necessary that this should be foretold";[14] "I foretold it long since that they might know that it is I (Is 48:5)."[15] Pascal also reaches beyond the Bible and examines prophecies in the Talmud, commentaries by Moses Maimonides, and even the mystical utterings of the pagan world recorded by Plutarch. We will examine the Messianic prophecy, "Great Pan is dead" in Plutarch's *The Obsolescence of Oracles* in *Moralia* (4.17), cited by Pascal.[16] Christian apologists understand "Great Pan is dead" as a Messianic prophecy coming from the pagan Gentile world that announced the end of paganism and the ushering in of a new era of the grace of the One True God.

Pascal also cleverly demonstrates that an omnipotent God was able to execute His will on earth even through the actions of unbelievers: he points out that the pagans Herod and Augustus Caesar unwittingly participated in the fulfillment of Messianic prophecy.[17] When Herod ordered the slayings of the children in Bethlehem, aged two years and under, he unwittingly fulfilled the prophecy that lamentation and bitter weeping would be heard in Ramah and Rahel would refuse to be comforted because her children were no more. Herod also fulfilled another OT prophecy: because Herod was killing children in Bethlehem, Joseph took Mary and Jesus to Egypt and they stayed there until an angel told them that it was safe to return. Hence, Herod was instrumental in the fulfillment of the prophecy "I...called my son out of Egypt." Moreover, despite all of Herod's efforts to kill Jesus, he was unable to stop the fulfillment of the prophecy that a ruler would come out of Bethlehem Ephratah, one "whose goings forth have been from of old, from everlasting."

Pascal also points out that another pagan, Augustus Caesar, unwittingly fulfilled biblical prophecy when he issued a decree that all the world be taxed. This was the reason that Joseph and Mary left Nazareth and journeyed to Bethlehem-they went there to be registered and taxed. Hence, Christ was born in Bethlehem, in fulfillment of prophecy.

Pascal, having painstakingly conducted extensive research, demonstrates that the fact that one man has fulfilled hundreds of Messianic prophecies to the utmost minutia lies outside the realm of statistical probability and clearly points to the Will of God. He declares that the greatest proofs of Christ are the prophecies.[18] He points out that a succession of men over 4,000 years announced the same event.[19] These people were born in various time periods and did not know each other, but they had visions and dreams and prophecized about the same event, each time offering specific

Introduction

information that, taken together, provided the life history, mission, and purpose of the Messiah.

Pascal cites numerous OT verses in which God explains that He will announce important events before they happen through the prophets so that the wise would watch for them and be able to identify them when they do occur. He cites the verses in which God advises that He will declare the end from the beginning, and from ancient times things that are not yet done because he wants people to know that He, God, has done these things and that it is not the work of idols (Is 48:3, 5). Pascal uses this argument, but modifies it to demonstrate that the fact that God announces events ahead of time proves that these occurrences, when they do happen, are not the work of random chance, but rather of Divine Will. Pascal has an excellent command of the Bible and cites a vast wealth of the passages in which God reiterates that he will warn people of events well in advance of their arrival.

Pascal also points out the plethora of prophecies in which God reiterates that He would extend His grace to the pagan Gentile world and that it, too, would one day glorify Him. There is an abundance of references in the OT to the salvation of the Gentiles: the calling of the Gentiles, the shaking of all nations, the desire of all nations would come, the isles shall wait for His law, He would be a light of the Gentiles, He would bring those that sit in darkness out of the prison house, He would bring the blind by a way that they knew not and lead them in paths that they have not known, those who trust in graven images would be ashamed and they would turn back, God would give Him for a light to the Gentiles and He would be His salvation to the ends of the earth, kings and princes would arise and worship Him, He would establish the earth and inherit the desolate heritages, they will come to Him from afar, from the north and east and the southern most part of Egypt, he will sprinkle many nations, kings will shut their mouths at him, idolatry will be overthrown, he will give strangers and eunuchs in his house a name better than of sons and daughters, He will give them an everlasting name and they will not be cut off, the Gentiles will come to His light and kings to the brightness of His rising, the forces of the Gentiles will come unto Him. God foretells that He will establish a new covenant: new wine will be found in the cluster and it should not be destroyed because there is a blessing in it.

Pascal also brings to the reader's attention the fact that Christianity has transformed the whole world in the areas of philosophy, religion, ethics, but more importantly, in the minds and hearts of believers themselves. Citing Joel 2:28, he declares, *"I will pour out my spirit...*The whole world now became fervent with love. Princes abandoned their pomp; maidens suffered martyrdom. Whence came this influence? The Messiah was come. These were the effect and signs of His coming."[20] The Holy Spirit indwells the believer and makes him a new creation: man turns away from sin and is renewed and regenerated; man becomes more like Christ and reflects His image (ie: His obedience to the Father). Hence, the foundations of Mosaic Law-holiness, love and virtue-are inscribed in the heart of every believer. Moreover, cowards become brave and are willing to be martyred for Christ because they are certain that His kingdom awaits them and that it is far superior to this temporal world.

Pascal finds it significant that God preserved the Book of Ruth and the story of Tamar and he holds them up as additional proofs of Christ. Pascal asks, "Why was the book of Ruth preserved? Why the story of Tamar?"[21] The answer is because Christ was a descendant of Ruth and also of Tamar, who were both two virtuous Gentiles. Ruth, a Moabitess, married Boaz and bore Obed; thus she was the great-grandmother of David (Ruth 4:13-22) and an ancestor of Jesus (Mat 1:5). The *NIV Study Bible* points out that it is significant that a Gentile was an ancestor of Christ-Ruth is an iconic representation of the fact that the Gentile world, through the saving blood of Christ, is grafted unto the tree of Israel: "She strikingly exemplifies the truth that participation into the coming kingdom of God is decided, not by blood and birth, but by the conformity of one's life to the will of God through the 'obedience that comes from faith' (Rom 1:5). Her place in the ancestry of David signifies that all nations will be represented in the kingdom of David's greater Son"[22]

Pascal also finds it significant that the story of Tamar was preserved. In order to understand why Tamar was considered to be a virtuous woman according to the Law, one must examine Deut 25:5. Here, God ordains that if a man dies without leaving a son, his brother is required to marry the widow he leaves behind so that she may bear him a son and carry on the family name. This is called a levirate marriage, from the Latin *levir*, meaning brother-in-

Introduction

law. In the story of Tamar (Gen 38:1-10), Tamar marries two men, first Er, who dies without leaving a son, and then Onan, his brother, who also dies without leaving a son. Their father, Judah, has a third surviving son, Shelah, and he promises him to her when he grows up. However, after Shelah does become an adult, Judah does not give him to her. Tamar disguises herself as a prostitute and tricks Judah into fathering children with her. When he learns that the children she is bearing are his, he exclaims, "She hath been more righteous than I; because that I gave her not to Shelah my son" (Gen 38:26).

Tamar carried twins, Perez and Zerah. When she was delivering them, Zerah put his hand out first and the midwife took a scarlet thread and tied it on his wrist. Then he withdrew his hand and his brother, Perez, was born first. Perez was to be an ancestor of David and ultimately, of Christ.

In asking the questions, "Why was the book of Ruth preserved? Why the story of Tamar?" Pascal is pointing out the importance of virtue and the extension of God's saving grace to the whole world. Both Ruth and Tamar were virtuous Gentiles and demonstrated obedience to the Law. It shows that God's presence in the Tabernacle was to go out to the entire world, in the person of Christ, who is our Tabernacle; God intended to offer everlasting life to the entire world regardless of ethnicity or race.

We will also examine the stunning accuracy of the timetable of the Messiah's appearance that is given by the prophet Daniel in Dan 9:25-26 and Pascal's discussion of it.[23] Pascal attempts to clarify the meaning of the prophecy, but he admits that he cannot because chronologists have differing opinions as to the "time of the commencement" or the year that the commandment went out to restore Jerusalem and rebuild the Temple. Although Pascal could not decipher Daniel's timetable, someone else has: in the 20th century, Grant R. Jeffrey has and we shall see that Jeffrey fulfilled Pascal's dream of solving the enigma. It is quite impressive that Jeffrey is able to employ Daniel's books of weeks to extrapolate that the first Palm Sunday, when the Messiah appeared (entered Jerusalem triumphantly on the back of a donkey) occurred in 32 AD.[24] Because the Orthodox Church teaches that Christ was crucified in 33 AD, we conclude that Jeffrey was only one year off in his calculations. His math is impressive, to say the least, and Pascal would have been proud of him because he managed to accomplish what he, himself, had attempted, but could not.

Chapter 2 ("Table of Messianic Prophecies Fulfilled in Christ") provides a bird's eye view at a glance of some of the vast abundance of Messianic prophecies that Christ fulfilled; it also shows Pascal's formidable command of the Bible, as he had labored diligently to cite as many as possible. The four columns of the Table indicate the chapter and verse of each Messianic prophecy, the KJV text, Pascal's commentary in quotation marks or else a very brief recapitulation of his criticism, and the Brunschvicg, Lafuma, and Sellier fragment numbers where the main idea is expressed. It must be pointed out that Pascal does not always cite the correct chapter and verse; nor does he provide the exact language of the Bible, but often paraphrases it. Therefore, the fragment numbers shown in the Table identify where the general concept of the prophecy is found in *Thoughts*.

The precision of Messianic prophecies that the OT provides is stunning: Bethlehem will be His birthplace; virgin birth; hands and feet pierced; they cast lots for His clothing; He would be given gall and vinegar to drink; resurrection on the third day; calling of the Gentiles; unto us a child is born, unto us a son is given: and the government shall be upon his shoulder: and his name shall be called Wonderful, Counsellor, the mighty God, the everlasting Father, the Prince of Peace; I gave my back to the smiters, and my cheeks to them that plucked off the hair: I hid not my face from shame and spitting; will be given for a covenant of the people; inherit the desolate heritages; visage was marred more than any man; will sprinkle many nations; He is despised and rejected of men; a man of sorrows, and acquainted with grief: and we hid as it were our faces from him; he was despised, and we esteemed him not; Surely he hath borne our griefs, and carried our sorrows: yet we did esteem him stricken, smitten of God, and afflicted; But he was wounded for our transgressions; he was bruised for our iniquities: the chastisement of our peace was upon him; and with his stripes we are healed; All we like sheep have gone astray; we have turned every one to his own way; and the LORD hath laid on him the iniquity of us all; He was oppressed and he was afflicted, yet he opened not his mouth: he is brought as a lamb to the slaughter, and as a sheep before her shearers is dumb, so he openeth not his mouth; he was taken from prison and from judgment; he was cut off out of the land of the living; he made his grave with the wicked, and with the rich in his death; made his soul an offering for

Introduction

sin; he shall prolong his days; he bare the sin of many; he hath sent me to bind up the brokenhearted; as the new wine is found in the cluster, and one saith, Destroy it not; for a blessing is in it; descendant of Jacob; I will cause the sun to go down at noon, and I will darken the earth in the clear day; I will make it as the mourning of an only son; the King cometh unto thee: he is just and having salvation; lowly, and riding upon an ass, and upon a colt the foal of an ass; they weighed for my price thirty pieces of silver; cast it unto the potter; I took the thirty pieces of silver, and cast them to the potter in the house of the LORD; they shall look upon me whom they have pierced, and they shall mourn for him, as one mourneth for his only son; my name shall be great among the Gentiles; I will send my messenger, and he shall prepare the way before me; he will ascend to heaven to sit at the right hand; he will sit on the right hand of the father; and the kings of the earth and all nations will worship him. It is remarkable that these prophecies provide razor sharp images of the events in Christ's life. It is equally astounding that they were uttered centuries before they happened (in the 8th century BC, in the case of Isaiah).

In fact, Ps 22:13-18 is so precise, it gives the reader the impression that the speaker is elevated on a cross, high above the ground, looking down at his enemies: "They gaped upon me with their mouths, as a ravening and a roaring lion. I am poured out like water, and all my bones are out of joint: my heart is like wax; it is melted in the midst of my bowels. My strength is dried up like a potsherd; and my tongue cleaveth to my jaws; and thou hast brought me into the dust of death. For dogs have compassed me: the assembly of the wicked have inclosed me: they pierced my hands and my feet. I may tell all my bones: they look up and stare upon me. They part my garments among them, and cast lots upon my vesture." This prophecy is truly remarkable: it has been written from the point of view of the one being crucified. The speaker is elevated and is looking down: "they look up and stare upon me"; "They gaped upon me." There is a crucifixion taking place: "they pierced my hands and my feet"; "all my bones are out of joint." The victim's lungs have collapsed and his internal organs have moved upward into his chest cavity due to gravity pulling his body downward: "my heart is like wax; it is melted in the midst of my bowels." He is surrounded by his enemies: "They gaped upon me with their mouths, as a ravening and a roaring lion"; "For dogs have compassed me: the assembly of the wicked have inclosed me." This is a high definition laser print of Christ's Crucifixion, written from the perspective of the One who is being crucified. The speaker is elevated over his enemies; he is the one who is experiencing weakness and faintness; whose tongue is cleaving to his jaws; whose hands and feet have been pierced.

The vast treasury of prophecies that Pascal enumerates indicates the amount of research and long hours he must have put into his project of proving his arguments. Pascal was a true mathematician: he wanted to prove Christ's Messianic identity with the accuracy and definitiveness of a geometric theorem.

Two prophecies are particularly significant because they indicate that the awaited Messiah will be God, Himself. The first is: "Who hath ascended up into heaven, or descended? who hath gathered the wind in his fists? who hath bound the waters in a garment? who hath established all the ends of the earth? what is his name, and what is his son's name, if thou canst tell?" (Prov 30:4). This prophecy is truly amazing because after it enumerates the activities of God and makes it clear that the persona described in the verse can be none other than God, it ends by asking, "and what is his son's name, if thou canst tell?" Hence, this verse alludes to the divine nature of the Son and reveals that God, does, indeed, have a Son. This particular prophecy was not cited by Pascal and therefore, I do not cite it within the Table. However, because of its undeniable significance, I gave it the most prominent place in the entire chapter: the epigraph.

There is another prophecy that the Eternal God has a Son and in this verse, God's Son will be born of the flesh: "But thou, Bethlehem Ephratah, though thou be little among the thousands of Judah, yet out of thee shall he come forth unto me that is to be ruler in Israel; whose goings forth have been from old, from everlasting" (Mic 5:2). This prophecy is significant because it links the birthplace, Bethlehem, with One "whose goings forth have been from old, from everlasting." This verse was cited by Pascal in fragment B727/L487/S734, and I do include it in the Table.

While these two prophecies, articulated by prophets centuries in advance of the fact, are striking, the wealth of Messianic prophecies that Christ has fulfilled and that are laid out neatly in the Table leave no doubt

Introduction

that Jesus is the Messiah. The wealth of Messianic prophecies cited by Pascal attest to His tireless efforts and his rationalistic mathematical mind: he set out to demonstrate the unity between the Old and New Testaments and the fact that hundreds of prophecies were fulfilled in one man is beyond the realm of statistical probability. Therefore, these facts provide clear evidence as to the Will of God.

Chapter 3 ("Christ's Miracles Prove His Divinity") examines the great wealth of miracles that Christ performed and Pascal's use of these miracles as proof of His divinity. First and foremost, Christ raised the dead: this is a feat that only God Himself can perform. Christ predicted His own resurrection and then raised Himself on Sunday morning, significantly, on the Feast of the First Fruits. Many people saw the resurrected Christ: He appeared to the women at the empty tomb, to Peter and Cleopas on the road to Emmaus, to the disciples in the Upper Room on two occasions; Thomas touched His pierced hands and put his hand in His pierced side; He appeared to the disciples in the fish boat on the Sea of Tiberius; Paul advises that more than 500 people saw Him at one time and that many of these witnesses were still alive (implying that they were still available for interview).

In addition, He resurrected the widow's son at Nain; Jairus' 12 year old daughter; His friend, Lazarus; and after He surrendered His Ghost on the Cross, the tombs opened and the bodies of many OT saints were resurrected and were seen by many in Jerusalem (Mat 27:52). Moreover, after He raised Lazarus from the dead, Lazarus lived another thirty years and went on to found a church at Kition (now Larnaca), Cyprus. After Lazarus' second death, most of his bones were taken to Constantinople, but it is believed that some fragments that have been unearthed beneath the altar of his church in Larnaca actually belong to the first human in history to be resurrected after having been dead for four days.

Ever since the time of Christ's ministry, Christians have witnessed miracles, have deduced that a spiritual realm must exist, and consequently, have lost their fear of death and willingly became martyrs for what they had seen and knew to be true. The fact that early Christians saw, believed, and were willing to be martyred for Christ, is evidence that the historicity of miracles is certain. For example, the Miracle of the Holy Thorn at Port

Royal is a documented fact and declared to be a miracle by the Archbishop of Paris in 1656. Moreover, the Orthodox Church points out that the Miracle of the Holy Flame is witnessed by thousands of Christian pilgrims each year in Jerusalem. Orthodoxy also points to the great healings that occur when God pours out His mercy and heals many through icons that cry.

Pascal recognized that miracles, which can be observed by the five senses, provide reality-based evidence of God's existence and of Christ's divinity. The miracles that he experienced in his personal life certainly concretized his own Christian faith. In addition to offering proof of the supernatural realm, he contemplated the significance of their meaning: he asked whether they constitute proof of sound theological doctrine and examined the pros and cons to that argument. On the one hand, they may indicate that God approves of the miracle worker because he is promulgating sound doctrine; on the other hand, they may not because Pharaoh's magicians also had a limited capability to perform magic. Of course, a third possibility is that the artifact heals because it is a true artifact of Christ, and the particular brand of theology of the person who has it in his possession is irrelevant. The reader surmises that Pascal's painstaking scrutiny of the validity of miracles was his attempt to ascertain whether or not the miracles effected by the Holy Thorn at Port Royal was evidence that God approved of the Jansenists' doctrine on predestination and their stance against Jesuit casuistry.

Pascal cites examples in Church history when God performed miracles to provide evidence in matters of doubt. For example, he alludes to the raising of the dead by Christ's True Cross discovered by Saint Helena: "Miracles furnish the test in matters of doubt…between the two crosses."[25] When Helena journeyed to Jerusalem in search of the True Cross, she was led to a site where there were buried three crosses: one of these was Christ's Cross and the other two belonged to the two thieves who were crucified alongside Him. Helena had a dead man brought to the site and she took turns, successively placing his body over each of the three crosses. When he was placed over the True Cross of Christ, he was raised from the dead. This is a historical fact documented by 4th century authors, passed down through the oral tradition of the Church, and slivers of this Cross have been acquired by people who have connections with the hierarchies of both the

Introduction

Orthodox and Catholic churches. Eusebius, Bishop of Caesarea, in *Life of Constantine* (*Vita Constantini*), 3.42-47, describes the journey that Helena made to Palestine during the years 327-328 AD. Although Eusebius does not mention that Helena had discovered the Cross, Cyril, Archbishop of Jerusalem, in *Catechetical Lectures* (*Catecheses*), 4.10, 10.19, and 13.4, tells us that pieces of the True Cross were venerated in the Church of the Resurrection (Church of the Holy Sepulcher) in Jerusalem at the end of the 340s. During the second half of the 4th century, it became widely known that Helena had discovered the True Cross during her pilgrimage to the Holy Land, how she had identified it, and the miracles that pieces of it brought about. It is discussed in the works of Rufinus, Socrates Scholasticus, Sozomen, Theodocretus, Ambrose, Paulinus of Nola, and Sulpicius Severus.

In another fragment, he briefly states, "The combinations of miracles."[26] This fragment points out the great variety of miracles that Christ performed (the raising of the dead, healings, exorcisms, the transformation of water into wine, the creation of enough food to feed 5,000 people from a few fish and loaves of bread); it also points to the continuation of miracles throughout time, from the time of Christ's ministry continuing to the present day.

In addition to being useful tools in deciding matters of controversy, miracles also serve to persuade skeptics. Pascal declares that God gave man miracles in order to draw them to Him. When people discern a miracle with their five senses, they do more than merely believe: they know. It is for this reason that Christ raised the dead, healed the sick, exorcized the possessed, and fed multitudes of thousands from a few fishes and loaves of bread. Pascal quotes Augustine, who said, "I should not be a Christian, but for the miracles."[27] In the *City of God*, 22.7, Augustine observes that the human mind cannot accept the Resurrection without the power of miracles confirming it. Pascal notes that Augustine was right about this and he also observes that God's remedy for skepticism is the continuity of miracles throughout the ages.

Chapter 3 recounts the most stunning miracle of all, one that Pascal does not mention and that is rarely discussed in the West. God proves the historicity of Christ's Resurrection every year when He causes the candles to miraculously light on Holy Saturday in the Church of the Resurrection (the Holy Sepulcher) in Jerusalem. Each year, after Christ's tomb has been inspected and sealed with wax by representatives of the Israeli government (to reenact the soldiers guarding the tomb), the Patriarch of Jerusalem enters it with an unlit candle. Thousands of Eastern Orthodox pilgrims travel to the site, also holding unlit candles, awaiting the miracle that is expected to happen. Indeed, this is the place where Heaven meets earth: each year God proves Christ's triumphant victory over death. The Miracle of the Holy Flame is chronicled as far back as 870 AD by the French monk Bernard in his itinerary. After prayer, the Patriarch of Jerusalem passes his unlit candle over the Lord's tomb and it miraculously lights. On some years, the pilgrims' unlit candles also miraculously light at precisely that moment. The Holy Spirit moves about the Sepulcher lighting the candles, first on one side, then on the other. The Orthodox await this miracle and they have come to expect it. Christ is faithful to the Church, His earthly bride. Seekers of truth can journey there to see for themselves. Many have and as a result, understand that this is a sign that the Orthodox Church is the true Church of Christ on earth.

Chapter 4 ("The Holy Trinity in the Old Testament") will provide an in depth analysis of Pascal's statement, "Moses first teaches the Trinity..."[28] We will explain why Pascal thought so and demonstrate that there is plenty of evidence in the OT that there is one God, comprised of the Father, the Son, and the Holy Spirit. One striking example is the Shema, "Hear, O Israel: The LORD our God is one LORD" (Deut 6:4). The Hebrew word for "one" in this verse is *echad*, which means cluster or unity, as in a cluster of grapes, and not the absolute numeric one. It is significant that *echad* appears again in Gen 2:24 which says, "Therefore shall a man leave his father and his mother, and shall cleave unto his wife: and they shall be one flesh." Here *echad* denotes a unity or cluster, not the absolute numeric one. It is significant that neither *yachid*, nor *bad* (both of which connote numeric oneness) are used. *Echad*, which connotes a unity or cluster appears many times in the OT. Significantly, it us used again to mean a cluster of grapes in Num 13:23: "and cut down from thence a branch with one [*echad*] cluster of grapes." Here a cluster, not one grape is being discussed. The original text of the Shema, written before the Talmud, used the term *echad*, and therefore, provides Maosaic evidence as to the triune nature of the Godhead.

Introduction

The Father is the Eternal Fountainhead from which the Son and the Holy Spirit proceed. Chapter 4 will provide many more examples where *echad* means unity and it will be distinguished from verses that employ *yachid* or *bad* (connoting numeric oneness).

Rabbis recognize that biblical verses can have many layers of meaning: the surface meaning or literal interpretation, the allegorical, the homiletical, and the mystical meanings. Pascal points out that some Messianic prophecies are on the surface and some are hidden. Teaching the skeptic that verses can have more than one meaning is Pascal's method of bringing him to Christ. For example, the mystical interpretation of Deut 6:4 is that *echad* sheds light on the nature of the Godhead.

There is evidence of the Holy Trinity throughout the OT. For example, Prov 30:4 asks: "Who hath ascended up into heaven, or descended? who hath gathered the wind in his fists? who hath bound the waters in a garment? who hath established all the ends of the earth? what is his name, and what is his son's name, if thou canst tell?" This verse is clearly describing God in a series of questions about an omnipotent Person and then concludes by asking the reader the names of this Person and His Son.

Messianic prophecies also exist in Ps 2:2 (the kings of the earth are plotting "against the LORD, and against his anointed") and in Ps 2:7 ("I will declare the decree: the LORD hath said unto me, Thou art my son; this day have I begotten thee"). Moreover, we have a high definition laser print of Christ on the Cross in Ps 22:13-18, Ps 69:21, Is 52:14-14, and Is 53:3-8.

A particularly significant example of the Father and the Son conversing with one another in Heaven is in Ps 110:1 "The LORD said unto my Lord, Sit thou at my right hand, until I make thine enemies thy footstool." Here the Father is inviting the Son to sit at His right hand until He returns to earth to judge the wicked. This judgment occurs in the next verse, Ps 110:2-"The LORD shall send the rod of thy strength out of Zion: rule thou in the midst of thine enemies." In Ps 110:4, the Father continues his conversation with the Son and declares Him to be the intercessor between Himself (the Father) and humanity: "The LORD hath sworn, and will not repent, Thou art a priest for ever after the order of Melchizedek." Here, the Father is telling the Son, "Thou art a priest for ever after the order of Melchizedek." After Christ surrendered His Ghost on the Cross, the curtain in the Temple was rent in two and God indicates that now man could have a relationship directly with the Father because Christ is man's High Priest after the order of Melchizedek. In Ps 110:5 we glimpse again the Son at the right hand of the Father as we did in Ps 110:1-"The Lord at thy right hand shall strike through Kings in the day of his wrath." This appears to be the intermediary period between the Ascension and His return when He will judge humanity.

The Son of God is seen again in Dan 3 in the story about the three Jewish boys, Shadrach, Meshach, and Abednego, whom Nebuchadnezzar throws into a furnace. It is significant that a fourth figure is seen walking in the fire with the boys. This omnipotent figure, who is not consumed by the flames of the furnace, is the anthropomorphosis of God, the Second Person of the Holy Trinity, and His appearance foreshadows His Advent. In fact, Nebuchadnezzar exclaims, "Lo, I see four men loose, walking in the midst of the fire, and they have no hurt; and the form of the fourth is like the Son of God" (Dan 3:25).

The Holy Spirit also is seen in the OT: Moses gathers 70 elders around the Tabernacle and God takes some of the Holy Spirit that is on Moses and places Him on the elders and they begin to prophecize (Num 11:25). This is clearly a foreshadowing of Pentecost when the Holy Spirit descended on the apostles and they spoke about all that they had seen in many foreign languages to people from many nations.

Chapter 5 ("Typology") addresses the notion that people, places, and events in the OT, even the Jewish Feast Days themselves, are symbols or shadows that point to a future reality, Christ. Christians have long held that typology is evidence of unity between the OT and New and therefore, of God's blueprint for man's salvation through Christ's redemptive work on the Cross. Typology concretizes the notion that God is unchanging; events in the OT are considered to be shadows that point to the reality of future events; they foreshadow the Advent, ministry, death, and Resurrection of Christ.

One significant type in the OT is the sacrifice of the red heifer in Num 19. This perfect, unblemished sacrifice, different from all others, is used for the ceremonial cleansing of people and objects that come into contact with the dead. The sacrifice of the red heifer foreshadows Christ's sacrifice

Introduction

on the Cross. The red heifer is a shadow of a future reality: it temporarily cleanses people who have been defiled (until they become defiled again), while Christ cleanses people from their sins forever. In fact, the composite of Mosaic Law is considered to be a type or shadow of Christian dispensation. Paul emphasizes that Mosaic Law was a shadow pointing to something perfect that would occur at a future date: "For the law having a shadow of good things to come, and not the very image of the things, can never with those sacrifices which they offered year by year continually make the comers thereunto perfect" (Heb 10:1).

Pascal declares that the Synagogue was a type of the Church.[29] The Synagogue was the site of animal sacrifice: this form of sacrifice covered sins, but did not take them away forever. When the priest in the Church offers his flock communion, it is partaking of the body and blood of Christ, who takes sins away forever. Christ said, "Whoso eateth my flesh, and drinketh my blood, hath eternal life; and I will raise him up at the last day. For my flesh is meat indeed, and my blood is drink indeed. He that eateth my flesh, and drinketh my blood, dwelleth in me, and I in him" (John 6:54-56). Hence, the Temple is a shadow of the Church, the curtain in the Temple was rent in two and marked the end of the separation between God and man; man can commune directly with God; in fact, Christ dwells in the believer and the believer dwells in Him.

In addition, the Jewish feast days themselves can be seen as symbols of Christ's mission of redemption. For example, Passover foreshadows the passage of man from sin and death to everlasting life through the Crucifixion and Resurrection of Christ. Each portion of the paschal meal has Christian symbolism. The paschal lamb is a foreshadowing of Christ, who is the perfect sacrifice; the bitter herbs remind us that everlasting life has been bought by the price of the suffering and agony of Christ on the Cross; the unleavened bread symbolizes one who is without malice or deceit, Christ, and that state of spiritual purity to which the Christian aspires. Another example of the typology of the Jewish feast days is the Feast of the First Fruits, when a sheaf of the first barley harvest is presented to God: this is a type of the Resurrection of Christ, which, significantly, occurred on the Feast of the First Fruits. The sheaf of the first harvest is a shadow of the reality that is Jesus, who was the first to enter Heaven, and who is followed by many more who are redeemed through Him.

However, as thorough a job as Pascal did of providing empirical, mathematical, reality-based evidence as to the existence of God and the Divinity of Christ, he also, tragically enough, sifted the truth with lies and gave his readers a sack of flour mixed with sand. Conscience dictates that any eulogy of Pascal's apologetics must also address his errors. Therefore, Chapter 6 ("Predestination vs. Free Will") will provide a criticism of Pascal's views on predestination and specifically, of his notion of the election of the damned. Pascal held the erroneous notion that God has predested most people to eternal damnation and punishment in the everlasting flames of hell through no fault of their own. This position is unscriptural, given the orginal Greek text of the NT, heretical, and also blasphemous, given its negation of God's goodness and justice. Pascal was influenced by the Jansenists' interpretation of Augustine-and Augustine, himself, who was not well versed in Greek, relied on a Latin mistranslation of the original Greek text of Rom 5:12. Hence, Pascal's mistaken view that man is 100% predestined and has no free will at all is the result of two layers of error that antecede him-the doctrine of Augustine, who relied on the mistranslation of Rom 5:12 (pertaining to the fall of man), and also on the theology of the Jansenists, who added another layer of error over Augustine's, in their zeal to break with the casuistry of the Jesuits.

Unfortunately, the Latin Vulgate (completed by Jerome in 405) and other Latin translations that existed during Augustine's time mistranslated a key Pauline verse, Rom 5:12, from the original Greek. The original Greek says, literally, "Therefore as through one man sin entered into the world and through sin death, so also to all men death came inasmuch as all sinned."[30] A synonym for "inasmuch as" is "because," so the last clause can also be translated "so also to all men death came because all sinned." The point here is that men have inherited death and disease, the consequences of Adam's sin, not Adam's sin itself. Each of us carries the sins that we commit, but not Adam's.

The Latin Vulgate translates Rom 5:12 as "Propterea sicut per unum hominem in hunc mundum peccatum intravit et per peccatum mors et ita in omnes homines mors pertransiit in quo omnes peccaverunt." It is significant and unfortunate that the Latin Bible translates the last clause as "in quo omnes peccaverunt" ("in whom all men have sinned). The original

Introduction

Greek says, "because," not "in whom." This is key. The Latin erroneously implies that guilt is inherited from Adam and carried from one generation to the next. The Greek, *eph ho*, is correctly translated as "inasmuch as" or "because." This concurs with "For the wages of sin is death" (Rom 6:23), which applies to Adam and to all who sin.

Therefore, the key difference between the East and the West is that the East does not teach that all generations subsequent to Adam inherit the guilt or even his sin; they commit their own sins. Rather, they inherit the consequences of sin, mortality (death and disease), which is the cause of all subsequent disobedience.

Because Augustine relied on the mistranslation of Rom 5:12 as "in whom all men have sinned," all of his subsequent hypotheses hinge on the notion that man is born carrying Adam's sin. From this the West's arguments are derived regarding the damnation of babies who die before they can get baptized, a notion that the East rejects.

Augustine posited that man is totally depraved because he inherited Adam's sin and God's grace is needed for salvation. Unless God gives a person the gift of "irresistible efficacious grace," he cannot believe, no matter how hard he tries, and he cannot conform himself to Christ's image. God chooses to impart His grace to some, who are relatively few in comparison to all the people who have ever been born. God chooses those to whom He will give grace (the elect) and those from whom He will withhold it (the damned). This heresy of double predestination or double election is the corollary of the Latin Vulgate's mistranslation of Rom 5:12 from the original Greek.

Pascal reiterates in *Thoughts* and in *Writings on Grace* that God imparts "irresistible efficacious grace" to those he wants to save and that He withholds it from those that he has decided to damn. We will examine this heresy and compare it to the earliest writings of Christianity regarding election. The Eastern Orthodox Church has relied upon the teachings of John Chrysostom, Gregory of Nazianzus, Gregory of Nyssa, Gregory Palamas, Macarius, Maximus the Confessor, Photius, and Symeon the New Theologian, to name just a few, rather than on those of Augustine. As a result, it has remained unchanged throughout the centuries and is untouched by the apostasies, heresies, schisms, and controversies that have torn Western

Christianity apart. Therefore, we will use it as a prism through which to observe the great divide that exists between early Christianity's beliefs about the relationship between predestination and free will and the controversies that erupted when western theologians began to interpret Augustine.

Pascal was a heretic who repeatedly expounded on the election of the damned. For this reason, Pascal was somewhat of a paradox: he was a man of reason who declared that reason should be the basis of morality; he had experienced God's goodness; he had the privilege of witnessing many miraculous healings performed by an original thorn of Christ's Crown of Thorns; and yet, he embraced a theology that taught that God chooses to damn people to the flames of everlasting hell through no fault of their own. For this reason, there is a great advantage to examining Pascal through the lens of the Orthodox Church: Orthodox theologians, relying on the original Greek text rather than a translation, can greatly clarify Paul's statement, "For whom he did foreknow, he also did predestinate to be conformed to the image of his Son, that he might be the firstborn among many brethren" (Rom 8:29) and Peter's phrase, "Elect according to the foreknowledge of God" (1 Pet 1:2); they can shine a halogen lamp to illuminate and expose the errors in Pascal's theology due to mistranslation.

Pierre Force points out that there is a vicious cycle inherent in Pascal's theology: a person receives grace by reading Scripture, but he needs grace in order to understand it.[31] We observe that this endless cycle promulgates an absurd theology and serves to concretize atheists' unbelief, rather than dispel it. For this reason, we are compelled to present the theology of the Eastern Orthodox Church, which is logical and free of this cycle.

Orthodoxy's position is this: God created man in His image, and therefore, man, like God, has free will. Moreover, modern man also knows that time and space are dimensions of the created universe. Therefore, one must necessarily extrapolate that when Christ spoke and caused the universe to come into existence, that was the moment when He created time and space. Therefore, God antecedes time. He exists outside of it and therefore He is not bound by it; the past, present, and future are all the same to Him. Because He is not limited by the confines of time, He knows the future before we make our choices. Orthodoxy posits that just because God knows

Introduction

the choices that we will make in the future, it does not mean that we do not have free will. We are still free to choose and we do have free will.

Rom 8:29 says, "For whom he did foreknow, he also did predestinate to be conformed to the image of his Son." God's foreknowledge of the future is based on the choices that we make of our free will. The future is fluid, liquid, subject to change from moment to moment, based on our decisions. Bishop Elias Minatios, in an article entitled, "On Predestination," provides three examples taken from the Bible in which God makes it clear that the future is fluid and that man is free to change it at any time.[32]

In one particularly striking example, King Hezekiah is told by the prophet Isaiah that he will soon die. When Hezekiah prays and pleads with God, God grants him an additional fifteen years of life (2 Ki 20:1-6). Minatios points out that here, the Bible clearly teaches that the future is fluid, subject to change from moment to moment, and contingent upon man's behavior.[33] Thus, Minatios brilliantly puts his finger on a biblical passage that shows that in God's scheme of things, the future can change, that it is open-ended, rather than predetermined. God's foreknowledge of the future is based on our choices. It is not the other way around: our choices are not determined by God's foreknowledge. When we take a step towards God, God reaches towards us. The moment that we believe, God infuses us with grace and we embark on a journey in which we will be conformed to the image of His Son.

Regarding election, the Church teaches that men are coworkers (*synergoi*) with God (1 Cor 3:8). The NT has many verses that warn believers to use their free will wisely. We find that Orthodoxy is closest to the Semi-Pelagian view (Jesuit) that sufficient grace is given to all and it only needs free will to make it efficient.

What Critics Have Written on Pascal's Apologetics

To date, there exists a substantial body of research that addresses Pascal's method of using reason as a tool to entice the skeptic to examine the Bible for the fulfillment of prophecy; on the paradox of Pascal's use of reason to save souls when he believed that they have already been predestined for Heaven or hell; on the endless cycle "people receive grace by reading Scripture, but grace is required in order to understand Scripture"; on the influence of Jansenism and the notion of double predestination in Pascal's theology. However, an analysis of Pascal's application of probability theory to the proofs of Christ has not been done. There are no studies that address Pascal's argument that the fulfillment of hundreds of Messianic prophecies in the person of one man, Jesus Christ, the historicity of miracles, and the absolute unity between the OT and New, clearly fall outside the realm of statistical probability, and that therefore, they provide evidence of the Will of God. Furthermore, a criticism of his heresies from the vantage point of the earliest writings of Christianity has not been done. There are no studies of his heresies (double predestination and his thesis that God has deliberately veiled Messianic prophecies so that the non-elect would not understand them) as seen through the prism of the Eastern Orthodox Church. This study will attempt to fill that void.

There are several excellent studies on Pascal and probability theory (ie: his work with Pierre Fermat, his triangle): Florence Nightingale David, *Gods, Games and Gambling*,[34] four criticisms by Anthony William Fairbank Edwards, "Pascal and the Problem of Points,"[35] *Pascal's Arithmetical Triangle*,[36] "Pascal's Problem: The 'Gambler's Ruin,'"[37] and "Pascal's Work on Probability,"[38] Ian Hacking, *The Emergence of Probability*,[39] Anders Hald, *A History of Probability and Statistics and their Applications before 1750*,[40] Oystein Ore, "Pascal on the Invention of Probability Theory,"[41] Laurent Thirouin, *Le hasard et les règles: Le modèle du jeu dans la pensée de Pascal*,[42] and Isaac Todhunter, *A History of the Mathematical Theory of Probability from the Time of Pascal to that of Laplace*.[43]

There are also many fine histories that provide a background on Jansenism: Antoine Adam, *Du mysticisme à la révolte: Les jansénistes du XVIIe siècle*;[44] Henri Bremond, *Histoire littéraire du sentiment religieux en France depuis la fin des guerres de religion jusqu'à nos jours* (volume 4, *L'Ecole Port-Royal*, treats Saint-Cyran, Mère Agnes Arnauld, and Pascal);[45] Augustin Gazier, *Histoire générale du mouvement janséniste depuis ses origines jusqu'à nos jours*;[46] Jean Marie Fréderic Laporte, *La doctrine de la grace chez Arnauld*;[47] and Charles-Augustin Sainte-Beuve, *Port-Royal* (2:379 and 3:7-464 address Pascal).[48] The histories of Gazier, Laporte, and Sainte-Beuve are pro-Jansenist. Bremond's is anti-Jansenist. In addition, Leszek Kolakowski, *God Owes Us Nothing: A Brief Remark on Pascal's*

Introduction

Religion and on the Spirit of Jansenism,[49] provides an excellent analysis of the influence of Augustine, Jansenius, Arnauld, and Saint-Cyran on Pascal, as well as explain the differences among the Molinists (Semi-Pelagians, Jesuits), Pelagians, Calvinists, and Jansenists. On Pascal's Augustinianism we also recommend Philippe Sellier, *Pascal et saint Augustin*[50] and Michael Moriarty, "Grace and Religious Belief in Pascal," in *The Cambridge Companion to Pascal*.[51]

Because Pascal believed that at the foundation of the world God elected those that he would save or damn, critics have examined the question as to whether Pascal was troubled by the apparent futility of trying to save anyone. The fact is that he did make a great effort to put together a thousand fragments that would one day be incorporated into a Christian apologetic designed to convince skeptics to believe. Harold Bloom, in *Blaise Pascal*, is able to reconcile Pascal's belief in predestination with the fact that he worked very hard to save souls through his apologetic project. Bloom explains that Pascal had written that it is the duty of every Christian to believe that he belongs to the small number of elect and also to believe the same thing about every other human being. The Book of Life, which contains the names of the saved, is God's secret. Therefore, the duty of the Christian is to believe that every man has the opportunity of being saved as long as he is alive.[52] Hence, Christians must work relentlessly to preach the Word as if all that they meet might be saved, and they should leave the judgment to God.

Pierre Force, in *The Hermeneutical Problem in Pascal's Writing* (*Le Problème herméneutique chez Pascal*), points out the cyclical dilemma of Pascal's belief system.[53] Force advises that it was Pascal's belief that it is in the Bible that God speaks to man and gives him reason to believe. However, he also held that the divine nature of these texts is evident only to those who already have faith. It is a cycle out of which there is no escape: man receives graces by reading Scripture, but grace is required in order to understand Scripture.[54] However, Force explains Pascal's way out of this dilemma. Pascal's approach to the problem is to use reason to entice the skeptic to read the Bible and place him in the position of reading Scriptures with the objective of interpreting them.[55] Having exposed the person to the Bible, the next step is to show him that there is a hidden meaning beneath the surface meaning.⁵⁶ Once the skeptic sees that, he will understand that hundreds of prophecies were fulfilled in Jesus Christ. When the skeptic sees that the OT was fulfilled in the New, the apologist will have proven the veracity of both texts to him. The Christian apologist can use reason to appeal to the mind; however, only God can plant the seed of faith in the heart. The most that the Christian apologist can do is to appeal to the mind until faith takes root in the heart.

Leszek Kolakowski, in *God Owes Us Nothing: A Brief Remark on Pascal's Religion and on the Spirit of Jansenism*, comments upon Pascal's heresies.⁵⁷ Kolakowski points out that in *Thoughts*, he continually reiterates that God veils his Messianic prophecies in the OT so that only the elect would understand them. Kolakowski says, "…the dominant theme of the *Pensées*: the hidden God. God discloses himself in part and conceals himself in part, and this is just. The prophecies, conforming to the same order of things, both enlighten and blind: they are understood unhesitatingly by those who are pure in heart and they portent doom to obdurate sinners. This is indeed both a Jansenist and a Calvinist principle: 'there is enough clarity to enlighten the elect…There is enough obscurity to blind the reproved and enough clarity to condemn and leave them without excuse' (B578/L236/S268).'"⁵⁸

Kolakowski also examines Pascal's tenet that God imparts grace to the elect in their hearts. This is possible as the heart, also called instinct and intuition, can grasp the notions of the dimensions of length, width, height, numbers, and mathematical abstractions. Therefore, if the Christian apologist can demonstrate that the fact that Christ fulfilled hundreds of Messianic prophecies is beyond the realm of statistical probability, the skeptic's instinct or intuition should be able to grasp that. Similarly, miracles such as those of the Holy Thorn constitute physical proof that God exists, and again, intuition or the heart can apprehend that.

Pierre Force, in *Self-Interest before Adam Smith*, points out that The Wager is not intended to convince anyone that God exists because wishing that something is so does not prove that it is.⁵⁹ Rather, Force advises that Pascal is showing the skeptic that it is a perfectly rational thing to bet that God exists.⁶⁰ If the skeptic replies, "I know that it is rational to wager that God exists, but I still cannot believe," Pascal would reply, "You admit that

Introduction

it is irrational to wager that God exists, but you do not act on this belief. You are not behaving rationally. If you still cannot believe, then diminish your passions."[61] Force demonstrates that for Pascal, the passions are blocks to faith: they take control of the person and rule over his power of reason. During the course of this study we will see that that is why early Christian mystics stressed the necessity of purging the passions by fasting, prayer, and silence in order to attain theosis (union with God).

Marvin R. O'Connell, in *Blaise Pascal: Reasons of the Heart*, observes that Pascal's method of apology is a marriage of faith and reason, of the heart and mind. The Christian apologist must recognize the importance of reason: "Submission is the use of reason in which consists true Christianity."[62] However, faith, which is the apologist's objective, is also important: "If we submit everything to reason, our religion will have no mysterious and supernatural event."[63]

O'Connell holds that Pascal decided that he would bring faith to the skeptic by speaking to his heart, as well as to his mind. The heart is a euphemism for intuition. People know the truth when they hear it: their intuition tells them when something is true. O'Connell explains the importance that Pascal placed on appealing to the heart: "In Pascal's vocabulary, 'the heart' is a term that means, not simply feelings or emotions, but intuition-immediate comprehension and understanding of certain things that we have without having to reason our way to them. Through 'the heart,' we immediately apprehend basic principles that reason cannot discover on its own, and that reason requires as givens for its own operation. Through the 'heart,' in fact, we apprehend truths that reason, if left to its own devices, would never touch. In one of the most famous portions of the *Pensées*, Pascal warns the lovers of reason that 'the heart has its reasons of which reason knows nothing...It is the heart which perceives God and not the reason. That is what faith is: God perceived by the heart, not by the reason.'"[64] Pascal describes Christianity as a religion of love whose God fills the heart of the believer with joy and peace. The Holy Spirit indwells the believer and teaches him all things; thus, the believer is never alone because the Holy Spirit lives within him. The believer has Christ, who is the Prince of Peace, and He fills his heart with peace: "The God of the Christians is not a God who is simply the author of mathematical truths, or of the order of the elements…But…is a God of love and comfort, a God who fills the soul and heart of those whom he possesses, a God…who unites Himself to their inmost soul, who fills it with humility and joy, with confidence and love, who renders them incapable of any other end than Himself."[65]

O'Connell points out that in The Wager, if the skeptic argues that he wants to believe, but he cannot, Pascal's response is that he should diminish his passions: "But at least learn your inability to believe, since reason brings you to this, and yet you cannot believe. Endeavour then to convince yourself, not by increase of proofs of God, but by the abatement of your passions."[66] Here we see a paradox: the heart is where the Kingdom of God is found. The heart is where the Holy Spirit makes His home and indwells the believer. Conversely, it is also a repository of filth and every vile passion. Pascal demonstrates that the passions are at war with God: the passions are obstacles to faith. The heart must be addressed and the passions that reside within must be nullified, disengaged, rendered powerless. The question arises as to how this may be done. The Desert Fathers have the answer.

An important Eastern Orthodox work, *The Philokalia*, makes an analogy which clarifies Pascal's point and instructs how to cleanse the heart of passions. *The Philokalia* is a compilation of the writings of early Christian mystics from the 4th century AD to the 15th century. This work teaches that God's ultimate purpose for man is to deify him and unite him with Himself. This deification or union with God is called theosis. The *Philokalia* explains that the process of theosis may be metaphorized as going to a well to draw water. If someone goes to a well to procure some water, but the well is cluttered with garbage, then the man will not be able to reach the water. The thirsty man must first remove the garbage from the well and then attempt to get water. Similarly, the heart is full of impurities (the emotions-anger, greed, covetousness). These must be addressed and removed before one can become an image of Christ or be pure enough in heart to see God. This leads us to recognize the brilliance in Pascal's assertion that the passions (which are emotions born of self-interest) are obstacles to God. The seeker of truth must set self-interest aside and feel that he has nothing to lose if he wishes to find God. During the course of this study we will examine the precious theological jewels in *The Philokalia* and they will shed light on why Pascal,

Introduction

and all those who choose a life of self-abnegation, hold that monasticism, renunciation of worldly pleasures, and the denial of the flesh, are necessary to see God and realize the spiritual state that God intended man to have.

However, despite Pascal's great efforts to write an apologetic that would save souls, he did embrace the Jansenist heresy that God foreordained the vast majority of all the people who have ever been born to be cast into the flames of an eternal hell. Anthony Levi comments upon the tragic consequences of Pascal's conversion to Jansenism. Levi brilliantly establishes a causality between the fact that Pascal left his *Pensées* unfinished, and the futility of trying to save anyone that is intrinsic to Jansenism. Levi hypothesizes that continually focusing on and arguing on behalf of the doctrine of election, which was an essential point in his *Pensées*, and the focus of his *Writings on Grace*, may have, ironically, caused Pascal to give up on trying to save the skeptic: if people have already been elected, his apology would be of no use in saving anyone.[67]

The futility of trying to save the non-elect may be one reason that Pascal left his *Pensées* unfinished. There is another reason that Levi also considers: perhaps Pascal, himself, questioned the rigid belief system that people are destined for non-election through no fault of their own. Levi speculates that perhaps Pascal questioned Jansenism and needed more time to consider whether he wanted to continue to promulgate this brand of theology.[68]

Pascal's flawed belief system, based on the Jansenists' interpretation of Augustine, was the reason for this study's Eastern Orthodox focus of Pascal. The Eastern Orthodox Church is an iconic representation of early Christianity. It has remained unchanged and unscathed by dissension throughout the centuries, while sharp divisions have torn western Christianity apart. It has seen many miracles in the past and continues to do so today. Like Pascal, it holds that self-denial is a step on the ladder to man's spiritual purification. Therefore, we will judge Pascal according to his century, but where his statements are antithetical to Christ's own words, we will compare his doctrine to that of the earliest Christians, embodied in Orthodoxy, and show his errors.

Endnotes

1. Blaise Pascal, *Thoughts*, translated by W.F. Trotter, Brunschvicg numbering system (New York: P.F. Collier & Son, 1910), fragment 707. "Et afin qu'on ne prît point ce concert pour un effet du hasard, il fallait que cela fût prédit." Blaise Pascal, *Pensées*, in *Œuvres de Blaise Pascal*, edited by Léon Brunschvicg, Pierre Boutroux, and Félix Gazier (Paris: Librairie Hachette & Cie, 1904-1914), fragment 707 (Lafuma 385; Sellier 4).
2. Pierre Force, *Le Problème herméneutique chez Pascal* (Paris: Librairie philosophique J. Vrin, 1989), 15.
3. Blaise Pascal, *Pensées*, translated and introduced by A.J. Krailsheimer, Lafuma numbering system (London: Penguin Books, 1995), fragment 913 (Sellier 742). "...Feu. Dieu d'Abraham, Dieu d'Isaac, Dieu de Jacob, non des philosophes et des savants. Certitude, certitude, sentiment, joie, paix. (*Dieu de Jésus-Christ*). Dieu de Jésus-Christ. '*Deum meum et deum vestrum*'...Père juste, le monde ne t'a point connu, mais je t'ai connu. Joie, joie, joie, pleurs de joie..." Blaise Pascal, *Penées*, edited by Louis Lafuma (Paris: Seuil, 1963), fragment 913 (Sellier 742).
4. Gilberte Périer, *La Vie de M. Pascal* in *Pensées de M. Pascal sur la Religion, et sur quelques autres sujets, qui ont esté trouvées aprés sa mort parmy ses papiers* (Amsterdam: Abraham Wolfgang, 1688), pp. 20-21.
5. Ibid., 21.
6. John 19:1-5. See also Matt 27:29 and Mark 15:17.
7. "Crown of Thorns," *Catholic Encyclopedia: An International Work of Reference on the Constitution, Doctrine, Discipline, and History of the Catholic Church*, edited by Charles G. Herbermann, Edward A. Pace, et al (New York: Robert Appleton Company, 1907-1912), 4:540-41.
8. Blaise Pascal, *Thoughts*, translated by W.F. Trotter, Brunschvicg numbering system (New York: P.F. Collier & Son, 1910), fragment 248. "La foi est différente de la preuve: l'une est humaine, l'autre est un don de Dieu...c'est de cette foi que Dieu lui-même met dans le cœur, dont la preuve est souvent l'instrument..." Blaise Pascal, *Pensées*, in *Œuvres de Blaise Pascal*, edited by Léon Brunschvicg, Pierre Boutroux, and Félix Gazier (Paris: Librairie Hachette & Cie, 1904-1914), fragment 248 (Lafuma 7; Sellier 41).
9. Ibid., fragment 185. "La conduite de Dieu, qui dispose toutes choses avec douceur, et de mettre la religion dans l'esprit par les raisons, et dans le cœur par la grâce..."
   Ibid., fragment 185 (Lafuma 172; Sellier 203).
10. Ibid. "mais de la vouloir mettre dans l'esprit et dans le cœur par la force et par les menaces, ce n'est pas y mettre la religion, mais la terreur..." Ibid.
11. Ibid., fragment 347. "L'homme n'est qu'un roseau, le plus faible de la nature; mais c'est un roseau pensant. Il ne faut pas que l'univers entier s'arme pour l'écraser: une vapeur, une goutte d'eau, suffit pour le tuer. Mais, quand l'univers l'écraserait, l'homme serait encore plus noble que ce qui le tue, parce qu'il sait qu'il meurt, et l'avantage que l'univers a sur lui; l'univers n'en sait rien." Ibid., fragment 347 (Lafuma 200; Sellier 231).

Introduction

12 Ibid. "Toute notre dignité consiste donc en la pensée. C'est de là qu'il faut pour relever et non de l'espace et de la durée, que nous ne saurions remplir. Travaillons donc a bien penser: voilà le principe de la morale." Ibid. (Ibid.; Sellier 232).
13 Ibid., fragment 694. "Et ce qui couronne tout cela est la prédiction, afin qu'on ne dît point que c'est le hasard qui l'a faite." Ibid., fragment 694 (Lafuma 326; Sellier 358).
14 Ibid., fragment 707. "Et afin qu'on ne prît point ce concert pour un effet du hasard, il fallait que cela fût prédit." Ibid., fragment 707 (Lafuma 385; Sellier 4).
15 Ibid., fragment 716. "Je l'ai prédit depuis longtemps afin qu'on sût que c'est moi (Is 48:5)." Ibid., fragment 716 (Lafuma 334; Sellier 366).
16 Ibid., fragment 695. "*Prophéties*.-Le grand Pan est mort." Ibid., fragment 695 (Lafuma 343; Sellier 375).
17 Ibid., fragment 700. "Beau de voir par les yeux de la foi l'histoire d'Hérode, de César." Ibid., fragment 700 (Lafuma 500; Sellier 737).
18 Ibid., fragment 706. "La plus grande des preuves de Jésus-Christ sont les prophéties." Ibid., fragment 706 (Lafuma 335; Sellier 368).
19 Ibid., fragment 710. "Mais il y a bien plus ici, c'est une suite d'hommes, durant quatre mille ans, qui, constamment et sans variation, viennent, l'un ensuite de l'autre, prédire ce même avènement." Ibid., fragment 710 (Lafuma 332; Sellier 364).
20 Ibid., fragment 772. "*Effundam spiritum meum*...toute la terre fut ardente de charité, les princes quittent leurs grandeurs, les filles souffrent le martyre. D'où vient cette force? c'est que le Messie est arrive; voilà l'effet et les marques de sa venue." Ibid., fragment 772 (Lafuma 302; Sellier 332).
21 Ibid., fragment 743. "*Preuves de Jésus-Christ*. Pourquoi le livre de Ruth conserve? Pourquoi l'histoire de Thamar?" Ibid., fragment 743 (Lafuma 304; Sellier 335).
22 *NIV Study Bible* (Grand Rapids: Zondervan, 2002), 483.
23 Blaise Pascal, *Thoughts*, translated by W.F. Trotter, Brunschvicg numbering system (New York: P.F. Collier & Son, 1910), fragment 722. "Sachez donc et entendez. Depuis que la parole sortira pour rétablir et rééditifiez Jérusalem, jusqu'au prince Messie, il y aura sept semaines et soixante-deux semaines." (*Les Hébreux ont accoutumé de diviser les nombres et de mettre le petit le premier; ces 7 et 62 font donc 69: de ces 70 il en restera donc la 70e, c'est-à-dire les sept dernières années, dont il parlera ensuite.*)

"Après que la place et les murs seront édifiés dans un temps de trouble et d'affliction, et après ces soixante-deux semaines (*qui auront suivi les 7 premières. Le Christ sera donc tué après les 69 semaines, c'est-à-dire en la dernière semaine*), le Christ sera tué, et un peuple viendra avec son prince, qui détruira la ville et le sanctuaire, et inondera tout; et la fin de cette guerre consommera la désolation." Blaise Pascal, *Pensées*, in *Œuvres de Blaise Pascal*, edited by Léon Brunschvicg, Pierre Boutroux, and Félix Gazier (Paris: Librairie Hachette & Cie, 1904-1914), fragment 722 (Lafuma 485; Sellier 720).
24 Grant R. Jeffrey, *Armageddon: Appointment with Destiny* (New York: Bantam Books, 1990), 26-33.

25 Blaise Pascal, *Thoughts*, translated by W.F. Trotter, Brunschvicg numbering system (New York: P.F. Collier & Son, 1910), fragment 841. "Les miracles discernent aux choses douteuses...entre les deux croix." Blaise Pascal, *Pensées*, in *Œuvres de Blaise Pascal*, edited by Léon Brunschvicg, Pierre Boutroux, and Félix Gazier (Paris: Librairie Hachette & Cie, 1904-1914), fragment 841 (Lafuma 901; Sellier 449).
26 Ibid., fragment 809. "Les combinaisons des miracles." Ibid., fragment 809 (Lafuma 302; Sellier 333).
27 Ibid., fragment 812. "Je ne serais pas chrétien sans les miracles, dit saint Augustin." Ibid., fragment 812 (Lafuma 169; Sellier 200).
28 Ibid., fragment 752. "Moïse d'abord enseigne la trinité, le péché originel, le Messie." Ibid., fragment 752 (Lafuma 315; Sellier 346).
29 Ibid., fragment 646. "La synagogue ne périssait point, parce qu'elle était la figure..." Ibid., fragment 646 (Lafuma 573; Sellier 476).
30 *The New Greek-English Interlinear New Testament*, translated by Robert K. Brown and Philip W. Comfort and edited by J. D. Douglas (Carol Stream: Tyndale House Publishers, Inc., 1993), 544.
31 Pierre Force, *Le Problème herméneutique chez Pascal* (Paris: Librairie philosophique J. Vrin, 1989), 15.
32 Bishop Elias Minatios, "On Predestination," *Orthodox Life*, translated by Father Gregory Naumenko 40, no. 6 (Nov-Dec 1990), 34-35.
33 Ibid., 35.
34 Florence Nightingale David, *Gods, Games and Gambling* (New York: Hafner Publishing Company, 1962).
35 Anthony William Fairbank Edwards, "Pascal and the Problem of Points," *International Statistical Review* 50 (1982):259-66.
36 Anthony William Fairbank Edwards, *Pascal's Arithmetical Triangle* (New York: Oxford University Press, 1987).
37 Anthony William Fairbank Edwards, "Pascal's Problem: The 'Gambler's Ruin,'" *International Statistical Review* 51 (1983):73-79.
38 Anthony William Fairbank Edwards, "Pascal's Work on Probability," in *The Cambridge Companion to Pascal*, edited by Nicholas Hammond (Cambridge: Cambridge University Press, 2003), 40-52.
39 Ian Hacking, *The Emergence of Probability* (London: Cambridge University Press, 1975).
40 Anders Hald, *A History of Probability and Statistics and their Applications before 1750* (New York: Wiley, 1990).
41 Oystein Ore, "Pascal and the Invention of Probability Theory," *American Mathematical Monthly* 67 (May 1960):409-19.
42 Laurent Thirouin, *Le hasard et les règles: Le modèle du jeu dans la pensée du Pascal* (Paris: J. Vrin, 1991).
43 Isaac Todhunter, *A History of the Mathematical Theory of Probability from the Time of Pascal to that of Laplace* (Cambridge: Macmillan and Company, 1865).
44 Antoine Adam, *Du mysticisme à la révolte: Les jansénistes du XVIIe siècle* (Paris: Fayard, 1968).

45 Henri Bremond, *Histoire littéraire du sentiment religieux en France depuis la fin des guerres de religion jusqu'à nos jours* (Paris: Bloud et Gay, 1916-1933).
46 Augustin Gazier, *Histoire générale du mouvement janséniste depuis ses origines jusqu'à nos jours* (Paris: E. Champion, 1922).
47 Jean Marie Fréderic Laporte, *La doctrine de la grace chez Arnauld* (Paris: Presses Universitaires de France, 1922).
48 Charles-Augustin Sainte-Beuve, *Port-Royal*, 3rd ed., 7 vols (Paris: Hachette, 1867).
49 Leszek Kolakowski, *God Owes Us Nothing: A Brief Remark on Pascal's Religion and on the Spirit of Jansenism* (Chicago: University of Chicago Press, 1998).
50 Philippe Sellier, *Pascal et saint Augustin*, second edition (Paris: Albin Michel, 1995).
51 Michael Moriarty, "Grace and Religious Belief in Pascal," in *The Cambridge Companion to Pascal*, edited by Nicholas Hammond (Cambridge: Cambridge University Press, 2003), 144-61.
52 Harold Bloom, *Blaise Pascal* (New York: Chelsea House Publishers, 1989), 61-62.
53 Pierre Force, *Le Problème herméneutique chez Pascal* (Paris: Librairie philosophique J. Vrin, 1989), 15.
54 Ibid.
55 Ibid., 16.
56 Ibid., 17.
57 Leszek Kolakowski, *God Owes Us Nothing: A Brief Remark on Pascal's Religion and on the Spirit of Jansenism* (Chicago: University of Chicago Press, 1998), 113.
58 Ibid., 142.
59 Pierre Force, *Self-Interest before Adam Smith* (Cambridge: Cambridge University Press, 2003), 116.
60 Ibid.
61 Ibid., 117. Force refers the reader to Blaise Pascal, *Thoughts*, B233/L418/S680.
62 Marvin R. O'Connell, *Blaise Pascal: Reasons of the Heart* (Grand Rapids: William B. Eerdmans Publishing Company, 1997), x. O'Connell cites Pascal, *Pensées*, fragment B269/L167. "Soumission et usage de la raison, en quoi consiste le vrai christianisme."
63 Ibid. O'Connell cites Pascal, *Pensées*, fragment B273/L173/S204. "Si on soumet tout à la raison, notre religion n'aura rien de mystérieux et de surnaturel."
64 Ibid., xi. O'Connell cites Pascal, *Pensées*, fragments B277/L423/S680 and B278/L424/S680. "Le cœur a ses raisons, que la raison ne connaît point…"; "C'est le cœur qui sent Dieu et non la raison. Voilà ce que c'est que la foi: Dieu sensible au cœur, non à la raison."
65 Ibid. O"Connell cites Pascal, *Pensées*, fragment B556/L449/S690. "Le Dieu des chrétiens ne consiste pas en un Dieu simplement auteur des vérités géométriques et de l'ordre des éléments…Mais…est un Dieu d'amour et de consolation; c'est un Dieu qui remplit l'âme et le cœur de ceux qu'il possède; c'est un Dieu…qui s'unit au fond de leur âme; qui la remplit d'humilité, de joie, de confiance, d'amour; qui les rend incapables d'autre fin que de lui-même."

66 Ibid., 188. O'Connell cites Blaise Pascal, *Pensées*, fragment B233/L418/S680. "Mais apprenez au moins votre impuissance à croire, puisque la raison vous y porte, et que néanmoins vous ne le pouvez. Travaillez donc, non pas à vous convaincre par l'augmentation des preuvres de Dieu, mais par la diminution de vos passions."
67 Anthony Levi, "Introduction," in *Pensées and Other Writings*, translated by Honor Levi and edited, introduced, and annotated by Anthony Levi (Oxford: Oxford University Press, 1999), ix.
68 Ibid., xix.

Christ's Fulfillment of Prophecy Proves His Divinity

Christ's Fulfillment of Prophecy Proves His Divinity
I am poured out like water, and all my bones are out of joint:
my heart is like wax; it is melted in the midst of my bowels.
— Ps 22:14

He is despised and rejected of men; a man of sorrows, and acquainted with grief...
Surely he hath borne our griefs, and carried our sorrows...
But he was wounded for our transgressions, he was bruised for our iniquities...
and with his stripes we are healed...
and the LORD hath laid on him the iniquity of us all...
for the transgression of my people was he stricken...
by his knowledge shall my righteous servant justify many; for he shall bear their iniquities...
he was numbered with the transgressors; and he bare the sin of many, and made intercession for the transgressors.
—Is 53:3-12

Prophecy vs. chance

Pascal understood that skeptics could argue that the universe is a product of random chance. This hypothesis dates back to antiquity. The concepts that motion is intrinsic to the atom, and that atoms randomly collide and form everything in the universe, date back to the works of Thales (6th century BC), Leucippus (5th century BC), Democritus (460-370 BC), and Epicurus (341-270 BC). Lucretius' *On the Nature of Things* (first century BC) is the fullest extant statement of the physical theory of Epicurus. In this work, Lucretius had argued that atoms are continually in motion and that it was this random molecular motion that caused them to eventually collide and form everything that exists in the world. Multitudinous atoms came together in every possible way and tested every possible combination; over a vast period of time these random atomic clashes resulted in the beginning of the earth, sea, sky and living creatures.[1] The motive property of matter eventually gave rise to consciousness: Lucretius said that we may infer that the conscious arises from the insensate because we see with our eyes "the eggs of birds turn into living chickens, and worms swarm out when mud has seized on the earth owing to immoderate rains.[2] Because Pascal was a probability theorist and had studied the outcomes of tosses of dice in games of chance, he was well aware of the fact that given an infinite number of throws and an infinite time frame, eventually all possible outcomes will occur. Hence, as a mathematician, he understood the argument that the universe is merely the product of the random collision of atoms.

As a student of probability, he also knew how to calculate the odds that a certain outcome would manifest. This process is called factoring. Factors are numbers that we multiply to get another number. For example, the odds that a number will eventuate on the roll of one die is 1/6 or 1:6 (since a die is comprised of 6 sides). The odds that a number will appear twice if the die were rolled twice consecutively is $P(A \times B)$ or $P(6 \times 6)$ or 1/36 or 1:36. The odds that a number will appear thrice after 3 consecutive rolls of one die is $P(A \times B \times C)$ or $P(6 \times 6 \times 6)$ or 1:216.

Pascal recognized that the statistical probability that hundreds of Messianic prophecies would be fulfilled in one person was astronomically remote. He held that the fact that they have, indeed, been fulfilled in one man, clearly indicates volition (the will of God) and not random chance.

Scrutinizing the Old Testament with great care, Pascal observed that the absolute precision and accuracy of the hundreds of Messianic prophecies that were fulfilled in Christ demonstrated that the will of God permeates not only molecular organization, but also human events. He declares, "And what crowns all this is prediction, so that it should not be said that it is chance which has done it."[3] It is the stunning accuracy of prediction [*la prédiction*] that renders void the skeptics' argument that chance [*le hasard*] has created everything in the universe. It is the spectacular precision of prediction that only the Bible offers, and no other book does, that demonstrates that Christianity is the true religion.

Chapter One: Christ's Fulfillment of Prophecy Proves His Divinity

Pascal enumerates with great patience and detail numerous Messianic prophecies that came true. Using the factoring method, he knew that the statistical probability that all of the predictions about the forgiveness of sin would come true in one person was exponentially remote. Furthermore, he demonstrates that the fact that a series of prophets, most of whom did not know each other, made predictions about the same event over the course of 1,600 years, indicates that the will of God had permeated the minds of the prophets: "In fact, all other sects come to an end, this one still endures, and has done so for four thousand years. They declare that they hold from their ancestors that man has fallen from communion with God, and is entirely estranged from God, but that He has promised to redeem them; that this doctrine shall always exist on earth; that their law has a double signification; that during sixteen hundred years they have had people, when they believed prophets, foretelling both the time and the manner…";[4] "So God has raised up prophets during sixteen hundred years…;"[5] "Here is a succession of men during four thousand years, who, consequently and without variation, come, one after another, to foretell this same event. Here is a whole people who announce it, and who have existed for four thousand years, in order to give corporate testimony of the assurances which they have, and from which they cannot be diverted by whatever threats and persecutions people may make against them."[6]

As a true mathematician and probability theoretician who takes care to enumerate every possibility, Pascal discusses in detail as many of the fulfilled prophecies of Christ as he can find. He casts his net wide: he not only enumerates and cites Old Testament prophecies that have been fulfilled in Christ, but he also incorporates into his work Talmudic texts, commentaries by Moses Maimonides, and prophecies from the Gentile world, as well. He is as thorough in his apologetics and he is in his great mathematical triangle that highlights all of the possibilities of a toss of the coin.

Pascal declares his methodology to be as follows:
Proof of the two Testaments at once.-To prove the two at one stroke, we need only see if the prophecies in one are fulfilled in the other. To examine the prophecies, we must understand them. For if we believe they have only one meaning, it is certain that the Messiah

has not come; but if they have two meanings, it is certain that He has come in Jesus Christ.

The whole problem then is to know if they have two meanings.

That the Scripture has two meanings, which Jesus Christ and the Apostles have given, is shown by the following proofs:
1. Proof by Scripture itself.
2. Proof by the Rabbis. Moses Maimonides says that it has two aspects, and that the prophets have prophesied Jesus Christ only.
3. Proof by the Kabbala.
4. Proof by the mystical interpretation which the Rabbis themselves give to Scripture.
5. Proof by the principles of the Rabbis, that there are two meanings; that there are two advents of the Messiah, a glorious and an humiliating one, according to their desert; that the prophets have prophesied of the Messiah only-the Law is not eternal, but must change at the coming of the Messiah-that then they shall no more remember the Read Sea; that the Jews and the Gentiles shall be mingled.[7]

He also urges the skeptic to *"Read the prophets. See what has been accomplished. Collate what is still to be accomplished."*[8] Here Pascal implores the skeptic to see with his own eyes [*cerno*]. Pascal recommends using reason and the scientific method to arrive at truth: read, see with one's own eyes, collate data. He does have logic and probability theory on his side: the number of prophecies that Christ fulfilled is too great to ignore and clearly falls outside the realm of statistical probability. In 1881 Alfred Edersheim, in *The Life and Times of Jesus the Messiah*, Appendix 9, would enumerate 456 Messianic prophecies that Christ fulfilled.[9] In 1958 Peter W. Stoner, in *Science Speaks*, would calculate that the statistical probability that one man would fulfill just eight Messianic prophecies is $1:10^{17}$.[10] He would also calculate that the statistical probability that one man would fulfill 48 prophecies is $1:10^{157}$.[11]

Pascal's approach will be to intrigue the skeptic to the point where he would be willing to search Scriptures to find agreement between the OT and the NT. This method of teaching relies on the premise that there are multiple levels of understanding the text. This notion is thousands of years old.

Chapter One: Christ's Fulfillment of Prophecy Proves His Divinity

Biblical verses often have several levels of interpretation, ranging from a surface meaning all the way to a hidden, mystical meaning. These four levels of interpretation are:

1. *P'shat* (also spelled *pashat, peshat*); literal interpretation; surface meaning; the plain meaning of the text. Rabbis place great importance on *p'shat* and regard this as having primary significance above all other levels of understanding. The Talmud teaches that no verse loses its *p'shat*. An example is "But thou, Bethlehem Ephratah, though thou be little among the thousands of Judah, yet out of thee shall he come forth unto me that is to be ruler in Israel; whose goings forth have been from old, from everlasting" (Mic 5:2). We may take this literally. The surface meaning of the text reveals a lot: the person who will come forth (be born) in Bethlehem will be the ruler in Israel and He has an everlasting, eternal nature ("whose goings forth have been from old, from everlasting"); this is God, Himself. Hence, we may take it literally when the Holy Spirit tells us that God will be born in Bethlehem. The verse immediately preceding this one, may also be taken literally and contains a stunning prophecy of Christ: "...they shall smite the judge of Israel with a rod upon the cheek" (Mic 5:1). "The judge of Israel" in Mic 5:1 is reiterated in Mic 5:2 ("ruler in Israel"). Furthermore, "whose goings forth have been from old, from everlasting" (Mic 5:1) is a reiteration of "the judge of Israel" immediately preceding it. The teleological relationship between "the judge of Israel" (Mic 5:1), "ruler in Israel" (Mic 5:2), and "whose goings fort have been from old, from everlasting" (Mic 5:2) hyperbolizes the sovereign identity of the one to be born in Bethlehem. The *p'shat* level of "they shall smite...with a rod upon the cheek" (Mic 5:1) and "Bethlehem" (Mic 5:2) identify Jesus Christ as the judge, the ruler, and the one whose goings forth have been from old, from everlasting, and provides a high resolution color print of the Incarnation of the Lord.

2. *Remez*-the allegorical meaning; symbolic explanation; philosophical or rationalistic, intellectual speculation. An example is "When Israel was a child, then I loved him, and called my son out of Egypt" (Hos 11:1). This is allegorical on several levels. First, "Israel" is a metaphor for the infant Christ who did return from Egypt with Joseph and Mary, after the angel told Joseph that it was safe to return and Herod's infanticide was over. Secondly, "child," "him," and "son" are metaphors for the nation of Israel that was freed from bondage in Egypt.
3. *D'rash* (also spelled *drash* or *drosh*); the homiletical or midrashic teaching behind the text. A minister may use the homiletical meaning of the text to teach a practical application to everyday life. The *d'rash* or teaching application of a verse can never contradict the *p'shat* or *remez* of that verse or any other in the Bible. Again, the Talmud states that no passage loses its *p'shat*. An example is "To open the blind eyes, to bring the prisoners from the prison, and them that sit in darkness out of the prison house" (Is 42:7). This can be construed as a literal prophecy which was fulfilled when Jesus healed the blind, exorcized the demoniac of the Gadarenes (who literally did dwell in chains in a prison cave) (Mark 5:1-13, Luke 8:26-33), and freed Peter from prison (Acts 12:1-11). On the *remez* level, "blind eyes," prisoners," "prison," "darkness," and "prison house" are metaphors connoting sin and bondage to it. Christ endows every believer with a new heart and a new spirit (prophecized in Ezek 11:19; 18:31; 36:26) and breaks the bonds that ties him to sin. In addition, it has a homiletic application. The clergy can use this text in a sermon about Christ giving drug addicts the grace to come out of addiction, smokers to give up smoking, or anyone who is addicted to any behavior to walk away from his destructive habit. The Holy Spirit enters the heart of the believer and provides counsel to help him in his exit from (self-) destructive behavior; Christ transforms the heart and gives the person strength.
4. *Sod*-hidden, secret, mystery. This level of interpretation holds a hidden, mystical meaning of the text. For example, it may shed

Chapter One: Christ's Fulfillment of Prophecy Proves His Divinity

light on the nature of the Godhead, as does *echad*, meaning unity or cluster in Deut 6:4. In "Hear, O Israel: The LORD our God is one LORD" (Deut 6:4), known as the *Shema*, the Hebrew word for "one" is *echad*. *Echad* means unity or cluster, not numeric oneness. *Echad* is used again in "Therefore shall a man leave his father and his mother, and shall cleave unto his wife: and they shall be one flesh" (Gen 2:24). Here, "one," *echad*, means a union or cluster comprised of two beings, not the absolute numeric one. Another example is "And they came unto the brook of Eshcol, and cut down from thence a branch with one [*echad*] cluster of grapes, and they bare it between two upon a staff…" (Num 13:23). Here, *echad* means a unity or cluster of grapes, not one grape. Hence, the *sod* level of the *Shema*, Deut 6:4, contains the secret or mystery of the nature of the Godhead, which is the Holy Trinity. There is one God, revealed to us as three distinct persons, who have an interpersonal relationship among themselves (ie: the Father speaks to the Son and invites Him to sit at His right hand until He makes His enemies His footstool (Ps 110:1). This union of three distinct persons is intrinsic to the terminology (*echad*) that the Holy Spirit has given us in Deut 6:4.

Pascal would rely on multiple levels of meaning in biblical verses, especially on the surface meaning (*p'shat*) and the allegorical representation of the Messiah (*remez*). His goal is to examine the Messianic prophecies in the OT and show that they are fulfilled in the NT. The statistical probability that hundreds of prophecies would be fulfilled in one person is infinitesimally remote and therefore, it cannot be ignored or discarded: it demonstrates the Will of God and rules out random chance.

There are four kinds of Messianic prophecies:

1. those that address only the Messiah's First Coming. An example is "After two days will he revive us: in the third day he will raise us up, and we shall live in his sight" (Hos 6:2). This is a literal prophecy (*p'shat*) of Christ's Resurrection (the First Coming):

"us" and "we" identify the Son who is resurrected and "he," the Father who raises Him up. On the *remez* level the pronouns "us" and "we" constitute an anthropomorphosis of the nation of Israel, which supposes that God's wrath would end. The Christological *p'shat* is strongly supported by the verse that follows, which alludes to two Comings: "…and his going forth is prepared as the morning; and he shall come unto us as the rain, as the latter and former rain unto the earth" (Hos 6:3). The "latter and former rain" (KJV), also expressed as "the winter and springs rains" in the NIV, metaphorizes two Comings.

2. those that address only the Messiah's Second Coming. An example is "And it shall come to pass in that day, that the Lord shall set his hand again the second time to recover the remnant of his people, which shall be left, from Assyria, and from Egypt, and from Pathros, and from Cush, and from Elam, and from Shinar, and from Hamath, and from the islands of the sea: (Is 11:11). This is understood to be a literal prophecy of the Second Coming of Christ. That the Messiah is prophecized to come twice is seen in the clause "the Lord shall set his hand again the second time." It is significant that in verses preceding this one, the wolf dwells with the lamb, the leopard lies down with the kid, the calf and the young lion and the fatling together, and a little child leads them (Is 11:6). The peaceful and utopic vision that the world awaits will happen only when "the Lord shall set his hand again the second time." The reality of two Comings is also evident in the fact that "he shall come unto us" in the former rain and the latter rain (Hos 6:3). Christ, Himself, spoke of His Second Coming, as He was leaving the Temple. He said, "O Jerusalem, Jerusalem, thou that killest the prophets, and stonest them which are sent unto thee, how often would I have gathered thy children together, even as a hen gathereth her chickens under her wings, and ye would not! Behold, your house is left unto you desolate. For I say unto you, Ye shall not see me henceforth, till ye shall say, Blessed is he that cometh in the name of the Lord" (Mat 23:37-39). This statement is significant for many

Chapter One: Christ's Fulfillment of Prophecy Proves His Divinity

reasons. First, Christ declares that He did want to minister unto the Jews, that He did not hide Himself from them, as Pascal blasphemes on many occasions. Secondly, the Jews' retribution for not receiving Him will be that their house will be rendered desolate, a prophecy of Israel's destruction by Titus in 70 AD. Thirdly, Christ indicates that He will be leaving and that He will return; when He does return, the Jews will eagerly receive Him; then He will judge humanity and establish His Kingdom. That the remnant of the Jews will believe in Christ only after much tribulation is prophecized in Zech 13:8.

3. those that address both His First and Second Comings. An example is "And I will bring forth a seed out of Jacob, an out of Judah an inheritor of my mountains; and mine elect shall inherit it, and my servants shall dwell there" (Is 65:9). This refers both to Christ's birth ("bring forth a seed") and His Second Coming when He will establish His rule over all the earth ("inheritor of my mountains" and "mine elect shall inherit it")

4. Complete career prophecies or those that address the time spanning His entire career, that is, His First Coming, the interval between the First and Second Coming, and His Second Coming. An example is "The LORD said unto my Lord, Sit thou at my right hand, until I make thine enemies thy footstool" (Ps 110:10). "Sit thou at my right hand" embraces the time span covering His First Coming and the Ascension. "Until" embraces the period of time between His First and Second Comings. "I make thine enemies thy footstool" addresses His Second Coming when He will return in judgment and establish His Kingdom. Hence, Ps 110:1 is an example of a complete career prophecy. In addition, it is an example of *p'shat*-it has a literal interpretation and we can understand the surface meaning of the text to be the level that the Holy Spirit intended when He spoke through David.

When Christ was teaching the Pharisees in the Temple, He alerted them to the fact that their visitation from the Son of God (Prov 30:4) was at hand. As God always does, He respected their free will to accept or reject

Him. Pointing out the significance of Ps 110:1, He asked them, "What think ye of Christ? whose son is he?" They replied, "The son of David." Then He asked, "How then doth David in spirit call him Lord, saying, The LORD said unto my Lord, Sit thou on my right hand, till I make thine enemies thy footstool? If David then call him Lord, how is he his son?" Matthew tells us, "And no man was able to answer him a word, neither durst any man from that day forth ask him any more questions" (Mat 22:41-46; Mark 12:35-37; Luke 20: 41-44). It was well known that the Messiah would be from the line of David. What Jesus was demonstrating was that He would also be David's Lord. He was talking to the Pharisees, who were the teachers of the Law. The reason that they did not ask Him any more questions was that it was evident from Jesus' question that the Messiah would also be the divine Son of God (being teachers of the Law, they knew Prov 30:4), and therefore, one in essence with the Father, that He would proceed from the Father, true God from true God, Light from Light, and that He would be worthy to be worshipped as the Creator of the universe and Lord of all created beings (Mic 5:2 and Prov 30:4). This was all implicit in "The Lord said to my Lord" and was concretized by Mic 5:2 and Prov 30:4.

Essay in opposites—darkness vs. light; death vs. immortality; terror vs. peace; blindness vs. signs that God has left of Himself

> When I see the blindness and the wretchedness of man, when I regard the whole silent universe, and man without light, left to himself, and, as it were, lost in this corner of the universe, without knowing who has put him there, what he has come to do, what will become of him at death, and incapable of all knowledge, I become terrified, like a man who should be carried in his sleep to a dreadful desert island, and should awake without knowing where he is, and without means of escape. And thereupon I wonder how people in a condition so wretched do not fall into despair. I see other persons around me of a like nature. I ask them if they are better informed than I am. They tell me that they are not. And thereupon these wretched and lost beings, having looked around them,

Chapter One: Christ's Fulfillment of Prophecy Proves His Divinity

and seen some pleasing objects, have given and attached themselves to them. For my own part, I have not been able to attach myself to them, and, considering how strongly it appears that there is something else than what I see, I have examined whether this God has not left some sign of Himself.

I see many contradictory religions, and consequently all false save one. Each wants to be believed on its own authority, and threatens unbelievers. I do not therefore believe them. Every one can say this; every one can call himself a prophet. But I see the Christian religion wherein prophecies are fulfilled; and that is what every one cannot do.[12]

Pascal begins by seizing the reader's attention and not relinquishing it for a single moment: he addresses the universal issue of man's anxiety when confronted by the inevitability of death. He employs the phrases "without knowing...what will become of him at death" [*sans savoir...ce qu'il deviendra en mourant*] and "I become terrified" [*j'entre en effroi*]. He evokes the horror and dread of the corruption of the human body, as well as the end of consciousness.

This fragment is a masterful exercise in hyperbole which serves to summon up every emotion associated with impending doom. It is a long enumeration of dark and gloomy terms that compound and exponentiate horror: "blindness," "wretchedness," "whole silent," "without light," "left to himself," "lost in this corner," "without knowing," "at death," "incapable," "terrified," "carried in his sleep," "dreadful," "without knowing," "without means," "so wretched," "despair," "wretched," and "lost." The spooky phraseology conjures up the imminence and inevitability of death, the horror of a decaying body, and the fact that death is a lonely encounter when it does happen.

The passage is striking because of the repetition of words connoting sight and the coinciding absence of light: "When I see," "when I regard," "should awake," "I see," "it appears," "some sign" "having looked around," "seen," "it appears," "I see," and "some sign" are interspersed with terms connoting darkness: "blindness," "without light," "death," and "sleep." We also have the absence of sound: "whole silent universe." In fact, all of our senses are removed in "incapable of all knowledge." Hence, the reader experiences sensory deprivation as he is suspended in a dark, silent universe (awaiting inevitable death).

In the first sentence our senses are gradually removed: first we are blind ("blindness"), then deaf ("silent universe"), and finally, we lose all five senses ("incapable of all knowledge"). Pascal then introduces a little bit of light, so that there is semi-obscurity. People see some pleasing objects and are drawn and attached to them. This is tragic and elicits pathos: people are awaiting what is ultimately nothing less than a death sentence and they are trying to distract themselves momentarily to forget their anxiety.

Clair-obscure is a technique used in painting and also in literature, in which clear or well-lit portions border next to dark portions in order to highlight or emphasize an activity; this can create sharp contrasts between the dark background and the well-lit foreground. In fragment B692/L198/S229, darkness permeates the scene, but then we are permitted to perceive a portion of space in which people are amusing themselves; the amusements could be gambling, hobbies, the vices of the big city, obsessions. Without the light of Christ, sinners believe that living from moment to moment, busying oneself with diversions is all that exists in life until the final curtain call.

The clair-obscure is reminiscent of Plato's cave. The *Oxford English Dictionary* defines Plato's cave thus: "An imaginary cave in which prisoners are kept in such a way that all they can see are shadows created by puppeteers behind them, used by Plato (*Republic* VII.) as an allegory to explain the relationship between our perception of reality and the realm of ideas or forms...the awareness of which is made possible by an 'escape' into the light of intellectual understanding."[13] Just as the prisoners in Plato's cave mistakenly believe that the shadows on the walls are all that there is in the universe, so do those without the light of Christ believe that this life is all that there is, and that all of the knowledge that they gain during the course of a lifetime is for naught when consciousness ends.

Pascal explains that it is this overwhelming sense of desolation that causes men to seek escape through diversions: they look around, find some pleasing objects, and attach themselves to them; this is done to temporarily forget one's anxiety, fear, despair, and desolation at the meaninglessness of

Chapter One: Christ's Fulfillment of Prophecy Proves His Divinity

life and the inevitability of death. Pascal, sympathizing with man, admits that he, himself, has been unable to attach himself to diversions, although he has tried. Some people are uninterested in distractions, finding them a waste of time; others get involved, but reach a point of satiety and move on to new frontiers when there is nothing more to be learned or gained. Sooner or later those who seek escape through diversions must return to reality. The reader identifies with Pascal and is thoroughly seduced by and drawn into the text when Pascal says 1) he has asked others if they are better informed than he regarding the meaning of it all and they say that they are not and 2) he has examined whether this God has not left some sign of Himself. Many readers, to be sure, must have asked their friends or coworkers, at one time or another, "What is the meaning of it all?" How many friends, however, have had the answer? Pascal invites the reader to explore with him whether God has left any evidence of Himself. This invitation intrigues the reader and heightens the suspense.

Pascal is able to write with certitude because the basis of his faith is personal experience and not reason. He experienced God as fire in his room for a period of two hours during which he was consumed by spiritual rapture; his niece had been miraculously cured of a hideous, disfiguring lachrymal fistula by a thorn from Christ's Crown of Thorns. However, since he was targeting his work to skeptics who either have not had personal encounters with God's mercy, or who have, but did not recognize it when they saw it, he would rely upon reasonable arguments with mathematical underpinnings, and especially, reason solidly founded on the basis of probability theory. When dealing with an atheist, a good way to intrigue him is to point out that the statistical probability that hundreds of Messianic prophecies would be fulfilled in one man is exponentially remote. Therefore, he would start with reason to gain entrance into the skeptic's mind and pray that God would provide the gift of faith afterwards.

In the second paragraph Pascal acknowledges that there are many religions in the world other than the Christian religion. Since they all contradict each other, they cannot all be true. This is a mathematical concept: if A is not equal to B, and one of them is true, they cannot both be true. The first question that the skeptic would ask is, "How do we know that one of them is true?" The problem, then, is to identify which of the world's religions, if any, articulates the truth and is the true religion. He observes that of all the religions in the world, the Christian religion is the only one in which prophecies are fulfilled with utmost accuracy. This is certainly true and the skeptic cannot argue the point. However, if he does, Pascal, who has examined the OT with the greatest scrutiny, will go on to enumerate some of the hundreds of Messianic prophecies that have come true in the person of Christ. He will demonstrate with the use of reason, as a geometrician proves a theorem, that Christianity is the one true religion in the world: the fulfillment of hundreds of prophecies in one man clearly falls outside the realm of statistical probability and is therefore, not a result of random chance. God has already declared in numerous places in the OT that he announces all things in advance of their occurence. This notion that prophecies can and have been completely fulfilled both intrigues and offers hope to the skeptical reader whose subconscious fear of death has just been brought to the surface in the first paragraph.

The opposite of chance is volition; prophecy and its subsequent fulfillment are irrefutable proof of the will of God

Pascal declares, "And what crowns all this is prediction, so that it should not be said that it is chance which has done it."[14] As a probability theorist, Pascal knew full well that the statistical probability that hundreds of Messianic prophecies would be fulfilled in one person were so astronomically remote that they would require countless zeros to the right of the decimal point to articulate the odds of realization. For example, the statistical probability that one person would be born of a virgin, in Bethlehem, that He would be born of the line of David, that he would appear at exactly the time predicted in Daniel's books of sevens, that He would die in our place for our inequities, that His legs would not be broken, that lots would be cast for His vestiture, etc., is astronomically miniscule, to the extent that design or volition is obvious.

A prophecy of the end of paganism recorded by Plutarch

One fragment is very brief and is comprised of just five words: "Prophecies.—Great Pan is dead."[15] Pascal was aware of many of the prophecies of Christ that circulated in the Gentile world. The statement,

Chapter One: Christ's Fulfillment of Prophecy Proves His Divinity

"Great Pan is dead," is taken from the historian Plutarch, who, in *The Morals* [*Moralia*] (first century A.D.), records a prophecy in which the end of paganism is announced. This prophecy/miracle was recounted by a highly credible witness and Plutarch indicates respect for this source. As Plutarch begins, he is discussing the mortality of the pagan gods:

> "As for death among such beings, I have heard the words of a man who was not a fool nor an impostor. The father of Aemilianus the orator, to whom some of you have listened, was Epitherses, who lived in our town and was my teacher in grammar. He said that once upon a time in making a voyage to Italy he embarked on a ship carrying freight and many passengers. It was already evening when, near the Echinades Islands, the wind dropped, and the ship drifted near Paxi. Almost everybody was awake, and a good many had not finished their after-dinner wine. Suddenly from the island of Paxi was heard the voice of someone loudly calling Thamus, so that all were amazed. Thamus was an Egyptian pilot, not known by name even to many on board. Twice he was called and made no reply, but the third time he answered; and the caller, raising his voice, said, 'When you come opposite to Palodes, announce that Great Pan is dead.' On hearing this, all, said Epitherses, were astounded and reasoned among themselves whether it were better to carry out the order or to refuse to meddle and let the matter go. Under the circumstances Thamus made up his mind that if there should be a breeze, he would sail past and keep quiet, but with no winds and a smooth sea about the place he would announce what he had heard. So, when he came opposite Palodes, and there was neither wind nor wave, Thamus from the stern, looking toward the land, said the words as he had heard them: 'Great Pan is dead.' Even before he had finished there was a great cry of lamentation, not of one person, but of many, mingled with exclamations of amazement. As many persons were on the vessel, the story was soon spread

abroad in Rome, and Thamus was sent for by Tiberius Caesar. Tiberius became so convinced of the truth of the story that he caused an inquiry and investigation to be made about Pan; and the scholars, who were numerous at his court, conjectured that he was the son born of Hermes and Penelope."

Moreover, Philip had several witnesses among the persons present who had been pupils of the old man Aemilianus.[16]

Pascal does not cite the story, but rather, jots down the short phrase "Great Pan is dead." Since he left the idea undeveloped, it is up to the read to investigate what this could possibly mean. This declaration/prophecy/miracle is striking for several reasons:

1. It is recorded by the historian Plutarch.
2. Plutarch wholeheartedly believes the source: "I have heard the words of a man who was not a fool nor an impostor." Plutarch can well attest to the character of this witness because this source lived in his town and was his grammar teacher.
3. There were many witnesses to this incident, since the voyagers aboard the vessel were still awake ("almost everybody was awake"), they were astonished ("so that all were amazed" and "on hearing this, all, said Epitherses, were astounded"), and they argued about it ("reasoned among themselves whether it were better to carry out the order or to refuse to meddle").
4. The name of the Egyptian pilot, Thamus, was scarcely known, even by many on board ("not known by name even to many on board").
5. This occurred during the reign of Tiberius Caesar (14-37 A.D.), which overlapped with the life, death, and resurrection of Christ. Tiberius was convinced of the truth of the story, summoned Thamus, and requested an inquiry and investigation.
6. The locations that Plutarch mentions indicate that the vessel was sailing in the Ionian Sea in a northerly direction along the west coast of Greece. The Echinades Islands are a group of 25 small islands in the Ionian Sea in the vicinity of the 38th parallel that

Chapter One: Christ's Fulfillment of Prophecy Proves His Divinity

extend to Oxia (38°N 21°E). Since the ship drifted to Paxoi, it travelled in a northerly direction to 39.12°N 20.12°E. Palodes Harbor (modern day Butrint, Albania) is situated north of Paxoi at 39.46°N 20.00°E. This seafaring route is realistic and probable because it takes the traveller north past Corfu, on a path that proceeds to Bari and Brindisi. Plutarch tells us that Epitherses was making a voyage to Italy.

7. The existence of Palodes is verified by the geographer Strabo. In his *Geography* Strabo states, "After Onchesmus comes Poseidium, and also Buthrotum (which is at the mouth of what is called Pelodes Harbour, is situated on a place that forms a peninsula, and has alien settlers consisting of Romans), and the Sybota."[17] Today ancient Onchesimus is called Sarandë (39.52°N 20.00°E); it is Albania's most southern city, situated opposite northern Corfu. Buthrotum is modern Butrint (39.46°N 20.00°E) in southern Albania, opposite the northern end of Corfu. Sybota is now Syvota (39.40°N 20.25°E) and is situated on the west coast of Greece, opposite the southern tip of Corfu. Strabo is taking us down the Albanian coast in a southern direction towards Greece. These are the waters that Epitherses' vessel was most probably covering, as it sailed in the opposite direction, headed north, along the west coast of Greece. Plutarch specifies that the vessel was near the Echinades Islands, then drifted to Paxoi; Palodes Harbor (modern day Butrint) is farther north on the course. Hence, Strabo corroborates the existence of Palodes and that it is situated north of Paxoi.

This statement of the death of Pan was a significant prophecy coming from the Gentile world because it announced the end of paganism and an ushering of light to the "desolate nations" outside of Israel (Is 49:8). The end of paganism marked a transition that would prove to be a cataclysmic shift in religion, philosophy, and morality. It marked the end of barbaric practices among the Gentiles such as infanticide. It heralded a transformation of the human spirit that made cowards brave and willing to die for Christ. Christ conquered spiritual death and sin on the Cross for all those who would embrace Him throughout the centuries. He was resurrected, significantly, on the Feast of the First Fruits. Thus, the brevity of the prophecy, "Great Pan is dead," indeed understates an event of apocalyptic proportions in the evolution of the human spirit.

The pagans Herod and Caesar also unwittingly participated in the fulfillment of prophecy

Another fragment is comprised of only one sentence: "It is glorious to see with the eyes of faith the history of Herod and of Caesar."[18] Not only were Herod and Caesar unbelievers, they were enemies of Christ (neither wanted a rival king) and would certainly not deliberately do anything to glorify Him. However, they unwittingly did glorify Him by fulfilling prophecy.

Herod had been instrumental in the fulfillment of two Old Testament prophecies—Jer 31:15 and Hos 11:1. First, Jer 31:15 says, "Thus saith the LORD; A voice was heard in Ramah, lamentation, and bitter weeping; Rahel weeping for her children, refused to be comforted for her children, because they were not." This prophecy was fulfilled, thanks to the barbarism of Herod, as Matthew tells us: "Then Herod, when he saw that he was mocked of the wise men, was exceedingly wroth, and sent forth, and slew all the children that were in Bethlehem, and in all the coasts thereof, from two years old and under, according to the time which he had diligently enquired of the wise men." Herod had been troubled by the news that a "King of the Jews" had been born and plotted to get rid of Him by relying on a two year time frame for His birth.

Herod also unwittingly fulfilled another Messianic prophecy: Hos 11:1 predicts, "When Israel was a child, then I loved him, and called my son out of Egypt." Because Herod was on the verge of killing the children in Bethlehem, an angel warned Joseph to take Mary and Jesus and go to Egypt. Mat 2:14-15 says, "When he arose, he took the young child and his mother by night, and departed into Egypt: And was there until the death of Herod: that it might be fulfilled which was spoken of by the Lord by the prophet, saying, Out of Egypt have I called my son." Herod knew that Jesus would be born in Bethlehem because the chief priests and scribes advised him of the prophecy in Mic 5:2: "But thou, Bethlehem Ephratah, though

Chapter One: Christ's Fulfillment of Prophecy Proves His Divinity

thou be little among the thousands of Judah, yet out of thee shall he come forth unto me that is to be ruler in Israel; whose goings forth have been from of old, from everlasting." Herod was foiled in his plot even though he had carefully planned to purge Bethlehem of any potential rivals. In doing so, he fulfilled the Messianic prophecy in Hos 11:1 that God would call His son out of Egypt, and hence, glorified the God of the Jews who predicts things in advance.

Pascal informs us that another pagan, Caesar, also unwittingly fulfilled prophecy and in doing so, glorified God, as well. Luke 2:1-2 advises that Augustus Caesar issued a decree that all the world should be taxed. This taxing was first made when Quirinius was the governor of Syria. Luke 2:3 explains that every person was required to return to his own city to be registered and taxed. "His own city" means the city in which he was born, had estate, and to which he belonged. Luke 2:4 specifies that Joseph and Mary had to leave Nazareth, which is in Galilee, and go to Bethlehem, which is in Judea, to be taxed because Joseph was of the house and lineage of David. Hence, Jesus was born in Bethlehem, in fulfillment of the prophecy in Mic 5:2 because Augustus Caesar issued a decree requiring people to travel to the cities of their ancestors to be taxed. Hence, Pascal shows that even pagans kings, like Herod and Augustus, who thought they were gods, unintentionally glorified their rival, the one true God.

The Messiah foretold as to the time and state of the world

Pascal points out that God gave humanity the precise year of the Messiah's appearance (Dan 9:25): "Jesus Christ foretold as to the time and the state of the world. The ruler taken from the thigh, and the fourth monarchy";[19] "The time foretold by the state of the Jewish people, by the state of the heathen, by the state of the temple, by the number of years";[20] "One must be bold to predict the same thing in so many ways. It was necessary that the four idolatrous or pagan monarchies, the end of the Kingdom of Judah, and the seventy weeks, should happen at the same time, and all this before the second temple was destroyed";[21] "Know therefore, and understand, that, from the going forth of the commandment to restore and to rebuild Jerusalem unto Messiah the Prince, shall be seven weeks, and three score and two weeks…The street shall be built again, and the wall, even in troublous times. And after three score and two weeks...the Christ shall be cut off, and a people of the prince that shall come shall destroy the city and the sanctuary, and overwhelm all, and the end of that war shall accomplish the desolation."[22]

In addition, Pascal cites Scriptures in which God repeatedly reiterates that He announces events far in advance so that people would remain vigilant and recognize them when they do transpire: "Behold, the former things are come to pass, and new things do I declare; before they spring forth I tell you of them" (Is 42:9);[23] "Behold, I will do a new thing; now it shall spring forth; shall ye not know it?" (Is 43:19);[24] "Come and let us reason together. Who hath declared this from ancient time? Who hath told it from that time? Have not I, the Lord?" (Is 45:21);[25] "Remember the former things of old, and know there is none like me, declaring the end from the beginning, and from ancient times the things that are not yet done, saying, My counsel shall stand, and I will do all my pleasure" (Is 46:9-10);[26] "I have declared the former things from the beginning; I did them suddenly; and they came to pass" (Is 48:3);[27] "I have even declared it to thee before it came to pass: lest thou shouldst say that it was the work of thy gods, and the effect of their commands" (Is 48:5).[28]

The Shiloh prophecy in Gen 49:10

In the following fragment, Pascal observes that the time of Christ's appearance was foretold: "Jesus Christ foretold as to the time and the state of the world. The ruler taken from the thigh, and the fourth monarchy. How lucky we are to see this light amidst this darkness!"[29] Here Pascal mentions two OT prophecies regarding the time of Christ's appearance, namely, "ruler taken from the thigh" and "fourth monarchy." The "ruler taken from the thigh" is a literal translation of Gen 49:10, "Non auferetur sceptrum de Juda, et dux de femora ejus." The KJV says, "The sceptre shall not depart from Judah, nor a lawgiver from between his feet, until Shiloh come; and unto him shall the gathering of the people be." In Gen 49:10 Jacob, on his deathbed, prophesizes that the Jews will retain their kingdom and their kings, until Shiloh (a metaphor for the Messiah) comes. The significance of Shiloh is this: Shiloh was where the tabernacle was built and where God dwelt. The tabernacle was comprised of two chambers, the sanctuary (first tabernacle) and the Holy of Holies (second tabernacle, which contained the ark). The tabernacle was originally at the encampment at Gilgal and remained there for seven years. Then it was moved to Shiloh (Josh 18:1) and remained there from the time of the Judges until the ark was taken by the Philistines. Shiloh, then, is highly symbolic: it was the site of the tabernacle where God dwelt and is therefore a metaphor for Christ, who is our tabernacle of God. Moreover, many Christians regard the Feast of the Tabernacles as a type of the Advent of Christ, who journeyed to earth and temporarily dwelt in a human body for our redemption from sin.

The prophecy in Gen 49:10 was fulfilled because Israel became a Roman province shortly before Christ's birth, Christ appeared at the precise time predicted in Dan 9:25, and He called all of the nations of the world into His fold; the temple was destroyed by Titus in 70 AD, and the Jews were dispersed from Judea and Israel, the two kingdoms of the Israeli people, into every known land of the ancient world under continual foreign invasion and repression. While Pascal alludes to the prophecy in fragment B700/L317/S348, he fully cites it in fragment B725/L483/S718: "The sceptre shall not depart from Judah, nor a lawgiver from between his feet, until Shiloh come, and unto him shall the gathering of the people be."[30] Regarding the timetable of Christ's arrival, Pascal also recognizes that the exact time of the Messiah's appearance was prophesized in Dan 9:25, but is unable to arrive at the date of His Crucifixion by means of Daniel's books of weeks.[31]

Christ would rule over Israel forever from the throne of David

Pascal mentions the prophecy that the Messiah "will be a descendant of the family of Judah and of David."[32] There are many prophecies that state that Christ will be an offspring of Judah and of King David: "And I will bring forth a seed out of Jacob, and out of Judah and inheritor of my mountains" (Is 65:9); "Behold, the days come, saith the LORD, that I will raise unto David a righteous Branch, and a King shall reign and prosper, and shall execute judgment and justice in the earth. In his days Judah shall be saved, and Israel shall dwell safely: and this is his name whereby he shall be called THE LORD OUR RIGHTEOUSNESS" (Jer 23:5-6); God promised King David, "And thine house and thy kingdom shall be established for ever before thee: thy throne shall be established for ever" (2 Sam 7:16); "I will set up thy seed after thee...He shall build an house for my name, and I will stablish the throne of his kingdom for ever: (2 Sam 7:12-13). Hence, the Bible prophecizes that the Messiah would be born of the line of David, that He would sit on David's throne and reign over Israel forever as its true king.

There is only one problem: God cursed Jehoiachin (his name in the NIV; Coniah and Jeconiah in the KJV), son of Jehoiakim, and declared that none of Jehoiachin's offspring would ever sit on the throne of David or ever rule in Judah. The prophet Jeremiah relates the curse thus: "Thus saith the LORD, Write ye this man childless, a man that shall not prosper in his days: for no man of his seed shall prosper, sitting upon the throne of David, and ruling any more in Judah" (Jer 22:30). God even went so far as to say that if Jehoiachin were a signet ring on His right hand, He would pluck him off (Jer 22:24). This was a pivotal point in history: none of Jehoiachin's children could ever sit on the throne of David. We know that Jehoiachin had seven sons: they were named Salathiel, Malchiram, Peddaiah, Shenazar, Jecamiah, Hoshama, and Nedabiah (KJV spelling) (1 Chr 3:17-18). After Jehoiachin was taken captive in Babylon by Nebuchadnezzar, not one of his sons succeeded him to the throne. The last king to sit on the throne in Judah was Josiah's son, Zedekiah (Jehoiachin's uncle).

Now we have a problem: if Jehoiachin's lineage was cursed by God and none of his progeny could ever inherit David's throne, how could we get a Messiah whom God had promised would be a son of David? God found a way to solve this problem. Christ tells us three times that with God all things are possible: "With men this is impossible; but with God all things are possible" (Mat 19:26); "Abba, Father, all things are possible unto thee" (Mark 14:36); "The things which are impossible with men are possible with God" (Luke 18:27).

This is how God did it: Matthew tells us that Joseph, the husband of Mary, was of royal blood: he was a descendant of Salathiel, the son of Jehoiachin (Mat 1:12). Joseph, therefore, was a direct descendant of King David. In fact, when the angel of the Lord announces to Joseph that Mary's child has been conceived by the Holy Ghost, he addresses him thus: "Joseph, thou son of David, fear not to take unto thee Mary thy wife" (Mat 1:20). Luke corroborates Matthew's testimony as to Joseph's royal blood: "To a

Chapter One: Christ's Fulfillment of Prophecy Proves His Divinity

virgin espoused to a man whose name was Joseph, of the house of David" (Luke 1:27).

However, Joseph could not sit on the throne and reign over Judah because he was a descendant of Jehoiachin, and Jehoiachin's lineage was cursed. Irenaeus, the Bishop of Lugdunum (Lyon) in Gaul, mentions this fact in his argument that Christ was conceived by the Holy Spirit. In *Irenaeus against Heresies* [*Adversus hæreses*] (c. 180 AD), he points out that in God's plan, Jesus could not have inherited David's throne through Joseph because Jechoiachin's bloodline was cursed. Irenaeus declares:

> But besides, if indeed He had been the son of Joseph, He could not, according to Jeremiah, be either king or heir. For Joseph is shown to be the son of Joachim and Jechoniah, as also Matthew sets forth in his pedigree. But Jechoniah, and all his posterity, were disinherited from the kingdom; Jeremiah thus declaring, "As I live, saith the Lord, if Jechoniah the son of Joachim king of Judah had been made the signet of my right hand, I would pluck him thence, and deliver him into the hand of those seeking thy life." And again: "Jechoniah is dishonoured as a useless vessel, for he has been cast into a land which he knew not. Earth, hear the word of the Lord: Write this man a disinherited person; for none of his seed, sitting on the throne of David, shall prosper, or be a prince in Judah." And again, God speaks of Joachiim his father: "Therefore thus saith the Lord concerning Joachim his father, king of Judea, There shall be from him none sitting upon the throne of David: and his dead body shall be cast out in the heat of the day, and in the frost of night. And I will look upon him, and upon his sons, and will bring upon them, and upon the inhabitants of Jerusalem, upon the land of Judah, all the evils that I have pronounced against them." Those, therefore, who say that He was begotten of Joseph, and that they have hope in Him, do cause themselves to be disinherited from the kingdom, falling under the curse and rebuke directed against Jechoniah

and his seed. Because for this reason have these things been spoken concerning Jechoniah, the [Holy] Spirit foreknowing the doctrines of the evil teachers; that they may learn that from his seed-that is, from Joseph-He was not to be born...[33]

For this reason, in God's plan, Jesus inherited the throne of David through His mother, Mary. Mary was also a direct descendant of King David, but through Nathan, not Jehoiachin. The Orthodox Church teaches that the genealogy in Luke is that of Mary and the one in Matthew is that of Joseph. This goes back to the earliest fathers of the Church, who held that Luke wrote his narrative from Mary's point of view: "But Mary kept all these things, and pondered them in her heart" (Luke 2:19). Luke gives us the genealogy of Jesus through Mary's line: her father is Heli.

Lev Gillet points out that Paul is among the earliest Church fathers who held that Luke's genealogy is that of Mary: "Perhaps it is necessary to admit that the genealogy given by Luke is, in reality, the genealogy of Mary, who would then have been a kinswoman of Joseph's, but that the name of Joseph had been substituted for that of Mary by virtue of the legal marriage. In any case, the Fathers of the Church admitted Davidic descent not only for Joseph, but also for Mary. The apostle Paul taught that Jesus is 'made of the seed of David according to the flesh' (Rom 1:5) and that 'Jesus Christ of the seed of David was raised from the dead' (2 Tim 2:8). The account of the Nativity of Christ according to Matthew is written more from the point of view of Joseph, whereas the same account according to Luke is more from the point of view of Mary."[34]

Mary's father, Heli, had descended from David through David's son, Nathan (Luke 3:31). Hence, Jesus was the direct descendant of David and the natural heir to the throne through His mother, Mary. Joseph, however, was a descendant of King Solomon. When Joseph married Mary and adopted her Child, conceived by the Holy Spirit, Jesus became David's legal royal heir. Hence, this is the way that God solved the problem of creating an heir to David's throne when Jehoiachin's line was cursed: Christ was not affected by the curse because Joseph was not his natural father. However, because Joseph was His adopted father, Jesus was the legal heir to David's throne through Solomon. In addition, Christ was the natural heir to David's throne through his mother, who was a direct descendant of David through Nathan.

Hence, Joseph was the King of Israel and Mary was the Queen of Israel not only because they married each other, but also because each one was an heir to the throne in his or her own right. Christ, therefore, was indeed, the King of the Jews. When one stops to think about it, because of God's plan to create a Messiah who would sit upon the throne of David during the Millennium, Joseph and Mary had to marry one another. They could not have married anyone else.

The Gospel writers tell us that many of the people that Christ healed knew that He was of the royal lineage of David. For example, the two blind men followed Him, crying, "Thou Son of David, have mercy on us" (Mat 9:27). The Canaanite woman, who asked Him to exorcize a demon from her daughter, addressed Him, "Have mercy on me, O Lord, thou Son of David" (Mat 15:22). The blind Bartimaeus cried out, "Jesus, thou son of David, have mercy on me" (Mark 10:47). Mark goes on to say, "And many charged him that he should hold his peace: but he cried the more a great deal, Thou son of David, have mercy on me" (Mark 10:48). Luke tells us that this blind man of Jericho "cried, saying, Jesus, thou son of David, have mercy on me" (Luke 19:38); "And they which went before rebuked him, that he should hold his peace: but he cried so much the more, Thou son of David, have mercy on me" (Luke 19:39).

4,000 years of prophecy is an undeniable proof of Christ

Pascal declares, "The prophecies are the strongest proof of Jesus Christ."[35] He observes, "If one man alone had made a book of predictions about Jesus Christ, as to the time and the manner, and Jesus Christ had come into conformity to these prophecies, this fact would have infinite weight."[36] Pascal hyperbolizes this scenario: "this fact would have infinite weight" [*ce serait une force infinie*]. He then surpasses even this "infinite weight": "But there is much more here. Here is a succession of men during four thousand years, who, consequently and without variation, come, one after another, to foretell this same event."[37] Pascal specifies 4,000 years because in the Judeao-Christian world view, based on the chronologies in the Bible, the universe was believed to be less than 6,000 years old. In 1644 John

Lightfoot calculated that the world was created at the equinox on 9 AM in September 3298 BC. In 1650 James Ussher reckoned that the universe was formed on Sunday, October 23, 4004 BC. Pascal finds it significant that an entire race of people announced the same event and that this race existed for 4,000 years to give testimony to it despite threats and persecution. Pascal notes, "This is far more important." [*ceci est autrement considérable*]. His objective, then, will be to explain the prophecies.

God declares that He will foretell events

Pascal enumerates with great care OT verses in which God declares that He predicts events with accuracy centuries and even millennia before they take place (B713/L489/S735). Because God predicts events, He expects people to be vigilant and to watch out for them. The most significant of all events, of course, is the appearance of the Messiah. Pascal cites, "Behold, the former things are come to pass, and new things do I declare; before they spring forth I tell you of them" (Is 42:9);[38] he cites God's challenge to anyone "who will equal himself to me" to "declare the things that are coming" (Is 44:7);[39] "...have I not told you all these things? Ye are my witnesses" (Is 44:8);[40] "Come and let us reason together. Who hath declared this from ancient time? Who hath told it from that time? Have not I, the Lord?" (Is 45:21);[41] "Remember the former things of old, and know there is none like me, declaring the end from the beginning, and from ancient times the things that are not yet done, saying My counsel shall stand, and I will do all my pleasure" (Is 46:9-10);[42] "I have declared the former things from the beginning; I did them suddenly; and they came to pass" (Is 48:3);[43] "I have even declared it to thee before it came to pass: lest thou shouldst say that it was the work of thy gods, and the effect of their commands" (Is 48:5);[44] "I have shewed thee new things from this time, even hidden things, and thou didst not know them. They are created now, and not from the beginning; I have kept them hidden from thee; lest thou shouldst say, behold, I knew them" (Is 48:6-7).[45]

Having established that God predicted events in advance, Pascal begins to address Old Testament prophecies in which God foretold that he would one day, very mercifully, call the Gentile world to be His people, bestow His grace upon it, and invite it to enter into His Kingdom. Pascal

Chapter One: Christ's Fulfillment of Prophecy Proves His Divinity

mentions the "conversion of the Gentiles" and cites Is 65:1: "I am sought of them that asked not for me; I am found of them that sought me not: I said, Behold me, behold me, unto a nation that did not call upon my name."[46] He also cites Is 65:8-9 in which a new wine is mentioned, foretelling the New Covenant: "Thus saith the Lord, As the new wine is found in the cluster, and one saith, Destroy it not, for a blessing is in it [and the promise of fruit]... Thus I will bring forth a seed out of Jacob and out of Judah, an inheritor of my mountains, and mine elect and my servants shall inherit it, and my fertile and abundant plains." The prophecy of the new wine is fulfilled in Mat 9:17: "Neither do men put new wine into old bottles: else the bottles break, and the wine runneth out, and the bottles perish: but they put new wine into new bottles, and both are preserved." This is reiterated in Mark 2:22 and Luke 5:37.

God extends His grace to the Gentiles and they glorify Him

Pascal points out that Mal 1:11 was a Messianic prophecy that was fulfilled in the person of Christ: "For from the rising of the sun even unto the going down of the same my name shall be great among the Gentiles; and in every place incense shall be offered unto my name, and a pure offering: for my name shall be great among the heathen, saith the LORD of hosts."[47] This prophecy came true, as the Lord of Lords is praised and worshipped throughout the world today. The pure offering is the sacrifice of the Lamb of God who was pure and without sin. Christ's name became great among the Gentiles from the moment of the Crucifixion when a centurion pierced His side, and blood and water poured out (John 19:34). His name was further glorified among the Gentiles when He surrendered His soul on the Cross: Matthew recounts how the tombs were opened and the bodies of many saints, having fallen asleep, arose and were seen in Jerusalem by many (Mat 27:52).

The calling of the Gentiles

Pascal continually reiterates that God had foretold that one day, all nations would belong to Him. Under the subtitle, "The calling of the Gentiles," he provides the chapter and verse numbers of OT passages that announce that one day the Gentile world would be invited to enter into

God's eternal kingdom. In fragment number B715/L498/S736 he mentions Joel 2:28, Hos 2:23, Deut 32:21, and Mal 1:11. The KJV declares, "And it shall come to pass afterward, that I will pour out my spirit upon all flesh; and your sons and your daughters shall prophesy, your old men shall dream dreams, your young men shall see visions" (Joel 2:28); "And I will sow her unto me in the earth; and I will have mercy upon her that had not obtained mercy; and I will say to them which were not my people, Thou art my people; and they shall say, Thou art my God" (Hos 2:23); "for from the rising of the sun even unto the going down of the same my name shall be great among the Gentiles; and in every place incense shall be offered unto my name, and a pure offering: or my name shall be great among the heathen, saith the LORD of hosts" (Mal 1:11).

He also mentions Hag 2:7-9 in two fragments. He enumerates the chapter and verses in fragment B715/L498/S736 and goes on to fully cite them in fragment B726/L483/S718. The KJV reads, "And I will shake all nations, and the desire of all nations shall come: and I will fill this house with glory, saith the LORD of hosts. The silver is mine, and the gold is mine, saith the LORD of hosts. The glory of this latter house shall be greater than of the former, saith the LORD of hosts: and in this place will I give peace, saith the LORD of hosts" (Hag 2:7-9). Here God promises to "shake all nations" and draw "the desire of all nations." Two houses are mentioned, symbolizing the Old and New Covenants, just as the metaphors of old and new wine is used in the Bible, and of these two houses, the latter shall be greater than the former.

When Pascal fully quotes Hag 2:7-9 in fragment B726/L483/S718, he inserts a citation from another biblical verse in order to make a point. Pascal renders Hag 2:7-9 thus: "'and I will shake all nations, and the desire of all the Gentiles shall come; and I will fill this house with glory,' saith the Lord. 'The silver is mine, and the gold is mine,' saith the Lord, (that is to say, it is not by that that I wish to be honoured; as it is said elsewhere: All the beasts of the field are mine, what advantages me that they are offered me in sacrifice?). 'The glory of this latter house shall be greater than of the former,' saith the Lord of hosts; and in this place will I establish my house,' saith the Lord."[48]

Chapter One: Christ's Fulfillment of Prophecy Proves His Divinity

It is significant that Pascal inserts in parentheses "(that is to say, it is not by that that I wish to be honoured; as it is said elsewhere: All the beasts of the field are mine, what advantages me that they are offered me in sacrifice?)" This is a reference to the biblical verse "I will take no bullock out of thy house, nor he goats out of thy folds. For every beast of the forest is mine, and the cattle upon a thousand hills" (Ps 50:9-10). The surface meaning here is that God instituted animal sacrifice only so that Israel would acknowledge its dependence on God and give Him thanks for His mercy. He did not want Israel to think that He had any need of the sacrificed animals. The ritual was for Israel's benefit, not God's. In fact, God goes on to say, "If I were hungry, I would not tell thee: for the world is mine, and the fullness thereof. Will I eat the flesh of the bulls, or drink the blood of the goats? Offer unto God thanksgiving; and pay thy vows unto the most High: And call upon me in the day of trouble: I will deliver thee, and thou shalt glorify me" (Ps 50:12-15). The point here is that God is not going to eat the animal sacrifices; they are merely a device to bring Israel closer to God, to teach the people obedience, that He is merciful, that He provides protection from enemies, and that He answers prayers. This is the *p'shat* meaning. On a deeper level, Ps 50:9-10, to which Pascal parenthetically refers, is a Messianic prophecy of the day when animal sacrifice would no longer be required because the perfect sacrifice, the Lamb of God who takes away the sins of the world forever, would arrive.

God provided five miracles to demonstrate that animal sacrifice was no longer required. These miracles are recorded in the Palestinian Talmud and the Babylonian Talmud and took place every year between 30 AD and 70 Ad when the Temple was destroyed. The Jerusalem Talmud states, "Forty years before the destruction of the Temple, the western light went out, the crimson thread remained crimson, and the lot for the Lord always came up in the left hand. They would close the gates of the Temple by night and get upon in the morning and find them wide op: (Jacob Neusner, The Yerushalmi, p. 156-57). The Babylonian Talmud states, "Our rabbis taught: During the last forty years before the destruction of the Temple the lot 'For the Lord' did not come up on the right hand; nor did the crimson-colored strip become white; nor did the western most light shine; and the doors of the Hekel [Temple] would open by themselves" (Soncino version, Yoma 39b).

The statistical probability of any one of these events occurring is miniscule, let alone all five of them. Clearly, random chance was not at work here, but rather, the will of God. However, another miracle replaced these and it is witnessed by thousands of pilgrims each year on Holy Saturday: when the Eastern Orthodox Patriarch of Jerusalem passes his candle over the Tomb of Christ, God miraculously lights his candle. This is a historical fact chronicled as far back as 870 AD by the French monk Bernard. It is documented in Timothy Ware's *The Orthodox Church* and pictures of the miracle are on numerous Internet websites. The signs in the Temple and the Miracle of the Holy Flame in the Church of the Resurrection will be discussed more fully in chapter 3.

The stunning accuracy of the timetable of the appearance of the Messiah

Besides the Shiloh prophecy in Gen 49:10, Pascal also cites Dan 9:25-26, in which Daniel furnishes the exact time of the Messiah's appearance. Pascal cites the two verses and interjects his own arithmetic aids in parenthetic remarks:

> "Know therefore, and understand, that, from the going forth of the commandment to restore and to build Jerusalem unto the Messiah the Prince, shall be seven weeks, and three score and two weeks." (The Hebrews were accustomed to divide numbers, and to place the small first. Thus, 7 and 62 make 69. Of this 70 there will then remain the 70th, that is to say, the 7 last years of which he will speak next.)"
>
> "The street shall be built again, and the wall, even in troublous times. And after three score and two weeks," (which have followed the first seven. Christ will then be killed after the
>
> sixty-nine weeks, that is to say, in the last week), "the Christ shall be cut off, and a people of the prince that shall come shall destroy the city and the sanctuary, and overwhelm all, and the end of that war shall accomplish the desolation."[49]

Chapter One: Christ's Fulfillment of Prophecy Proves His Divinity

Pascal argues that the fulfillment of this prophecy, which Daniel made in the sixth century BC, provides evidence that God exists, that He gives man foreknowledge of coming events (in this case, 600 years in advance), and that Christianity is the true religion, as no other religion can fulfill such predictions. Pascal had faith that Dan 9:25-26 was accurate. The problem was that he did not know how to prove it. He admits with disappointment, "The seventy weeks of Daniel are ambiguous as regards the term of commencement, because of the terms of the prophecy; and as regards the term of conclusion, because of the differences among chronologists. But all this difference extends only to two hundred years."[50]

Pascal found the time of commencement of the seventy weeks problematic because four decrees were issued to restore Jerusalem. They are:

1. The decree of Cyrus in March 538 BC.[51] Ezra 1:1-4.
2. The decree of Darius during his second year of reign—Nisan 1 (Apr. 3), 520 BC-Feb. 21, 519 BC.[52] Ezra 6:1-12.
3. The decree of Artaxerxes in 458 BC.[53] Ezra 7:1-28. See also Ezra 4:24.
4. The decree of Artaxerxes in Nisan (March-April) 444 BC.[54] Neh 2:1-8.

Although Pascal could not perform the calculations, someone else, more recently, has. It is relevant to interject here that in the 20th century, Dr. Grant R. Jeffrey conducted research using the observatory in Greenwich, England and has succeeded in arriving at the arithmetic explanation behind the prophecy.[55] Jeffrey explains Dan 9:25-26 thus: in biblical prophecy, a prophetic day represents a year. Therefore, a prophetic week symbolizes 7 years. Furthermore, the Jews used a lunar calendar consisting of 360 days. Jeffrey holds that although four decrees were issued to restore Jerusalem, the decree of Artaxerxes Longanimus to Nehemiah (Neh 2:1-8) is the only one that mentions rebuilding the walls of Jerusalem and therefore, not coincidentally, it is the only decree, when calculating the appearance of Messiah, that yields results. Dr. Jeffrey's research indicates that the commandment to restore and rebuild Jerusalem was given by Artaxerxes on March 14, 445 BC. From that date until the appearance of Messiah was to be 7 prophetic weeks + 62 prophetic weeks or 69 prophetic weeks. Since a prophetic day represents a year, 7 prophetic days or one prophetic week represents 7 years. Hence, 69 prophetic weeks = 483 years. However, we may not simply add 483 years to 445 BC to arrive at the appearance of the Messiah because the Hebrew lunar calendar consists of 360 days and our modern calendar consists of 365.25 days. Therefore, we must perform the following conversion: 483 x 360 days = 173,880 days. 173,880 ÷ 365.25 = 476.05749, which, when added to March 14, 445 BC brings us to the first Palm Sunday, April 6, 32 AD, when the Lord entered Jerusalem triumphantly on the back of a donkey! Daniel gave us the prophecy in the sixth century BC. Blaise Pascal offered it as a proof of Christ in 1656. It would not be until the 20th century, when Jeffrey would conduct the research and arrive at the mathematic explanation in this paragraph.[56]

It should be noted here that the *NIV Study Bible* points out that the solar calendar can be applied to the decree of Artaxerxes in 458 BC: "By using either a solar calendar with the former date (458 BC) or a lunar calendar with the latter date (444), one can arrive remarkably close to the date of Jesus' public ministry."[57] Therefore, -458 + 483 = 25 - 1 = 24 AD. We must subtract 1 because there was no year 0. Hence, applying the solar calendar to Artaxerxes first decree does place us in 24 AD, squarely in the Lord's life on earth.

Prophecies in the OT of Christ calling the Gentiles into His fold

Pascal cites the entire chapters of Is 49 and 50, and Is 51:1-4 in fragment B726/L483/S718. In these passages Christ is speaking in the first person to the Gentile nations that would one day embrace Him; Pascal's renditions of the Bible are cited below. Significant verses are as follows:

1. "Listen, O isles, unto me, and hearken, ye people, from afar: The Lord hath called me by my name from the womb of my mother…Thou art my servant in whom I will be glorified…I have raised thee up for a light to the Gentiles, that thou mayest be my salvation unto the ends of the earth. Thus saith the Lord to him whom man despiseth, to him whom the nation abhorrest… Princes and kings shall worship thee…and I will preserve thee for

a covenant of the people, to cause to inherit the desolate nations, that thou mayest say to the prisoners: Go forth…Behold, I will lift up mine hand to the Gentiles, and set up my standard to the people; and they shall bring thy sons in their arms and in their bosoms. And kings shall be their nursing fathers, and queens their nursing mothers: they shall bow down to thee with their face toward the earth, and lick up the dust of thy feet; and thou shalt know that I am the Lord; for they shall not be ashamed that wait for me" (Is 49:1-23)[58]

2. "For I came, and no man received me; I called, and there was none to hear. Is my arm shortened, that I cannot redeem? Therefore I will show the tokens of mine anger; I will clothe the heavens with darkness, and make sack cloth their covering…The Lord hath revealed His will, and I was not rebellious. I gave my body to the smiters, and my cheeks to outrage; I hid not my face from shame and spitting" (Is 50:2-6).[59]

3. "and I will make my judgment to rest for a light of the Gentiles" (Is 51:4).[60]

4. "and I will make this nation mourn as for an only son" (Amos 8:10).[61]

5. "All these things shall be finished, when the scattering of the people of Israel shall be accomplished" (Dan 12:7).[62]

6. "and I will shake all nations, and the desire of all the Gentiles shall come…The glory of this latter house shall be greater than of the former, saith the Lord of Hosts; and in this place will I establish my house, saith the Lord" (Hag 2:7-9).[63]

7. "I will raise them up a prophet from among their brethren, like unto thee, and will put my words in his mouth; and he shall speak unto them all that I shall command him. And it shall come to pass, that whosoever will not hearken unto my words which he will speak in my name, I will require it of him" (Deut 18:18-19).[64]

8. "The sceptre shall not depart from Judah, nor a lawgiver from between his feet, until Shiloh come; and unto him shall the gathering of the people be" (Gen 49:10).[65]

In verse 1 "Listen" [*Ecouter*] in the initial position and the imperative hyperbolizes the authority of the speaker, who, we will see, is Jesus Christ. In the apostrophe, "O isles," the speaker is calling to the Gentiles. The sermon in the previous chapter, Is 48, was directed to Jacob and the people of Israel (Is 48:1, 12). Chapter 49 begins at a point in time when He is extending His grace to the Gentile world in far away lands. "Isles" is the English translation of the original word, pronounced *ya*, which means coast, island, shore, region. *Ya* refers back to the isles of the Gentiles in Gen 10:5, which says, "By these were the isles of the Gentiles divided in their lands; every one after his tongue, after their families, in their nations." In Is 49:1 "isles" is a metaphor for the heathen in distant regions.

"Hearken" reiterates "listen" and "ye people, from far" repeats "O isles." The tautology hyperbolizes the authority of the speaker, who is giving a command and the object of His concern, the Gentile world in far away regions.

"The Lord hath called me from the womb" is a prophecy of Christ's physical birth into the world, to his preelection by the Father before His physical birth and it connotes the will of the Father and a conversation between the Father and the Son: the Father calls out to the Son who hears Him. Here we have a conversation between two persons of the Holy Trinity, as we do in Ps 2, which says, "Thou art my Son: this day have I begotten thee. Ask of me, and I shall give thee the heathen for thine inheritance, and the uttermost parts of the earth for thy possession. Thou shalt break them all with a rod of iron; thou shalt dash them in pieces like a potter's vessel" (Ps 2:7-9).

Is 49:3 says, "Thou art my servant, O Israel, in whom I will be glorified." Israel is a metaphor for Christ and the entire body of faithful believers. Therefore, God the Father will be glorified in His servant, Christ and the body of believers. God the Father is talking to God the Son: "I have raised thee up for a light to the Gentiles" and this light will be seen and worshipped among many nations. Princes and kings all over the earth will be come to Christ and will worship the Son of God. Christ will inherit the Gentile world, metaphorized as "the desolate nations." The prisoners that he will set free are those who are prisoners to sin and death: he will transform souls and they will abruptly turn away from sin and also inherit eternal life.

Chapter One: Christ's Fulfillment of Prophecy Proves His Divinity

The kings and queens that will come to Christ will recognize Him and be subordinate to Him and their kingdoms will be Christian countries.

Is 50:2 clearly and unmistakably foretells Israel's response to the Messiah: "For I came, and no man received me; I called, and there was none to hear." Is 50:2-3, "Therefore I will show the tokens of mine anger; I will clothe the heavens with darkness, and make sack cloth their covering" describes what happened immediately after Christ surrendered His soul on the cross: the skies were darkened, the temple curtain was torn in two from top to bottom, the earth shook and rocks split. Mark 15:33 states, "at noon, darkness covered the whole land for three hours." Israel did not receive Him; He obeyed the Father's will and did not rebel; He allowed Himself to be beaten and spat upon (Is 50:2, 5-6).

Is 51:4 reiterates that Christ will be a light to the Gentiles: "and I will make my judgment to rest for a light of the Gentiles."

Hag 2:7 reiterates: "and I will shake all nations, and the desire of all the Gentiles shall come; and I will fill this house with glory, saith the Lord." Christ will be the "desire of all the Gentiles"; the nations will be shaken in that Christianity will profoundly transform morality, philosophy, religion and ethics: barbaric pagan practices such as infanticide will stop, cowards will gladly die for Christ, the mark of Christ will be the transformation that takes place in the heart of the individual; the law will be written in the human heart.

Hag 2:9 continues, "The glory of this latter house shall be greater than of the former, saith the Lord of hosts" prophesizes that the New Testament will be the fulfillment of the promises in the Old; Christ is the perfect sacrifice that abolishes sin for all time, not merely covers it as does the sacrifice of the red heifer in Number 19; spiritual death is defeated on the Cross and believers have everlasting life; Christ opened the gates of Hades and released OT saints who had died before His advent and resurrection.

Pascal also cites Deut 18:18-19, which specifies that the Messiah will be also be "a prophet from among their brethren" and that the Lord will put His "words in His mouth"; those who do not listen to His words which He will speak in the Lord's name, will be punished.

The abundance of fulfilled prophecies makes it clear that it is not random chance that one man fulfilled hundreds of predictions; the opposite of chance is volition; it is evident that the will of God has permeated the course of human events and the advent of the Messiah. This is good news: since it is obvious that the coming of Christ was no accident, but a deliberate act of God, there is more to life than meets the eye, God does exist, He keeps promises, and gives everlasting life, as is evidenced by the Resurrection of Christ.

Pascal reiterates the Shiloh prophecy: "The sceptre shall not depart from Judah, nor a lawgiver from between his feet, until Shiloh come; and unto him shall the gathering of the people be" (Gen 49:10). Shiloh, the site of the tabernacle in which God dwelt, the Holy of Holies (the second or inner tabernacle) is a metaphor for Christ on the *sod* level: it represents Christ who came to earth to be our tabernacle, our temple of the Living God, in our midst. He said that He is in the Father and the Father is in Him; those who have seen Him have seen the Father. Therefore, the tabernacle of Shiloh came to earth and dwelt among us. He promised that when He ascended to Heaven He would ask the Father to send the Holy Spirit to indwell us. Therefore, all believers are tabernacles of the Holy Spirit.

The time of the Messiah's coming was fixed precisely by Jacob's prophecy on his deathbed. John Wesley, in the *Explanatory Notes upon the Old Testament* advises, "Till the captivity, all along from David's time, the scepter was in Judah, and from thence governors of that tribe, or of the *Levites* that adhered to it, which was equivalent; till *Judea* became a province of the *Roman* empire just at the time of our Saviour's birth, and was at that time taxed as one of the provinces, *Luke* ii:1..."[66] *WEN* also interprets "the sceptre shall not depart from Judah until Shiloh come" as meaning all of the following things:

1. "That the sceptre should come into the tribe of *Judah*, which was fulfilled in David, on whose family the crown was entailed."[67]

2. "That *Shiloh* should be of this tribe; that seed in whom the earth should be blessed. That *peaceable prosperous one*, or, the Saviour, so others translate it, shall come of *Judah*."[68]

3. "That the *sceptre* should continue in that tribe, till the coming of the *Messiah*, in whom as the king of the church, and the great High-priest, it was fit that both the priesthood and the royalty should determine."[69]

Chapter One: Christ's Fulfillment of Prophecy Proves His Divinity

The Holy Land became a Roman province shortly before Christ's birth; when the Messiah was among them, the Jews declared that Caesar alone was their king, indicating that the scepter had departed from Judah, and the Jews soon after were dispersed into every known land of the ancient world.

In summation, Pascal's position was that if Christianity is amply supported by prophecy and miracles, then that is evidence that it is true and that it should be embraced by all men. Christ's fulfillment of hundreds of Messianic prophecies, most significantly that of His anticipated time of arrival in Daniel's books of weeks, provides mathematical evidence that God exists and that Christ is His Anointed. Pascal, who painstakingly and with great care and precision, enumerated as many prophecies as he could identify, recognized that the statistical probability that one man would fulfill so many prophecies is astronomically remote, and therefore, must be ruled out as coincidental or inconsequential. Three centuries after his death, Peter W. Stoner, following in Pascal's footsteps in an effort to bring mathematical certainty to faith, ascertained that the statistical probability that one man would fulfill eight prophecies is $1:10^{17}$ and that one man would fulfill 48 prophecies is $1:10^{157}$.[70] Alfred Edersheim, in 1883, was able to identify 456 Messianic prophecies in the OT.[71]

Pascal demonstrates that the precision with which prophecies are fulfilled in Christ, especially those addressing the time of His appearance and His mission as sacrificial lamb to atone for the sins of all those who believe on Him, are evidence that it is not random chance, but rather the volition of God that has brought them about, that Christianity is the true religion, that everything that is said about the Messiah in the Old and New Testaments is true, that Christ is, indeed, the Word of God that created the universe and that He, alone, is worthy of worship, thanks, and praise.

Endnotes

1. sed quia multa modis multis primordia rerum ex infinito iam tempore percita plagis ponderibusque suis consuerunt concita ferri omnimodisque coire atque omnia pertemptare, quæcumque inter se possent congressa creare, propterea fit uti magnum volgata per ævom, omne genus coctus et motus experiundo, tandem conveniant ea quæ convecta repente magnarum rerum fiunt exordia sæpe, terrai maris et cæli generique animantum. (5.422-31) Titus Lucretius Carus, De rerum natura, edited by H.A.J. Munro (London: George Bell and Sons; Cambridge: Deighton Bell and Company, 1905), 1:215.

   but because many first-beginnings of things in many ways, driven on by blows from time everlasting until now, and moved by their own weight, have been wont to be borne on, and to unite in every way and essay everything that they might create, meeting one with another, therefore it comes to pass that scattered abroad through a great age, as they try meetings and motions of every kind, at last those come together, which, suddenly cast together, become often the beginnings of great things, of earth, sea and sky, and the race of living things. (5.422-31) Titus Lucretius Carus, On the Nature of Things, translated by Cyril Bailey (Oxford: Clarendon Press, 1910), 200.

2. quatinus in pullos animalis vertier ova cernimus alituum vermisque effervere terra, intempestivos quam putor cepit ob imbris, scire licet gigni posse ex non sensibu' sensus. (2.927-30) Ibid., 1:110.

   Then, moreover, as we saw before, inasmuch as we perceive the eggs of birds turn into living chickens, and worms swarm out when mud has seized on the earth owing to immoderate rains, we may know that sensations can be begotten out of that which is not sensation. (2.927-30) Ibid., 97.

3. Blaise Pascal, *Thoughts*, translated by W.F. Trotter, Brunschvicg numbering system (New York: P.F. Collier & Son, 1910), fragment 694. "Et ce qui couronne tout cela est la prédiction, afin qu'on ne dît point que c'est le hasard qui l'a faite." Blaise Pascal, *Pensées*, in *Œuvres de Blaise Pascal*, edited by Léon Brunschvicg, Pierre Boutroux, and Félix Gazier (Paris: Librairie Hachette & Cie, 1904-1914), fragment 694 (Lafuma 326; Sellier 358).

4. Ibid., fragment 618. "En effet, toutes les autres sectes cessent, celle-là dure toujours, et depuis quatre mille ans.

   Ils déclarent qu'ils tiennent de leurs ancêtres que l'homme est déchu de la communication avec Dieu, dans un entier éloignement de Dieu, mais qu'il a promis de les racheter; que cette doctrine serait toujours sur la terre; que leur loi

Chapter One: Christ's Fulfillment of Prophecy Proves His Divinity

a double sens; que durant mille six cents ans, ils ont eu des gens qu'ils ont cru prophètes, qui ont prédit le temps et la manière…" Ibid., fragment 618 (Lafuma 456; Sellier 696).

5 Ibid., fragment 706. "Aussi Dieu a suscité des prophètes durant seize cents ans…" Ibid., fragment 706 (Lafuma 335; Sellier 368).

6 Ibid., fragment 710. "C'est une suite d'hommes, durant quatre mille ans, qui, constamment et sans variation, viennent, l'un ensuite de l'autre, prédire ce même avènement. C'est un peuple tout entier qui l'annonce, et qui subsiste depuis quatre mille années, pour rendre en corps témoignage des assurances qu'ils en ont, et dont ils ne peuvent être divertis par quelques menaces et persécutions qu'on leur fasse…" Ibid., fragment 710 (Lafuma 332; Sellier 364).

7 Ibid., fragment 642. "*Preuve des deux Testaments à la fois.*-Pour prouver tout d'un coup les deux, il ne faut que voir si les prophéties de l'un sont accomplies en l'autre. Pour examiner les prophéties, il faut les entendre. Car, si on croit qu'elles n'ont qu'un sens, il est sûr que le Messie ne sera point venu; mais si elles ont deux sens, il est sûr qu'il sera venu en Jésus-Christ. Toute la question est donc de savoir si elles ont deux sens.

Que l'Ecriture a deux sens, que Jésus-Christ et les apôtres ont donnés dont voici les preuves.
1. Preuve par l'Ecriture meme;
2. Preuves par les rabbins: Moïse Maymon dit qu'elle a deux faces, et que les prophètes n'ont prophétisé que de Jésus-Christ;
3. Preuves par la cabale;
4. Preuves par l'interprétation mystique que les rabbins mêmes donnent à l'Ecriture;
5. Preuves par des principes des rabbins, qu'il y a deux sens, qu'il y a deux avènements, glorieux ou abject, du Messie, selon leur mérite, que lesprophètes n'ont prophétisé que du Messie-la loi n'est pas   éternelle, mais doit changer au Messie-qu'alors on ne se souviendra plus de la mer Rouge, que les Juifs et les gentils seront mêlés…"
Ibid., fragment 642 (Lafuma 274; Sellier 305).

8 Blaise Pascal, *Pensées*, translated and introduced by A.J. Krailsheimer, Lafuma numbering system (London: Penguin Books, 1995), fragment 312 (Brunschvicg 697; Sellier 343). We used Krailsheimer here because Trotter does not translate the Latin into English. "*Prodita lege.-Impleta cerne.-Implenda collige.*" Ibid., fragment 697 (Lafuma 312; Sellier 343).

9 Alfred Edersheim, *The Life and Times of Jesus the Messiah* (New York: Anson D.F. Randolph, 1883), appendix 9, 707-38.

10 Peter W. Stoner, *Science Speaks* (Chicago: Moody Press, 1958). This book is available online at http://www.geocities.com/stonerdon/science_speaks.html (February 14, 2007).

11 Ibid.

12 Blaise Pascal, *Thoughts*, translated by W.F. Trotter, Brunschvicg numbering system (New York: P.F. Collier & Son, 1910), fragment 693. "En voyant l'aveuglement et la misère de l'homme, en regardant tout l'univers muet, et l'homme sans lumière,

abandonné à lui-même et comme égaré dans ce recoin de l'univers, sans savoir qui l'y a mis, ce qu'il y est venu faire, ce qu'il deviendra en mourant, incapable de toute connaissance, j'entre en effroi, comme un homme qu'on aurait porté endormi dans une île déserte et effroyable et qui s'éveillerait sans connaître où il est, et sans moyen d'en sortir. Et, sur cela, j'admire comment on n'entre point en désespoir d'un si misérable état. Je vois d'autres personnnes auprès de moi, d'une semblable nature: je leur demande s'ils sont mieux instruits que moi; ils me disent que non; et sur cela, ces misérables égarés, ayant regardé autour d'eux, et ayant vu quelques objets plaisants, s'y sont donnés et s'y sont attachés. Pour moi, je n'ai pu y prendre d'attache et, considérant combien il y a plus d'apparence qu'il y a autre chose que ce que je vois, j'ai recherché si ce Dieu n'aurait point laissé quelque marque de soi.

Je vois plusieurs religions contraires, et partant toutes fausses, excepté une. Chacune veut être crue par sa propre autorité et menace les incrédules. Je ne les crois donc pas là-dessus. Chacun peut dire cela, chacun peut se dire prophète. Mais je vois la chrétienne où je trouve des prophéties, et c'est ce que chacun ne peut pas faire." Blaise Pascal, *Pensées*, in *Œuvres de Blaise Pascal*, edited by Léon Brunschvicg, Pierre Boutroux, and Félix Gazier (Paris: Librairie Hachette & Cie, 1904-1914), fragment 693 (Lafuma 198; Sellier 229).

13 "Plato's cave," *Oxford English Dictionary Online*, http://dictionary.oed.com (Jan. 24, 2007).
14 Blaise Pascal, *Thoughts*, translated by W.F. Trotter, Brunschvicg numbering system (New York: P.F. Collier & Son, 1910), fragment 694. "Et ce qui couronne tout cela est la prédiction, afin qu'on ne dît point que c'est le hasard qui l'a faite." Blaise Pascal, *Pensées*, in *Œuvres de Blaise Pascal*, edited by Léon Brunschvicg, Pierre Boutroux, and Félix Gazier (Paris: Librairie Hachette & Cie, 1904-1914), fragment 694 (Lafuma 326; Sellier 358).
15 Ibid., fragment 695. "*Prophéties*.-Le grand Pan est mort." Ibid., fragment 695 (Lafuma 343; Sellier 375).
16 Plutarch, *The Obsolescence of Oracles* in *Moralia*, translated by Frank Cole Babbitt (Cambridge, MA: Harvard University Press, 2003), 4.17 (pp. 399, 401, 403).
17 Strabo, *Geography*, translated by Horace Leonard Jones (Cambridge, MA: Harvard University Press, 1924), 7.7.5 (p. 299).
18 Blaise Pascal, *Thoughts*, translated by W.F. Trotter, Brunschvicg numbering system (New York: P.F. Collier & Son, 1910), fragment 700. "Beau de voir des yeux de la foi l'histoire d'Hérode, de César." Blaise Pascal, *Pensées*, in *Œuvres de Blaise Pascal*, edited by Léon Brunschvicg, Pierre Boutroux, and Félix Gazier (Paris: Librairie Hachette & Cie, 1904-1914), fragment 700 (Lafuma 500; Sellier 737).
19 Ibid., fragment 701. "Jésus-Christ prédit quant au temps et à l'état du monde: le duc ôté de la cuisse et la quatrième monarchie." Ibid., fragment 701 (Lafuma 317; Sellier 348).
20 Ibid., fragment 708. "Le temps prédit par l'état du peuple juif, par l'état du peuple païen, par l'état du temple, par le nombre des années." Ibid., fragment 708 (Lafuma 333; Sellier 365).

Chapter One: Christ's Fulfillment of Prophecy Proves His Divinity

21 Ibid., fragment 709. "Il faut être hardi pour prédire une même chose en tant de manières: il fallait que les quatre monarchies, idolâtres ou païennes, la fin du règne de Juda, et les soixante-dix semaines arrivassent en même temps, et le tout avant que le deuxième temple fût détruit." Ibid., fragment 709 (Lafuma 336; Sellier 367).
22 Ibid., fragment 722. "Sachez donc et entendez. Depuis que la parole sortira pour rétablir et réédifier Jérusalem, jusqu'au prince Messie, il y aura sept semaines et soixante-deux semaines…

Après que la place et les murs seront édfiés dans un temps de trouble et d'affliction, et après ces 62 semaines…le Christ sera tué, et un peuple viendra avec son prince, qui détruira la ville et le sanctuaire, et inondera tout; et la fin de cette guerre consommera la désolation." Ibid., fragment 722 (Lafuma 485; Sellier 720).
23 Ibid., fragment 713. "Les premières choses sont arrivées comme elles avaient été prédites; et voici maintenant, j'en prédis de nouvelles et vous les annonce avant qu'elles soient arrivées." Ibid., fragment 713 (Lafuma 489; Sellier 735).
24 Ibid. "Voici, je prépare de nouvelles choses qui vont bientôt paraître, vous les connaîtrez…" Ibid.
25 Ibid. "Venez et disputons ensemble. Qui a fait entendre les choses depuis le commencement? Qui a prédit les choses dès lors? N'est-ce pas moi, qui suis le Seigneur?" Ibid.
26 Ibid. "Ressouvenez-vous des premiers siècles, et connaissez qu'il n'y a rien de semblable à moi, qui annonce dès le commencement les choses qui doivent arriver à la fin, en disant l'origine du monde. Mes décrets subsisteront, et toutes mes volontés seront accomplies." Ibid.
27 Ibid. "J'ai fait prédire les premières, et je les ai accomplies ensuite, et elles sont arrivées en la manière que j'avais dit…" Ibid.
28. Ibid. "…c'est pourquoi je les ai voulu annoncer avant l'événement, afin que vous ne puissiez pas dire que ce fût l'ouvrage de vos dieux et l'effet de leur ordre." Ibid.
29 Ibid., fragment 701. "Jésus-Christ prédit quant au temps et à l'état du monde: le duc ôté de la cuisse et la quatrième monarchie. Qu'on est heureux d'avoir cette lumière dans cette obscurité." Ibid., fragment 701 (Lafuma 317; Sellier 348).
30 Ibid., fragment 726. "Le sceptre ne sera point ôté de Juda, ni le législateur d'entre ses pieds, jusqu'à ce que Silo vienne; et les nations s'assembleront à lui, pour lui obéir." Ibid., fragment 726 (Lafuma 483; Sellier 718).
31 Ibid., 722. "Sachez donc et entendez. Depuis que la parole sortira pour rétablir et réédifier Jérusalem, jusqu'au prince Messie, il y aura sept semaines et soixante-deux semaines…

Après que la place et les murs seront édfiés dans un temps de trouble et d'affliction, et après ces 62 semaines…le Christ sera tué, et un peuple viendra avec son prince, qui détruira la ville et le sanctuaire, et inondera tout; et la fin de cette guerre consommera la désolation." Ibid., fragment 722 (Lafuma 485; Sellier 720).
32 Ibid., fragment 727. "Il paraîtra principalement en Jérusalem et naîtra de la famille de Juda et de David." Ibid., fragment 727 (Lafuma 487; Sellier 734).

33 Irenaeus, *Irenaeus against Heresies*, 3.21.9, in *The Apostolic Fathers with Justin Martyr, Irenaeus*, vol. 1 of *Ante-Nicene Fathers*, edited by Alexander Roberts and James Donaldson (New York: The Christian Literature Company, 1890-1897), 453-54 [Irenaeus, *Adversus hæreses*, 3.21.9, in Jacques-Paul Migne, ed., *Patrologiæ cursos completus...Series græca*, 161 vols. (Paris: Migne, 1857-1866), 7:953C-954C].
34 Father Lev Gillet, *The year of the Grace of the Lord: A Scriptural and Liturgical Commentary on the Calendar of the Orthodox Church*, translated by Deborah Cowan (Crestwood: St. Vladimir's Seminary Press, 1980), 64-65.
35 Blaise Pascal, *Thoughts*, translated by W.F. Trotter, Brunschvicg numbering system (New York: P.F. Collier & Son, 1910), fragment 706. "La plus grande des preuves de Jésus-Christ sont les prophéties." Blaise Pascal, *Pensées*, in *Œuvres de Blaise Pascal*, edited by Léon Brunschvicg, Pierre Boutroux, and Félix Gazier (Paris: Librairie Hachette & Cie, 1904-1914), fragment 706 (Lafuma 335; Sellier 368).
36 Ibid., fragment 710. "Quand un seul homme aurait fait un livre des prédictions de Jésus-Christ, pour le temps et pour la manière, et que Jésus-Christ serait venu conformément à ces prophéties, ce serait une force infinie." Ibid., fragment 710 (Lafuma 332; Sellier 364).
37 Ibid. "Mais il y a bien plus ici. C'est une suite d'hommes, durant quatre mille ans, qui, constamment et sans variation, viennent, l'un ensuite de l'autre, prédire ce même avènement." Ibid.
38 Ibid., fragment 713. "Les premières choses sont arrivées comme elles avaient été prédites; et voici maintenant, j'en prédis de nouvelles et vous les annonce avant qu'elles soient arrivées." Ibid., fragment 713 (Lafuma 489; Sellier 735).
39 Ibid. "Je suis le premier et le dernier, dit le Seigneur; qui s'égalera à moi, qu'il raconte l'ordre des choses depuis que j'ai formé les premiers peuples, et qu'il annonce les choses qui doivent arriver." Ibid.
40 Ibid. "...ne vous ai-je pas fait entendre toutes ces choses? Vous êtes mes témoins." Ibid.
41 Ibid. "Venez et disputons ensemble. Qui a fait entendre les choses depuis le commencement? Qui a prédit les choses dès lors? N'est-ce pas moi qui suis le Seigneur?" Ibid.
42 Ibid. "Ressouvenez-vous des premiers siècles, et connaissez qu'il n'y a rien de semblable à moi, qui annonce dès le commencement les choses qui doivent arriver à la fin, en disant l'origine du monde. Mes décrets subsisteront, et toutes mes volontés seront accomplies." Ibid.
43 Ibid. "J'ai fait prédire les premières, et je les ai accomplies ensuite; et elles sont arrivées en la manière que j'avais dite..." Ibid.
44 Ibid. "...c'est pourquoi je les ai voulu annoncer avant l'événement, afin que vous ne puissiez pas dire que ce fût l'ouvrage de vos dieux et l'effet de leur ordre." Ibid.
45 Ibid. "Maintenant je vous annonce des choses nouvelles, que je conserve en ma puissance, et que vous n'avez pas encore vues; ce n'est que maintenant que je les prépare et non pas depuis longtemps: je vous les ai tenues cachées de peur que vous ne vous vantassiez de les avoir prévues par vous-mêmes." Ibid.

Chapter One: Christ's Fulfillment of Prophecy Proves His Divinity

46   Ibid. "Ceux-là m'ont cherché qui ne me consultaient point. Ceux-là m'ont trouvé qui ne me cherchaient point; j'ai dit: Me voici! me voici! au peuple qui n'invoquait pas mon nom." Ibid.

47   "*Prophecies fulfilled*...Malachi I,11. The sacrifice of the Jews rejected, and the sacrifice of the heathen, (even out of Jerusalem,) and in all places." Blaise Pascal, *Thoughts*, translated by W.F. Trotter, Brunschvicg numbering system (New York: P.F. Collier & Son, 1910), fragment 714. "*Prophéties accomplies...Malach., I, 11. Le sacrifice des Juifs réprouvé, et le sacrifice des païens (même hors de Jérusalem) et en tous les lieux.*" Blaise Pascal, *Pensées*, in *Œuvres de Blaise Pascal*, edited by Léon Brunschvicg, Pierre Boutroux, and Félix Gazier (Paris: Librairie Hachette & Cie, 1904-1914), fragment 714 (Lafuma 493; Sellier 736). Pascal does not quote from the Bible, but merely furnishes the chapter and verse number.

48   Ibid., fragment 726. "L'argent et l'or sont à moi, dit le Seigneur (c'est-à-dire que ce n'est pas de cela que je veux être honoré; comme il est dit ailleurs: 'Toutes les bêtes des champs sont à moi; à quoi sert de me les offrir en sacrifice?'); la gloire de ce nouveau temple sera bien plus grande que la gloire du premier, dit le Seigneur des armées; et j'établirai ma maison en ce lieu-ci, dit le Seigneur." Ibid., fragment 726 (Lafuma 483; Sellier 718).

49   Ibid., fragment 722. "Sachez donc et entendez. Depuis que la parole sortira pour rétablir et réédifiez Jérusalem, jusqu'au prince Messie, il y aura sept semaines et soixante-deux semaines." (*Les Hébreux ont accoutumé de diviser les nombres et de mettre le petit le premier; ces 7 et 62 font donc 69: de ces 70 il en restera donc la 70e, c'est-à-dire les sept dernières années, dont il parlera ensuite.*)

"Après que la place et les murs seront édifiés dans un temps de trouble et d'affliction, et après ces soixante-deux semaines (*qui auront suivi les 7 premières. Le Christ sera donc tué après les 69 semaines, c'est-à-dire en la dernière semaine*), le Christ sera tué, et un peuple viendra avec son prince, qui détruira la ville et le sanctuaire, et inondera tout; et la fin de cette guerre consommera la désolation." Blaise Pascal, *Pensées*, in *Œuvres de Blaise Pascal*, edited by Léon Brunschvicg, Pierre Boutroux, and Félix Gazier (Paris: Librairie Hachette & Cie, 1904-1914), fragment 722 (Lafuma 485; Sellier 720).

50   Ibid., fragment 723. "Les septante semaines de Daniel sont équivoques pour le terme du commencement, à cause des termes de la prophétie; et pour le terme de la fin, à cause des diversités des chronologistes. Mais toute cette différence ne va qu'à deux cents ans." Ibid., fragment 723 (Lafuma 341; Sellier 373).

51   *NIV Study Bible* (Grand Rapids: Zondervan, 2002), 896note1:11.
52   Ibid., 906note4:24.
53   Ibid., 911note 7:11.
54   Ibid., 911note7:11 and 924note2:1
55   Grant Jeffrey, *Armageddon: Appointment with Destiny* (New York: Bantam Books, 1990), 26-33.
56   Ibid.
57   *NIV Study Bible* (Grand Rapids: Zondervan, 2002), 911.
58   Blaise Pascal, *Thoughts*, translated by W.F. Trotter, Brunschvicg numbering system (New York: P. F. Collier & Son, 1910), fragment 726. "Ecoutez, peuples éloignés, et vous habitants des îles de la mer: le Seigneur m'a appelé par mon nom dès le

ventre de ma mère...Tu es mon serviteur; c'est par toi que je ferai paraître ma gloire...je t'ai suscité pour être la lumière des Gentils, et pour être mon salut jusqu'aux extrémités de la terre. Ce sont les choses que le Seigneur a dites à celui qui a humilié son âme, qui a été en mépris et en abomination aux Gentils et qui s'est soumis aux puissants de la terre. Les princes et les rois t'adoreront...Je t'ai exaucé les jours de salut et demiséricorde, et je t'ai établi pour être l'alliance du peuple, et te mettre en possession des nations les plus abandonees; afin que tu dises à ceux qui sont dans les chaînes: Sortez en liberté...Voici, j'ai fait paraître ma puissance sur les Gentils, et j'ai élevé mon étendard sur les peuples, et ils t'apporteront des enfants dans leurs bras et dans leurs seins; les rois et les reines seront tes nourriciers, ils t'adoreront le visage contre la terre, et baiseront la poussière de tes pieds; et tu connaîtras que je suis le Seigneur, et que ceux qui espèrent en moi ne seront jamais confondus..." Blaise Pascal, *Pensées*, in *Œuvres de Blaise Pascal*, edited by Léon Brunschvicg, Pierre Boutroux, and Félix Gazier (Paris: Librairie Hachette & Cie, 1904-1914), fragment 726 (Lafuma 483; Sellier 718).

59   Ibid. "Le Seigneur dit ces choses: Quel est ce libelle de divorce par lequel j'ai répudié la synagogue? et pourquoi l'ai-je livrée entre les mains de vos ennemis? n'est-ce pas pour ses impiétés et pour ses crimes que je l'ai répudiée?

Car je suis venu, et personne ne m'a reçu; j'ai appelé, et personne n'a écouté. Est-ce que mon bras est accourci, et que je n'ai pas la puissance de sauver?

C'est pour cela que je ferai paraître les marques de ma colère; je couvrirai les cieux de ténèbres et les cacherai sous des voiles...

Le Seigneur m'a révélé ses volontés et je n'y ai point été rebelle.

J'ai livré mon corps aux coups et mes joues aux outrages; j'ai abandonné mon visage aux ignominies et aux crachats..." Ibid.

60   Ibid. "...car une loi sortira de moi, et un jugement qui sera la lumière des Gentils." Ibid.

61   Ibid. "...et je mettrai cette nation en une désolation pareille à celle de la mort d'un fils unique...Ils iront errants d'une mer jusqu'à l'autre, et se porteront d'aquilon en orient; ils tourneront de toutes parts en cherchant qui leur annonce la parole du Seigneur, et ils n'en trouveront point." Ibid.

62   Ibid. "Toutes ces choses s'accompliront lorsque la dispersion du peuple d'Israël sera accomplie." Ibid.

63   Ibid. "...et j'ébranlerai toutes les nations. Alors viendra celui qui est désiré par tous les Gentils..."
...la gloire de ce nouveau temple sera bien plus grande que la gloire du premier, dit le Seigneur des armées; et j'établirai ma maison en ce lieu-ci, dit le Seigneur." Ibid.

64   Ibid. "...je leur susciterai un prophète tel que vous du milieu de leurs frères, dans la bouche duquel je mettrai mes paroles; et il leur dira toutes les choses que je lui aurai ordonnées; et il arrivera que quiconque n'obéira point aux paroles qu'il leur portera en mon nom, j'en ferai moi-même le jugement." Ibid.

65 Ibid. "Le sceptre ne sera point ôté de Juda, ni le législateur d'entre ses pieds, jusqu'à ce que Silo vienne; et les nations s'assembleront à lui, pour lui obéir." Ibid.
66 John Wesley, *Wesley's Explanatory Notes upon the Old Testament*, 3 vols. (Bristol: William Pine, 1765), 1:188.
67 Ibid., 187.
68 Ibid.
69 Ibid., 1:187-88.
70 Peter W. Stoner, *Science Speaks* (Chicago: Moody Press, 1958). This book is available online at http://www.geocities.com/stonerdon/science_speaks.html (February 14, 2007).
71 Alfred Edersheim, *The Life and Times of Jesus the Messiah* (New York: Anson D.F. Randolph, 1883), appendix 9, 707-38.

Table of Messianic Prophecies Fulfilled in Christ

Who hath ascended up into heaven,
or descended?
who hath gathered the wind in his fists?
who hath bound the waters in a garment?
who hath established all the ends of the earth?
what is his name,
and what is his son's name,
if thou canst tell?
—Prov 30:4

BIBLICAL VERSE	KJV TEXT	PASCAL IN QUOTATION MARKS; OTHERWISE, MY EXPLICATION	FRAGMENT NUMBER BRUNSCHVICG/ LAFUMA/SELLIER
Gen 3:15	And I will put enmity between thee and the woman, and between thy seed and her seed; it shall bruise thy head, and thou shalt bruise his heel	"That a deliverer should come, who would crush he demon's head, and free His people from their sins"	B736/L609/S504
Gen 14:18	And Melchizedek king of Salem brought forth bread and wine: and he was the priest of the most high God	Foreshadowing of Christ; that the order of Aaron's priesthood would end, and that of Melchizedek, introduced by the Messiah	B610/L453/S693
Gen 49:10	The sceptre shall not depart from Judah, nor a lawgiver from between his feet, until Shiloh come; and unto him shall the gathering of the people be	"Jesus Christ foretold as to the time and the state of the world"; the end of the kingdom of Judah would not occur until after His advent; to Him shall the obedience of believers	B701/L317/S348; B708/L333/S365; B709/L336/S367; B711/L484/S719; B722/L485/S720; B723/L341/S373; B726/L483/S718

Chapter Two: Table of Messianic Prophecies Fulfilled in Christ

Biblical Verse	KJV Text	Pascal in quotation marks; otherwise, my explication	Fragment number Brunschvicg/ Lafuma/Sellier
Deut 6:4	Hear, O Israel: The LORD our God is one LORD	"Moses first teaches the Trinity, original sin, the Messiah"; the Hebrew word for "one," echad, means cluster, as in Gen 2:24, "Therefore shall a man leave his father and his mother, and shall cleave unto his wife: and they shall be one flesh." Here, echad, one, is a union or cluster comprised of 2 beings	B752/L315/S346
Deut 18:18	I will raise them up a Prophet	He will be a prophet	B726/L483/S718
Deut 18:18	from among their brethren	He will be a Jew	B726/L483/S718
Deut 32:21	I will move them to jealousy with those which are not a people; I will provoke them to anger with a foolish nation	Moses, before dying, foretold the conversion of the Gentile world	B714/L493, L497/ S736; B715/L498/ S736; B724/L338/ S370; B726/L483/ S718; B727/L487/ S734
Ps 2:5	Then shall he speak unto them in his wrath, and vex them in his sore displeasure	He will be victorious over His enemies	B727/L487/S734
Ps 2:9	Thou shalt break them with a rod of iron; thou shalt dash them in pieces like a potter's vessel	He will be victorious over His enemies	B727/L487/S734
Ps 16:10	For thou wilt not have my soul in hell; neither wilt thou suffer thine Holy One to see corruption	"He will rise again the third day."	B727/L487/S734
Ps 22:13	They gaped upon me with their mouths, as a ravening and a roaring lion	Crucifixion scene written from the perspective of the One being crucified: Christ is surrounded by His enemies, by the individuals who condemned Him. The speaker is situated above the ground, looking down at them	B727/L487/S734

Biblical Verse	KJV Text	Pascal in quotation marks; otherwise, my explication	Fragment Number Brunschvicg/ Lafuma/Sellier
Ps 22:14	I am poured out like water, and all my bones are out of joint: my heart is like wax; it is melted in the midst of my bowels	Crucifixion scene: again, written in the first person. Christ's lungs have collapsed and His internal organs have moved upward into His chest cavity	B727/L487/S734
Ps 22:15	My strength is dried up like a potsherd; and my tongue cleaveth to my jaws; and thou hast brought me into the dust of death	Crucifixion scene: His strength has left Him and death is imminent	B727/L487/S734
Ps 22:16	For dogs have compassed me: the assembly of the wicked have inclosed me: they pierced my hands and my feet	Crucifixion scene; He is surrounded by His enemies; His hands and feet have been pierced	B727/L487/S734
Ps 22:18	They part my garments among them, and cast lots upon my vesture	they cast lots for His clothing	B727/L487/S734
Ps 22:22	I will declare thy name unto my brethren: in the midst of the congregation will I praise thee	Resurrection scene: Christ has risen! [Χριστός ανέστη!] (Mat 28:6; Mark 16:6; Luke 24:6). Christ is victorious over death. The tone and content of this verse is significantly different from preceding verses: Christ has conquered death on behalf of the faithful; He will be the firstborn among many brethren in Heaven. He has confirmed the victory of life over death, of love over hatred, and quells our terror and anxiety at death.	B727/L487/S734
Ps 30:3	thou hast brought up my soul from the grave: thou hast kept me alive, that I should not go down to the pit	"He will rise again the third day."	B727/L487/S734
Ps 69:21	They gave me also gall for my meat; and in my thirst they gave me vinegar to drink	He will be given gall and vinegar to drink	B727/L487/S734

Chapter Two: Table of Messianic Prophecies Fulfilled in Christ

Biblical Verse	KJV Text	Pascal in quotation marks; otherwise, my explication	Fragment number Brunschvicg/ Lafuma/Sellier
Ps 110:1	The LORD said unto my Lord, Sit thou at my right hand, until I make thine enemies thy footstool	A Divine Counsel takes place in Heaven between two Persons of the Holy Trinity; the Son will ascend to Heaven; the Father invites the Son to sit at His right hand; the Father promises the Son that He will be victorious over His enemies.	B727/L487/S734; B731/L624/S517
Ps 110:4	The LORD hath sworn, and will not repent, Thou art a priest for ever after the order of Melchizedek	continuation of the Divine Counsel in Heaven; foreshadowing of Christ; that the order of Aaron's priesthood should be ended, and that of Melchizedek, introduced by the Messiah	B610/L453/S693
Ps 118:22	The stone which the builders refused is become the head stone of the corner	He will be rejected, only to be worshipped by the faithful	B713/L489/S735; B726/L483/S718; B727/L487/S734
Is 5:2	And he fenced it, and gathered out the stones thereof, and planted it with the choicest vine, and built a tower in the midst of it, and also made a winepress therein: and he looked that it should bring forth grapes, and it brought forth wild grapes	the Son of God (the choicest vine) came, sinless and perfectly obedient to the Father, He bore the wrath of God (winepress) on our behalf at the Cross (tower), but was rejected	B713/L489/S735; B735/L347/S379
Is 6:9	And he said, Go, and tell this people, Hear ye indeed, but understand not; and see ye indeed, but perceive not	He will be rejected	B727/L487/S734
Is 8:14-15	And he shall be for a sanctuary; but for a stone of stumbling and for a rock of offence to both the houses of Israel, for a gin and for a snare to the inhabitants of Jerusalem. And many among them shall stumble, and fall, and be broken, and be snared, and be taken	He will provide protection from God's wrath; will be a deliverer from the powers of darkness; He will be rejected	B713/L489/S735; B726/L483/S718

Biblical Verse	KJV Text	Pascal in quotation marks; otherwise, my explication	Fragment number Brunschvicg/ Lafuma/Sellier
Is 9:6	For unto us a child is born, unto us a son is given: and the government shall be upon his shoulder: and his name shall be called Wonderful, Counsellor, The mighty God, The everlasting Father, The Prince of Peace	The Messiah will be born an infant; a son; declared to be the son of God with power; The Wonderful One; The Counsellor, The Mighty God; The Everlasting Father; The Prince of Peace	B727/L487/S734
Is 19:19-22	In that day shall there be an altar to the LORD in the midst of the land of Egypt, and a pillar at the border thereof to the LORD. And it shall be for a sign and for a witness unto the LORD of hosts in the land of Egypt: for they shall cry unto the LORD because of the oppressors, and he shall send them a saviour, and a great one, and he shall deliver them. And the LORD shall be known to Egypt, and the Egyptians shall know the LORD in that day, and shall do sacrifice and oblation; yea, they shall vow a vow unto the LORD, and perform it. And the LORD shall smite Egypt: he shall smite and heal it: and they shall return even to the LORD, and he shall be intreated of them, and shall heal them.	conversion of the Egyptians; an altar in Egypt to the true God	B725/L330/S362
Is 28:16	I lay in Zion for a foundation a stone, a tried stone, a precious corner stone, a sure foundation	He is the precious cornerstone	B727/L487/S734

Chapter Two: Table of Messianic Prophecies Fulfilled in Christ

Biblical Verse	KJV Text	Pascal in quotation marks; otherwise, my explication	Fragment number Brunschvicg/ Lafuma/Sellier
Is 29:9-10	Stay yourselves, and wonder; cry ye out, and cry: they are drunken, but not with wine; they stagger, but not with strong drink. For the LORD hath poured out upon you the spirit of deep sleep, and hath closed your eyes: the prophets and your rulers, the seers hath he covered.	He will be rejected; there will be no more prophets, rulers or seers under the Old Covenant	B713/L489/S735; B726/L483/S718; B727/L487/S734
Is 29:14	Therefore, behold, I will proceed to do a marvellous work among this people, even a marvellous work and a wonder	The Messiah will perform astounding miracles (ie: raise the dead, cure the sick); Christ will give believers a new heart and a new spirit	B713/L489/S735; B726/L483/S718
Is 42:4	and the isles shall wait for his law	He will carry His law to the Gentile world	B727/L345, L487/S734
Is 42:6	and give thee for a covenant of the people, for a light of the Gentiles	the Messiah's covenant will be a light to the Gentiles	B727/L345, L487/S734
Is 42:7	To open the blind eyes, to bring out the prisoner from prison, and them that sit in darkness out of the prison house	the Messiah will open the eyes of the blind (literally, he will heal the blind, and figuratively, He will bring understanding and truth to the pagan world); he will transform lives and free prisoners to sin	B727/L345, L487/S734
Is 42:9	Behold, the former things are come to pass, and new things do I declare: before they spring forth I tell you of them	God announces all things of significance in advance through prophecy	B706/L335/S368; B714/L493/S736

Biblical Verse	KJV Text	Pascal in quotation marks; otherwise, my explication	Fragment Number Brunschvicg/ Lafuma/Sellier
Is 42:16	And I will bring the blind by a way that they knew not; I will lead them in paths that they have not known: I will make darkness light before them, and crooked things straight. These things will I do unto them, and not forsake them.	He will correct all those who believe on Him, significantly, the pagan world, and establish a cataclysmic change in men's hearts and behavior; He will never forsake those who follow Him; idolatry will be overthrown; the Messiah will cast down all idols and bring people to worship the One True God	B727/L345, L487/ S734; B730/L324/ S355
Is 42:17	They shall be turned back, they shall be greatly ashamed, that trust in graven images, that say to the molten images, Ye are our gods	He will establish a hitherto unforeseen change in the pagan world and it will abandon idolatry; the Messiah will cast down all idols and bring people to worship the One True God	B727/L345, L487/ S734; B/730/L324/ S355
Is 42:18	Hear, ye deaf; and look, ye blind, that ye may see	He is calling to all unbelievers	B727/L345, L487/ S734
Is 42:19	Who is blind, but my servant: or deaf, as my messenger that I sent? Who is blind as he that is perfect, and blind as the LORD's servant?	the Messiah will be rejected	B727/L487/S734
Is 42:20	Seeing many things, but thou observest not; opening the ears, but he heareth not	He will be rejected even though He will have performed many miracles (ie: raising Lazarus, Jairus' daughter, the widow's son, Himself, and many dead saints after the Crucifixion; healing the sick) and teaching with great wisdom and authority	B727/L487/S734

Chapter Two: Table of Messianic Prophecies Fulfilled in Christ

Biblical Verse	KJV Text	Pascal in quotation marks; otherwise, my explication	Fragment number Brunschvicg/ Lafuma/Sellier
Is 44:7-8	And who, as I, shall call, and shall declare it, and set it in order for me, since I appointed the ancient people? and the things that are coming, and shall come, let them shew unto them. Fear ye not, neither be afraid: have not I told thee from that time, and have declared it? ye are even my witnesses	God announces things in advance through prophecy: "The prophecies are the strongest proof of Jesus Christ. It is for them also that God has made the most provision; for the event which has fulfilled them is a miracle existing since the birth of the Church to the end. So God has raised up prophets during 1600 years, and, during 400 years afterwards"; "If one man alone had made a book of predictions about Jesus Christ, as to the time and the manner, and Jesus Christ had come in conformity to these prophecies, this fact would have infinite weight. But there is much more here. Here is a succession of men during 4,000 years, who constantly and without variation, come, one after another, to foretell this same event. Here is a whole people who announce it, and who have existed for 4,000 years, in order to give corporate testimony of the assurances which they have, and from which they cannot be diverted by whatever threats and persecutions people may make against them. This is far more important."	B706/L335/S368; B710/L332/S364; B714/L493/S736
Is 45:21	who hath declared this from ancient time? who hath told it from that time? have not I the LORD?	God announces all things in advance through prophecy	B706/L335/S368; B714/L493, L497/ S736

An Eastern Orthodox View of Pascal

Biblical Verse	KJV Text	Pascal in quotation marks; otherwise, my explication	Fragment number Brunschvicg/ Lafuma/Sellier
Is 46:9-10	Remember the former things of old…Declaring the end from the beginning, and from ancient times the things that are not yet done	God announces all things in advance through prophecy	B706/L335/S368; B714/L493/S736
Is 48:3, 5-7	I have declared the former things from the beginning; and they went forth out of my mouth, and I shewed them; I did them suddenly, and they came to pass…I have even from the beginning declared it to thee; before it came to pass I shewed it thee…I have shewed thee new things from this time, even hidden things, and thou didst not know them. They are created now, and not from the beginning; even before the day when thou heardest them not; lest thou shouldest say, Behold, I knew them	God announces all things in advance through prophecy	B706/L335/S368; B714/L493/S736
Is 49:1	Listen, O isles, unto me; and hearken, ye people, from afar; The LORD hath called me from the womb; from the bowels of my mother hath he made mention of my name	Christ is speaking in the first person and He is calling to the Gentile nations; He is relating that the Father has called Him by name while He was still in His mother's womb; conversion of the Gentile world (isles, people from afar); the Messiah will be born of a woman	B714/L493/S736; B715/L498/S736; B724/L338/S370; B726/L483/S718; B727/L345, L487/S734
Is 49:2	And he hath made my mouth like a sharp sword	the Messiah is the Word who both saves and condemns; allusion to the Second Coming when He will judge all of humanity	B714/L493/S736; B715/L498/S736; B724/L338/S370; B726/L483/S718; B727/L345, L487/S734

Chapter Two: Table of Messianic Prophecies Fulfilled in Christ

Biblical Verse	KJV Text	Pascal in quotation marks; otherwise, my explication	Fragment number Brunschvicg/ Lafuma/Sellier
Is 49:3	And said unto me, Thou art my servant, O Israel, in whom I will be glorified	Israel is a metaphor for Christ; the Messiah is God's servant and will glorify Him; Christ is speaking and is relating a Divine Counsel that takes place in Heaven: the Father has said to Him, "Thou are my servant" and "in whom I will be glorified"; the fact that Christ is relating what the Father has told Him is evident in v. 1, 3, 5, 6, 8, 9 (called me from the womb, from the bowels of my mother, my mouth like a sharp sword, shadow of his hand hath he hid me, a light to the Gentiles, that thou mayest be my salvation unto the end of the earth, I will preserve thee, give thee for a covenant of the people, establish the earth, cause to inherit the desolate heritages)	B714/L494/S736; B715/L498/S736; B724/L338/S370; B726/L483/S718; B727/L345, L487/ S734
Is 49:4	Then I said, I have laboured in vain, I have spent my strength for nought, and in vain	Christ continues to relate the Divine Counsel that takes place in Heaven: the Son tells the Father that He will be rejected	B714/L493/S736; B715/L498/S736; B724/L338/S370; B726/L483/S718; B727/L487/S734
Is 49:5	And now, saith the LORD that formed me from the womb to be his servant	Christ relates what the Father has told Him: that He will be born of a woman in order to serve the Father and carry out His will	B714/L493/S736; B715/L498/S736; B724/L338/S370; B726/L483/S718; B727/L487/S734
Is 49:6	I will also give thee for a light to the Gentiles, that thou mayest be my salvation unto the end of the earth	Christ relates what the Father has told Him: that He will convert the Gentile world; that salvation will be carried to every country; that idolatry will be overthrown; that He will cast down all idols and bring people to worship the One True God	B714/L493/S736; B715/L498/S736; B724/L338/S370; B726/L483/S718; B727/L345, L487/ S734; B/730/L324/ S355

Biblical Verse	KJV Text	Pascal in quotation marks; otherwise, my explication	Fragment number Brunschvicg/ Lafuma/Sellier
Is 49:7	Thus saith the LORD, the redeemer of Israel, and his Holy One, to him who man despiseth, to him whom the nation abhorreth, to a servant of rulers, Kings shall see and arise, princes also shall worship, because of the LORD that is faithful, and the Holy One of Israel, and he shall choose thee	Isaiah is relating, from his own point of view, what the Father has said to the Son; the Son will be despised and abhorred; He will be submissive and judged by the rulers who reject Him; kings and princes will worship the Messiah	B714/L493/S736; B715/L498/S736; B724/L338/S370; B726/L483/S718; B727/L345, L487/ S734
Is 49:8	And I will preserve thee, and give thee for a covenant of the people, to establish the earth, to cause to inherit the desolate heritages	conversion of the Gentile world; idolatry will be overthrown; the Messiah will cast down all idols and bring people to worship the One True God	B714/L493/S736; B715/L498/S736; B724/L338/S370; B726/L483/S718; B727/L345, L487/ S734; B730/L324/ S355
Is 49:9	That thou mayest say to the prisoners, Go forth; to them that are in darkness, Shew yourselves	The Messiah will free prisoners from sin; conversion of the Gentile world; the Messiah will overthrow idolatry and bring people to worship the One True God	B726/L483/S718; B730/L324/S355
Is 49:12	Behold, these shall come from far: and, lo, these from the north and from the west; and these from the land of Sinim	conversion of the Gentile world	B714/L493/S736;, B715/L498/S736; B724/L338/S370; B726/L483/S718; B727/L345, L487/ S734
Is 50:2	Wherefore, when I came, was there no man? When I called, was there none to answer? Is my hand shortened at all, that it cannot redeem? Or have I no power to deliver?	The Messiah will be rejected; He has all of God's powers: when He heals the sick, he will forgive sins so that all may know that He has the power to forgive sins; He has the power to redeem people from their sins and to deliver them both spiritually and physically; He holds the keys to life and death in His hands: He will raise Lazarus, Jairus' daughter, the widow's son, Himself, many saints after the Crucifixion	B713/L489/S735; B726/L483/S718

Chapter Two: Table of Messianic Prophecies Fulfilled in Christ

Biblical Verse	KJV Text	Pascal in quotation marks; otherwise, my explication	Fragment number Brunschvicg/ Lafuma/Sellier
Is 50:3	I clothe the heavens with blackness, and I make sackcloth their covering	after He is rejected (the Crucifixion), the sky will be darkened	B726/L483/S718
Is 50:4	The Lord GOD hath given me the tongue of the learned, that I should know how to speak a word in reason to him that is weary	the Messiah has the tongue of the learned; He will comfort the weary and heavy laden	B726/L483/S718
Is 50:5	and I was not rebellious, neither turned away back	The Messiah will not be rebellious; He will do the will of God; He will accept the cup that is before Him; he will be silent before His accusers and be led as a lamb to the slaughter	B726/L483/S718
Is 50:6	I gave my back to the smiters, and my cheeks to them that plucked off the hair: I hid not my face from shame and spitting	the Messiah will be beaten and spat upon	B726/L483/S718
Is 50:7	Therefore shall I not be confounded: therefore have I set my face like a flint, and I know that I shall not be ashamed	the Messiah will not be confounded by His enemies	B726/L483/S718
Is 50:8	He is near that justifieth me; who will contend with me?	the Messiah will be justified by God	B726/L483/S718
Is 51:4	Hearken unto me, my people; and give ear unto me, O my nation: for a law shall proceed from me, and I will make my judgment to rest for a light of the people	a light of the Gentiles	B714/L493, L497/ S736; B715/L498/ S736; B724/L338/ S370; B726/L483/ S718; B727/L345, L487/S734
Is 51:5	the isles shall wait upon me, and on mine arm shall they trust	conversion of the Gentile world	B726/L483/S718
Is 52:10	The LORD hath made bare his holy arm in the eyes of all the nations; and all the ends of the earth shall see the salvation of our God	The Messiah will be worshipped in every country on earth; conversion of the pagan world; He will bring the forgiveness of sin to all nations	B711/L484/S719

Biblical Verse	KJV Text	Pascal in quotation marks; otherwise, my explication	Fragment Number Brunschvicg/ Lafuma/Sellier
Is 52:14	As many were astonied at thee; his visage was so marred more than any man, and his form more than the sons of men	the Passion of Christ foretold; Crucifixion scene	B727/L487/S734
Is 52:15	So shall he sprinkle many nations; the kings shall shut their mouths at him: for that which had not been told them shall they see; and that which they had not heard shall they consider	Baptism of many nations foretold; conversion of the Gentile world; kings will obey Him; He is master of the nations	B714/L493/S736; B715/L498/S736; B724/L338/S370; B726/L483/S718; B727/L345, L487/ S734
Is 53:1	Who hath believed our report? and to whom is the arm of the LORD revealed?	the Messiah will be rejected	B714/L493/S736; B727/L345, L487/ S734
Is 53:2	For he shall grow up before him as a tender plant, and as a root out of a dry ground: he hath no form nor comeliness; and when we shall see him, there is no beauty that we should desire him	He will grow up as a child, will be humble, and will not be recognized as the Messiah	B727/L487/S734; B736/L609/S504
Is 53:3	He is despised and rejected of men; a man of sorrows, and acquainted with grief: and we hid as it were our faces from him; he was despised, and we esteemed him not	Passion and Crucifixion: despised by men; rejected; man of sorrows; acquainted with grief; the people turned away from him; despised; not esteemed	B727/L487/S734
Is 53:4	Surely he hath borne our griefs, and carried our sorrows: yet we did esteem him stricken, smitten of God, and afflicted	Passion and Crucifixion: borne our griefs; carried our sorrows; stricken; smitten of God; afflicted. What is key here is that Isaiah is telling us why He is stricken: He is bearing our sins; He is bearing our griefs; carrying our sorrows	B727/L487/S734

Chapter Two: Table of Messianic Prophecies Fulfilled in Christ

Biblical Verse	KJV Text	Pascal in quotation marks; otherwise, my explication	Fragment number Brunschvicg/ Lafuma/Sellier
Is 53:5	But he was wounded for our transgressions, he was bruised for our iniquities: the chastisement of our peace was upon him; and with his stripes we are healed	Passion and Crucifixion: wounded; bruised; chastisement was upon Him; his stripes; Again, Isaiah is repeating that He is being punished in our place, for our transgressions: He was wounded for our transgression; He was bruised for our iniquities; He was chastised so that we would have peace; we are spiritually healed through His stripes. At this point it is obvious that He is the Lamb of God that takes away the sins of the world	B727/L487/S734
Is 53:6	All we like sheep have gone astray; we have turned every one to his own way; and the LORD hath laid on him the iniquity of us all	This is the third time that Isaiah is telling us that He is being punished for our sins: because all we like sheep have gone astray, and have turned to our own ways, God has laid the blame for all of our sins on Him	B727/L487/S734
Is 53:7	He was oppressed, and he was afflicted, yet he opened not his mouth: he is brought as a lamb to the slaughter, and as a sheep before her shearers is dumb, so he openeth not his mouth	Passion and Crucifixion: oppressed; afflicted; analogy with the sacrifice of the red heifer in Numbers 19: He is brought as a lamb to the slaughter, and like a lamb, He does not open His mouth; as a sheep before the shearers is silent, so he does not open His mouth	B727/L487/S734

Biblical Verse	KJV Text	Pascal in quotation marks; otherwise, my explication	Fragment Number Brunschvicg/ Lafuma/Sellier
Is 53:8	He was taken from prison and from judgment: and who shall declare his generation? for he was cut off out of the land of the living: for the transgression of my people was he stricken	Passion and Crucifixion: taken from prison; judgment; cut off from the land of the living; stricken. This is the fourth time that Isaiah is telling us why He is stricken: for the transgressions of sinners was he stricken. He died in our place, for our transgressions.	B727/L487/S734
Is 53:9	And he made his grave with the wicked, and with the rich in his death; because he had done no violence, neither was any deceit in his mouth	He was crucified with two thieves; the rich man, Nicodemus, gave Him his tomb; He is the perfect sacrifice to which the red heifer in Num 19 foreshadows: he has done no violence, there is no deceit in His mouth, He is without sin.	B727/L487/S734
Is 53:10	Yet is pleased the LORD to bruise him; he hath put him to grief: when thou shalt make his soul an offering for sin, he shall see his seed, he shall prolong his days, and the pleasure of the LORD shall prosper in his hand	This is the fifth time that Isaiah explains why He is stricken: He is an offering for sin; when the nations believe on Him and are clothed in His righteousness (because they, themselves, are unrighteous), He shall see His progeny and prosper.	B727/L345, L487/ S734
Is 53:11	He shall see of the travail of his soul, and shall be satisfied: by his knowledge shall my righteous servant justify many; for he shall bear their iniquities	This is the sixth time that Isaiah explains why He is stricken: by His knowledge, many will be justified; He shall bear their iniquities.	B726/L345, L487/ S734
Is 53:12	Therefore will I divide him a portion with the great, and he shall divide the spoil with the strong; because he hath poured out his soul unto death: and he was numbered with the transgressors; and he bare the sin of many, and made intercession for the transgressors	This is the seventh time that Isaiah explains why this righteous servant of God was stricken: He bare the sin of many and made intercession for sinners.	B727/L487/S734

Chapter Two: Table of Messianic Prophecies Fulfilled in Christ

Biblical Verse	KJV Text	Pascal in quotation marks; otherwise, my explication	Fragment number Brunschvicg/ Lafuma/Sellier
Is 55:3	Incline your ear, and come unto me: hear, and your soul shall live	the Messiah will give everlasting life to the soul	B727/L487/S734
Is 55:5	Behold, thou shalt call a nation that thou knowest not, and nations that knew not thee shall run unto thee because of the LORD thy God, and for the Holy One of Israel; he hath glorified thee	conversion of the Gentile world; idolatry will be overthrown; the Messiah will cast down all idols and bring people to worship the One True God	B714/L493/S736; B715/L498/S736; B724/L338/S370; B726/L483/S718; B727/L345, L487/ S734; B730/L324/ S355
Is 56:3-5	Neither let the son of the stranger, that hath joined himself to the LORD, speak, saying, The LORD hath utterly separated me from his people: neither let the eunuch say, Behold, I am a dry tree. For thus saith the LORD unto the eunuchs that keep my sabbaths, and choose the things that please me, and take hold of my covenant; Even unto them will I give in mine house and within my walls a place and a name better than of sons and of daughters: I will give them an everlasting name, that shall not be cut off	conversion of the Gentile world; foreshadows that the first person saved in the Book of Acts is the eunuch of Ethiopia of the Court of Queen Candace	B610/L453/S693; B714/L493/S736; B715/L498/S736; B724/L338/S370; B726/L483/S718; B727/L345, L487/ S734
Is 59:9-11	Therefore is judgment far from us, neither doth justice overtake us: we wait for light, but behold obscurity; for brightness, but we walk in darkness. We grope for the wall like the blind, and we grope as if we had no eyes: we stumble at noon day as in the night; we are in desolate places as dead men. We roar all like bears, and mourn sore like doves: we look for judgment, but there is none; for salvation, but it is far off from us	the Messiah will be rejected	B713/L489/S735; B726/L483/S718

Biblical Verse	KJV Text	Pascal in quotation marks; otherwise, my explication	Fragment number Brunschvicg/ Lafuma/Sellier
Is 60:1-5	Arise, shine; for thy light is come, and the glory of the LORD is risen upon thee. For, behold, the darkness shall cover the earth, and gross darkness the people: but the LORD shall arise upon thee, and his glory shall be seen upon thee. And the Gentiles shall come to thy light, and kings to the brightness of thy rising. Lift up thine eyes round about, and see: all they gather themselves together, they come to thee: thy sons shall come from far, and thy daughters shall be nursed at thy side. Then thou shalt see, and flow together, and thine heart shall fear, and be enlarged; because the abundance of the sea shall be converted unto thee, the forces of the Gentiles shall come unto thee	The calling of the Gentiles; the Messiah will be a light unto the Gentile world; the flourishing state of Christianity under the Messiah shall be evident and unmistakable; the Lord arises to light the spiritual darkness covering the earth and He dispels the darkness of the pagan world. The Resurrection of the Christ is implied: the Lord shall arise upon thee, and his glory shall be seen and the Gentiles shall come to thy light	B716/L334/S366
Is 61:1	The Spirit of the Lord GOD is upon me; because the LORD hath anointed me to preach good tidings unto the meek; he hath sent me to bind up the brokenhearted, to proclaim liberty to the captives, and the opening of the prisons to them that are bound	the Holy Spirit is upon Him; He is anointed (as King) by God; He preaches the goods news about everlasting life to the meek; He binds up the brokenhearted; He frees people who have been prisoner to sin	B727/L345, L487/ S734
Is 65:1	I am sought of them that asked not for me; I am found of them that sought me not: I said, Behold me, behold me, unto a nation that was not called by my name	conversion of the Gentile world	B714/L493, L497/ S736; B715/L498/ S736; B724/L338/ S370; B726/L483/ S718; B727/L345, L487/S734

Chapter Two: Table of Messianic Prophecies Fulfilled in Christ

Biblical Verse	KJV Text	Pascal in quotation marks; otherwise, my explication	Fragment number Brunschvicg/Lafuma/Sellier
Is 65:8	Thus saith the LORD, As the new wine is found in the cluster, and one saith, Destroy it not; for a blessing is in it: so I will do for my servants' sakes, that I may not destroy them all	God will establish a new covenant	B713/L489/S735; B715/L498/S736; B726/L483/S718; B729/L346/S378
Is 65:9	And I will bring forth a seed out of Jacob, and out of Judah an inheritor of my mountains; and mine elect shall inherit it, and my servants shall dwell there	the Messiah will be of the seed of Jacob and of Judah	B711/L484/S719; B713/L459/S735; B727/L487/S734
Is 65:13	Therefore thus saith the Lord GOD, Behold, my servants shall eat, but ye shall be hungry: behold, my servants hall drink, but ye shall be thirsty: behold, my servants shall rejoice, but ye shall be ashamed	the Messiah will be rejected	B713/L459/S735, B726/L483/S718
Is 66:18-19	For I know their works and their thoughts: it shall come, that I will gather all nations and tongues; and they shall come, and see my glory. And I will set a sign among them, and I will send those that escape of them unto the nations, to Tarshish, Pul, and Lud, that draw the bow, to Tubal, and Javan, to the isles afar off, that have not heard my fame, neither have seen my glory; and they shall declare my glory among the Gentiles	conversion of the Gentile world	B714/L493, L497/S736; B715/L498/S736; B724/L338/S370; B726/L483/S718; B727/L345, L487/S734

Biblical Verse	KJV Text	Pascal in quotation marks; otherwise, my explication	Fragment number Brunschvicg/ Lafuma/Sellier
Amos 8:9	And it shall come to pass in that day, saith the Lord GOD, that I will cause the sun to go down at noon, and I will darken the earth in the clear day	"He says this: 'And it shall come to pass Pascal cites this verse verbatim because it prophecizes the darkening of the sky during the Crucifixion	B726/L483/S718
Dan 2:39	And after thee shall arise another kingdom inferior to thee, and another third kingdom of brass, which shall bear rule over all the earth	The first kingdom is that of Nebuchadnezzar; the second, that of the Medes and Persians; the third, the Grecian monarchy under Alexander the Great	B708/L333/S365; B709L336/S367; B722/L485/S720; B724/L338/S370
Dan 2:40	And the fourth kingdom shall be strong as iron: forasmuch as iron breaketh in pieces and subdueth all things: and as iron breaketh all these, shall it break in pieces and bruise	The fourth kingdom is that of the Romans	B708/L333/S365; B709/L336/S367; B722/L485/S720; B724/L338/S370
Dan 2:44	And in the days of these kings shall the God of heaven set up a kingdom, which shall never be destroyed: and the kingdom shall not be left to other people, but it shall break in pieces and consume all these kingdoms, and it shall stand for ever	The Messiah's advent will be during the fourth monarchy (Roman). "And in the days of these kings" is the iron kingdom; Christ was born during the reign of Augustus Caesar; Christ's kingdom has no boundaries, as earthly kingdoms do, it is universal; it will stand forever, never be destroyed or given to others, as are earthly kingdoms	B708/L333/S365; B709/L336/S367; B722/L485/S720; B724/L338/S370

Chapter Two: Table of Messianic Prophecies Fulfilled in Christ

Biblical Verse	KJV Text	Pascal in quotation marks; otherwise, my explication	Fragment number Brunschvicg/ Lafuma/Sellier
Dan 9:5-24	We have sinned, and have committed iniquity, and have done wickedly, and have rebelled, even by departing from thy precepts and from thy judgments: Neither have we hearkened unto thy servants the prophets…through all the countries whither thou hast driven them, because of their trespass that they have trespassed against thee. Because we have sinned against thee…Yea, all Israel have transgressed thy law…Therefore hath the LORD watched upon the evil…we obeyed not his voice…we have sinned, we have done wickedly…And while I was…confessing my sin and the sin of my people…the man Gabriel… informed me…Seventy weeks are determined upon thy people and upon thy holy city, to finish the transgression, and to make an end of sins, and to make reconciliation for iniquity, and to bring in everlasting righteousness, and to seal up the vision and prophecy, and to anoint the most Holy	"Daniel (Chap. ix.) prays for the deliverance of the people from the captivity of their enemies. But he was thinking of sins, and to show this, he says that Gabriel came to tell him that his prayer was heard, and that there were only seventy weeks to wait, after which the people would be freed from iniquity, sin would have an end, and the Redeemer, the Holy of Holies, would bring eternal justice, not legal, but eternal."	B692/L269/S300
Dan 9:25-26	from the going forth of the commandment to restore and to rebuild Jerusalem unto the Messiah the Prince shall be seven weeks, and threescore and two weeks: the streets shall be built again, and the wall, even in troublous times. And after threescore and two weeks shall Messiah be cut off, but not for himself: and the people of the prince that shall come shall destroy the city and the sanctuary	Jesus Christ foretold as to the time and the state of the world; the first Palm Sunday announced to His people 483 lunar years to the exact day, after the decree to rebuild the wall of Jerusalem; executed for the sins of others, not for Himself; His execution will occur before the destruction of the Temple	B701/L317/S348; B708/L333/S365; B709/L336/S367; B711/L484/S719; B722/L485/S720; B723/L341/S373; B726/L483/S718

An Eastern Orthodox View of Pascal

Biblical Verse	KJV Text	Pascal in quotation marks; otherwise, my explication	Fragment number Brunschvicg/ Lafuma/Sellier
Dan 12:10	Many shall be purified, and made white, and tried; but the wicked shall do wickedly: and none of the wicked shall understand; but the wise shall understand	"tried" implies the persecution and/or testing of the early Church; believers are made pure by the Blood of Christ; the wise will understand; the wicked will not	B713/L459/S735; B726/L483/S718
Hos 2:23	And I will sow her unto me in the earth; and I will have mercy upon her that had not obtained mercy; and I will say to them which are not my people, Thou art my people; and they shall say, Thou art my God	conversion of the Gentile world	B714/L493/S736; B715/L498/S736; B724/L338/S370; B726/L483/S718; B727/L345, L487/S734
Hos 6:3	After two days will he revive us: in the third day he will raise us up, and we shall live in his sight	"He will rise again the third day."	B727/L487/S734
Mic 5:2	But thou, Bethlehem Ephratah, though thou be little among the thousands of Judah, yet out of thee shall he come forth unto me that is to be ruler in Israel; whose goings forth have been from old, from everlasting	He will be born in Bethlehem	B727/L487/S734
Hag 2:7-9	And I will shake all nations, and the desire of all nations shall come: and I will fill this house with glory, saith the LORD of hosts. The silver is mine, and the gold is mine, saith the LORD of hosts. The glory of this latter house shall be greater than of the former, saith the LORD of hosts: and in this place will I give peace, saith the LORD of hosts	conversion of the Gentile world; the New Covenant is greater and more glorious than the Old	B714/L493/S736; B715/L498/S736; B724/L338/S370; B726/L483/S718; B727/L345, L487/S734

Chapter Two: Table of Messianic Prophecies Fulfilled in Christ

Biblical Verse	KJV Text	Pascal in quotation marks; otherwise, my explication	Fragment number Brunschvicg/ Lafuma/Sellier
Zech 9:9	Thy King cometh unto thee: he is just, and having salvation; lowly, and riding upon an ass, and upon a colt the foal of an ass	"The prophecies, which represent Him as poor, represent Him as master of the nations"; foretells that the Messiah will enter Jerusalem triumphantly on a donkey	B727/L487/S734
Zech 11:12-13	So they weighed for my price thirty pieces of silver. And the LORD said unto me, cast it unto the potter: a goodly price that I was prised at of them. And I took the thirty pieces of silver, and cast them to the potter in the house of the LORD	He is to be sold for thirty pieces of silver; it will be cast to the potter	B727/L487/S734
Zech 12:10	and they shall look upon me whom they have pierced, and they shall mourn for him, as one mourneth for his only son	Crucifixion scene; He will be pierced; an only son	B727/L487/S734
Mal 1:11	For from the rising of the sun even unto the going down of the same my name shall be great among the Gentiles; and in every place incense shall be offered unto my name, and a pure offering: for my name shall be great among the heathen, saith the LORD of hosts	conversion of the Gentile world; Christians will burn incense at His altar in every nation; Christ is a pure offering, for He is without sin; His name is great among the Gentiles; the Messiah will overthrow idolatry and bring people to worship the One True God	B714/L493/S736; B715/L498/S736; B724/L338/S370; B726/L483/S718; B727/L345, L487/S734; B730/L324/S355
Mal 3:1	Behold, I will send my messenger, and he shall prepare the way before me	the Messiah will have a forerunner (John the Baptist)	B727/L487/S734

Christ's Miracles Prove His Divinity

Then saith he to Thomas,
Reach hither thy finger, and behold my hands;
and reach hither thy hand, and thrust it into my side:
and be not faithless, but believing.
And Thomas answered and said unto him,
My LORD and my God.
— John 20:27-28

When Pascal set out to write his defense of Christianity, he recognized that the two greatest proofs of the existence of a Divine Being who created the universe, came to earth, and revealed Himself to men, are miracles and the fulfillment of prophecy. If Christ's mission was supported by miracles and the fulfillment of prophecy to the most miniscule detail, then it was divine and it should be accepted by the whole world. There exists a vast treasury of material on the miracles that Christ performed both in the Bible and in the history of the Church since Pentecost. Pascal was well aware of this fact, and yet, however, he chose to set his bundles of fragments on miracles aside rather than include them in his larger grouping of 27 bundles. In this chapter we will show that Pascal's flawed Jansenist theology regarding double election caused him to view miracles as opportunities that God took to save the elect and to condemn the damned to hell: this is blasphemy, a denial of God's goodness and justice, and a twisting of Scripture. His fragments on miracles do not glorify Christ; they are an essay in circular reasoning that argues that man has as much reason to disbelieve as he does to believe. The reader readily observes that Pascal is being deliberately confusing in order to undermine reason, that he questions whether miracles have any value at all in bringing people closer to God, and that therefore, he missed an excellent opportunity to use the historical evidential reality of miracles as a tool to bring people to Christ.

Let us begin, then, by reviewing the great miracles performed by Christ and then contrast these events to Pascal's meager, pathetic presentation of them in *Thoughts*. The Lord's miracles are ample testimony as to His divinity, His authority to forgive humanity's sins, His love, and His willingness to provide. The Lord, who compassionately fed more than 4,000 and 5,000 people on two occasions from a few fish and loaves of bread, is the same Lord who provided manna from Heaven and water from a split rock to the people in the desert.

Christ's Power to Resurrect the Dead

Among Christ's greatest miracles were those in which He resurrected the dead. He did this a number of times, both during His ministry and after He surrendered His Ghost on the Cross. There are five instances in the NT in which Christ resurrected the dead (including Himself) and if we address them in chronological order, we will see that a pattern arises in which the glorification of God gradually increases and reaches a crescendo. In the first example, Christ resurrected a woman's son at Nain. She was a widow and she was mourning the loss of her only son. When the bier of the young man was brought to Jesus, He touched it and said, "Young man, I say unto thee, Arise." The man sat up in the coffin and began to speak (Luke 7:11-17). Christ also raised Jairus' twelve year old daughter from the dead (Mat 9:24-25, Mark 5:39-42, Luke 8:49-55). Another resurrection took place when Christ raised his beloved friend, Lazarus, from the dead. After his resurrection, Lazarus went on to found a church in Kition, Cyprus (now Larnaca) and he lived another thirty years. The Eastern Orthodox Church believes that remains discovered beneath the altar of the Church of Saint Lazarus in Larnaca belong to Lazarus and that therefore, this site bears physical evidence of the first man in human history to be resurrected and to die again after he had already been dead and buried for four days. This burial site is held as physical proof of Christ's power to resurrect the dead and therefore, of His divinity.

A fourth example of the resurrection of the dead occurred immediately after Christ surrendered His Ghost on the Cross. The apostle Matthew tells us that the bodies of many OT saints who had died arose and were seen by many in Jerusalem. Since this is an apocalyptic event in human history, let us examine a literal translation of the original Greek text: "And the tombs were opened and many bodies of the saints having fallen asleep were raised, and having gone out from the tombs after the resurrection of him they entered into the holy city and they appeared to many" (Mat 27:52-53).[1] In this powerful statement, Matthew informs us that the graves of OT saints, such as Abraham and Sarah, must be empty today. These graves are well guarded and no one is allowed to open them to see whether they still contain the remains of those who had died. However, physical evidence of the veracity of Matthew's account of the resurrection of OT saints does reside in the tombs of Abraham and Sarah and one only need open them to verify the miracle that God had done immediately after Christ surrendered His Ghost on the Cross.

Christ had journeyed to *sheol* and released the OT saints who had died before His advent. In Hebrew *sheol* means "the abode of the dead." It is the Semitic equivalent to the Greek concept of Hades. Christians consider it to be the destination of the dead prior to Christ's Resurrection. *Strong's Concordance* indicates that *sheol* appears 31 times in the OT when the KJV translates it as "hell" and another 30 times when the KJV translates it as "grave." The meaning of *sheol* can be readily inferred from Ps 16:10: "For thou will not leave my soul in *sheol*; neither wilt thou suffer thine Holy One is see corruption." This verse is helpful in understanding what *sheol* means because we see that it is a place where the soul goes. The sentence is divided into two parts: in the first half, the soul goes to *sheol*; in the second, the physical part, the flesh, suffers corruption. We see a division of the parts of the person after death. This verse can be understood on at least three levels: the surface level and two deeper levels. On the surface, the psalmist, David, is confident that when he dies, his soul will not remain in *sheol*, but that His Savior will release him and take him to Heaven. On a deeper level, this verse is a prophecy of the Resurrection of Christ. In addition, it is also a prophecy of Mat 27:52-53 in which Christ releases the OT saints from *sheol*. We can be confident that the grave of David is empty and that God raised him after Christ surrendered His Ghost on the Cross and resurrected "many bodies of the saints having fallen asleep."

Paul advises, since the Lord was the first to rise from the dead and because He set free the souls in *sheol* that had been awaiting Him, believers in Christ can be certain that when they die they will be with Him: "Therefore we are always confident, knowing that, whilst we are at home in the body, we are absent from the Lord" (2 Cor 5:6) and "We are confident, I say, and

Chapter Three: Christ's Miracles Prove His Divinity

willing rather to be absent from the body, and to be present with the Lord (2 Cor 5:8). There are only two possibilities for the follower of Christ: either he is in the body or else he is with the Lord. That is because "to be absent in the body is to be present with the Lord."

Finally, the fifth, greatest and most significant resurrection was that of Christ Himself, which occurred, not coincidentally, on the Feast of the First Fruits. The fact that He had gone to *sheol* (Hades) and released OT believers who had died before His Advent and Crucifixion, was proven by the fact that there were many in Jerusalem who saw resurrected dead people and also, many who saw the resurrected Christ.

The resurrection of Christ was prophesied in the OT, was predicted by Christ, Himself, and was witnessed by more than five hundred people at one time, including the apostles (1 Cor 15:6). The fact that men and women became courageous and were willing to die for what they had observed and knew to be true is evidence of the transformative power that His Resurrection had on all who saw Him. Early believers who had seen the resurrection of the dead, the healing of the sick, and the Risen Lord, lost their fear of death and were certain of immortality, despite the imminent thread of persecution.

A good place to begin an examination of Christ's miracles is Mat 9 because this chapter begins with His healing of the sick and includes His resurrection of a young girl from the dead. Matthew takes care to point out that the Lord's healing was intimately intertwined with the forgiveness of sin. He also notes that there was a certain ruler of the synagogue who prostrated himself before Him in adoration and asked for the resurrection of his little girl who had died; Christ, in his compassion, granted the man's prayer. Mark and Luke tells us that this ruler's name was Jairus.

Matthew begins chapter 9 by recalling that Christ healed a man sick with the palsy (Mat 9:2-7). The *OED* defines "palsy" as "paralysis or paresis (weakness) of all or part of the body, sometimes with tremor."[2] In the six verses that comprise Mat 9:27, we have five declarations of Christ's divinity. The first occurs just prior to the paralytic's healing. Jesus declares, "Be of good cheer; thy sins be forgiven thee" (Mat 9:2). He made it clear that he had the authority to forgive sin and this was an affirmation of His deity. The scribes understood the significance of this (God alone has the authority to forgive sin) and they said among themselves that this was blasphemy. Jesus knew what they were thinking and asked, "Wherefore think ye evil in your hearts? For whether is easier to say, Thy sins be forgiven thee; or to say, Arise, and walk?" (Mat 9:4-5). The question, "Wherefore, think ye evil in your hearts?" is a second declaration of His divinity for two reasons. First, he demonstrated that he knew what they were thinking and what was in their hearts. Secondly, he held that equating His forgiveness of sin with blasphemy is intrinsically evil because it refuses to acknowledge His divine nature. The equation forgiveness = blasphemy is intrinsically flawed and evil because it is a conscious denial of Christ's divine nature. Thirdly, Christ acknowledges that His forgiveness is just as easy to grant as is His healing because He is God. He can rearrange the physical matter in a person's body and make him whole because He is God incarnate. Therefore, He has the authority to forgive sin. The apostle John will tell us that He created everything that there is and that there is nothing which is that he did not create (John 1:3). Fourthly, Jesus explains, "But that ye may know that the Son of man hath power on earth to forgive sins..." Fifthly, Jesus commands the sick man, "Arise, take up thy bed, and go unto thine house." Matthew tells us that when the multitudes saw the miracles, they marveled and glorified God.

In Mat 9:9 Jesus is walking past the customs table and calls Matthew. Matthew was a customs officer and tax collector. Jesus said only two words: "Follow me." Matthew informs us that at that moment he arose from the customs table (he left his job) and followed the Lord; Matthew traveled with Him during His 3½ year ministry.

Jesus went to Matthew's house and sat down to eat with tax collectors and sinners. When His disciples were asked why He was dining with tax collectors and sinners, Jesus heard the question and declared, "I am not come to call the righteous, but sinners to repentance" (Mat 9:13). Hence, He points out that all have sinned and have fallen short of the glory of God. Christ came to minister unto those who had the humility to admit that they were sinners. All that was required was for the individual to own up to the fact that he was a sinner in need of forgiveness: Christ always forgave those who asked for forgiveness. Hence, the statement, "I am not come to call the righteous" is a statement that recognizes that man has free will: either he can declare himself to be perfect or else he can admit that he has shortcomings and that he needs to be forgiven.

Chapter Three: Christ's Miracles Prove His Divinity

Then Christ makes a series of prophecies. First, He is asked why the Pharisees fast and His disciples do not. He responds, "Can the children of the bridechamber mourn, as long as the bridegroom is with them? but the days will come, when the bridegroom shall be taken from them, and then shall they fast" (Mat 9:15). This is a prediction of His own execution. Furthermore, the metaphors of bride and bridegroom recur throughout the NT. The Church is metaphorized as the bride of Christ. The metaphors bride, bride chamber or bridegroom appear in Mat 9:15; 25:1; 25:5-6; 25:10; Mark 2:19-20; Luke 5:34-35; 3:29; Rev 21:2; 21:9; 22:17. These metaphors imply faithfulness, protection and concern about the people of God. In human relationships, marriage implies the extension of ego boundaries so that both parties are concerned about the happiness and welfare of each other. The marriage metaphor provides a hint, an allusion to the ultimate theosis or union with God that awaits every believer. Just as in Gen 2:24 Adam and Eve become a unity, one flesh, so also in theosis, Christians will one day achieve spiritual union with God. Orthodox teaching on theosis will be discussed more fully in Chapter 6. He prophesizes the fasting that will take place during Lent for two millennia in remembrance of His Passion and Crucifixion.

Following the metaphorization of God's people as the bride of Christ, He makes a declaration of the New Covenant and distinguishes it from the Old Covenant: "No man putteth a piece of new cloth unto an old garment, for that which is put in to fill it up taketh from the garment, and the rent is made worse. Neither do men put new wine into old bottles: else the bottles break, and the wine runneth out, and the bottles perish: but they put new wine into new bottles, and both are preserved" (Mat 9:16-17). Here the Old Covenant is metaphorized both as an old garment and an old wine bottle; the New Covenant is likened to a piece of new cloth that is used to make a new garment and also to a new wine bottle. He makes it clear that from that moment on that the covenant that God made with Abraham had metamorphosed into its fullness. Christ is the fulfillment of the Law and all the promises that God made to humanity through His prophets.

This is in fulfillment of the prophecy uttered by the prophet Jeremiah: "Behold, the days come, saith the LORD, that I will make a new covenant with the house of Israel, and with the house of Judah: Not according to the covenant that I made with their fathers in the day that I took them by the hand to bring them out of the land of Egypt...But his shall be the covenant that I will make with the house of Israel; After those days, saith the LORD, I will put my law in their inward parts, and write it in their hearts; and will be their God, and they shall be my people. And they shall teach no more every man his neighbour, and every man his brother, saying Know the LORD: for they shall all know me, from the least of them unto the greatest of them, saith the LORD: for I will forgive their iniquity, and I will remember their sin no more" (Jer 31:31-34).

At this point a ruler of a synagogue came forward and worshipped Christ. Matthew says, "...there came a certain ruler, and worshipped him..." (Mat 9:18). The original Greek uses the verb *proskineo* [προσκυνέω], meaning to prostrate oneself in homage, reverence, adoration, worship. The *OED* defines "prostrate" thus: "In strict use, Lying with the face to the ground, in token of submission or humility"[3] While the KJV says, "and worshipped him," the Greek word is much more graphic and indicates that the ruler of the synagogue, who must have been thoroughly acquainted with Hebrew Scriptures and prophecies that the healing of the sick would occur during the Messianic age, humbly prostrated himself on the ground in adoration of the Lord.

Proskineo is used again to identify the adoration of the three magi before the infant Jesus: "And when they were come into the house, they saw the young child with Mary his mother, and fell down, and worshipped him: and when they had opened their treasures, they presented unto him gifts; gold, and frankincense, and myrrh" (Mat 2:11). Here, *proskineo*, to worship, is preceded by "fell down"; the tautology hyperbolizes the great humility that the magi had and that they recognized Him as a king. Also, in the following verse, *proskineo* is preceded by "falling down on his face": "And thus are the secrets of his heart made manifest; and so falling down on his face he will worship God, and report that God is in you..." (1 Cor 14:25). Again, the tautology of "falling down on his face" and *proskineo* hyperbolizes the act of worshipping God. This form of worship is also seen in Heaven before Christ: "And the four and twenty elders, which sat before God on their seats, fell upon their faces, and worshipped God" (Rev 11:16).

Chapter Three: Christ's Miracles Prove His Divinity

The Greek language also has two other words meaning "worship": *latreo* [λατρεύω] and *sevomai* [σέβομαι]. *Latreo* [λατρεύω] means to pay homage, to worship. It is used in Phil 3:3, which says, "For we are the circumcision, which worship God in the spirit, and rejoice in Christ Jesus, and have no confidence in the flesh." Here, worship is used in the general sense and does not graphically illustrate the act of lying face down on the ground. In fact, "worship God in the spirit" denotes a spiritual adoration, not a physical act. The other Greek word for worship, *sevomai* [σέβομαι], means to revere, to adore, to worship. It is used in Acts 18:7, in which the apostle Paul "entered into a certain man's house, named Justus, one that worshipped God, whose house joined hard to the synagogue." Again, *sevomai*, like *latreo*, means worship in the general sense and does not connote physical prostration. Hence, the original Greek in Mat 9:18, that specifies that the ruler of the synagogue fell on the ground in prostration, tells us that the Father had revealed to him the divinity of Christ. Mark and Luke tell us that the man's name was Jairus.

The Father in Heaven had opened this man's eyes and had revealed to him that Christ was God incarnate on earth. When the faithful came to Christ and asked for help, He never turned them away. This man, who worshipped Him, made the ultimate declaration of faith: he declared that he believed that Christ had the power to resurrect the dead. The man said, "My daughter is even now dead: but come and lay thine hand upon her, and she shall live" (Mat 9:18). This declaration also indicates that Jairus recognized Christ's divine nature: only God can raise the dead. Hence, the fact that he worshipped him and his confidence that Christ could resurrect his daughter from the dead are two signs that he acknowledged Christ to be God Incarnate.

When Jesus entered the ruler's house, he encountered professional mourners who were making noise and playing the flute. The flute players were professional musicians hired to play in mourning ceremonies. When Jesus said, "The maid is not dead, but sleepeth," the musicians and professional mourners in the house scornfully laughed and mocked Him. Jesus had them removed from the house and then "he went in, and took her by the hand, and the maid arose" (Mat 9:25). Matthew informs us that His fame spread throughout the whole land.

The other gospel writers also relate this story, but include other details (Mark 5:39-42; Luke 8:49-55). Mark tells us that the father was the ruler of the synagogue and that the people in the house were weeping and wailing greatly. Christ put the visitors out, took the father, mother, and those that were in His company, and entered where the girl was lying. Mark tells us that Christ took her by the hand and said, "Talitha Cumi," which, in Aramaic, means, "Damsel, I say unto thee, arise." The girl immediately arose and walked; she was twelve years old; Christ commanded that she be given something to eat.

Luke's account of the miracle provides more information. Christ said, "Fear not: believe only, and she shall be made whole." Here we have the command not to fear and also a statement as to the direct causality between belief and cure. We are also told that He allowed only Peter, James, John, and the parents of the girl to enter the house. The mourners that were there scornfully laughed when He said, "Weep not; she is not dead, but sleepeth" and he removed them from the house. He took her by the hand and commanded, Maid, arise," "and her spirit came again, and she arose straightway."

Matthew informs us that after Jesus performed this miracle and left the ruler's home, He healed two blind men (Mat 9:27). He asked them, "Do you believe that I am able to do this?" They replied, "Yes, Lord," and he restored their vision. This event, along with many other times when He restored vision to the blind, were a fulfillment of Isaiah's prophecy that during the Messianic age, the blind will see, the deaf will hear, the lame will leap like deer, and the mute will shout with joy (Is 35:5).

A third resurrection of the dead and a striking testimony as to the divine nature of Christ occurred when He restored His friend Lazarus to life (John 11:1-44; 12:10-11; Acts 11:19). Lazarus and his sisters, Martha and Mary, lived in Bethany. The apostle John, who traveled with the Lord during His 3½ year ministry and who witnessed the raising of Lazarus from the dead, informs us, "Now a certain man was sick, named Lazarus, of Bethany, the town of Mary and his sister Martha. (It was that Mary which anointed the Lord with ointment, and wiped his feet with her hair, whose brother Lazarus was sick.)" and "Now Jesus loved Martha, and her sister, and Lazarus (John 11:1-2, 5).

Chapter Three: Christ's Miracles Prove His Divinity

Lazarus was not only sick, he was dying. When Jesus was told this, He replied, "This sickness is not unto death, but for the glory of God, that the Son of God might be glorified thereby" (John 11:4). Two days later, Jesus informed the apostles, "Our friend Lazarus sleepeth; but I go, that I may awake him out of sleep" (John 11:11). Jesus used the term "sleep" in the metaphoric sense, but the apostles thought that He meant that Lazarus was resting. Then Jesus spoke to them plainly, "Lazarus is dead."

We can consider the raising of Lazarus to be an eyewitness account on the part of the apostle John. John informs us that Jesus was traveling with His disciples when He was told that Lazarus was sick: "Then after that saith he to his disciples, Let us go into Judaea again" (John 11:7). Since Jesus was traveling with His disciples and John relates the events that occurred, we have every reason to believe that John's testimony is his own eyewitness account.

By the time the Lord arrived at Bethany, Lazarus had been buried for four days. When Martha had heard that Jesus was on the way to her house, she ran out and met Him along the way. She declared, "Lord, if thou hadst been here, my brother had not died. But I know, that even now, whatsoever thou wilt ask of God, God will give it thee" (John 11:21-22). Jesus said to her, "Thy brother shall rise again." Martha replied, "I know that he shall rise again in the resurrection at the last day." Jesus said, "I am the resurrection, and the life: he that believeth in me, though he were dead, yet shall he live: And whosoever liveth and believeth in me shall never die. Believest thou this?" Here Martha made an astounding declaration of faith: "Yea, Lord: I believe that thou art the Christ, the Son of God, which should come into the world" (John 11:27). Martha has always been remembered as the one who was busy fixing up her home, while Mary, the wiser of the two, preferred to sit at the Lord's feet and learn (Luke 10:38-41). However, here, we see that Martha was a woman of great faith and that the Father in Heaven had revealed to her the identity of Christ.

Jesus went to the tomb, which was a cave with a stone in front of it. Jesus ordered, "Take ye away the stone." Martha said, "Lord, by this time he stinketh: for he hath been dead four days." Jesus asked her, "Said I not unto thee, that, if thou wouldest believe, thou shouldest see the glory of God?" The stone that was covering the entrance to the cave was removed and then Jesus raised His gaze up to Heaven and thanked the Father for having heard Him. Then He commanded, "Lazarus, come forth." The apostle John informs us, "And he that was dead came forth, bound hand and foot with graveclothes: and his face was bound about with a napkin. Jesus saith unto them, Loose him, and let him go" (John 11:44).

After His execution, many believed and became His followers. However, these early Christians had to flee from Judea because the persecutions began. They traveled throughout the Mediterranean world and founded the original seven churches of Christ that are mentioned in Rev 1 (those in Ephesus, Smyrna, Pergamos, Thyatira, Sardis, Philadelphia, and Laodicea). Mary, the mother of Christ, and the apostle John settled in Ephesus; the resurrected Lazarus, in Cyprus. Paul advises that it was to the Gentiles' great advantage that the setting up of God's kingdom was postponed: the pagan world had not yet been saved and more time was necessary to carry the Good News across the world.

Lazarus fled Judea and went to Cyprus to found a church in Kition, which is now Larnaca. In 52 AD Mary, the mother of Christ, voyaged to Cyprus to visit Lazarus and brought with her a bishop's stole with cuffs that she had woven herself to present to him as a gift.[4] He lived another thirty years after his resurrection and was buried in Kition. In 890 AD Emperor Leo VI erected a magnificent church on his tomb, but carried the remains of Lazarus that he found in a marble sarcophagus to Constantinople. In 1204 the Frank Crusaders captured Constantinople and ransacked the Church of Holy Wisdom (Agia Sophia), carrying many holy things back to Europe with them. The journey of Lazarus' body was traced up to Marseille and then it disappeared.

On Nov. 2, 1972 renovation was being done to the Church of Saint Lazarus in Larnaca and some of his remains were discovered in a marble sarcophagus beneath the altar. These are believed to be genuine: it turns out that the people of Kition had not buried Lazarus all in one place and that therefore, they had not surrendered all of his relics to Leo VI.

A fifth and pivotal example of the resurrection of the dead is Christ's own Resurrection from the tomb that Joseph of Arimathea had given Him. This resurrection should come as no surprise to anyone well acquainted with Hebrew Scriptures, as it was prophesized many times:

1. "For thou wilt not leave my soul in hell; neither wilt thou suffer thine Holy One to see corruption" (Ps 16:10).
2. "thou hast brought up my soul from the grave: thou hast kept me alive, that I should not go down to the pit" (Ps 30:3).
3. "and his name shall be called…everlasting Father…" (Is 9:6).
4. "And I will preserve thee, and give thee for a covenant of the people…" (Is 49:8).
5. "when thou shalt make his soul an offering for sin, he shall see his seed, he shall prolong his days, and the pleasure of the LORD shall prosper in his hand" (Is 53:10).
6. "After two days will he revive us: in the third day he will raise us up, and we shall live in his sight" (Hos 6:3).
7. "whose goings forth have been from old, from everlasting" (Mic 5:2). This verse is particularly significant because it is a declaration of the awaited Messiah's immortality and hence, of His divinity.

Moreover, Jesus prophesized His own Resurrection many times before His Crucifixion:

1. "For as Jonas was three days and three nights in the whale's belly; so shall the Son of man be three days and three nights in the heart of the earth" (Mat 12:40).
2. "A wicked and adulterous generation seeketh after a sign; and there shall no sign be given unto it, but the sign of the prophet Jonas" (Mat 16:4).
3. "From that time forth began Jesus to show unto his disciples, how that he must go unto Jerusalem, and suffer many things of the elders and chief priests and scribes, and be killed, and be raised again the third day" (Mat 16:21).
4. "And as they came down from the mountain, Jesus charged them saying, Tell the vision to no man, until the Son of man be risen again from the dead" (Mat 17:9). This occurred after the transfiguration on the mountain; Jesus took Peter, James, and John up a mountain and he was transfigured before them; His

face shone as the sun and His clothing was as white light; they saw Moses and Elias talking to the Lord.

5. "And while they abode in Galilee, Jesus said unto them, The Son of man shall be betrayed into the hands of men: And they shall kill him, and the third day he shall be raised again. And they were exceeding sorry" (Mat 17:22-23).

6. "Behold, we go up to Jerusalem; and the Son of man shall be betrayed unto the chief priests and unto the scribes, and they shall condemn him to death, And shall deliver him to the Gentiles to mock, and to scourge, and to crucify him: and the third day he shall rise again" (Mat 20:18-19).

7. "Then saith Jesus unto them, All ye shall be offended because of me this night: for it is written, I will smite the shepherd, and the sheep of the flock shall be scattered abroad. But after I am risen again, I will go before you into Galilee" (Mat 26:31-32).

8. "And he began to teach them, that the Son of man must suffer many things, and be rejected of the elders, and of the chief priests, and scribes, and be killed and after three days rise again" (Mark 8:31).

9. "And they came down from the mountain, he charged them that they should tell no man what things they had seen, till the son of man were risen from the dead. And they kept that saying with themselves, questioning one with another what the rising from the dead should mean" (Mark 9:9-10).

10. "And they were in the way going up to Jerusalem; and Jesus went before them: and they were amazed; and as they followed, they were afraid. And he took again the twelve, and began to tell them what things should happen unto him, Saying, Behold, we go up to Jerusalem; and the Son of man shall be delivered unto the chief priests, and unto the scribes; and they shall condemn him to death, and shall deliver him to the Gentiles" (Mark 10:32).

11. "Then he took unto him the twelve, and said unto them, Behold, we go up to Jerusalem, and all things that are written by the prophets concerning the son of man shall be accomplished. For he shall be delivered unto the Gentiles, and shall be mocked, and

Chapter Three: Christ's Miracles Prove His Divinity

spitefully entreated, and spitted on: And they shall scourge him, and put him to death: and the third day he shall rise again" (Luke 18:31-33).

12. "And his disciples remembered that it was written, The zeal of thine house hath eaten me up. Then answered the Jews and said unto him, What sign showest thou unto us, seeing that thou doest these things? Jesus answered and said unto them, Destroy this temple, and in three days I will raise it up. Then said the Jews, Forty and six years was this temple in building, and wilt thou rear it up in three days? But he spoke of the temple of his body. When therefore he was risen from the dead, his disciples remembered that he had said thus unto them; and they believed the scripture, and the word which Jesus had said" (John 2:17-22).

13. "Therefore doth my Father love me, because I lay down my life, that I might take it again. No man taketh it from me, but I lay it down of myself. I have power to lay it down, and I have power to take it again. This commandment have I received of my Father" (John 10:17-18).

14. "Jesus said unto her, I am the resurrection, and the life: he that believeth in me, though he were dead, yet shall he live: And whosoever liveth and believeth in me shall never die. Believest thou this?" (John 11:25-26).

The risen Lord was witnessed by thousands of people who, because they had seen Him, believed and were willing to die for what they knew to be true. First He appeared to Mary Magdalene in the garden in Jerusalem on Resurrection Sunday (Mark 16:9-11; John 20:11-18); then to Mary, the mother of James, Salome, and Joanna in Jerusalem on Resurrection Sunday (Mat 28:9-10; Mark 16:1; Luke 24:9); to Peter and Cleopas on Resurrection Sunday on the seven mile road from Jerusalem to Emmaus and He discussed Scriptures with them (Mark 16:12; Luke 24:13-35); to Peter (also called Cephas, as *kephas* is Aramaic for "rock") in Jerusalem on Resurrection Sunday (Luke 24:34; 1 Cor 15:5); to the ten assembled disciples in the Upper Room in Jerusalem on Sunday (Mark 16:14; Luke 24:36-49; John 20:19-25); to eleven assembled disciples in the Upper Room in Jerusalem one week later (John 20:26-31); to the doubting Thomas, who touched His pierced hands, put his hand in His pierced side, and believed (John 20:26-29); to seven disciples (Simon, Thomas, Nathaniel, the sons of Zebedee, and two others) while fishing in the Sea of Tiberius (John 21:1-25); to the eleven on a mountain in Galilee (Mat 28:16-20); Mark 16:14-18); to the doubting James (1 Cor 15:7); to the disciples in Jerusalem (Luke 24:36-49); to the disciples who witnessed His ascension to Heaven forty days later from the Mount of Olives (Mat 28:16-20; Mark 16:19-20; Luke 24:50-53; Acts 1:3-11); to Saul of Tarsus on the road to Damascus (Acts 9:1-19; 22:3-16; 26:9-18; 1 Cor 9:1); His voice was heard by the men traveling with Saul (Acts 9:7); He appeared to Ananias (Acts 9:10-16); to more than five hundred people, who saw Him at the same time (1 Cor 15:6).

In Mat 28:9 Jesus met the women who had come to bring Him spices and said, "Rejoice!" The original Greek says, "Χαίρετε." [Rejoice!]. The verb χαίρω means to rejoice, to be of cheer. It is significant that the word is in the imperative: the command implies, "Rejoice! I have conquered death on the Cross; you have everlasting life; there is much to be happy about." The first word that the Lord spoke on the Sunday of His Resurrection has come to mean "hello" and it has been used as a greeting down through the millennia among Greeks.

Miracles Performed by Christ that Prove His Divinity

The apostles Matthew, Mark, Luke, and John provide eyewitness testimony to the vast wealth of miracles that the Lord performed. John ends his gospel by declaring, "And there are also many other things which Jesus did, the which, if they should be written every one, I suppose that even the world itself could not contain the books that should be written" (John 21:25). Below is an enumeration, in chronological order, of some of the many miracles that Christ performed:

1. performs His first miracle: turns water into wine at the wedding feast at Cana in Galilee (John 2:1-11)
2. prophesizes that He will raise His body three days after His life is taken (John 2:19-22)
3. He miraculously cures someone despite the great distance

Chapter Three: Christ's Miracles Prove His Divinity

between Himself and the sick person: while at Cana, He gives the word and heals a nobleman's son who is dying of a fever at Capernaum. When the father returns to Capernaum, he learns that his son recovered from his illness at 7:00 the previous day, precisely the time when the Lord had promised him that his son would be healed (John 4:46-54).

4. "passing through the midst of them," evades a hostile multitude in Nazareth that led Him to the brow of a hill with the intention of pushing Him down a cliff (Luke 4:28-30)
5. enables Peter to catch a first draught of fish (Luke 5:4-10)
6. exorcizes an unclean spirit from a man in the synagogue at Capernaum on the Sabbath (Mark 1:21-28; Luke 4:31-37)
7. heals Peter's mother-in-law of a fever at Capernaum (Mat 8:14-15; Mark 1:30-31; Luke 4:38-39)
8. lays hands on many sick people and heals them at Capernaum (Mat 8:16-17; Mark 1:32-34; Luke 4:40)
9. exorcizes demons from the possessed at Capernaum (Mat 8:16-17; Mark 1:32-34; Luke 4:41)
10. cleanses a man with leprosy (Mat 8:2-4; Mark 1:40-45; Luke 5:12-14)
11. forgives and heals a paralytic at Capernaum (Mat 9:2; Mark 2:3-12; Luke 5:18-26)
12. heals a man who had been an invalid for 38 years in Jerusalem on the Sabbath (John 5:5-13)
13. restores a man's withered hand and makes it whole in the synagogue on the Sabbath (Mat 12:10-13; Mark 3:1-5; Luke 6:6-10)
14. heals a centurion's servant of the palsy in Capernaum (Mat 8:5-13; Luke 7:1-10)
15. prophesizes that the Gentile world will believe and enter the Kingdom of Heaven: many will come from the east and the west and will sit down with Abraham, Isaac, and Jacob in the Kingdom of Heaven (Mat 8:10-12)
16. raises a widow's son from the dead at Nain; the young man sits up in his bier and begins to speak (Luke 7:11-15)

17. calms a fierce storm on the sea of Galilee (Mat 8:23-27; Mark 4:35-41; Luke 8:22-25)
18. exorcizes unclean spirits from a demoniac at the Gadarenes; casts the demons into a herd of 2,000 swine that runs down a cliff into the sea and is drowned (Mat 8:28-34; Mark 5:1-20; Luke 8:26-39)
19. heals a woman who has been bleeding for twelve years; she touches the hem of His garment and is restored to health (Mat 9:20-22; Mark 5:25-34; Luke 8:43-48)
20. raises Jairus' daughter from the dead at Capernaum (Mat 9:18-19; 9:23-26; Mark 5:22-24; 5:35-43; Luke 8:41-42; 8:49-56)
21. restores sight to two blind men (Mat 9:27-31)
22. restores speech to a mute and exorcizes a demon from him (Mat 9:32-33)
23. heals every sickness and every disease among the people (Mat 8:35)
24. heals the sick (Mat 14:14; Luke 9:11)
25. given five barley loaves and two small fish, He feeds 5,000 men, besides women and children in a desert in Bethsaida; twelve baskets of fragments are left over (Mat 14:15-21; Mark 6:33-44; Luke 9:12-17; John 6:1-13
26. walks on the sea when the wind is fierce (Mat 14:22-33; Mark 6:45-52; John 6:16-21)
27. enables Peter to walk on the sea and catches him when his faith waivers (Mat 14:28-32)
28. all the diseased that touch the hem of His garment are healed of their illnesses at Gennesaret (Mat 14:34-36; Mark 6:53-56)
29. exorcizes a demon from the Canaanite woman's daughter (Mat 15:22-28, Mark 7:24-30)
30. heals the lame, the blind, the mute, the maimed, and many others at Decapolis (Mat 15:29-31)
31. restores hearing and speech to a deaf mute at Decapolis (Mark 7:31-37)
32. given seven loaves and a few fish, feeds 4,000 men, besides women and children at Decapolis; seven baskets of broken meat are left over (Mat 15:32-39; Mark 8:1-9)

Chapter Three: Christ's Miracles Prove His Divinity

33. heals a blind man at Bethsaida (Mark 8:22-26)
34. at Caesarea Philippi, prophesizes for the first time His rejection by the elders, chief priests, and scribes, Crucifixion, and Resurrection after three days (Mat 16:21-24; Mark 8:31-34; Luke 9:22-23)
35. the transfiguration of Christ: Christ is seen with Moses and Elijah on the mountain (Mat 17:1-9; Mark 9:2-9; Luke 9:28-36)
36. exorcizes demons out of a man's son (Mat 17:14-21; Mark 9:14-29; Luke 9:37-43)
37. prophesizes a second time his death and Resurrection (Mat 17:22-23; Mark 9:9-10; 9:31-32; Luke 9:43-45)
38. enables Peter to find the Temple tax ($δίδραχμα$, a two-drachma piece) in a fish's mouth (Mat 17:24-27)
39. During the Feast of Tabernacles, hostile mobs seek to take Him, but cannot because His hour has not yet come (John 7:30-33; 7:44).
40. evades a hostile multitude that tries to stone Him (John 8:59)
41. heals a man who was born blind in Jerusalem (John 9:1-41)
42. heals the infirm, bent woman who had been stooped over for 18 years (Luke 13:11-13)
43. evades another hostile multitude in Jerusalem that tries to take Him (John 10:39)
44. prophesizes His death and resurrection on the third day (Luke 13:31-33)
45. heals a man with dropsy (Luke 14:1-4)
46. resurrects Lazarus from the dead at Bethany (John 11:1-44)
47. heals ten lepers while passing through Samaria and Galilee (Luke 17:11-19)
48. while going to Jerusalem, prophecizes for the third time that He will be condemned, delivered to be mocked, scourged and crucified, and that He will be resurrected on the third day (Mat 20:17-19; Mark 10:32-34; Luke 18:31-34)
49. heals the blind Bartimaeus at Jericho (Mat 20:29-34; Mark 10:46-52; Luke 18:35-43)
50. curses the fig tree and it immediately withers away (Mat 21:19; Mark 11:13-14; 11:20-21)

51. identifies Judas as being the one who will betray Him (Mat 26:21-25; Mark 14:18-21; Luke 22:21-23; John 13:21-30)
52. At the Last Supper before His Crucifixion, He transforms wine into His Blood and bread into His Body and prophesizes that this will be the last time that He will taste wine before He drinks it again in Heaven; this is a miracle; it is also a prophesy of His imminent execution; moreover, it is a prophesy that this miracle will continue to be done in His Church until His return (Mat 26:26-29; Mark 14:22-25; Luke 22:16-20; John 6:51-58)
53. predicts Peter's denial of Him (Mat 26:31-35; Mark 14:27-31; Luke 22:31-38; John 13:31-34)
54. prophesizes His Resurrection and the disciples' joy to see Him again (John 16:16-22)
55. restores the ear of Malchus, a servant of the high priest, after Peter draws a sword and cuts it off (Mat 26:51-54; Mark 14:47-49; Luke 22:49-51; John 18:10-11)
56. enables the apostles to catch a second draught of fish (John 21:5-11)[5]

Miracles attending His Conception, Birth, Childhood, Crucifixion, Resurrection, and Ascension

1. the angel Gabriel's Annunciation to Mary of the Birth of Christ (Luke 1:26-38)
2. an angel of the Lord's Annunciation to Joseph that Mary's Child has been conceived by the Holy Ghost (Mat 1:18-25)
3. an angel of the Lord proclaims the Birth of Jesus to the shepherds; a multitude of angels praises God (Luke 2:8-20)
4. the three magi arrive from the East having followed a star that miraculously appears over His birthplace (Mat 2:1-12)
5. an angel of the Lord warns Joseph in a dream to take Mary and Jesus to Egypt (Mat 2:13-18)
6. an angel of the Lord tells Joseph to bring them back to Israel; Joseph is warned in a dream to turn away from Judea; he goes to Nazareth (Mat 2:19-23; Luke 2:39)

Chapter Three: Christ's Miracles Prove His Divinity

7. At the age of 12 He both hears and asks questions of renown teachers in the Temple in Jerusalem; all that hear Him are astonished at his understanding and answers (Luke 2:42-47). Many believe that Hillel, the foremost scholar of biblical commentary and interpreter of the Law, must have been present in the Temple in Jerusalem on Passover, and that Jesus taught Hillel, it was not the other way around.
8. when Jesus is baptized by John, the Father speaks from Heaven and the Holy Spirit descends like a dove (Mat 3:13-17; Mark 1:9-11; Luke 3:21-23)
9. first miracle attending His Crucifixion: the sky becomes dark for three hours over the whole land (Mat 27:45; Mark 15:33; Luke 23:44)
10. second miracle attending His Crucifixion: the curtain in the Temple is torn in two. This is indeed a miracle of God because it is six inches thick and requires 300 men to carry it (Mat 27:51; Mark 15:38; Luke 23:45)
11. third miracle attending His Crucifixion: the earth was shaken and the rocks were split: "the earth did quake, and the rocks rent…Now the centurion, and they that were with him, watching Jesus, saw the earthquake, and those things that were done…" (Mat 27:51, 54)
12. fourth miracle attending His Crucifixion: the tombs were opened and the dead were resurrected: "And the graves were opened; and many of the bodies of the saints which slept arose, And came out of the graves after his resurrection, and went into the holy city, and appeared unto many" (Mat 27:52-53)
13. fifth miracle attending His Crucifixion: the Roman centurion, a pagan, is converted and declares, "Truly, this man was the Son of God!" (Mat 27:54; Mark 15:39; Luke 23:47)
14. angels announce the Resurrection to certain women; Peter and John enter the empty tomb (Mat 28:1-8; Mark 16:1-8; Luke 24:1-8; John 20:1-10)
15. first and second appearances of the Risen Lord (Mat 28:9-10; Mark 16:9-11; Luke 24:9-11; John 20:11-18)

16. third and fourth appearances of the Risen Lord (Mark 16:12-13; Luke 24:13-35; 1 Cor 15:5)
17. fifth appearance of the Risen Lord (Mark 16:4; Luke 24:36-43; John 20:19-25)
18. sixth appearance of the Risen Lord (John 20:26-31; 1 Cor 15:5)
19. seventh appearance of the Risen Lord (John 21:1-15)
20. eighth appearance of the Risen Lord (Mat 28:16-17; 1 Cor 15:6)
21. ninth and tenth appearances of the Risen Lord (Luke 24:44-49; Acts 1:3-8; 1 Cor 15:7)
22. the Ascension (Mark 16:19-20; Luke 24:50-53; Acts 1:9-12)
23. first appearance after His Ascension is to Paul (Acts 9:1-9; 22:6-11; 26:12-18; 1 Cor 15:8)
24. second appearance after His Ascension is to Ananias (Acts 1:10-16)
25. third appearance after His Ascension is in a vision to Stephen (Acts 7:55)
26. He speaks to Peter, telling him to eat of all living things (Acts 10:10-16; 11:5-10)
27. vision of John (Rev 1-5; 6:1; 14:1; 22)[6]

Signs in the Temple 30 AD-70 AD

In addition to the miracles that Christ performed, there are some stunning miracles that occurred in the Temple during the years 30 AD-70 AD that the Talmud records. Centuries after the destruction of the Temple in 70 AD, the Jews began to write their religious history and commentary in two works: one was written in Palestine and is called the Palestinian Talmud or the Jerusalem Talmud (translated orally for centuries prior to its compilation by Jewish scholars between the 3rd-4th century); the other is called the Babylonian Talmud (compiled by Jewish scholars about 499 AD, with some later additions). It is significant that both versions of the Talmud indicate that each year during the period 30 AD-70 AD, God provided five great miracles to demonstrate that something had changed in the relationship between man and God. It is the testimony of the Gospel writers who had traveled with Christ during His ministry, the writings of Paul, and

Chapter Three: Christ's Miracles Prove His Divinity

the testimony of the early martyrs that explain that this "something" that had changed was the fact that the Lamb of God had come to earth and that animal sacrifice was no longer required. The five miracles that the Talmud records are as follows:

1. The Miracle of the Lots. On the Day of Atonement (Yom Kippur), lots were cast to decide which of two goats would be sacrificed and which would be set free. During this ritual, two goats were brought before the High Priest, as well as a container bearing two stones. One stone was white and was called the "Lot for the Lord"; the other stone was black and was called the "Lot for the Scapegoat." Without looking into the container, the priest reached into it with his right hand, selected a stone, and held it over the goat that was standing on his right hand side. If the stone was white, the goat on the priest's right hand side would be called "For the Lord" and would be sacrificed; the other goat would be called "Azazel" or the scapegoat and would be set free. If the stone was black, the goat on the priest's right hand side would be set free and the other would be sacrificed. The statistical probability that the High Priest would pick either color is 50-50 and history bore this out. During the 200 years before 30 AD, the High Priest picked one color or the other 50 percent of the time. However, beginning in 30 AD and continuing each year until 70 AD, a black stone always turned up in the High Priest's right hand. The statistical probability of this happening in forty consecutive years is 1:1,099,511,627,776 or more than a trillion to one. The way to calculate the chances of this happening are as follows: the chances of getting one of two colors after one throw are 1:2. The chances of getting the same color after two consecutive throws are 1 in 2x2 or 1:4. The chances of getting the same color after three consecutive throws are 1 in 2x2x2 or 1:8. If we continue on to forty consecutive throws, we get 1:1,099,511,627,776. The Jews regarded this phenomenon to be a harbinger of ill fortune and they were afraid that something terrible was going to happen.

2. The Miracle of the Crimson Cloth. On Yom Kippur the High Priest dipped a white cloth in the blood of the animal that had been sacrificed and placed this bloody cloth on the door of the Temple overnight. In the morning it was discovered that God had turned the crimson cloth white again, as a sign that He had accepted the animal sacrifice and that the people's sins were covered by it. This miracle has an antecedent reference in Isaiah: "Come now, and let us reason together, saith the LORD: though your sins be as scarlet, they shall be as white as snow; though they be as red as crimson, they shall be as wool" (Is 1:18). However, the Talmud indicates that during the years 30 AD until the destruction of the Temple in 70 AD, this miracle had ceased and the crimson cloth no longer turned white. Christians understand that God was indicating that he had created something new, a New Covenant in which the ritual sacrifice of animals was no longer necessary, and that He required all of humanity to be justified by the blood that removes sin, not merely covers it (as does animal sacrifice), namely, the blood of Christ. The miracle of the crimson cloth ceased forever.
3. The Miracle of the Crimson Thread. On Yom Kippur the High Priest wore a crimson thread into the Temple's Holy of Holies (the second tabernacle) and God turned the crimson thread white. After 30 AD, this crimson thread never turned white again.
4. The Miracle of the Temple Doors. Beginning in 30 AD, the Temple doors swung open every night by themselves. This continued each night for forty years until 70 AD. This miracle could be interpreted in a few ways. Christians saw this as a sign that humanity could now enter the Holy of Holies and commune with the Living God through our High Priest, Jesus Christ. The Bible tells us that when Christ surrendered His Ghost on the Cross, the veil in the Temple was rent in two. This was, indeed, a miracle performed by God, and not the work of man, because the veil was six inches thick and 300 priests were required to carry it. The tearing of the veil indicated that a human high priest was no longer needed to be the intercessor between the Living

God and man. The Living God came to earth and now Christ is our Tabernacle of the Living God. Those who believe in Him are indwelt by the Holy Spirit and have God residing within them. They are born of the Spirit. They can commune directly with the Father through the intercession of the Son. On the other hand, there was another way of interpreting the Miracle of the Temple Doors. This second interpretation need not be considered to be an alternative to the first; both can be accepted concurrently. Some considered this miracle to be an ominous sign because the prophet Zechariah had predicted, "Open thy doors, O Lebanon, that the fire may devour thy cedars" (Zech 11:1). The doors were made of cedars of Lebanon and covered with gold. The entire eleventh chapter of Zechariah describes the judgment that God would one day mete out to Israel. One verse predicts that the people will be smitten by the king of their neighbors: "For I will no more pity the inhabitants of the land, saith the LORD: but, lo, I will deliver the men every one into his neighbor's hand, and into the hand of his king: and they shall smite the land, and out of their land I will not deliver them" (Zech 11:6). A few verses later Zechariah announces that at this time Israel will suffer the worst punishment of all, cannibalism: "Then said I, I will not feed you: that that dieth, let it die; and that that is to be cut off, let it be cut off; and let the rest eat every one the flesh of another" (Zech 11:9). The Jerusalem Talmud notes that the Miracle of the Temple Doors was regarded as a sign of great impending destruction and devastation: "Said [to the Temple] Rabban Yohanan ben Zakkai, O Temple, why do you frighten us? We know that you will end up destroyed. For it has been said, Open your doors, O Lebanon, that the fire may devour your cedars! (Zech 11:1)."[7]

5. The Miracle of the Temple Menorah. After Christ's Crucifixion, the seven candlestick menorah in the Temple self-extinguished every night for forty years (on over 12,500 consecutive nights). This happened every night despite the precautions that the priests took to keep the candles lit.

Now let us examine the passages in both the Jerusalem Talmud and the Babylonian Talmud that cite these miracles. The Jerusalem Talmud states, "It has been taught: Forty years before the destruction of the Temple the western light went out, the crimson thread remained crimson, and the lot for the Lord always came up in the left hand. They would close the gates of the Temple by night and get up in the morning and find them wide open. Said [to the Temple] Rabban Yohanan ben Zakkai, O Temple, why do you frighten us? We know that you will end up destroyed. For it has been said, Open your doors, O Lebanon, that the fire may devour your cedars! (Zech. 11:1)."[8] The Babylonian Talmud states, "Our Rabbis taught: During the last forty years before the destruction of the Temple the lot ['For the Lord'] did not come up in the right hand; nor did the crimson-coloured strap become white; nor did the westernmost light shine; and the doors of the *Hekal* would open by themselves, until R. Johanan b. Zakkai rebuked them, saying: *Hekal, Hekal*, why wilt thou be the alarmer thyself? I know about thee that thou wilt be destroyed, for Zechariah ben Ido has already prophesied concerning thee: *Open thy doors, O Lebanon, that the fire may devour thy cedars.*"[9]

It is significant that both Talmuds indicate that these astonishing Temple miracles commenced in 30 AD: the Lord began His 3½ year ministry in 30 AD. Hence, God was alerting man that it was time to take the next step in the unfolding of the God-man relationship (which would ultimately lead to theosis or unification with God): the King of Kings and Lord of Lords had arrived in the flesh to forgive sins in person. Prior to healing people, He forgave them their sins. Hence, the start of the Temple miracles in 30 AD indicated that the Tabernacle of the Living God had come to earth and that the forgiveness of sin had begun. God's plan for man's redemption reached its fulfillment when Christ declared, just prior to surrendering His Ghost on the Cross, *tete'lestai* ($\tau\varepsilon\tau\acute{\varepsilon}\lambda\varepsilon\sigma\tau\alpha\iota$) (the original Greek text, John 19:30), which is an accounting term meaning "the debt has been paid in full." Christ's sacrifice, in our place for our transgressions, did not merely cover men's sins, as animal sacrifice had done, but took them away forever, in fulfillment of the prophecy, "As far as the east is from the west, so far hath he removed our transgressions from us" (Ps 103:12).

Chapter Three: Christ's Miracles Prove His Divinity

It is highly significant that God uttered this word prior to leaving us and an examination of its meaning reveals why He chose a language as rich and as vast as Greek in which to record the events of His sojourn on earth. Liddell and Scott's *A Greek-English Lexicon* indicates that τετέλεστο, a form of τελέω, means "fulfill one's word...*to be fulfilled*...pay what one owes, what is due...esp. tax, duty, toll...Pass. Of money, etc., *to be paid*... bring to an end, finish...lay out, spend."[10] Hence, the Lord's words on the Cross, in the original Greek, means three things that all have immense theological significance. First, the word does mean "It is finished," as the KJV translation indicates. Christ accomplished His mission on earth and realized all of the OT prophecies that had been written about Him. Secondly, it means "the debt has been paid in full." Τετέλεσται is an accounting term meaning that a debt or obligation has been fully paid. The obligation here is Christ's payment in full, for each believer's sins. This is in fulfillment of the prophecy dating back to God's exhortation to the snake in the Garden of Eden: "And I will put enmity between thee and the woman, and between thy seed and her seed; it shall bruise thy head, and thou shalt bruise his heel" (Gen 3:15). The surface level meaning of this verse (*p'shat*) is that the snake must crawl on his belly and be subject to being stepped on by humans. However, on a deeper level (*sod*), it is a Messianic prophecy: Christ, a descendant of Eve, will conquer spiritual death on the Cross and proclaim victory over the powers of darkness. He will forgive the sins of Adam and Eve and once more give humanity the opportunity to enter God's kingdom. Paul reiterates this in Rom 16:20. Thirdly, τετέλεσται means "the word has been fulfilled," "the word has been kept." Christ has kept his promise, indeed. Is 6:8 reads, "And I heard the voice of the Lord, saying, Whom shall I send, and who will go for us? Then said I, Here am I; send me." On the surface level, (*p'shat*), Isaiah is offering to carry God's message to man. On a deeper level (*sod*), God is having a Divine Counsel in Heaven and Christ is offering to do the will of the Father, and condescend to go to earth and suffer and die in our place, for our transgressions. He kept His promise: His word, "Here am I; send me," has been kept. Moreover, His promise in Is 61:1 has also been kept: "The Spirit of the Lord GOD is upon me; because the LORD hath anointed me to preach good tidings unto the meek; he hath sent me to bind up the brokenhearted, to proclaim liberty to the captives, and the opening of the prisons to them that are bound."

An Eastern Orthodox View of Pascal

Luke tells us that at the outset of His ministry, Jesus stood in the synagogue in Nazareth on the Sabbath day and read Is 61:1 (Luke 4:16-21). Then he closed the book, sat down to teach and announced to the congregation that on that day this scripture was fulfilled: "This day is this scripture fulfilled in your ears." This statement had incalculable significance in human history: Christ was revealing that the Holy Spirit was upon Him, that the Holy Spirit had anointed Him to preach the gospel to the poor; that the Holy Spirit had sent Him to heal the brokenhearted, to proclaim liberty to captives (those in bondage to sin), give sight to the blind (both physically and spiritually), to free those held bound in prisons (again, meaning held in bondage to sin). Hence, when he said, "Τετέλεσται," "the word has been kept," He was declaring that He had kept His word and accomplished all of the things that He had promised that He would do.

Miracle of the Holy Flame

A great new miracle took place that demonstrated to the whole world that Christ is truly risen, and this miracle has been continuing for 2,000 years: when the Greek Orthodox Patriarch of Jerusalem passes his unlit candle across the tomb of Christ on Holy Saturday, it miraculously lights. The miracle of the Holy Flame is well known and well documented both in Church history and in the present day.

The miracle of the Holy Flame is chronicled in the 9th century itinerary of the French monk Bernard who saw it in 870 AD. Bernard was a Breton monk from the monastery of Mont St.-Michel. He was also known as Bernardus Francus, Bernardus Sapiens (Bernard the Wise), and Bernardus Monachus (Bernard the Monk; Monachus is derived from the 4th century Byzantine Greek μοναχός, monk, via the post classical Latin *monachus*, monk). In his journal Bernard recalls, "I must not, however, omit to state, that on Holy Saturday, which is the eve of Easter, the office is begun in the morning in this church, and after it is ended the *Kyrie Eleison* is chanted, until an angel comes and lights the lamps which hang over the aforesaid sepulchre; of which light the patriarch gives their shares to the bishops and to the rest of the people, that each may illuminate his own house. The present patriarch is called Theodosius, and was brought to this place on account of his piety from his monastery, which is fifteen miles from

Chapter Three: Christ's Miracles Prove His Divinity

Jerusalem, and was made patriarch over all the Christians in the Land of Promise."[11] Bernard's text was discovered by Jean Mabillon in a manuscript of the library at Rheims and printed in the *Acts of the Saints of the Order of St. Benedict* [*Acta sanctorum Ordinis Sancti Benedicti*, 9 vols. (Paris, 1668-1710)]. Mabillon's text indicates that the year of authorship is 870 AD. Bernard's departure from Europe is fixed at 867. Theodosius was the Patriarch of Jerusalem from 863-879.

In modern times thousands of pilgrims travel to Jerusalem from all over the world and sit faithfully with unlit candles outside the tomb of Christ on Holy Saturday (according to the Julian calendar). In some eyewitness accounts, a flash of light descends and remains over the tomb. On some years, the unlit candles of the pilgrims who are seated outside the tomb miraculously light by themselves at the moment when the Patriarch's candle lights. Timothy Ware, in *The Orthodox Church*, chronicles an early 12th century account of this annual miracle: "A Russian pilgrim at Jerusalem in 1106-7, Abbot Daniel of Tchernigov, found Greeks and Latins worshipping together in harmony at the Holy Places, though he noted with satisfaction that at the ceremony of the Holy Fire the Greek lamps were lit miraculously while the Latin had to be lit from the Greek.[12] It is a historical fact that the candle does not miraculously light for the Vatican or Anglican envoys, when they pass their candles over the Holy Sepulcher, but rather, they have to turn and receive their light from an Orthodox priest.

Let us examine Abbot Daniel's account of the Holy Flame. In his narrative of 1107 AD, the Russian Orthodox monk declares:

> The following is a description of the Holy Light, which descends upon the Holy Sepulchre, as the Lord vouchsafed to show it to me, his wicked and unworthy servant. For in very truth I have seen with my own sinful eyes how that Holy Light descends upon the redeeming Tomb of our Lord Jesus Christ. Many pilgrims relate incorrectly the details about the descent of that Holy Light. Some say that the Holy Ghost descends upon the Holy Sepulchre in the form of a dove; others that it is lightning from heaven which kindles the lamps above the Sepulchre of the Lord. This is all untrue,

for neither dove nor lightning is to be seen at that moment; but the Divine grace comes down unseen from heaven, and lights the lamps of the Sepulchre of our Lord. I will only describe it in perfect truth as I have seen it. On Holy Friday, after Vespers, they clean the Holy Sepulchre and wash all the lamps that are there; they fill the lamps with pure oil without water and after having put in the wicks, leave them unlighted they affix the seals to the Tomb at the second hour of the night. At the same time they extinguish all the lamps and wax candles in every church in Jerusalem. Upon that same Friday, at the first hour of the day, I, the unworthy, entered the presence of Prince Baldwin, and bowed myself to the ground before him. Seeing me, as I bowed, he bade me, in a friendly manner, come to him, and said, "What dost thou want, Russian abbot?" for he knew me and like me, being a man of great kindness and humility and not given to pride. I said to him, "My prince...allow me to place my lamp on the Holy Sepulchre in the name of the whole Russian country." Then with peculiar kindness and attention he gave me permission to place my lamp on the Sepulchre of the Lord, and sent one of his chief retainers with me to the custodian of the Resurrection, and to the keeper of the keys of the Holy Sepulchre. The custodian and the keeper of the keys directed me to bring my lamp filled with oil. I thanked them, and hastened, with much joy, to purchase a very large glass lamp; having filled it with pure oil, I carried it to the Holy Sepulchre towards evening, and was conducted to the afore-mentioned keeper, who was alone in the chapel of the Tomb. Opening the sacred portal for me, he ordered me to take off my shoes; and then having admitted me barefooted to the Holy Sepulchre, with the lamp that I bore, he directed me to place it on the Tomb of the Lord. I placed it, with my sinful hands, on the spot occupied by the sacred feet of our Lord Jesus Christ; the lamp of the Greeks being where the head lay, and that of St. Sabbas and all the monasteries in the position of

Chapter Three: Christ's Miracles Prove His Divinity

the breast; for it is the custom of the Greeks and of the Monastery of St. Sabbas to place their lamps there each year. By God's grace these three lamps kindled on that occasion, but not one of those belonging to the Franks, which hung above, received the light. After having placed my lamp on the Holy Sepulchre, and after having adored and kissed, with penitence and pious tears, the sacred place upon which the body of our Lord Jesus Christ lay; I left the Holy Tomb filled with joy, and retired to my cell…

At the end of the ninth hour, when they commenced chanting the Canticle of the passage (of the Red Sea), "Cantabo Domino," a small cloud, coming suddenly from the east, rested above the open dome of the church; fine rain fell on the Holy Sepulchre, and wet us and all those who were above the Tomb. It was at this moment that the Holy Light suddenly illuminated the Holy Sepulchre, shining with an awe-aspiring and splendid brightness. The bishop, who was followed by four deacons, then opened the doors of the Tomb, and entered with the taper of Prince Baldwin so as to light it first at the Holy Light; he afterwards returned it to the Prince, who resumed his place, holding, with great joy, the taper in his hands. We lighted our tapers from that of the Prince, and so passed on the flame to everyone in the church.

This Holy Light is like no ordinary flame, for it burns in a marvellous way with indescribable brightness, and a ruddy colour like that of cinnabar. All the people remain standing with lighted tapers, and repeat in a loud voice with intense joy and eagerness: "Lord, have mercy upon us!" Man can experience no joy like that which every Christian feels at the moment when he sees the Holy Light of God. He who has not taken part in the glory of that day will not believe the record of all that I have seen. It is only wise, believing men who will place complete trust in the truth of this narrative, and who will hear with delight all the details concerning the holy places. He who is faithful in little will also be faithful in much; but to the wicked and incredulous the truth seems always a lie. God and the Holy Sepulchre of our Lord bear witness to my stories and to my humble person; so do my companions from Russia, Novgorod, and Kief: Iziaslav Ivanovitch, Gorodislav Mikhailovitch, the two Kashkitch, and many others who were there the same day.

But to return to my narrative. Directly the light shone in the Holy Sepulchre, the chant ceased, and all, crying out "Kyrie Eleison," moved towards the church with great joy, bearing the lighted tapers in their hands, and protecting them from the wind. Everyone then goes home; and the people after lighting the lamps of the churches with their tapers, remain in them to terminate the Vespers; whilst the priests alone, and without assistance, finish the Vespers in the great Church of the Holy Sepulchre. Carrying the lighted tapers, we returned to our monastery with the abbot and the monks; we finished the Vespers there and then retired to our cells, praising God for having condescended to show us unworthy ones His Divine grace. The morning of Holy Sunday…the abbot, cross in hand, and all monks singing the hymn, "Immortal One, Thou hast deigned to go down into the Tomb." Having entered the Holy Sepulchre, we covered the life-giving tomb of the Lord with kisses and scorching tears; we breathed with ecstasy the perfume which the presence of the Holy Ghost had left; and we gazed in admiration on the lamps which still burned with a bright and marvelous splendour. The custodian and the keeper of the keys told us, and the abbot, that the three lamps had kindled. The five other lamps suspended above were also burning, but their light was different from that of the three first, and had not that marvelous brightness. We afterwards left the tomb by the west door, and having proceeded to the high altar, kissed the orthodox and received absolution; we then, with the abbot and the monks, left the Temple of the Holy Resurrection, and returned to our monastery to rest until it was time for mass.

The third day after the Resurrection of our Lord I went, after mass, to the keeper of the keys of the Holy Sepulchre, and said, "I wish to take away my lamp." He received me kindly, and made me enter the Tomb quite alone. I saw my lamp on the Holy Sepulchre still burning with the flame of that holy light; I prostrated myself before the sacred Tomb, and, with penitence, covered the sacred pace where the pure body of our Lord Jesus Christ lay with kisses and tears. I afterwards measured the length, width, and height of the Tomb as it now is a thing which no one can do before witnesses. I gave (the keeper of the keys) of the Tomb of the Lord as much as I could, and offered him, according to my means, a small, poor gift. The keeper of the keys, seeing my love for the Holy Sepulchre, pushed back the slab that covers the part of the sacred Tomb on which Christ's head lay, and broke off a morsel of the sacred rock; this he gave me as a blessed memorial, begging me at the same time not to say anything about it at Jerusalem. After again kissing the Tomb of the Lord, and greeting the keeper, I took up my lamp, filled with holy oil, and left the Holy Sepuchre full of joy, enriched by the Divine grace, and bearing in my hand a gift from the sacred place, and a token from the Holy Sepulchre of our Lord. I went on my way rejoicing as if I were the bearer of vast wealth, and returned to my cell full of great joy.[13]

Having witnessed the descent of the Holy Flame in the Church of the Resurrection on Easter Sunday 1107 AD, and having procured a precious piece of rock cut off from the Lord's Tomb, Abbot Daniel began his journey home to Russia.

In modern times thousands of pilgrims continue to travel to Jerusalem each year to witness the Miracle of the Holy Flame. Many Internet websites describe the miracle and provide eyewitness testimonies of some of these pilgrims.[14] One website summarizes the miracle thus:

At a certain moment the Holy Light flashes from the depth of the Holy Sepulchre in a supernatural way, miraculously, and lights up the little lamp of olive oil put on the edge of it... The Holy Light is not only distributed by the Archbishop, but operates also by itself. It emits from the Holy Sepulchre having a gleam of a hue completely different from that on natural light. It sparkles, it flashes like lightning. It flies like a dove around the tabernacle of the Holy Sepulchre, and lights up the unlit lamps of olive oil hanging in front if it. It whirls from one side of the church to the other. It enters into some of the chapels inside the church, as for instance the chapel of the Calvary (at a higher level than the Holy Sepulchre) and lights up the little lamps. It lights up also the candles of certain pilgrims. In fact there are some very pious pilgrims who, every time they attended this ceremony, noticed that their candles it up on the own accord! ...As soon as it appears it has a bluish hue and does not burn. At the first moments of its appearance, if it touches the face, or the mouth, or the hands, it does not burn. This is proof of its divine and supernatural origin.[15]

Prof. Niels Christian Hvidt has traveled to the Church of the Resurrection and provides the following eyewitness account in his Internet article:

In order to find out, I traveled to Jerusalem to be present at the ceremony in which the Miracle of the Holy Fire occurs, and I can testify that it did not only happen in the ancient Church and throughout the Middle Ages but also on the 18th of April, 1998. The Greek-Orthodox Patriarch of Jerusalem, Diodorus I, is the man who every year enters the tomb to receive the Holy Fire...the Israeli authorities on this Easter Saturday come and seal the tomb with wax. Before they seal the door it is customary that they enter the tomb to check for any hidden source of fire, which could produce the miracle through fraud. Just as the Romans were to guarantee that there was no manipulation after the death of Jesus, likewise the Israeli Local Authorities are to guarantee that there be no trickery in 1998...[16]

Hvidt procured an interview with His Beatitude, Diodorus I, the Patriarch of Jerusalem, who described his experience inside the tomb of the Lord. This is what how Patriarch, who experiences the miracle every year, describes it:

> "From the core of the very stone on which Jesus lay an indefinable light pours forth. It usually has a blue tint, but the color may change and take many different hues. It cannot be described in human terms. The light rises out of the stone as mist may rise out of a lake. It almost looks as if the stone is covered by a moist cloud, but it is light. This light each year behaves differently. Sometimes it covers just the stone, while other times it gives light to the whole sepulchre, so that people who stand outside the tomb and look into it will see it filled with light. The light does not burn. I have never had my beard burnt in all the sixteen years I have been Patriarch in Jerusalem and have received the Holy Fire. The light is of a different consistency than normal fire that burns in an oil lamp. At a certain point the light rises and forms a column in which the fire is of a different nature, so that I am able to light my candles from it. When I thus have received the flame on my candles, I go out and give the fire first to the Armenian Patriarch and then to the Coptic. Hereafter I give the flame to all people present in the Church... For me personally it is of great comfort to consider Christ's faithfulness towards us, which he displays by giving us the holy flame every year in spite of our human frailties and failures. We experience many wonders in our Churches, and miracles are nothing strange to us. It happens often that icons cry, when Heaven wants to display its closeness to us..."[17]

Mr. Hvidt concludes:

> The miracle is not confined to what actually happens inside the little tomb, where the Patriarch prays. What may be even more significant, is that the blue light is reported to appear and be active outside the tomb. Every year many believers claim that this miraculous light ignites candles, which they hold in their hands, of its own initiative. All in the church wait with candles in the hope that they may ignite spontaneously. Often closed oil lamps take fire by themselves before the eyes of the pilgrims. The blue flame is seen to move in different places in the Church. A number of signed testimonies by pilgrims, whose candles lit spontaneously, attest to the validity of these ignitions.[18]

What Pascal has to say about Christ's miracles

The preparatory material above, on the history of Christian miracles, provides a basis for understanding the awe and gratitude that the miracles in Pascal's life must have inspired in him. Pascal was a man who was deeply touched by miracles: God came to him late one night and he experienced God as a fire in his soul; a Holy Thorn from the Crown of Christ came into his life and miraculously healed his niece; this same Holy Thorn performed numerous other healings at Port Royal and this further concretized his faith.

One of the greatest miracles in Pascal's life was a spiritual experience: on the night of Monday, November 23, 1654, from about 10:30 PM until 12:30 AM, Blaise Pascal had a personal encounter with God, in which he described God as fire. During this time his soul was enraptured by the presence of the Lord. Pascal wrote down his experience on a small piece of folded paper and inserted it in parchment on which he recorded a slightly longer version. According to his nephew, Louis Périer, the parchment contained a few extra lines at the end that did not appear on the folded paper. The parchment text includes, at the end, "Total submission to Jesus Christ and my director. Everlasting joy in return for one day's effort on earth. I will not forget thy word. Amen."[19] Pascal sewed both the parchment and the paper into his doublet and wore them during the remained of his lifetime. This was an effort to hold on to the memory, to immortalize the event and to be able to remember and relive it, if that were possible, again in the future. Scholars refer to this text, which describes his stream of consciousness as he experienced the presence of God, as the "The Memorial."

"The Memorial" may be divided into two parts: a statement as to the time of the event, followed by a stream of consciousness of the experience. He begins "The Memorial" by stating the year, the day of the week, the date, the feast days on the Catholic calendar, and the time that the experience began and ended. In this way he is anchoring the spiritual encounter as one anchors a boat in the sea: the time, date, and feast days are an attempt to return his soul to the exact time and place of the event, to recapture what has been lost, to grasp that which is ephemeral and eludes capture, to paint a picture of a fleeting, kaleidoscopic event.

Having anchored the experience in time, he proceeds to give us the title of the piece, "Fire" [*Feu*], on a line by itself, in the middle of the page. The title of the piece is hyperbolic, and by itself, it puzzles the reader and builds suspense. It is not until we read the next line, beneath the title, "God of Abraham, God of Isaac, God of Jacob, not of philosophers and scholars," that we understand that the fire is God and that it must be the presence of the Lord that is permeating his consciousness.[20]

Marvin R. O'Connell, in *Blaise Pascal: Reasons of the Heart*, observes that he refers to three very important biblical passages.[21] "The God of Abraham, God of Isaac, God of Jacob" refers to the manner in which God identified Himself to Moses in Ex 3. God appeared to Moses as a burning bush and instructed him not to draw near and to remove his shoes "for the place whereon thou standest is holy ground. Moreover he said, I am the God of thy father, the God of Abraham, the God of Isaac, and the God of Jacob. And Moses hid his face; for he was afraid to look upon God" (Ex 3:5-6). Secondly, Pascal cites "My God and your God" [*Deum meum et deum vestrum*]. This calls to mind two biblical references: first, Ruth's pledge to Naomi, "Entreat me not to leave thee, or to return from following after thee: for whither thou goest, I will go; and where thou lodgest, I will lodge: thy people shall be my people, and thy God my God:" (Ruth 1:16). The phrase "your God and my God" was repeated by the Risen Lord on Resurrection

Sunday when He appeared to Mary Magdalene: "...go to my brethren, and say unto them, I ascend unto my Father, and you Father; and to my God, and you God" (John 20:17).

O'Connell finds it significant that neither Moses, nor Mary Magdalene were able to identify, at the outset, whom it was that was speaking to them. It took a while for both of them to achieve that awareness. O'Connell points out that it took Pascal eight years to understand that true Christianity was definitely neither the philosophy of the savant, nor that of the *honnête homme* (the successful man of the world).[22]

When Pascal says, "God of Abraham, God of Isaac, God of Jacob, not of philosophers and scholars, he is expressing that the True God is a Living God and that He is a personal God; that He manifests Himself to men; that He is not a distant God who brought the universe into existence and now remains uninvolved with it; that He interacts with His created beings and manifests Himself through miracles and/or personal encounters. For example, Paul was blinded by a powerful light on the road to Damascus, Christ transformed him from a murderer into a saint, and recruited him to be an apostle; 500 people saw the Risen Lord at one time and many were still alive to verify what they had seen at the time that Paul wrote; when Saint Helena wanted to identify the true Cross of Christ among three, God gave her the miracle she needed (a dead man was raised when he was placed over the Cross of Christ); the candles in the Holy Sepulcher miraculously light every year, as do the unlit candles held in the hands of many pilgrims who make the journey there. God is alive and present, not distant and uninvolved in human affairs as philosophers might think.

The language in the Memorial, "God of Abraham, God of Isaac, God of Jacob, not of philosophers and scholars," is similar to that in fragment B430/L149/S182, in which Pascal points out that the philosophy of the world's greatest thinkers is unable to change the human heart or cure man of his unrighteousness. In the latter, he asks whether the true religion is that of philosophers; philosophers can only offer humanity the good that resides in man himself. He asks, "Shall it be that of the philosophers, who put forward as the chief good, the good which is in ourselves? Is this the true good? Have they found the remedy for our ills? Is man's pride cured by placing him on an equality with God? Have those who have made us equal to the brutes, or the Mahomedans who have offered us earthly pleasures as the chief good even in eternity, produced the remedy for our lusts?"[23] The salient point here is that Christianity revolutionized the human spirit and gave man the keys to achieving things that Aristotle and Plato could have only wished for: the Holy Spirit, who indwells the believer, made cowards brave and willing to die for the Risen Lord that they had seen; He inspires young people to leave worldly pleasures and devote themselves to the things pertaining to God. Despite the persecutions of the early Church, the fledgling religion spread like wildfire around the world. Early Christians were not afraid to die because they had seen the Risen Lord and they knew that He had conquered death on the Cross.

The phrase "not of philosophers and scholars" refutes the notion that God can be known only through the power of reason and intellect. Pascal's point is that the path to God is not through reason, not through the casuistry of the Jesuits, not through the philosophy of Montaigne, but rather, through the heart. The Risen Lord is the "I am" who spoke to Moses and men can know His presence in their hearts.

The question arises that if God is "not of philosophers and scholars," why does Pascal go to great lengths to employ reason to prove His existence (ie: the statistical probability of the fulfillment of prophecy, the historicity of miracles, the agreement between the OT and New). The Eastern Orthodox would reply that the answer is that theosis is a process that requires time and hard work. Theosis is deification or union with God. Although Pascal did not have a word for the process and theosis was not spoken of by Catholics, he readily understood that drawing close to God is a process. The Orthodox explain that union with God is the purpose of man. Although the term "theosis" must have been foreign to Pascal, who was a Catholic, he undertook all of the steps recommended by the Desert Fathers necessary to achieve union with God. He gave up the world in exchange for treasure in the life to come. He worked hard at cleaning out his mind and heart of all impurity. Christ taught us that the pure in heart will see God. Pascal tackled the problem of achieving that purity. On that fateful night of 1654, God took the initiative and the Holy Spirit filled Pascal's soul with joy.

The language, "God of Abraham, God of Isaac, God of Jacob, not of philosophers and scholars," is also similar to fragment B556/L449/S690, in which Pascal declares, "But the God of Abraham, the God of Isaac, the God of Jacob, the God of Christians, is a God of love and of comfort, a God who fills the soul and heart of those whom He possesses, a God who makes them conscious of their inward wretchedness, and His infinite mercy, who unites Himself to their inmost soul, who fills it with humility and joy, with confidence and love, who renders them incapable of any other end than Himself."[24] The God of the people that Pascal enumerates-Abraham, Isaac, Jacob, and Christians, seeks to have a personal relationship with His created beings. He was a friend to the people of the Old Covenant who eagerly awaited the advent of the Messiah and in the age of grace, He is a friend to the people of the New Covenant who are deemed righteous by His Blood. The memorial that Pascal sewed inside his clothing and wore for the remainder of his life is a testimonial to the God "who fills the soul and heart of those whom He possesses…who fills it with humility and joy… who renders them incapable of any other end than Himself."

That night Pascal was certain that God exists because his heart was filled with the Holy Spirit. Hence, the second sentence, "Certainty, certainty, heartfelt, joy, peace."[25] Before Jesus left, He promised His disciples that He would ask the Father in Heaven to send a Comforter to walk alongside each believer so that he would never be alone. The Holy Spirit indwells each believer and walks alongside him, counseling him, reminding him of lessons he has forgotten: "And I will pray the Father and he shall give you another Comforter, that he may abide with you for ever; Even the Spirit of truth; whom the world cannot receive, because it seeth him not, neither knoweth him: but ye know him; for he dwelleth with you, and shall be in you" (John 14:16-17); "I will not leave you comfortless: I will come to you" (John 14:18); "I am in my Father, and ye in me, and I in you" (John 14:20); "If a man love me, he will keep my words: and my Father will love him, and we will come unto him, and make our abode with him" (John 14:23); "But the Comforter, which is the Holy Ghost, whom the Father will send in my name, he shall teach you all things, and bring all things to your remembrance, whatsoever I have said unto you: (John 14:26).

This is a good opportunity to note that the Bible specifies three times that the Holy Spirit proceeds from the Father: "And I will pray the Father, and he shall give you another Comforter, that he may abide with you for

Chapter Three: Christ's Miracles Prove His Divinity

ever" (John 14:16) (here the Son does the praying and the Father does the giving); "But the Comforter, which is the Holy Ghost, whom the Father will send in my name, he shall teach you all things, and bring all things to your remembrance, whatsoever I have said unto you" (John 14:26) (here the Father does the sending); "But when the Comforter is come, whom I will send unto you from the Father, even the Spirit of truth, which proceedeth from the Father, he shall testify of me" (John 15:26) (here the Bible specifies that the Son sends someone from the Father, a person who proceeds from the Father; hence, this verse specifies twice that the Holy Spirit originates from the Father).

The Father is the eternal fountainhead from which the Son and the Holy Spirit spring forth. The Orthodox Church stresses the importance of maintaining the integrity of the Holy Trinity as it has been revealed to us three times by the Lord in John 14:16, John 14:26, and John 15:26. It warns that to do otherwise 1) adds or subtracts from the Bible, which Rev 22:18-19 exhorts us not to do, and 2) distorts the distinct relationship that each Person of the Godhead has with the other Two.

Furthermore, we know that the Holy Spirit is a distinct Person of the Godhead, since Jesus says, "he shall testify of me": the pronoun "he" and the verb "testify" indicate personhood. Anyone who can testify is a person. Also, in Acts 8:29, the Holy Spirit speaks to Philip: "Then the Spirit said unto Philip, Go near, and join thyself to this chariot." Anyone who can speak is a person and this verse also provides proof that the Holy Spirit is the third Person of the triune Godhead.

As the Holy Spirit filled Pascal's soul, he began to praise his Savior. Hence, the third and fourth lines, "God of Jesus Christ. God of Jesus Christ."[26] Pascal's double apostrophe is a testimony to the Son of God. He is the eternal being who was prophecized to have been born in Bethlehem, whose goings forth have been from old, from everlasting (Mic 5:2); He is the one by whom all things were made and without whom there was not anything made that was made (John 1:3). Christ manifests His presence through space and time and fills the believer's heart with joy. He told the apostles may times that He abides in them and they abide in Him (John 15:4-5, 7; John 17:21-23). He promised that His presence would fill them with joy: "These things have I spoken unto you, that my joy might remain in you, and that your joy might be full" (John 15:11); "ask and ye shall receive, that you joy may be full" (John 16:24).

Christians hold that the NT is the fulfillment of the promises that God made in the Old; that the nation of Israel under the Law was a shadow pointing to a future reality, namely, the fulfillment of the Law in Christ, the Lord. In the New Covenant, God created something new and extended His grace throughout the Gentile world and has made it possible for all nations to receive the gift of everlasting life through faith in His Son. Christians have inherited the promise, "And ye shall know that I am in the midst of Israel… your sons and your daughters shall prophesy, your old men shall dream dreams, your young men shall see visions" (Joel 2:27-28). The Church age, beginning with Pentecost, is characterized by prophecy, visions, and miracles. On the night of Nov. 23, 1654, the Lord Jesus Christ manifested Himself to Blaise Pascal as a rapturous fire burning in his soul and Pascal was forever transformed by it. He resolved to withdraw from the world of science, mathematics, and the philosophy of men and devoted himself to the things that belong to the Lord. His only desire was to glorify Christ to the best of his ability. The inventor of the barometer and the calculator, the probability theorist, turned his back on men's learning and set out to write a book proving that Christianity is the one true religion on earth and that the Lord Jesus Christ is risen from the grave and rules over men forever.

Pascal writes, "He can only be found by the ways taught in the Gospels."[27] That is, by humbly admitting that one is a sinner and by asking for forgiveness. Christ never turned anyone away who came to Him in need. The way taught in the Gospels is the way that Jesus declared to Nicodemus when he came to visit him at night: one must be born again of water and of the Spirit. Baptism is an act of faith; the Father will send the Holy Spirit to indwell the believer, teach him all things, and walk alongside him forever. The only path to God is through the Lord Jesus Christ. He said, "I am the way, the truth, and the life: no man cometh unto the Father, but by me" (John 14:6).

What follows is the most touching sequence of words in his memorial: "Joy, joy, joy, tears of joy."[28] Happiness flooded his consciousness; sickness, pain, loneliness, despair, all vanished and he was bathed in the ecstasy of God's presence. Did Pascal's soul enter the Throne Room of God? Perhaps.

Chapter Three: Christ's Miracles Prove His Divinity

Perhaps the barrier between Heaven and earth was lifted and He was in the presence of God in Heaven.

In the lines that follow it becomes evident that Pascal does find himself in the presence of the Son of God. His soul is filled with the joy and peace that only the Prince of Peace can bring: "And this is life eternal, that they might know thee, the only true God, and Jesus Christ who thou hast sent. Jesus Christ. Jesus Christ."[29] This is a profession of faith. Pascal declares that he believes on the only begotten Son of God and he surrenders his life to Him. He places his life on Christ's altar so that He may use it according to His will and for His greater glory. Pascal declares, "Sweet and total renunciation. Total submission to Jesus Christ and my director."[30] Pascal's *raison d'être* was to glorify Christ and write a book carrying the Good News across the world. Pascal knew that he belonged to God forever and he lost his fear of death "Everlasting joy in return for one day's effort on earth. I will not forget thy word. Amen."[31]

Pascal was not afraid to die. The curtain between Heaven and earth was lifted and he knew what it was to be in God's presence. His certainty and joy would remain with him the rest of his days. His life was transformed in more ways than one: not only did he lose his fear of death, not only was he certain that his consciousness would continue on after the death of his physical body, but he resolved to give God a gift in return for His very generous gift of Salvation on the Cross: Blaise would write a book for God to carry the Good News to the ends of the earth. Blaise received his Great Commission that night: he would prove that Christianity is the true religion and thus offer back to God a small token in gratitude for His gift of eternal life.

Pascal's' night of fire was the greatest miracle in his life and turned his life around. He resolved to retreat from the world of science, math and reason to lead a monastic lifestyle. He never forgot the joy that he experienced in God's presence and he wanted more of it. He wanted to relive it, if it were possible. He wrote down his feelings on parchment and again on a piece of paper and sewed the two items in his clothing; he wore "The Memorial" for the rest of his life.

Pascal carefully examined the purpose of miracles: God provides them for a reason. For example, miracles bring people to faith and they serve to glorify God. Pascal found another purpose: they can also be used to resolve a conflict. He observes, "Miracles furnish the test in matters of doubt...between the two crosses."[32] This is a reference to the fact that Helena, the mother of Constantine, journeyed to Calvary in search of the original Cross of Christ.

Constantine and Helena had a profound influence on the history of Christianity and its spread across the known world. Both Constantine and Helena had witnessed miracles and these signs from God served to strengthen both their faith and that of others. In 312 AD when Constantine was riding with his army in France, he saw the miraculous sign of a brilliant light in the form of the cross in the sky with the inscription, in Greek, "$Εν$ $τούτο$ $Νικα$" (in this, conquer). Lactantius claims that the event occurred in a dream when he relates it in his work, *Of the Manner in which the Persecutions Died* [*De mortibus persecutorum*], 44;[33] Eusebius records it as a reality that occurred during prayer in the *Life of Constantine* [*De vita Constantini*], 1.28;[34] Eusebius also speaks of it as a historical event in *Oration in Praise of Constantine* [*Oratorio de laudibus Constantini*], 6.21.[35] Constantine understood that the appearance of the Cross in the sky was a sign from God and he established Christianity as the religion of his empire. This was significant not only because it initiated the evolution of Europe into a Christian empire, but also because it marked the end of the persecution of the Church. He also declared Sunday to be the official Sabbath day throughout the Empire, although Christians had already been celebrating it on Sunday since the first century. Henceforth, he also placed the sign of the Cross on his military standard representing it as a long spear, overlaid with gold, and with a transverse bar that formed a cross. At the top of the Cross there appeared a wreath of gold and precious stones and within the wreath he placed *P* (the Greek letter *rho*, pronounced *ro*) intersected by *X* (*chi*, pronounced *hee*) to represent the first two letters of $ΧΡΙΣΤΟΣ$ (Christos). From the crossbar of the spear there was suspended a purple banner with the inscription "$Εν$ $τούτο$ $Νικα$."[36]

During the years 327-328 AD, Constantine's mother, Helena, traveled to Jerusalem in search of the original Cross of Christ. There she conducted an inquiry and was led to a place where she found three crosses buried in the ground. One of the crosses belonged to Christ and the other two, to the thieves who had been crucified alongside Him. In order to ascertain which of the three crosses was Christ's, Helena brought a dead body over to the crosses and took turns placing the corpse on each of the three artifacts. The dead man was resurrected when he was placed on the True Cross, that is, the Cross on which the Lord had been crucified. This is a historical fact and part of Church history.

Eusebius, Bishop of Caesarea, in *Life of Constantine* [*De vita Constantini*], 3.42-47, describes the journey that Helena made to Palestine during the years 327-328 AD.[37] Although Eusebius does not mention that she discovered the True Cross, it is significant that in 327 AD Macarius, Bishop of Jerusalem, had excavations performed in order to find the holy sites. Twenty years later, in 347 AD, Cyril of Jerusalem, in *Catechetical Lectures* 1-18 [*Catecheses illuminandorum*], 4.10, 10.19, and 13.4, discloses that pieces of the True Cross were venerated in the Church of the Resurrection (Church of the Holy Sepulcher) in Jerusalem.[38] For example, in *Catechetical Lectures*, 4.10, Cyril writes, "He was truly crucified for our sins. For if thou wouldest deny it, the place refutes thee visibly, this blessed Golgotha, in which we are now assembled for the sake of Him who was here crucified; and the whole world has since been filled with pieces of the wood of the Cross."[39] After May 7, 351, Cyril wrote to the Emperor Constantinus II that the True Cross had been discovered during the reign of Constantine I, although he does not specify who had discovered it. In the *Letter to Constantine on the Appearance of the Cross* [*Epistula ad Constantium de visione crucis*], Cyril writes, "In the time of your blessed father Constantine of happy memory and most favoured by God, the saving wood of the Cross was found in Jerusalem whom God's grace rewarded the piety of his noble search with the discovery of the hidden holy places."[40] In 362-363 AD, Julian, the pagan Emperor of Rome, rebukes Christians for venerating the relic. In *Against the Galileans* [*Contra Galilaeos*], 194C-D, Julian says, "...but you adore the wood of the cross and draw its likeness on your foreheads and engrave it on your housefronts."[41] Helena's discovery of the True Cross is discussed by Rufinus of Aquileia, in *Church History* [*Historia ecclesiastica*], 10.7-8;[42] Socrates Scholasticus, in *Ecclesiastical History* [*Historia ecclesiastica*], 1.17;[43] Sozomen, in *Ecclesiastical History* [*Historia ecclesiastica*], 2.1-2);[44] Theodoretus, in *Ecclesiastical History*

[*Historia ecclesiastica*], 1.17;[45] Ambrose *On the Death of Theodosius* [*De obitu Theodosii*], 40-49;[46] Paulinus of Nola, *Letters* [*Epistulæ*], 31.4-5;[47] and Sulpicius Severus (or Sulpitius Severus) *Chronicles in Two Books* [*Chronicorum libri duo*] or *Sacred History* [*Historia sacra*], 2.33-34.[48]

Pascal uses Helena's discovery of the True Cross to point out that miracles can be used to distinguish among things in matters of doubt. The fact that the True Cross raised a dead man proves that Christ is Lord of Lords, that He raised Himself and that His Cross continues to raise the dead.

Therefore, one is led to wonder why, after several readings of his thoughts on miracles (fragments B803-856/L830-912/S419-451), the reader is left puzzled by the long list of continual contradictions in Pascal's work. One must necessarily extrapolate that Pascal, on the surface, appears to contradict himself because he is trying to accomplish the following:

1. show the reader that reason has limits (What better way is there to do this, than to continuously contradict oneself or to engage in circular reasoning?)
2. place himself in the skeptic's shoes and articulate the skeptic's arguments so that he can better refute them
3. glorify Christ by demonstrating that He continues to provide His Church with miracles throughout the centuries as evidence of the bride/groom relationship that He has with the Church and to strengthen the faith of His followers
4. recreate a scenario in which some believe, while others do not, even though the miracles occur in front of their eyes: both sides are confronted by the exact same phenomena. Pascal recreates this situation by stating that miracles bring people to faith and then by refuting this and stating that people have reason to disbelieve them. The case for belief becomes a throw of the die having 50-50 odds: which side to bet on? The answer is that Pascal is suggesting is that God takes the initiative and gives the elect faith and withholds his gift from the reprobate. The reader is thus confronted with the Jansenist heresy that underlies Pascal's belief system—that God chooses those to whom He will

give the gift of grace and those from whom He will withhold it, through no fault of their own. Pascal employed this heresy to explain why some believe and others do not. In chapter 6 we will examine and refute Pascal's heretical reiteration that God blinds people. We will show that Orthodoxy teaches that God has given man free will and that man is free to believe or disbelieve. The moment that man reaches towards God, God reaches towards him. When man accepts Christ as his Lord and Savior, God infuses him with grace. Christ knocks on the door to everyone's heart: it is up to man to open the door to Christ.

Miracles vs. Magic

Pascal examines the issue of the authenticity of miracles for several reasons. First, it is one of the arguments that Christ's contemporaries used against Him. Pascal declares, "Miracles enable us to judge of doctrine, and doctrine enables us to judge of miracles."[49] Miracles must be approached with a critical mind because not all miracles are of God; there is a difference between miracles and magic. We see this in the story of the dueling staffs of Moses and Pharaoh's sorcerers.

More importantly, however, the underlying reason that he devotes so much time and space to settling the issue of miracles vs. magic is because his Jansenist companions at Port Royal had many miracles from the Holy Thorn and they were at odds with the established Church because they stressed the doctrine of predestination. Therefore, his concern about the holiness of those who perform miracles is really an effort to legitimize his belief that God graced his Jansenist group with miracles in order to affirm their doctrine to the world. Hence, the Lord's conflict with the Pharisees over doctrine becomes a metaphor for the Jansenists' battle with the Jesuits also over doctrine. The miracles that the Lord performed in the Bible becomes a metaphor for the miracles that that He performed through the Holy Thorn at Port Royal.

Pascal advises further that people "were forbidden to believe every worker of miracles; and they were further commanded to have recourse to the chief priests and to rely on them."[50] While the OT affirms that miracles do, indeed, exist, it distinguishes between miracles and magic (sorcery) and gives examples of both.

For example, Moses casts his rod on the ground and it becomes a serpent (Ex 4:3). Then he puts forth his hand, catches the serpent by the tail and it becomes a rod again (Ex 4:4). He puts his hand in his bosom, withdraws it and it is as leprous as snow (Ex 4:6). He puts his hand back into his bosom, withdraws it again, and it is healed (Ex 4:7). Moses and Aaron go before Pharaoh: Aaron casts down his rod and it becomes a serpent (Ex 7:10). However, the reader is surprised to learn that Pharaoh's sorcerers can do the same thing: "they also did in like manner with their enchantments" (Ex 7:11). Here we see that while servants of the one true God can perform miracles, sorcerers can perform magic by the power of the prince of darkness.

However, then there is still yet another surprise: Aaron's rod swallows up the rods of Pharaoh's sorcerers: "For they cast down every man his rod, and they became serpents: but Aaron's rod swallowed up their rods" (Ex 7:12). Here we see a sharp distinction between the infinite power of the Living God and the finite abilities of the prince of darkness. God is the Creator; the prince of darkness is merely a created being. God is limitless; the latter is limited. The OT offers this event as an iconic representation of the existence of an evil created being that has been given limited power on the earth. Hence, in Ex 7:8-12, the Bible distinguishes between miracles and magic (sorcery).

Then the OT narrates the ten plagues that God sends to Egypt. It is significant that Pharaoh's sorcerers can duplicate the first two plagues, but not the remaining eight: their powers are limited. In the first plague, Aaron lifts up his rod and the water in the Nile River turns into blood (Ex 7:20). The fish die, the river stinks, the water becomes undrinkable; there is blood in all the vessels in Egypt as well, in both the wooden ones and in those made of stone (Ex 7:21). Pharaoh's sorcerers were able to duplicate this first plague: "And the magicians of Egypt did so with their enchantments" (Ex 7:22).

In the second plague, Aaron stretches his hand over the waters of Egypt and frogs come forth and cover the land of Egypt (Ex 8:6). Pharaoh's sorcerers are able to duplicate this feat: "And the magicians did so with their enchantments, and brought up frogs upon the land of Egypt" (Ex 8:7).

Chapter Three: Christ's Miracles Prove His Divinity

However, Aaron and Moses perform eight more miracles (plagues upon Egypt), but Pharaoh's sorcerers are unable to duplicate them. This shows that the powers and principalities of darkness are limited, as they are created beings. In the third plague, Aaron stretches out his hand with his rod and turns the dust of the earth into lice (the KJV says "lice"; the NIV, "gnats"). This lice infects man and beast throughout all of Egypt (Ex 8:17). However, Pharaoh's sorcerers cannot duplicate this feat: "And the magicians did so with their enchantments to bring forth lice, but they could not" (Ex 8:18). The fourth plague was flies (Ex 8:20-32); the fifth plague was against livestock (Ex 9:1-7); the sixth plague was boils (Ex 9:8-12); the seventh plague was hail (Ex 9:13-35); the eighth plague was locusts (Ex 10:1-20); the ninth plague was darkness (Ex 10:21-29); the tenth plague was the death of the firstborn (Ex 11:1-10).

The fact that Pharaoh's sorcerers were limited is essential to understanding why unbelievers are apostate in their rejection of Christ. Christ raised the dead and only God can do that. Hence, He has fulfilled the prophecy, "I will dwell in the midst of thee": "Sing and rejoice, O daughter of Zion: for, lo, I come, and I will dwell in the midst of thee, saith the LORD. And many nations shall be joined to the LORD in that day, and shall be my people: and I will dwell in the midst of thee, and thou shalt know that the LORD of hosts hath sent me unto thee" (Zech 2:10-11). Nicodemus recognized that Jesus had been sent by God: "Rabbi, we know that thou art a teacher come from God: for no man can do these miracles that thou doest, except God be with him" (John 3:2).

Regarding lesser miracles (short of raising the dead), God proscribed certain rules so that one can discern miracles (performed by men of God) from magic (performed by pagans), true prophets from false ones. Pascal discusses these rules in his fragments addressing miracles.

Pascal advises, "Moses has given two rules: that the prediction does not come to pass (Deut 18), and that they do not lead to idolatry (Deut 13), and Jesus Christ one."[51] In Deut 13 Moses advises that if there arises a prophet or one who predicts the future through dreams and this person announces a sign or wonder, and the sign or wonder actually does comes to pass, and then he says, "Let us go follow other gods," this prophet or seer must be put to death. God is testing to see if the people love Him with all of their heart and all of their soul. In Deut 13:1-4 Moses discusses the scenario; in Deut 13:5 he proscribes death to the prophet or seer. The litmus test is doctrine: if the doctrine is false, then the miracle worker must be put to death.

In Deut 18:17-22 Moses describes three future scenarios. In the first, God will raise up a prophet from among the brethren of His own nation; God will put His words in his mouth, and he will tell the people everything that God commands him; if anyone does not listen to this prophet who speaks in the name of God, God will call him to task. These verses can be understood on two levels of interpretation. The surface meaning is that there will be a series of prophets to arise after Moses. On a deeper level, this a Messianic prophecy: the Messiah will be raised up among the brethren of His own nation; he will have prophetic abilities; he will speak the words that God puts in His mouth; he will tell the people everything that the Father commands, he will speak words in the name of God; those who do not listen to him will be taken to task. All of these conditions were fulfilled by Christ.

The second scenario that Moses proposes is that a prophet arises who speaks in God's name things that God has not commanded him to say or a prophet who speaks in the name of other gods. This prophet must be put to death. The third scenario is that a prophet predicts things that do not come to pass. Moses does not proscribe the death penalty in this case. He merely advises that this prophet has spoken presumptuously and that the people should not fear him.

Pascal advises, "Moses has given two rules: that the prediction does not come to pass (Deut 18), and that they do not lead to idolatry (Deut 13)..."[52] Using Deut 13:1-5 and Deut 18:22 Pascal summarizes the distinguishing hallmarks by which one must judge prophetic statements: if the prophecy does not come to pass, it is false; if it leads to idolatry, it is false. If it comes true, it is to be judged by its doctrine: does it bring one closer to the one true God? Is it in agreement with the Bible? Does it glorify God?

This takes us back to the first sentence of fragment B803/L832/S421: "Miracles enable us to judge of doctrine, and doctrine enable us to judge of miracles."[53] This statement is problematic because both clauses in the sentence, the first and the second, can be proven to be either true or false. In fact, Pascal shows the error in both and the truth in both. He refutes the first

Chapter Three: Christ's Miracles Prove His Divinity

clause, "miracles enable us to judge of doctrine" in fragment B808/L846/S429: "They were forbidden to believe every worker of miracles; and they were further commanded to have recourse to the chief priests and to rely on them."[54] Then he goes on to prove that it is true: "And yet they were very sinful in rejecting the prophets and Jesus Christ because of their miracles; and they would not have been culpable, if they had not seen the miracles. *Nisi fecissem...peccatum non haberrent.* [John 15: 24 'If I had not done... they had not had sin.'] Therefore all belief rests upon miracles."[55]

Then taking the second clause, "and doctrine enables us to judge of miracles," he refutes it in fragment B843/L840/S428: "Jesus Christ cured the man born blind and performed a number of miracles on the Sabbath day. In this way He blinded the Pharisees, who said that miracles must be judged by doctrine."[56] Conversely, the truth of this second clause is seen in the dueling staffs of Ex 7:8-12.

Pascal is showing the weakness of reason. Reason alone cannot enable man to arrive at the truth. The questions, then, that arise are "What is Pascal advising? Should the reader judge miracles by doctrine? Should he judge doctrine by miracles? Is there any value at all in the first sentence of fragment B803/L832/S421, 'Miracles enable us to judge of doctrine, and doctrine enables us to judge of miracles?'" Pascal suggests that there is, indeed, value in the sentence: it shows the shortcomings of reason.

What Pascal shows is the limitations and inadequacy of reason. He does this by making a statement that is perfectly reasonable and then making a second statement that is also perfectly reasonable, but which contradicts the first. His favorite technique is to make statements that can be proven to be both true and false. If the reader finds this confusing, it is, and it is done deliberately. Pascal does this in order to undermine the notion that reason is absolute, reliable, trustworthy. How difficult it is then, for man to know and understand things relating to God.

However, Pascal holds that it is possible for man, who is finite and limited, to know and understand the truth about God: the only way that this can be accomplished is through His Son, Jesus. Pascal declares, "Jesus Christ is the end of all, and the centre to which all tends. Whoever knows Him knows the reason of everything."[57] He declares, "The heart has its reasons of which reason knows nothing."[58] Pascal knew that Christ is risen and that He is Lord of the universe because he witnessed many miracles that the Holy Thorn performed at Port Royal. Like the apostles, he saw and he believed. However, he recognizes that there are those who see, but do not believe. What Pascal is promulgating here is his vile doctrine of double predestination: that God predestines people to Heaven or hell based on whether He chooses to give or withhold grace through no fault of their own. This is intrinsically blasphemous because it negates God's goodness. In chapter 6 we will see how the Augustinians of Pascal's time promulgated a flawed theology based on a mistranslation of the original Greek Bible into the Latin vulgate.

In 1658 (according to Philippe Sellier) or 1660 (according to Jean Mesnard) Pascal chose 27 bundles of fragments for his apology and set aside seven other bundles. His material on miracles were found in the bundles that he set aside. Perhaps he put his fragments on miracles aside because they required more work and he needed time to decide how to develop them. Another possibility is this: perhaps he was agonizing over the notion that miracles serve to condemn as well as to save. He does say, "they would not have been culpable, if they had not seen the miracles" and he cites John 15:24, which says, "If I had not done among them the works which none other man did, they had not had sin: but now have they both seen and hated both me and my Father." After all, he did embrace the heresy of double predestination. The path to destruction is wide and very few find the narrow gate. Because he held that some can see miracles and not believe because God withholds grace from them through no fault of their own, he may have wondered how he could ever portray God in a favorable light. Pascal's flawed theology created a lot of problems for any reasonable man and perhaps that is why he left his worked unfinished.

When Pascal originally set out to write his apology, he planned to approach it from the vantage point of Christ's fulfillment of prophecy and miracles. However, as time went on, he expanded his perspective and included more material, such as that on the wretchedness and misery of man. An argument can be made that Pascal set aside his material on miracles because his flawed theology led him to surmise that miracles serve to condemn as well as to save. This is a pity: if he had not started out with the mistaken premise that people are already saved or damned and that man's

Chapter Three: Christ's Miracles Prove His Divinity

free will is absent from the decision that God makes, perhaps he would have argued that miracles are evidence of the will of God, of God's recognition that man, too, has free will to believe or disbelieve, and of God's effort to appeal to man's free will to think as he chooses. Then Pascal might have taken a different approach: he might have argued that if men see miracles and disbelieve, it is because they are exercising their free will to choose separation from God; it is not because of the heretical notion that God hides Himself from most of humanity.

Nevertheless, he did set out on the Great Commission and endeavored to spread the Good News through his writing. He began by intending to use the same method as God uses in the Bible: miracles and prophecy. The Gospel writers themselves stressed the historical basis of Christ's miracles (they specified the names of people, towns, and rulers in order to triangulate a point in time); Pascal examines miracles and mentions that Nicodemus, a member of the Sanhedrin, confessed to the Lord when he visited him secretly at night, "Rabbi, we know that thou art a teacher come from God: for no man can do these miracles that thou doest, except God be with him" (John 3:2). Nicodemus saw the miracles and he believed. So did Joseph of Arimathea; together, Nicodemus and Joseph buried Christ. Augustine also declared the saving power of miracles: "I should not believe except for the miracles."

If unbelievers had not seen the miracles, they could not stand condemned

Pascal explains that those who had seen the miracles, but did not believe, rejected the work that the Father had done in the Son. If they had not seen the miracles, they would not be guilty: but because God's grace had been poured out before them, plainly and clearly in full view, and they rejected it, they stood condemned. Pascal explains, "And yet they were very sinful in rejecting the prophets and Jesus Christ because of their miracles; and they would not have been culpable, if they had not seen the miracles."[59] He cites John 15:24: "If I had not done among them the works which none other man did, they had not had sin: but now have they both seen and hated both me and my Father." Pascal might have also cited John 15:22 in which Christ also advises that those who have heard him and still reject Him also stand condemned precisely because they have had the opportunity to hear Him: "If I had not come and spoken unto them, they had not had sin: but now they have no cloak for their sin." John 15:24 is a statement as to the authority that miracles point to: true miracles, in agreement with the teachings of the Bible, that teach people to worship the one true God in Heaven, indicate that the miracle worker has been sent by God and that therefore, people should heed his teaching and obey his commands. "Pascal says, "Therefore all belief rests upon miracles."[60]

Christ goes on to say, "But this cometh to pass, that the word might be fulfilled that is written in their law, "They hated me without a cause" (John 15:25). This is also a declaration as to the authenticity of the miracles that He performed. He always gave the glory to the Father in Heaven; His teachings are in agreement with Scripture; His miracles pass the tests proscribed by Moses. His rejection is a fulfillment of biblical prophecy.

Pascal examines the importance of the rule that enables men to discern miracles from magic. He advises, "Now the rule which is given to us must be such that it does not destroy the proof which the true miracles give of the truth, which is the chief end of the miracles."[61] Pascal points out that God has provided in Deut 13:1-5 and 18:22 all of the information that is necessary for men to discern miracles from magic. Jesus always gave thanks and the glory to the Father in Heaven; He never instructed the masses to go after other gods.

Fragment B808/L846/S429 addresses Nicodemus, who confessed to Christ that he believed that He had been sent by God: Nicodemus says, "Rabbi, we know that thou art a teacher come from God: for no man can do these miracles that thou doest, except God be with him" (John 3:2). Jesus told him that in order to enter the Kingdom of Heaven, he must be born again, of water and of the Spirit (John 3:5). This implies baptism and being indwelt by the Holy Spirit. Nicodemus' conversation with the Lord is related in John 3:1-21.

Pascal engages in an exercise in which he contradicts himself in order to show man's inability to rely on reason or on himself. Pascal cites Nicodemus profession of faith: "We know that thou are a teacher come from God; for no man can do these miracles that thou doest, except God be with him."[62] Pascal adds, "Nicodemus does not judge of the miracles by the teaching, but of the teaching by the miracles."[63]

Chapter Three: Christ's Miracles Prove His Divinity

Then Pascal utterly confuses the reader by doubting the wisdom of judging the teaching by the miracles. He adds that people "were forbidden to believe every worker of miracles; and they were further commanded to have recourse to the chief priests and to rely on them."[64] However, as a Christian apologist, Pascal must have believed that the masses were right in judging the teaching by the miracles; the leaders were the ones who were in error by rejecting Him, and so the masses could not rely on their leaders for guidance. Then Pascal contradicts himself again, "And yet they were very sinful in rejecting the prophets and Jesus Christ because of their miracles; and they would not have been culpable if they had not seen the miracles."[65] He cites Christ's words, "If I had not done among them the works which no other man did, they had not had sin: but now have they both seen and hated both me and my Father."[66] Pascal concludes, "Therefore all belief rests upon miracles."[67]

However, this is not Pascal's final conclusion. In fragments B817/L734/S615 and B818/L735/S616 he toys with the reader some more, creating more confusion, reiterating the difficulty of relying on reason to arrive at the truth. In fragment B817/L734/S615 Pascal declares, "How it happens that men believe so many liars, who say that they have seen miracles..."[68] He elaborates on the existence of liars, false miracles, and sorcerers. In fragment B818/L735/S616 he reiterates that there are many false miracles, false revelations, sorceries, etc. He thoroughly disorients the reader and demonstrates that man, left to his own resources, can distinguish neither miracles from magic, nor truth tellers from liars. There are no resolutions to the questions that this continual stream of antitheses creates. Pascal gives scriptural justification for believing in miracles, and then he undoes his proofs by contradicting himself. What this continual stream of thesis-antithesis does is demonstrate that God is the tie-breaker. As a Jansenist Pascal believed that God chooses those He will save from the vast ocean of unsaved sinners. Pascal's position is that reason does not save sinners, it does not open up people's understanding so that they can comprehend miracles. Only God can do that. The missing piece here is God: when a person performs miracles, only God can open up the observers' spiritual eyes and give them the wisdom to acknowledge that the miracle worker has been sent from God. Hence, Pascal's circular reasoning and exposition of continual thesis-antithesis expose the limitations of reason as a means by which to arrive at truth and to know God; his method suggests that God's illumination is required in the midst of confusion.

However, the reader is left to wonder whether something else was going on here, whether Pascal, himself, was going through a period of spiritual crisis. He was a man of reason: how could he justify the election of the damned? How could he argue that a loving God performed miracles, but withheld the gift of faith to those who observed these miracles? It is no surprise at all that Pascal put his bundles of fragments on miracles aside. Not only did he need more time to develop them, he needed more time to examine where his theology was taking him and how he could justify it.

As a Christian apologist Pascal would have done better to have enumerated the miracles that Christ performed, much as we have done in the beginning of this chapter. He used the method of enumeration in his fragments on Christ's fulfillment of Messianic prophecy. Pascal painstakingly researched and incorporated into his work as many prophecies as he could find and demonstrated that Christ's fulfillment of so many prophecies is beyond the realm of statistical probability, it is evidence of the will of God. By analogy, he could have enumerated the miracles that Christ performed and pointed out that the gospel writers took care to identify names, places, and rulers in power at that time in order to render a credible witness to Christ's life. The miracles speak for themselves. Pascal's confusing casuistry belittle the very efforts of Christ's work that he was attempting to glorify.

What critics say about Pascal's treatment of miracles

Hugh M. Davidson, in *The Origins of Certainty: Means and Meanings in Pascal's Pensées*, comments upon how Pascal employs miracles as proofs of Christ. First, Davidson advises that miracles, like prophecy, require the intervention of God. However, unlike prophecy, "miracles are not usually foretold, and correlation with past saying is less important than relevance to a present situation, to an immediate crisis that calls for a remedy or a doctrine that needs spectacular confirmation."[69] We must interject here that to the Jansenist, "correlation with past saying is less important than relevance to a present situation" applies only to the elect; for the non-elect, who judge miracles by doctrine, correlation with past saying is very important and determines their decision to reject the miracle worker.

Chapter Three: Christ's Miracles Prove His Divinity

Secondly, Davison observes that Pascal's proofs are interconnected and rely on each other. He examines the sequence in fragment B290/L402/S21, in which Pascal outlines his plan. Pascal writes, "Proofs of religion" as a title and beneath this he enumerates, "Morality, Doctrine, Miracles, Prophecies, Types." Davidson points out that the relationship among these five items is intimately intertwined. He uses the terms "interlocking," "linking" and "connects" to describe it: "Interlocking series of proofs are not very long and are few in number. By far most of the proofs are discrete acts of the mind, single, significant acts of linking a supposition to its presupposition. Pascal *states* proofs, and on rare occasions he *connects* them explicitly."[70] Regarding the sequence "Morality, Doctrine, Miracles, Prophecies, Types," Davidson has two comments to make: "In the first place, these headings appear to stem mainly from the Scripture side of the distinction Pascal makes early in the Apology (in fragment B60/L6/S40), where nature is to supply the proofs of man's corruption and Scripture will do the same in establishing the counterthesis, that there is a redeemer. In the second place, these headings, if one examines them in pairs and in linear fashion, seem to have logical relations to each other and to fall into a kind of sequence. They are not simply isolated topics. *Morale*, which has to do with practice and conduct, follows from *doctrine*, which is a matter of theory or explanation. (As we shall see below in fragment B289/L482/S717, Pascal's second list of proofs, "doctrine" suggests to Pascal at once this development: "qui rend raison du tout.") From this correlation we move to the pair *doctrine/miracles*, and note once more a close relationship, for one function of the latter is to justify the former; more than once Pascal affirms that miracles confirm doctrines and not vice versa. In turn, *miracles* and *prophéties* have a special connection, for a prophecy is, strictly speaking, the announcement of a miracle; and a miracle, though extraordinary in its own right, becomes all the more so when predicted. Finally, *prophéties* depend on *figures*, for without the double sense that figurative interpretation provides, one cannot establish that the prophecy has in fact been realized. This list faces, therefore, in two directions, upward toward one of the two basic sources of proofs (Scripture), and downward towards particular passages in the *Pensées* where proofs become explicit…"[71]

Of course we differ with Davidson's claim "more than once Pascal affirms that miracles confirm doctrine and not vice versa." Pascal declares that miracles may confirm doctrine and doctrine may confirm miracles in order to demonstrate the inadequacy and limitations of reason: Pascal declares, "Miracles enable us to judge of doctrine, and doctrine enables us to judge of miracles."[72] Pascal advises further that people "were forbidden to believe every worker of miracles; and they were further commanded to have recourse to the chief priests and to rely on them."[73] The implication here is that one cannot believe every miracle worker and must weigh the miracles against the soundness of doctrine. Hence, we maintain that the argument that the function of the miracle is to justify doctrine applies only to the elect; according to Jansenism, miracles also function to invalidate doctrine in the eyes of the non-elect. The continual thesis-antithesis (*contrariétés*) in Pascal's work recreates the scenario of doubt surrounding miracles and the dilemma of choosing whether to believe or disbelieve. For the heretical Jansenist, God is the deciding factor and the tie-breaker: the miracle justifies doctrine only for the elect; it serves to condemn the non-elect who have already been condemned from the foundation of the world.

Jean Mesnard, in *Pascal*, also offers a criticism of Pascal's treatment of miracles. Like Davidson, he, too, discusses the value that miracles have in convincing and redeeming. Again, it must be interjected that this applies only to the elect. In his analysis Mesnard makes a number of points. The first is that miracles constitute a language in which God speaks to man: "The miracle is a language that God speaks to us. It is not a useless anarchical manifestation of the supernatural; its essence is to signify. It settles contestations: 'Miracles, the mainstay of religion. They were the mark of the Jews. They were the mark of the Christians, the saints, the Innocents, the true believers' (B851/L903/S450)."[74] Hence, miracles prove the existence of a Divine Interlocutor and are not the result of random chance.

As an example of a situation in which God may choose to speak to man through miracles is to settle a dispute. Again, this indicates the intelligence and volition of an interlocutor that exists: "The miracle distinguishes the true from the false doctrine; it gives assurance to those who are in truth; it invites those who are in error to detach themselves from it. Oftentimes it even symbolizes this doctrine whose mainstay it is. Jesus Christ proves that he forgives sins by performing a miracle" (B808/L846/S429; cf. B643/L275/S306). Thus, the curing of the paralytic reported by Saint Mark expresses, in the bodily order, the healing of the soul procured by the remission of sins. The power of Jesus, manifest in visible things, guarantees His power over the invisible things that He simultaneously attributes to Himself. Generally, 'miracles prove the power which God has over hearts by the power which He exercises over bodies' (B851/L903/S450. In more profound but also more obscure terms: 'Miracles and truth are necessary because man must be convinced entirely in body and in soul' (B806/L848/S430)."[75]

Secondly, Mesnard points out that in order for the observer of the miracle to believe and be saved, he must be willing to submit to the authority of the miracle worker. This is key. Those who believe are willing to be submissive to Christ; those who disbelieve do not want to submit to His authority: "It is proper for any language to require interpretation, and so it is with the language of miracles. To distinguish the real miracles from the false, to determine what God meant by them-Pascal undertook to propose rules concerning all of these matters. But what he particularly wished to point out was that the most shining and clearest true miracles can be warded off, in a way, by whoever refuses to welcome the declared truth that they consider unpleasant."[76] Pascal makes the point, "To be understood, all divine signs demand an attitude of submission."[77] That is why followers of Christ are referred to as sheep and the Lord as the Shepherd. The metaphor of the sheep connotes submission, obedience, the conforming of the will of the disciple to that of the Master.

Thirdly, Mesnard points out the temporal significance of the miracle. He advises that Pascal associates the miracle with a specific time, place, situation, and divine purpose in human history. God chooses to perform a specific miracle at a certain time and place, in front of certain people, because He has a purpose in mind: "Finally, the significance of the miracle is tied to the circumstances in which it appears. It places itself in a precise manner in time; it constitutes God's answer to the questions of the moment: it aims at certain witnesses and addresses itself to determined interlocutors…Pascal affirmed very clearly that miracles, in the restrictive sense of the word, are necessary only at certain stages of revelation… 'Jesus Christ performed miracles, and the Apostles after Him, and the first saints in great numbers, because, as the prophecies were not yet fulfilled and were being fulfilled by them, only miracles testified. It had been foretold that the Messiah would convert the nations. How would this prophecy have been accomplished without the conversion of the nations, and how would the nations have been converted to the Messiah had they not seen this final effect of the prophecies which prove it? Therefore, before His death, rise from the dead, and conversion of the nations, all this was not accomplished and thus miracles were necessary during all of that time. Now they are no longer necessary...(B838/L180/S211).'"[78]

God has a timetable of events that must unfold at specific times, in chronological order, in order to restore the God-man relationship that was ruptured when Adam disobeyed. From the Eastern Orthodox point of view, Davidson is right when he observes that morality, doctrine, miracles, prophecy, and types are interlocking. Mesnard is right that miracles have temporal significance in the unfolding of God's plan for man's redemption. God began by giving man free will because he wants sons and daughters, not robots, in His Kingdom. When Adam disobeyed, God began the redemptive process by choosing a group of people that He wanted to keep holy and set apart from the pagan world. The Second Person of the Holy Trinity, the Creator of the world, chose to come to earth and pay the price for men's sins Himself. When men believe that He did this and they choose to follow where He leads them, they take the first step on a ladder that ultimately leads to theosis or unification with God. Theosis was God's original goal for man before Adam's disobedience. Submission to Christ is necessary (He advised that those who believe and are baptized will be saved) because through this submission they will be conformed to Christ's image, that is, conform their will to God's. God's Kingdom will be filled with sons and daughters who are obedient to the Father and Christ-like and therefore, Christ will be the firstborn in heaven among many brethren.

In the next chapter we will examine the nature of the Godhead and what Pascal had to say about evidence of the Holy Trinity in the OT. We have seen that he has done extensive work in Messianic prophecy in the OT. Pascal was well aware that the OT also provides ample testimony as to the Holy Spirit.

Endnotes

1. *The New Greek-English Interlinear New Testament*, translated by Robert K. Brown and Philip W. Comfort and edited by J. D. Douglas (Carol Stream: Tyndale House Publishers, Inc., 1993), 114.
2. "Palsy," *Oxford English Dictionary Online*, 1a, http://dictionary.oed.com (Mar. 9, 2007).
3. "Prostrate," *Oxford English Dictionary Online*, 1, http://dictionary.oed.com (Mar. 7, 2007).
4. Father Demetrios Serfes, "St. Lazarus the Friend of Christ and First Bishop of Kition, Cyprus." http://www.serfes.org/lives/stlazarus.htm (Mar. 6, 2007).
5. This collation has been assembled using the following tools: the cross-references in the *Holy Bible*, KJV (Grand Rapids: Zondervan, 2000); Archibald Thomas Robertson, *A Harmony of the Gospels for Students of the Life of Christ: Based on the Broadus Harmony in the Revised Version* (New York: George H. Doran Company, 1922), 1-252, the list on 294; J.W. McGarvey and Philip Y. Pendleton, *The Fourfold Gospel or A Harmony of the Four Gospels* (Cincinnati: The Standard Publishing Company, 1914), 1-767; the cross-references in the *NIV Study Bible* (Grand Rapids: Zondervan, 2002), and "The Life of Christ" chart on 2010-12 and "The Harmony of the Gospels" table on 2224-29; "Harmony of the Gospels" and "The Miracles of Jesus Christ" in James Strong, ed., *The New Strong's Exhaustive Concordance of the Bible* (Nashville: Thomas Nelson Publishers, 1990), unnumbered, unpaginated appendices.
6. Ibid.
7. *Yoma*, 6:3, in *The Talmud of the Land of Israel: A Preliminary Translation and Explanation*, translated by Jacob Neusner (Chicago: The University of Chicago Press, 1990), 14:176.
8. Ibid.
9. *Yoma*, 39b, in *Seder Mo'ed*, 4 vols., in *The Babylonian Talmud, Translated into English with Notes, Glossary and Indices under the Editorship of Rabbi Dr I. Epstein, Seder Mo'ed*, (London: The Soncino Press, 1938), 3:186.
10. "Τετέλεστο," *A Greek-English Lexicon*, edited by Henry George Liddell and Robert Scott, revised and unabridged (Oxford: Clarendon Press, 1958), 1772.
11. Bernard, *The Voyage of Bernard the Wise, A.D. 867* in *Early Travels in Palestine, comprising the Narratives of Arculf, Willibald, Bernard, Sæwulf, Sigurd, Benjamin of Tudela, Sir John Maundeville, De La Brocquière, and Maundrell*, edited and annotated by Thomas Wright (London: Henry G. Bohn, 1848), 27.
12. Timothy Ware, *The Orthodox Church*, revised edition (London: Penguin Books, 1997), 59.
13. Abbot Daniel of Tchernigov, *The Pilgrimage of the Russian Abbot Daniel in the Holy Land 1106-1107 AD*, translated from the French by Madame Sophie de Khitrowo, edited by C.W. Wilson (London: Palestine Pilgrims' Text Society, 1895), 74-75, 78-81.
14. A plethora of websites can be procured by triangulating "Holy Flame" and "Orthodox Church" on your search engine. Below are some websites. Note that some addresses are case sensitive:

http://www.ocf.org/OrthodoxPage/reading/light.html (Mar. 22, 2007)
www.orthodoxinfo.com/general/holyfire.asp (Mar. 22, 2007)
www.holyfire.org/eng/doc_MiracleEncounters.htm (Mar. 22, 2007)
www2.cytanet.com.cy/gogreek/miracle.htm (Mar. 22, 2007)
15 http://www.ocf.org/OrthodoxPage/reading/light.html (Mar. 22, 2007)
16 www.orthodoxinfo.com/general/holyfire.asp (Mar. 22, 2007)
17 Ibid.
18 Ibid.
19 Blaise Pascal, *Pensées*, translated by A.J. Krailsheimer, Lafuma numbering system (London: Penguin Books, 1995), fragment 913. "Soumission totale à Jésus-Christ et à mon directeur. Eternellement en joie pour un jour d'exercice sur la terre. *Non obliviscar sermons tuos*. Amen." Blaise Pascal, *Pensées*, in *Œuvres completes*, edited by Louis Lafuma (Paris: Seuil, 1963), fragment 913 (Sellier 742).
20 Ibid.
21 Marvin R. O'Connell, *Blaise Pascal: Reasons of the Heart* (Grand Rapids: William B. Eerdmans Publishing Company, 1997), 98-100.
22 Ibid., 100.
23 Blaise Pascal, *Thoughts*, translated by W.F. Trotter, Brunschvicg numbering system (New York: P.F. Collier & Son, 1910), fragment 430. "Sera-ce les philosophes, qui nous proposent pour tout bien les biens qui sont en nous? Est-ce là le vrai bien? Ont-ils trouvé le remède à nos maux? Est-ce avoir guéri la presomption de l'homme que de l'avoir mis à l'égal de Dieu? Ceux qui nous ont égalés aux bêtes, et les mahométans qui nous ont donné les plaisirs de la terre pour tout bien, meme dans l'éternité, ont-ils apporté le remède à nos concupiscences?" Blaise Pascal, *Pensées*, in *Œuvres de Blaise Pascal*, edited by Léon Brunschvicg, Pierre Boutroux, and Félix Gazier (Paris: Librairie Hachette & Cie, 1904-1914), fragment 430 (Lafuma 149; Sellier 182).
24 Ibid., fragment 556. "Mais le Dieu d'Abraham, le Dieu d'Isaac, le Dieu de Jacob, le Dieu des chrétiens, est un Dieu d'amour et de consolation; c'est un Dieu qui remplit l'âme et le cœur de ceux qu'il possède; c'est un Dieu qui leur fait sentir intérieurement leur misère, et sa miséricorde infinie; qui s'unit au fond de leur âme; qui la remplit d'humilité, de joie, de confiance, d'amour; qui les rend incapables d'autre fin que de lui-même." Ibid., fragment 556 (Lafuma 449; Sellier 690).
25 Blaise Pascal, *Pensées*, translated by A.J. Krailsheimer, Lafuma numbering system (London: Penguin Books, 1995), fragment 913. "Certitude, certitude, sentiment, joie, paix." Blaise Pascal, *Pensées*, in *Œuvres completes*, edited by Louis Lafuma (Paris: Seuil, 1963), fragment 913 (Sellier 742).
26 Ibid. "(*Dieu de Jésus-Christ*). Dieu de Jésus-Christ." Ibid.
27 Ibid. "Il ne se trouve que par les voies enseignées dans l'Evangile." Ibid.
28 Ibid. "Joie, joie, joie, pleurs de joie." Ibid.
29 Ibid. "'Cette est la vie éternelle, qu'ils te connaissent seul vrai Dieu et celui que tu as envoyé J-C. Jésus-Christ.' Jésus-Christ. Jésus-Christ." Ibid.
30 Ibid. "Renonciation totale et douce. Etc. Soumission totale à Jésus-Christ et à mon directeur." Ibid.
31 Ibid. "Eternellement en joie pour un jour d'exercice sur la terre. *Non obliviscar sermones tuos*. Amen." Ibid.

Chapter Three: Christ's Miracles Prove His Divinity

32 Blaise Pascal, *Thoughts*, translated by W.F. Trotter, Brunschvicg numbering system (New York: P.F. Collier & Son, 1910), fragment 841. "Les miracles discernent aux choses douteuses...entre les deux croix." Blaise Pascal, *Pensées*, in *Œuvres de Blaise Pascal*, edited by Léon Brunschvicg, Pierre Boutroux, and Félix Gazier (Paris: Librairie Hachette & Cie, 1904-1914), fragment 841 (Lafuma 901; Sellier 449).

33 Lactantius, *Of the Manner in which the Persecutions Died*, 44, in *Fathers of the Third and Fourth Centuries: Lactantius, Venantius, Asterius, Victorinus, Dionysius, Apostolic Teaching and Constitutions, Homily*, vol. 7 of *Ante-Nicene Fathers*, edited by Alexander Roberts and James Donaldson (New York: The Christian Literature Company, 1890-1897), 318 [Lactantius, *De mortibus persecutorum*, 44, in Jacques-Paul Migne, ed., *Patrologiæ cursos completus...Series latina*, 221 vols. (Paris: Migne, 1844-1879), 7:261A].

34 Eusebius Pamphilus, *Life of Constantine*, 1.28, in *Eusebius Pamphilus: Church History, Life of Constantine, Oration in Praise of Constantine*, vol. 1 of *Nicene and Post-Nicene Fathers of the Christian Church*, 2nd series, edited by Philip Schaff and Henry Wace (New York: Christian Literature Publishing Company, 1890), 490 [Eusebius Pamphilus, *De vita Constantini*, 1.28, in Jacques-Paul Migne, ed., *Patrologiæ cursos completus...Series græca*, 161 vols. (Paris: Migne, 1857-1866), 20:944A-C].

35 Eusebius Pamphilus, *Oration in Praise of Constantine*, 6.21, in *Eusebius Pamphilus: Church History, Life of Constantine, Oration in Praise of Constantine*, vol. 1 of *Nicene and Post-Nicene Fathers of the Christian Church*, 2nd series, edited by Philip Schaff and Henry Wace (New York: Christian Literature Publishing Company, 1890), 589 [Eusebius Pamphilus, *Oratorio de laudibus Constantini*, 6.21, in Jacques-Paul Migne, ed., *Patrologiæ cursos completus... Series græca*, 161 vols. (Paris: Migne, 1857-1866), 20:1349D-1352A].

36 Eusebius Pamphilus, *Life of Constantine*, 1.31, in *Eusebius Pamphilus: Church History, Life of Constantine, Oration in Praise of Constantine*, vol. 1 of *Nicene and Post-Nicene Fathers of the Christian Church*, 2nd series, edited by Philip Schaff and Henry Wace (New York: Christian Literature Publishing Company, 1890), Ibid., 490-91 [Eusebius Pamphilus, *De vita Constantini*, 1.31, in Jacques-Paul Migne, ed., *Patrologiæ cursos completus...Series græca*, 161 vols. (Paris: Migne, 1857-1866), 20:945A-948A].

37 Ibid., 3.42-47, 530-32 [Ibid., 20:1101B-1108B].

38 Cyril of Jerusalem, *Catechetical Lectures*, 4.10, 10.19, 13.4, in *Cyril of Jerusalem, Gregory Nazianzen*, vol. 7 of *Nicene and Post-Nicene Fathers of the Christian Church*, 2nd series, edited by Philip Schaff and Henry Wace (New York: Christian Literature Publishing Company, 1893), 21, 63, 83 [Cyril of Jerusalem, *Catecheses illuminandorum*, 4.10, 10.19, 13.4, in Jacques-Paul Migne, ed., *Patrologiæ cursos completus...Series græca*, 161 vols. (Paris: Migne, 1857-1866), 33:468B-469A; 685A-688C; 776B-777A].

39 Ibid., 21 [Ibid., 33:468B-469A].

40 Cyril of Jerusalem, *Letter to Constantinus*, 3, in Edward Yarnold, *Cyril of Jerusalem* (London and New York: Routledge, 2000), 69 [Cyril of Jerusalem, *Epistula ad Constantium de visione crucis*, 3, in Jacques-Paul Migne, ed.,

Patrologiæ cursos completus...Series græca, 161 vols. (Paris: Migne, 1857-1866), 33:1168B-1169A]. It should also be mentioned that on May 7, 351 AD, the sign of the Cross appeared in the sky in Jerusalem. Cyril writes to Constantius II, "Our purpose is to bring with all speed to your Piety's attention the display of divine energy that took place in the sky over Jerusalem during your reign so favoured by God...in your time miracles have now appeared no longer from the ground but in the heavens: the trophy of the victory which our Lord and Saviour Jesus Christ-the Only-begotten Son of God, won over death-I refer to the blessed Cross-has been seen flashing like lightning over Jerusalem.

In these holy days of the Eastern season, on 7 May at about the third hour, a huge cross made of light appeared in the sky above holy Golgotha extending as far as the holy Mount of Olives. It was not revealed to one or two people alone, but it appeared unmistakably to everyone in the city. It was not as if one might conclude that one had suffered a momentary optical illusion; it was visible to the human eye above the earth for several hours. The flashes it emitted outshone the rays of the sun, which would have outshone and obscured it themselves if it had not presented the watchers with a more powerful illumination than the sun." Cyril of Jerusalem, *Letter to Constantinus*, 2-4, in Edward Yarnold, *Cyril of Jerusalem* (London and New York: Routledge, 2000), 68-69 [Cyril of Jerusalem, *Epistula ad Constantium de visione crucis*, 2-4, in Jacques-Paul Migne, ed., *Patrologiæ cursos completus... Series græca*, 161 vols. (Paris: Migne, 1857-1866), 33:1165A-1169C].

41 Julian, Emperor of Rome, *Against the Galileans*, 194C-D, in *The Works of the Emperor Julian*, 3 vols., translated by Wilmer Cave Wright (London: William Heinemann, 1913-1923, 3:373.

42 Rufinus, *Church History*, 10.7-8, in *The Church History of Rufinus of Aquileia: Books 10 and 11*, translated by Philip R. Amidon (New York: Oxford University Press, 1997), 16-18 [Rufinus, *Historia ecclesiastica*, 10.7-8, in Jacques-Paul Migne, ed., *Patrologiæ cursos completus...Series latina*, 221 vols. (Paris: Migne, 1844-1879), 21:475C-478A].

43 Socrates Scholasticus, *Ecclesiastical History*, 1.17, in *The Ecclesiastical History of Socrates Scholasticus*, vol. 2 of *Nicene and Post-Nicene Fathers of the Christian Church*, 2nd series, edited by Philip Schaff and Henry Wace (New York: Christian Literature Publishing Company, 1886), 21-22 [Socrates Scholasticus, *Historia ecclesiastica*, 1.17, in Jacques-Paul Migne, ed., *Patrologiæ cursos completus... Series græca*, 161 vols. (Paris: Migne, 1857-1866), 67:117B-121A].

44 Sozomen, *Ecclesiastical History*, 2.1-2, in *The Ecclesiastical History of Sozomen, comprising a History of the Church, from A.D. 323 to A.D. 425*, vol. 2 of *Nicene and Post-Nicene Fathers of the Christian Church*, 2nd series, edited by Philip Schaff and Henry Wace (New York: Christian Literature Publishing Company, 1886), 258-59 [Sozomen, *Historia ecclesiastica*, 2.1-2, in Jacques-Paul Migne, ed., *Patrologiæ cursos completus...Series græca*, 161 vols. (Paris: Migne, 1857-1866), 67:929B-936B].

45 Theodoretus, *Ecclesiastical History*, 10.17, in *The Ecclesiastical History, Dialogues, and Letters of Theodoret*, vol. 3 of *Nicene and Post-Nicene Fathers of the Christian Church*, 2nd series, edited by Philip Schaff and Henry Wace (New York: Christian Literature Publishing Company, 1892), 54-55.

Chapter Three: Christ's Miracles Prove His Divinity

46 Ambrose, *On the Death of Theodosius*, 40-49, in *Ambrose of Milan: Political Letters and Speeches*, translated, introduced, and annotated by J.H.W.G. Liebeschuetz (Liverpool: Liverpool University Press, 2005), 196-201 [Ambrose, *De obitu Theodosii*, 40-49, in Jacques-Paul Migne, ed., *Patrologiæ cursos completus... Series latina*, 221 vols. (Paris: Migne, 1844-1879), 16:1462A-1466A].

47 Paulinus of Nola, *Letters of St. Paulinus of Nola*, 31.4-6, translated and annotated by P.G. Walsh, 2 vols. (Westminster, MD: The Newmann Press, 1966-1967, 2:129-33 [Paulinus of Nola, *Epistulæ*, 31.4-6, in Jacques-Paul Migne, ed., *Patrologiæ cursos completus...Series latina*, 221 vols. (Paris: Migne, 1844-1879), 61:327B-330B].

48 Sulpitius Severus, *The Sacred History of Sulpitius Severus*, 2:33-34, in *Sulpitius Severus, Vincent of Lerins, John Cassian*, vol. 11 of *Nicene and Post-Nicene Fathers of the Christian Church*, 2nd series, edited by Philip Schaff and Henry Wace (New York: Christian Literature Publishing Company, 1890-1900), 112-13 [Sulpitius Severus, *Historia sacra*, 2:33-34, in Jacques-Paul Migne, ed., *Patrologiæ cursos completus...Series latina*, 221 vols. (Paris: Migne, 1844-1879), 20:147C-148C].

49 Blaise Pascal, *Thoughts*, translated by W.F. Trotter, Brunschvicg numbering system (New York: P.F. Collier & Son, 1910), fragment 803. "Les miracles discernent la doctrine, et la doctrine discerne les miracles." Blaise Pascal, *Pensées*, in *Œuvres de Blaise Pascal*, edited by Léon Brunschvicg, Pierre Boutroux, and Félix Gazier (Paris: Librairie Hachette & Cie, 1904-1914), fragment 803 (Lafuma 832; Sellier 421).

50 Ibid., fragment 808. "...et défense de croire à tous faiseurs de miracles, et, de plus, ordre de recourir aux grands-prêtres, et de s'en tenir à eux." Ibid., fragment 808 (Lafuma 846; Sellier 429).

51 Ibid., fragment 803. "Moïse en a donné deux: que la prédiction n'arrive pas, *Deut*., XVIII, et qu'ils ne mènent point à l'idolâtrie, *Deut*., XIII; et Jésus-Christ une." Ibid., fragment 803 (Lafuma 832; Sellier 421).

52 Ibid. Ibid.

53 Ibid. "Les miracles discernent la doctrine et la doctrine discerne les miracles." Ibid.

54 Ibid., fragment 808. "...et défense de croire à tous faiseurs de miracles, et, de plus, ordre de recourir aux grands-prêtres, et de s'en tenir à eux." Ibid., fragment 808 (Lafuma 846; Sellier 429).

55 Ibid. "Et cependant ils étaient très coupables de refuser les prophètes, à cause de leurs miracles, et Jésus-Christ; et n'eussent pas été coupables s'ils n'eussent point vu les miracles: *Nisi fecissem..., peccatum non haberent*. Donc toute la créance est sur les miracles." Ibid.

56 Ibid., fragment 843. "Jésus-Christ guérit l'aveugle-né, et fit quantité de miracles, au jour du sabbat.

Par où il aveuglait les pharisiens qui disaient qu'il fallait juger des miracles par la doctrine." Ibid., fragment 843 (Lafuma 840; Sellier 428).

57 Ibid., fragment 556. "...Jésus-Christ est l'objet de tout, et le centre où tout tend. Qui le connaît, connaît la raison de toutes choses." Ibid., fragment 556 (Lafuma 449; Sellier 690).

58 Ibid., fragment 277. "Le cœur a ses raisons, que la raison ne connaît point…" Ibid., fragment 277 (Lafuma 423; Sellier 680).
59 Ibid., fragment 808. "Et cependant ils étaient très coupables de refuser les prophètes, à cause de leurs miracles, et Jésus-Christ; et n'eussent pas été coupables s'ils n'eussent point vu les miracles: *Nisi fecissem…, peccatum non haberent.* Donc toute la créance est sur les miracles." Ibid., fragment 808 (Lafuma 846; Sellier 429).
60 Ibid. "Donc toute la créance est sur les miracles." Ibid.
61 Ibid., fragment 803. "Or, il faut que la règle qu'il nous donne soit telle, qu'elle ne détruise la preuve que les vrais miracles donnent de la vérité, qui est la fin principale des miracles." Ibid., fragment 803 (Lafuma 832; Sellier 421).
62 Ibid., fragment 808. "Nicodème reconnaît, par ses miracles, que sa doctrine est de Dieu: *Scimus quia venisti a Deo magister, nemo enim potest haec signa facere quæ tu facis nisi Deus fuerit cum eo.*" Ibid., fragment 808 (Lafuma 846; Sellier 429).
63 Ibid. "Il ne juge pas des miracles par la doctrine, mais de la doctrine par les miracles." Ibid.
64 Ibid. "…et défense de croire à tous faiseurs de miracles, et, de plus, ordre de recourir aux grands-prêtres, et de s'en tenir à eux." Ibid.
65 Ibid. "Et cependant ils étaient très coupables de refuser les prophètes, à cause de leurs miracles, et Jésus-Christ; et n'eussent pas été coupables s'ils n'eussent point vu les miracles…" Ibid.
66 Ibid. "*Nisi fecissem…, peccatum non haberent.*" Ibid.
67 Ibid. "Donc toute la créance est sur les miracles." Ibid.
68 Ibid., fragment 817. "*D'où vient qu'on croit tant de menteurs qui disent qu'ils ont vu des miracles…*" Ibid., fragment 817 (Lafuma 734; Sellier 615).
69 Hugh M. Davidson, *The Origins of Certainty: Means and Meanings in Pascal's Pensées* (Chicago: The University of Chicago Press, 1979), 26.
70 Ibid., 30.
71 Ibid., 30-31.
72 Blaise Pascal, *Thoughts*, translated by W.F. Trotter, Brunschvicg numbering system (New York: P.F. Collier & Son, 1910), fragment 803. "Les miracles discernent la doctrine, et la doctrine discerne les miracles." Blaise Pascal, *Pensées*, in *Œuvres de Blaise Pascal*, edited by Léon Brunschvicg, Pierre Boutroux, and Félix Gazier (Paris: Librairie Hachette & Cie, 1904-1914), fragment 803 (Lafuma 832; Sellier 421).
73 Ibid., fragment 808. "…et défense de croire à tous faiseurs de miracles, et, de plus, ordre de recourir aux grands-prêtres, et de s'en tenir à eux." Ibid., fragment 808 (Lafuma 846; Sellier 429).
74 Jean Mesnard, *Pascal*, translated by Claude and Marcia Abraham (University, AL: University of Alabama Press, 1969), 61.
75 Ibid.
76 Ibid., 61-62.
77 Ibid., 62.
78 Ibid., 62-63.

The Holy Trinity in the Old Testament

Go ye therefore, and teach all nations,
baptizing them in the name of the Father,
and of the Son, and of the Holy Ghost.
—Mat 28:19

Pascal declared, "*Moses first teaches the Trinity, original sin, the Messiah.*"[1] His assertion that Moses was the first biblical author to declare the triune nature of the Godhead is supported by the Pentateuch. The Pentateuch is comprised of the first five books of the Old Testament (Genesis, Exodus, Leviticus, Numbers, and Deuteronomy). These books are ascribed to Moses and are sometimes called the Books of Moses. In the chapter we will see that just as Pascal said, the Books of Moses do, indeed, distinguish among the three Persons of the Trinity and provide snapshots of all three Persons in action. Pascal considered these glimpses of the Holy Trinity in the OT to provide additional proof that Christianity is the true religion: just as the OT provides Messianic prophecies that Christ would one day fulfill, it also furnishes evidence of the triune Godhead that Christ would one day explain and greatly clarify.

An especially revealing statement of the Holy Trinity in the Books of Moses is in Deut 6:4, in which Moses declares, "Hear, O Israel: The LORD our God is one LORD." This verse is known as the *Shema*, which is Hebrew for "Hear" and it is declared in synagogues every Sabbath. What is significant about this verse is God's choice of terminology. The Hebrew word for "one" here, *echad*, connotes a cluster or a unity, and it is used many times in the OT to mean just that. For example, it is used in Gen 2:24: "Therefore shall a man leave his father and his mother, and shall cleave unto his wife: and they shall be one flesh." Here "one," *echad*, means a union or cluster comprised of two beings, not the absolute numeric one. *Echad*, meaning one in unity (cluster) is to be distinguished from the Hebrew word *yachid*, which means one in number. It is significant that in the Old Testament *yachid*, meaning solitary oneness or the number one, is never used in reference to God.

Echad is used again in Num 13:23 to mean a cluster of grapes: "And they came unto the brook of Eshcol, and cut down from thence a branch with one [*echad*] cluster of grapes, and they bare it between two upon a staff..." Here, *echad* clearly means a cluster of grapes, not one grape.

Conversely, *yachid*, meaning "only" or "an absolute numeric one," is used when God told Abraham to offer his only [*yachid*] son as a burnt offering: "And he said, Take now thy son, thine only son Isaac, whom thou lovest..." (Gen 22:2); "And he said, Lay not thine hand upon the lad, neither do thou any thing unto him: for now I know that thou fearest God, seeing thou hast not withheld thy son, thine only son from me" (Gen 22:12); "And said, By myself have I sworn, saith the LORD, for because thou hast done this thing, and hast not withheld thy son, thine only son" (Gen 22:16). In these verses *yachid* clearly implies the numeric one. See also, "And Jephthah came to Mizpeh unto his house, and, behold, his daughter came out to meet him with timbrels and with dances: and she was his only child; beside her he had neither son nor daughter" (Judg 11:34); "make thee mourning, as for an only son, most bitter lamentation: for the spoiler shall suddenly come upon us" (Jer 6:26); "and they shall look upon me whom they have pierced, and they shall mourn for him, as one mourneth for his only son" (Zech 12:10).

Another Hebrew word that connotes numeric oneness, like *yachid*, is *bad*. *Bad* is used to identify the oneness of God. Examples are "thou art the God, even thou alone, of all the kingdoms of the earth; thou hast made heaven and earth" (2 Ki 19:15); "Thou, even thou, art LORD alone" (Neh 9:6); "that all the kingdoms of the earth may know that thou art the LORD, even thou only" (Is 37:20).

Therefore, it is significant that in the *Shema*, "Hear O Israel...," Moses used *echad*, cluster or unity, and neither *yachid*, nor *bad*, absolute number one. It is also significant that *yachid* is never used in the OT to describe God.

After Christianity began to take hold in the ancient world, Jews, anxious to establish their identity apart from it, replaced *echad* with *yachid* in Deut 6:4. The Talmud, which contains *yachid*, did not exist before the second century, when Christianity took hold; it was written after the rise of Christianity as a response to the fledgling religion, and when it was, *echad* was replaced with *yachid*. Furthermore, when Moses Maimonides, the 12th century Jewish rabbi and philosopher, compiled a creed of 13 articles, he made sure that *yachid* replaced *echad* in his creed: "I believe with a perfect faith that the Creator, blessed be His name, is an absolute one [*yachid*]." In addition, modern Jewish prayer books use *yachid* to describe the oneness of God.

Distinction within the Godhead: The Son

It has been said that the OT provides candlelight as to the nature of God, while the NT sheds full blown daylight on it. There are notable examples in the OT where the Father, the Son and the Holy Spirit appear as distinct persons, and several in which the Father and the Son are conversing among themselves. David, Isaiah, and Daniel provide snapshots of Christ. For example, in Ps 2 David portrays the two persons of the Holy Trinity, the Father and the Son. In Ps 2:2, "the rulers take counsel together, against the LORD, and against his anointed." Here we have two distinct persons, the Lord and His Anointed. The scene is set in Heaven: Ps 2:4 says, "He that sitteth in the heavens shall laugh. In Ps 2:7-9 we have a conversation between the Father and the Son. Christ is speaking in the first person and He is relating what the Father has said to Him: "the LORD hath said unto me, Thou art my son; this day have I begotten thee. Ask of me, and I shall give thee the heathen for thine inheritance, and the uttermost parts of the earth for thy possession. Thou shalt break them with a rod of iron; thou shalt dash them in pieces like a potter's vessel." David advises, in Ps 2:12, "Kiss the Son, lest he be angry, and ye perish from the way, when his wrath is kindled but a little. Blessed are all they that put their trust in him." "Kiss the Son," according to John Wesley's *Explanatory Notes upon the Old Testament*, is explained as "In token of your subjection and adoration; whereof this was a sign among the eastern nations."[2] Hence, David is issuing a warning in advance of the advent of Christ that the Lord of Lords demands obedience and submission to His will; disobedience will kindle His wrath and "ye then shall perish from the way."

In Ps 110:1, we have two Persons of the Holy Trinity conversing once more: "The LORD said unto my Lord, Sit thou at my right hand, until I make thine enemies thy footstool." Not only is David relating that the Father is speaking to the Son, but the Father is inviting the Son to sit at His right hand in Heaven, until He returns to earth to judge the wicked. That is what happens in Ps 110:2: "The LORD shall send the rod of thy strength out of Zion: rule thou in the midst of thine enemies." In Ps 110:4, the Son is the intercessor between the Father and humanity, a high priest and man can now go directly into the Holy of Holies without a mortal priest: "thou art a priest for ever after the order of Melchizedek." And so the curtain in the Temple was rent after Christ surrendered His Ghost on the Cross and man could directly converse with God because Christ is his High Priest. Again, Christ is sitting at the right hand of the Father in Ps 110:5: "The Lord at thy right hand shall strike through kings in the day of his wrath." His kingdom is eternal, not temporal as are the kingdoms of men; it will not be overthrown and replaced as are human kingdoms.

This psalm embraces a time span from the Ascension to the Second Coming. In Ps 110:1 the Father invites the Son to sit at His right hand until the time comes when He will judge the reprobate. In Ps 110:2 He establishes His eternal kingdom and rules over His subjects. Because God antecedes time, He exists outside of it; the past, the present, and the future are all the same to Him. Therefore, when the prophets articulated the future through the power of the Holy Spirit, they presented it in a continuous stream; there was no delineation between the First and Second Comings. However, we know that the Messiah has come and is risen from the dead because 1) the Patriarch's candle miraculously lights in Jerusalem every year, 2) the time of His arrival in Dan 9:25 has come and gone, 3) there were signs in the Temple from 30 AD-70 AD that indicated that the sacrifice of Yom Kippur was no longer what God wanted, and 4) the Gentile world has been called to the one true God of Israel, in fulfillment of prophecy.

In Ps 118:16 Christ is identified as the "right hand of the Lord": "The right hand of the LORD is exalted: the right hand of the LORD doeth valiantly." We also have the Crucifixion scene: "I called upon the LORD in distress'" (Ps 118:5); "The LORD is on my side; I will not fear: what can man do unto me?" (Ps 118:6); "upon them that hate me" (Ps 118:7); "All nations compassed me about" (Ps 118:10); "They compassed me about; yea, they compassed me about" (Ps 118:11); "They compassed me about like bees" (Ps 118:12); the Resurrection is implied here: "The LORD hath chastened me sore: but he hath not given me over unto death" (Ps 188:18);

Chapter Four: The Holy Trinity in the Old Testament

"Open to me the gates of righteousness" (Ps 118:19). It is significant that David specifies, "The stone which the builders refused is become the head stone of the corner" (Ps 118:22): therefore, we know that the entire psalm describes Christ's generous gift of salvation on the Cross. Moreover, in that same psalm, David identifies the persona as One who comes in the name of God: "Blessed be he that cometh in the name of the LORD" (Ps 118:26).

Isaiah is another prophet in the OT who describes Christ. The Book of Isaiah is especially significant because although he wrote during the 8th century BC, he provided a startling photograph depicting the crucified Christ to the utmost minutia, details of His life, and His purpose for coming to earth. Is 49 begins, "Listen, O isles, unto me; and hearken, ye people, from far; The LORD hath called me from the womb; from the bowels of my mother hath he made mention of my name" (Is 49:1). Here Christ is speaking in the first person and He is calling to the Gentile nations, metaphorized as "isles." He is relating the fact that the Father has called Him by name while He was still in His mother's womb. The chapter continues, "And he hath made my mouth like a sharp sword" (Is 49:2). Christ is continuing to speak in the first person. He is the Word (sharp sword) who saves and condemns. "Sword" also alludes to His Second Coming when He will judge all of humanity (Rev 1:16, "and out of his mouth went a sharp two-edged sword").

Is 49:3 states, "Thou are my servant, O Israel, in whom I will be glorified." Christ is relating what the Father has said to Him. Just as God sometimes used the word "David" to refer to successors of David, here, the Father is referring to Christ as the successor of Jacob (first called Israel). The *NIV Study Bible* advises, "'Servant' here cannot mean literally national Israel, since in v. 5 this servant has a mission to Israel. Rather, the Messianic servant is the ideal Israel through whom the Lord will be glorified. He will succeed where national Israel failed."[3]

Is 49:4 continues, "Then I said, I have laboured in vain, I have spent my strength for nought, and in vain: yet surely my judgment is with the LORD, and my work with my God." Christ is relating what he said to the Father. The *NIV Study Bible* explains, "Christ would encounter strong opposition during his ministry and would temporarily suffer apparent failure. The 'suffering servant' theme is developed in the third and fourth of the four servant songs (50:4 – 9 or 50: 4 – 11, 52:13 – 53:12). *What is due me...my reward.* Perhaps referring to the spiritual offspring of the servant (see 53:10) – Jews and Gentiles alike who believe in him (vv. 5 – 6)...In any case, he will be vindicated and rewarded (50:8; 53:10 – 12; 1Ti 3:16)."[4]

Is 49:5-"And now, saith the LORD that formed me from the womb to be his servant, to bring Jacob again to him, Though Israel be not gathered, yet shall I be glorious in the eyes of the LORD, and my God shall be my strength." Christ is still speaking in the first person and He is relating that the Father has said to Him: the Father has promised Him that He, Christ, will be glorious in His Father's eyes, even though Israel is not gathered. This prophesizes the Jewish diaspora ("though Israel be not gathered") and the Gentiles' conversion ("yet shall I be glorious in the eyes of the LORD") during that period, just under two millennia. It is evident that this chapter is about Christ's mission on earth during His First and Second Coming, the calling of the righteous to God, the Father ("to bring Jacob again to him"), and the deliverance from sin.

Is 49:6-"And he said, It is a light thing that thou shouldest be my servant to raise up the tribes of Jacob, and to restore the preserved of Israel: I will also give thee for a light to the Gentiles, that thou mayest be my salvation unto the end of the earth." Christ is speaking here and He is relating words that the Father has spoken to Him: the Father has said that Christ will restore the preserved of Israel, and that Christ will be a light to the Gentiles and the Father's salvation unto the end of the earth. "End of the earth" predicts that the Gospel will one day be carried to every country on earth.

Is 49:7-"Thus saith the LORD, the Redeemer of Israel, and his Holy One, to him who man despiseth, to him whom the nation abhorreth, to a servant of rulers, Kings shall see and arise, princes also shall worship, because of the LORD that is faithful, and the Holy One of Israel, and he shall choose thee." Isaiah begins to speak for the first time on his own behalf, and he is announcing that he is about to relate what the Father has said to the Son. When Isaiah says, "Thus saith the LORD, the redeemer of Israel, and his Holy One, to him whom man despiseth, to him whom the nation abhorreth, to a servant of rulers," he is alerting the reader or the listener that what is about to follow is a promise that the Father has made to the Son. The Father is "the LORD," "the Redeemer of Israel" and "his

Chapter Four: The Holy Trinity in the Old Testament

Holy One" The Son is the one whom man despises, Israel abhors, subject to the authority of its rulers. This verse is really quite prophetic: Christ, will, indeed, be despised, abhorred, and subject to the rulers who would condemn Him to death. In the second half of verse 7, Isaiah continues to address Israel in his own words: "Kings shall see and arise, princes also shall worship, because of the LORD that is faithful, and the Holy One of Israel, and he shall choose thee." The key here is "thee," indicating that someone is speaking to the Son. The person who is speaking is Isaiah, on his own behalf. Isaiah is praising the Son and engaging in worship. Filled with the Holy Spirit, he is exultant that one day, kings shall see Christ and arise, princes also shall worship Him, because the Father has chosen Him to do His will, to do His mission, to restore fallen humanity. By the power of the Holy Spirit, he is relating a Divine Counsel that takes place in Heaven, in which the Father addresses the Son. However, the conversation is related in the second person, through Isaiah's point of view. He has the facts of the conversation; he is relating them as he addresses Christ.

Is 49:8-"Thus saith the LORD, In an acceptable time have I heard thee, and in a day of salvation have I helped thee: and I will preserve thee, and give thee for a covenant of the people, to establish the earth, to cause to inherit the desolate heritages.: Isaiah is relating what the Father has said to the Son. The Father has told Christ that He has heard Him and that He will give Him for a covenant of the people, to establish the earth, to cause to inherit the Gentile world (the desolate heritages).

Is 49:9-"That thou mayest say to the prisoners, Go forth; to them that are in darkness, Shew yourselves. They shall feed in the ways, and their pastures shall be in all high places." Verse 9 is a continuation of verse 8 and Isaiah is still recounting what the Father has said to the Son. The Father has also told Christ that He (Christ) will one day say to the prisoners, "Go forth." This means that Christ will free those who are prisoners to sin and who are in spiritual darkness (His Precious Blood alone can justify the sinner, give him a new mind and heart, and cause him to leave sin behind).

Is 49:22-"Thus saith the Lord GOD, Behold, I will lift up mine hand to the Gentiles, and set up my standard to the people: and they shall bring thy sons in their arms, and thy daughters shall be carried upon their shoulders." Isaiah is relating what the Father has said to the Son. The Father has promised the Son that the Gentile world will brings its sons and daughters to Him as well as its kings and princes. Kings and princes will bow down to the Son and worship Him.

Is 49:23-"And kings shall be thy nursing fathers, and their queens thy nursing mothers: they shall bow down to thee with their face toward the earth, and lick up the dust of thy feet; and thou shalt know that I am the LORD: for they shall not be ashamed that wait for me." The father is continuing to speak to the Son: kings and queens will genuflect before the Son in a sign of submission and they will profess that they are Christians (they will not be ashamed that wait for me).

Hence, Is 49 relates a conversation that takes place in Heaven between the Father and the Son. It is highly prophetic and announces events that will take place during the First Coming of Christ, the interim until His Return, and His Second Coming. This chapter reveals that there is Divine Counsel in the Throne Room of Heaven, that the Persons of the Trinity converse among themselves, and that they have specific relationships among one another.

Is 50 provides a remarkably accurate depiction of the Son's rejection, His Passion and Crucifixion. In Is 50:2 Christ is speaking in the first person: "Wherefore, when I came, was there no man? when I called, was there none to answer? Is my hand shortened at all, that it cannot redeem?" He came, right on schedule, as prophesized in Dan 9:25, but He was rejected. It is significant that Christ uses the term "redeem." His purpose for coming to earth is to redeem believers from sin and to be the perfect offering that was foreshadowed by the unique sacrifice of the red heifer in Num 19 (offered to cleanse people and objects that had been defiled by contact with the dead).

Is 50:3, "I clothe the heavens with blackness" is a sign of rebuke for disobedience as is the drying up of the sea and the ruin of the rivers in Is 50:2. It is a sign that God disproves of rebellion. It also predicts the darkness of the sky after He surrenders His Ghost on the Cross. This is exactly what happens in Luke 23:44-45: "And it was about the sixth hour, and there was darkness over all the earth until the ninth hour. And the sun was darkened, and the veil of the temple was rent in the midst."

In Is 50:4 Christ relates how, as He is growing up, the Father will gradually give Him an understanding of the Bible and of His mission: "The

Lord GOD hath given me the tongue of the learned" and "he wakenth mine ear to hear as the learned" relates the process by which the Father taught the Son and prepared Him to teach the learned in the Temple and to persuade the masses: "he wakeneth morning by morning." Luke tells us that when He was twelve years old, Christ taught the rabbis: "and the child grew, and waxed strong in spirit, fill with wisdom: and the grace of God was upon him" (Luke 2:40); "And it came to pass, that after three days they found him in the temple, sitting in the midst of the doctors, both hearing them, and asking them questions, And all that heard him were astonished at his understanding and answers" (Luke 2:46-47). Many believe that Christ taught the renown biblical scholar Hillel in the Temple on Passover, and that it was not the other way around.

By Is 50:5-6 it becomes crystal clear that the speaker is Christ: "I was not rebellious…I gave my back to the smiters, and my cheeks to them that plucked off the hair: I hid not my face from shame and spitting." This prophecizes Christ's Passion just before His Crucifixion.

The material extending from the end of Is 52 and continuing all through Is 53 provides a razor sharp color print of Christ on the Cross. There is no question that Isaiah, who wrote during the 8th century BC, was describing someone who had been physically elevated over the people (Isaiah's gaze is directed upward), who had been pierced, and who died so that the trespasses of others would be forgiven. Is 52:9 announces that the subject that he will be addressing is the Lord's redemption. Isaiah is speaking about God in the third person and advises that "he hath redeemed Jerusalem." In Is 52:10 the Lord extends salvation to "all the nations" and "all the ends of the earth." Here we have the notion of the forgiveness of sins and that it will be extended to the Gentile world; this implies a conversion from paganism. In Is 52:13 the Father is speaking about His Son: "my servant shall deal prudently" will be "exalted and extolled, and be very high."

In Is 52:14 we have our first glimpse of the Crucifixion scene. It begins here and continues throughout Is 53: "his visage was so marred more than any man, and his form more than the sons of men." Is 52:15 prophecizes baptism ("so shall he sprinkle many nations") and that he will be worshipped by kings.

Is 53 provides a high definition laser print of Christ on the Cross. Is 53:1 begins by addressing the key issue governing the fulfillment of God's promise of redemption from sin and the establishment of an eternal kingdom in which death is abolished forever: the key issue is that of belief. Is 53:1 begins by asking the fundamental issue regarding salvation: "Who hath believed our report? and to whom is the arm of the LORD revealed?" Those who believe on Him enjoy a vicarious forgiveness from sin due to His suffering, crucifixion and resurrection. Throughout the NT it is reiterated that belief is something that God reveals, that it is a gift that God bestows. For example, "At that time Jesus answered and said, I thank thee, O Father, Lord of heaven and earth, because thou hast hid these things from the wise and prudent, and hast revealed them unto babes" (Mat 11:25). In another example, Jesus asked the apostles, "But whom say ye that I am?" and Peter answered, "Thou art Christ, the Son of the living God." Jesus replied, "Blessed art thou, Simon Barjona: for flesh and blood hath not revealed it unto thee, but my Father which is in heaven" (Mat 16:15-17). In another example, Simeon entered the Temple to see the baby Jesus because "it was revealed unto him by the Holy Ghost, that he shall not see death, before he had seen the Lord's Christ" (Luke 2:26). This last example provides an especially good analogy with Is 53:1 because here, the elderly Simeon recognizes his Saviour only because the Holy Ghost had revealed it to him.

Is 53:3 a detailed description of the Passion of Christ begins: "He is despised and rejected of men; a man of sorrows, and acquainted with grief: and we hid as it were our faces from him; he was despised, and we esteemed him not."

Is 53:4 is significant because this is the first of seven verses in which Isaiah explains why He will be stricken and what His mission is on earth: "Surely he hath borne our griefs, and carried our sorrows..." Is 53:5 is the second verse in which the reason for punishment is given: "But he was wounded for our transgressions, he was bruised for our iniquities: the chastisement of our peace was upon him; and with his stripes we are healed." It is clear that there is an exchange that occurs: the Messiah is stricken because He bears the sins of humanity. He is a sacrificial lamb. However, unlike the unique sacrifice of the red heifer in Num 19 (offered to cleanse people and objects that had been defiled by contact with the dead), He is the perfect sacrifice; He is without blemish (sin); because He is both man and God, He alone is qualified to die in our place for our transgressions; hence, He takes sins away forever, not merely covers them, as does the sacrifice of animals.

Is 53:6 is the third verse in which Isaiah explains why the Messiah is stricken: "the LORD hath laid on him the iniquity of us all." Furthermore, no one can keep the Law perfectly, all of the time; it is impossible to keep the Law: "we have turned every one to his own way," which is to say that everyone is guilty of breach of the Law.

Is 53:7 metaphorizes the Messiah as a sacrificial lamb: "he opened not his mouth," "he is brought as a lamb to the slaughter," "as a sheep before her shearers is dumb," and "so he openeth not his mouth."

Having metaphorized the Messiah as a sacrificial lamb four times, Isaiah prophesizes Christ's imprisonment, judgment before Pilate, and death. Is 53:8 says, "He was taken from prison," "from judgment," and "cut off out of the land of the living." Then Isaiah articulates the reason for the punishment a fourth time: "for the transgression of my people was he stricken."

Is 53:9 prophesizes that He would be condemned with thieves and His burial in Nicodemus' tomb: "he made his grave with the wicked" and "with the rich in his death." Isaiah reiterates that He was punished precisely because He was without sin: "because he had done no violence, neither was any deceit in his mouth."

In Is 53:10 the prophet explains for the fifth time why He is stricken: he is an offering for sin: "when thou shalt make his soul an offering for sin." It also predicts His Resurrection and that He will have generations upon generations of followers: "he shall see his seed," "he shall prolong his days," and "the pleasure of the LORD shall prosper in his hand." Christ will be glad when, on Judgment Day, He looks upon the sea of countless believers who have embraced Him throughout the ages: "He shall see of the travail of his soul, and shall be satisfied." Again, for the sixth time, Isaiah tells us why the Messiah is stricken: "by his knowledge shall my righteous servant justify many; for he shall bear their iniquities" (Is 53:11).

The Resurrection of the Lord is implied in Is 53:12 because He will reap the benefits of His work after death: "Therefore will I divide him a portion with the great, and he shall divide the spoil with the strong, because he hath poured out his soul unto death." His kingdom, which is not of this world, is eternal and cannot be overthrown by men. Again, for the seventh time in this chapter, Isaiah articulates why the Messiah was stricken: "he bare the sin of many, and made intercession for the transgressors."

In Is 61:1 Christ is speaking and He is declaring that He has been anointed by the Holy Spirit: "The Spirit of the Lord GOD is upon me; because the LORD hath anointed me to preach good tidings unto the meek; he hath sent me to bind up the brokenhearted, to proclaim liberty to the captives, and the opening of the prison to them that are bound." In the OT Christ is announcing His future mission: when He comes He will bind up the brokenhearted (one of His names is Counsellor). "Captives" and "them that are bound" are metaphors for sinners, the unsaved. "Prison" is a metaphor for sin. When He arrives He will forgive sins and give people a new life, a new heart, a new spirit, and everlasting life in His Father's Kingdom.

It is highly significant that Luke informs us that at the outset of His ministry, after His temptation on the mountain, Christ entered the synagogue in Nazareth on the Sabbath, and standing, read Is 61:1 to the congregation. Then He closed the book, returned it to the minister, and sat down. Sitting down was a rabbinical custom-it indicated that the rabbi was going to teach. Luke tells us "And the eyes of all of them that were in the synagogue were fastened on him. And he began to say unto them, This day is this scripture fulfilled in your ears" (Luke 4:20-21). His declaration astonished the congregation. These words were of monumental importance in the history of humanity. Christ was announcing that the long awaited Messiah, the Savior, Counsellor, Prince of Peace whose goings forth have been from everlasting, had arrived at last. What He was declaring was that He was the Messiah: that the Holy Spirit proceeding from the Father was upon Him; that the Holy Spirit had anointed Him to preach good tidings to the meek. Already at the inception of His ministry, he made it clear that the meek would inherit the earth, not the bold, aggressive or violent. He was proclaiming that the Holy Spirit has sent Him to bind up the brokenhearted. At a future time He would invite the brokenhearted and the wearing to come to Him so that He may give them rest. The Holy Spirit anointed Him to proclaim liberty to the captives and open the prisons to those that are bound, that is, those that are held captive in bondage to sin. He would forgive sins, tell people to go and sin no more, and give them a new heart and a new mind so that they could, indeed, begin their lives again. He would make men and women new creations in the Lord, very different from their former selves that had been held captive to sin. The language and the promise in Is 61:1 is the same as that in Is 42:7: "To open the blind eyes, to bring out the prisoners from the prison, and them that sit in darkness out of the prison house." Again "blind eyes" and "prisoner" are metaphors for the unsaved, for the sinner and "prison" and "prison house," for sin.

The promises are always in the context of a new covenant: "Behold, the days come, saith the LORD, that I will make a new covenant with the house of Israel, and with the house of Judah: Not according to the covenant that I made with their fathers in the day that I took them by the hand to bring them out of the land of Egypt; which my covenant they brake, although I was an husband unto them, saith the LORD: but this shall be the covenant that I will make with the house of Israel; After those days, saith the LORD, I will put my law in their inward parts, and write it in their hearts..." (Jer 31:31-33). The Second Person of the Holy Trinity is announcing in advance that He will establish a New Covenant in which the law will be inscribed in the heart of every believer and sins will be forgiven by His Precious Blood.

The prophet Daniel recalls the stunning event in which the Second Person of the Holy Trinity comes to earth to save three boys in a hot furnace. Christ, the anthropomorphosis of God, is the fourth figure seen walking through the fire with the three boys, Shadrach, Meshach, and Abednego in Dan 3. These three boys refused to worship the idols of Nebuchadnezzar and so, in his anger, the king ordered that his furnace be heated seven times hotter than usual and that the three boys be thrown into it. It is significant that a fourth figure was seen walking through the flames with them and this was Christ. In fact, the OT says that this Person "was like the Son of God": "Then Nebuchadnezzar the king was astonished, and rose up in haste, and spake, and said unto his counsellors, Did not we cast three men bound into the midst of the fire? They answered and said unto the king, True, O king.

An Eastern Orthodox View of Pascal

He answered and said, Lo, I see four men loose, walking in the midst of the fire, and they have no hurt; and the form of the fourth is like the Son of God" (Dan 3:24-25).

Distinction with the Godhead: The Holy Spirit

In the aforementioned verses in the OT we have seen prophecies that the Second Person of the Holy Trinity would one day come to earth to accomplish a mission, complete it, and return to His place in Heaven, seated on the right hand of the Father. The OT also mentions the Holy Spirit a number of times and even foreshadows Pentecost. In Num 11 Moses gathered 70 elders around the Tabernacle and God took some of the Holy Spirit that was on Moses and put Him on the elders and they began to prophesize: "And the LORD came down in a cloud, and spake unto him, and took of the spirit that was upon him, and gave it unto the seventy elders: and it came to pass, that, when the spirit rested upon them, they prophesized, and did not cease" (Num 11:25). In addition, two men, Eldad and Medad, who remained in the camp and did not join the others, also received the Holy spirit and prophesized: "but there remained two of the men in the camp… and the spirit rested upon them…and they prophesized I the camp" (Num 11:26).

Moses said, "Would God that all the LORD's people were prophets, and that the LORD would put his spirit upon them!" (Num 11:29). This wish became a prophecy by Joel and was fulfilled at Pentecost. Joel 2:28-29 says, "And it shall come to pass afterward, that I will pour out my spirit upon all flesh; and your sons and your daughters shall prophecy, your old men shall dream dreams, your young men shall see visions: And also upon the servants and upon the handmaids in those days will I pour out my spirit." Joel goes on to say that whoever calls on the Lord will be delivered (from sin and judgment) and also, that there will be deliverance in the remnant that God calls (Joel 2:32).

This is a prophecy of Pentecost in which the Holy Spirit would one day descend upon the apostles and they would speak in many languages to the people of many nations who would come to hear them: "And suddenly there came a sound from heaven as of a rushing mighty wind, and it filled al the house where they were sitting. And there appeared unto them cloven tongues like as of fire, and it sat upon each of them. And they were all filled with the Holy Ghost, and began to speak with other tongues, as the Spirit gave them utterance" (Acts 2:2-4).

In summation, the OT provides images of the Son and the Holy Spirit in Deut, Ps, Is, and Dan, just to name a few books. While the OT provides some candlelight on the triune nature of the Godhead, the NT sheds full blown daylight on it. It would not be until Christ came to earth that we would be told that God is one, and at the same time, comprised of three distinct Persons who have a relationship amongst themselves. The apostle John, who traveled with Christ during His 3 ½ year ministry, personally testifies as to the deity of Christ and of the Holy Spirit: "In the beginning was the Word, and the Word was with God, and the Word was God" (John 1:1); "The same was in the beginning with God" (John 1:2); "All things were made by him; and without him was not any thing made that was made" (John 1:3); "He was in the world, and the world was made by him, and the world knew him not" (John 1:10); "And the Word was made flesh, and dwelt among us, (and we beheld his glory, the glory as of the only begotten of the Father,) full of grace and truth" (John 1:14); "we believe that thou camest forth from God" (John 16:30). In addition, John cites the following statements made by Christ, Himself: "Your father Abraham rejoiced to see my day: and he saw it, and was glad" (John 8:56); "Jesus said unto them, Verily, verily, I say unto you, Before Abraham was, I am" (John 8:58); "If ye had known me, ye should have known my Father also: and from henceforth ye know him, and have seen him: (John 14:7); "he that hath seen me hath seen the Father" (John 14:9); "Believe me that I am in the Father, and the Father in me: (John 14:11); "And I will pray the Father, and he shall give you another Comforter, that he may abide with you for ever…for he dwelleth with you, and shall be in you" (John 14:16-17); "But the Comforter, which is the Holy Ghost, whom the Father will send in my name, he shall teach you all things, and brings all things to your remembrance, whatsoever I have said unto you" (John 14:26); "For the Father himself loveth you, because ye have loved me, and have believed that I came out from God" (John 16:27); "I came forth from the Father, and am come into the world: again, I leave the world, and go to the Father" (John 16:28); "These words spake Jesus, and lifted up his eyes to heaven, and said, Father, the hour is come; glorify thy Son, that thy Son also may glorify thee: As thou hast given him power over all flesh, that he should give eternal life to as many as thou hast given him": (John 17:1-2); "And now, O Father, glorify thou me with thine own self with the glory which I had with thee before the world was" (John 17:5); "Father, I will that they also, whom thou hast given me, be with me where I am; that they may behold my glory, which thou hast given me: for thou lovedst me before the foundation of the world" (John 17:24); "O righteous Father, the world hath not known thee: but I have known thee, and these have known that thou hast sent me" (John 17:25).

In the next chapter we will examine the view of Pascal and of many Christians that the people, places, and events in the OT, even the Jewish feast days themselves, are all symbols that point to Christ's mission, namely, the spiritual redemption of man from sin and his justification so that he can gain entry into God's eternal kingdom.

Endnotes

1. Blaise Pascal, *Thoughts*, translated by W. F. Trotter, Brunschvicg numbering system (New York: P. F. Collier & Son, 1910), fragment 752. "Moïse d'abord enseigne la trinité, le péché originel, le Messie." Blaise Pascal, *Pensées*, in *Œuvres de Blaise Pascal*, edited by Léon Brunschvicg, Pierre Boutroux, and Félix Gazier (Paris: Librairie Hachette & Cie, 1904-1914), fragment 752 (Lafuma 315; Sellier 346).
2. John Wesley, *Explanatory Notes upon the Old Testament*, 3 vols. (Bristol: William Pine, 1765), 2:1628.
3. *NIV Study Bible* (Grand Rapids: Zondervan, 2002), 1473n49:3.
4. Ibid., 1473n49:4

Typology

For the law having a shadow of good things to come,
is not the very image of the things,
can never with those sacrifices which they offered year by year
continually make the comers thereunto perfect.
—Heb 10:1

A type foreshadows or points to an event or person that will appear in the future. The *Oxford English Dictionary* defines "type" as "1a. That by which something is symbolized or figured; anything having a symbolical signification; a symbol, emblem; *spec.* in *Theol.* A person, object, or event of Old Testament history, prefiguring some person or thing revealed in the new dispensation."[1] Type is derived from the Greek τύπος, meaning impression, figure, type, from the root of τύπτειν, to beat, strike, via the Latin *typus*. Hence, a type is a shadow that points to a future reality. This future event or person in known as an antitype. For example, Christ's resurrection after three days and three nights is the antitype of Jonah's emergence from the whale after the same amount of time. The *OED* defines "typology" as "1. The study of symbolic representation, *esp.* of the origin and meaning of Scripture types."[2]

Typology is founded upon two premises: first, on the unchanging nature of God and secondly, on the principle that the events in the OT are all part of God's plan for man's ultimate redemption from sin and his eventual theosis and therefore, that they lead up to and point to the fulfillment of Mosaic Law in the life, death, and resurrection of Christ.

The most significant type in the OT is the sacrifice of the unblemished red heifer in Num 19 because it foreshadows or points to the perfect sacrifice of Christ. In Num 19 God tells Moses and Aaron to instruct the children of Israel to bring them "a red heifer without spot, wherein is no blemish, and upon which never came yoke" (Num 19:2). Moses and Aaron are instructed to take the red heifer to the priest Eleazar, who will lead the red heifer outside the camp and slay it there. After this unblemished red heifer has been slain, it is to be burned and its ashes, along with water of separation, will be used for 1) the ceremonial cleansing of people who have been defiled by contact with a dead body (Num 19:11-12) and 2) the purification of the tent, vessels, and persons that came in contact with the dead (Num 19:18-19).

The sacrifice of the red heifer is a type or foreshadowing of Christ's sacrifice on the Cross. The red heifer is unblemished; Christ is without sin. However, the red heifer merely covers sins, while Christ's sacrifice takes them away forever, "as far as the east is from the west, so far hath he removed our transgressions from us" (Ps 103:12). God says that if any man touches a corpse, but does not purify himself in this manner, "that soul shall be cut off from Israel: because the water of separation was not sprinkled upon him, he shall be unclean; his uncleanliness is yet upon him" (Num 19:13). Here Israel is a type or shadow of the Kingdom of God, which will be a nation of all peoples, regardless of ethnicity or race, who have been redeemed by the Blood of Christ. The Children of Israel in the OT, kept separate and pure from the pagan world, is a type or shadow of the Kingdom of God, whose inhabitants have eternal life because their sins have been forgiven by Christ. In the OT it says that those who are unclean and have not been cleansed "shall be cut off from Israel" (Num 19:13) and that "that soul shall be cut off from among the congregation" (Num 19:20); in the age of dispensation, the Blood of Christ alone forgives sins and permits entry into the Kingdom of Heaven. The "water of separation" is a foreshadowing of baptism, which separates man from his sins. In the OT both the blood of the red heifer and the water of separation are required to have sin covered; once the Law was fulfilled in Christ, God requires the Blood of Christ and baptism to take sin away forever.

John Wesley's *Explanatory Notes upon the Old Testament* comments on the significance of the requirement that the heifer be red, that it has never been placed in a harness, and that it be slain outside the camp: "V. 2 *Red*-A fit colour to shadow forth the bloody nature of sin, and the blood of Christ; from which this water and all other rites had their purifying virtue. *No blemish*-A fit type of Christ. *Upon which never came yoke*-Whereby may be signified, either that Christ in himself was free from all the yoke or obligation of God's command, till for our sakes he put himself under the law, or that Christ was not forced to undertake our burden and cross, but did voluntarily chuse it. He was bound and held with no other cords but those of his own love V. 3...*Without the camp*-Partly because it was reputed an unclean and accursed thing, being laden with the sins of all the people; and partly to signify that Christ should suffer without the camp, in the place where malefactors suffered."[3]

The apostle Paul asks, "For if the blood of bulls and of goats, and the ashes of an heifer sprinkling the unclean, sanctifieth to the purifying of the flesh: How much more shall the blood of Christ, who through the eternal Spirit, offered himself without spot to God, purge your conscience from dead works to serve the living God?" (Heb 9:13-14).

Paul goes on to compare the Holy Place in the Temple where God dwells with Heaven; the High Priest to Christ; the sacrifice to the Crucifixion. Paul declares, "For Christ is not entered into the holy places made with hands, which are the figures of the true; but into heaven itself, now to appear in the presence of God for us: Nor yet that he should offer himself often, as the high priest entereth into the holy place every year with blood of others; For then must he often have suffered since the foundation of the world: but now once in the end of the world hath he appeared to put away sin by the sacrifice of himself. And as it is appointed unto men once to die, but after this the judgment: So Christ was once offered to bear the sins of many…" (Heb 9:24-28); "For the law having a shadow of good things to come, and not the very image of the things, can never with those sacrifices which they offered year by year continually make the comers thereunto perfect. For then would they not have ceased to be offered?" (Heb 10:1-2); "But this man, after he had offered one sacrifice for sins for ever, sat down on the right hand of God; From henceforth expecting till his enemies be made his footstool" (Heb 10:12-13) (This was prophecized in Ps 110:1-"The Lord said unto my Lord, Sit thou at my right hand, until I make thine enemies thy footstool").

Another type or shadow is the exodus of the Children of Israel from bondage in Egypt: this points to the release from sin and death and the entrance into everlasting life through Christ. Bondage to Pharaoh represents bondage to sin; Moses represents Christ; walking through the water represents separation from sin and points to the cleansing of baptism; leaving the Egyptians behind represents leaving principalities and powers behind.

The Church has used typology to illuminate the unity of the divine plan in the two testaments since apostolic times. The apostles Paul and Peter engaged in typological analogies in their letters. For example, Paul says, "Moreover, brethren, I would not that ye should be ignorant, how that all our fathers were under the cloud, and all passed through the sea; And were all baptized unto Moses in the cloud and in the sea; And did all eat the same spiritual meat; And did all drink the same spiritual drink: for they drank of that spiritual Rock that followed them and that Rock was Christ. But with many of them God was not well pleased: for they were overthrown in the wilderness. Now these things were our examples...Now all these things happened unto them for examples..." (1 Cor 10:1-6, 11). Paul teaches the Corinthians that God went before the Israelites in a pillar of cloud (*shekinah*) to guide them by day and as a pillar of fire to guide them by night, so that they could travel by day or night (Ex 13:21-22); they escaped through the Red Sea. The cloud and the pillar of fire are pre-incarnate manifestations of Christ. This is a foreshadowing of the baptism of the Holy Spirit and water. Paul uses the word "examples" twice to emphasize that these events in the OT point towards Christ: "Now these things were our examples" (1 Cor 10:11) and "Now all these things happened unto them for examples" (1 Cor 10:11).

In addition, Paul states outright that Mosaic Law was a foreshadowing of the day when the Law would be inscribed in the hearts of Christians and that the sacrifice of the red heifer was a type of the Lamb of God who takes away the sins of the world: "For the law having a shadow of good things to come, and not the very image of the things, can never with those sacrifices which they offered year by year continually make the comers thereunto perfect" (Heb 10:1).

The apostle Peter also engages in typological analogy and indicates that the Noachian Flood was a type of baptism: "...when once the longsuffering of God waited in the days of Noah, while the ark was a preparing, wherein few, that is, eight souls were saved by water. The like figure whereunto even baptism doth also now save us (not the putting away of the filth of the flesh, but the answer of a good conscience toward God,) by the resurrection of Jesus Christ" (1 Pet 3:20-21). Hence, typological

Chapter Five: Typology

analogy goes back to apostolic times and has been a tradition of the Church in both its oral and written teaching.

Pascal devoted considerable effort in engaging in typological references and made this kind of analogy a solid part of his Christian apology (see fragment ranges B642-692; L223-L276, L501-L502; S256-S307, S737-S738). For example, he discusses the Jews' flight from Egypt as a type pointing to Christ's Redemption. Pascal says "The Red Sea an image of the Redemption…God, wishing to show that He could form a people holy with an invisible holiness, and fill them with an eternal glory, made visible things…Therefore He saved this people from the deluge…The object of God was not to save them from the deluge…only…to bring them into a rich land."[4] Hence, salvation from the Egyptians points to salvation from the power of sin; the Promised Land foreshadows everlasting life, which Adam would have had if he had not disobeyed. It is the alternative method of achieving immortality, since it could not be attained in the Garden of Eden.

Pascal also compares the Temple to the Church: "The Synagogue did not perish, because it was a type. But because it was only a type, it fell into servitude. The type existed till the truth came, in order that the Church should be always visible, either in the sign which promised it, or in substance."[5] The synagogue was the site of imperfect animal sacrifice; the Church reenacts the Last Supper and offers communion, the body and blood of Christ, the perfect sacrifice, to its communicants. Orthodoxy recognizes that God changes the substance of the bread and wine into His actual Body and Blood. This is because at the Last Supper, Christ said, "This is my body" (Mat 26:26; Mark 14:22; Luke 22:19) and "This is my blood" (Mat 26:28; Mark 14:24; Luke 22:20). Christ taught, "Whoso eateth my flesh, and drinketh my blood, hath eternal life; and I will raise him up at the last day. For my flesh is meat indeed, and my blood is drink indeed. He that eateth my flesh, and drinketh my blood, dwelleth in me, and I in him" (John 6:54-56). It is for this reason that Paul issues a stern warning to reprobates not to take communion: if they do and they are unrepentant, they will get sick and/or die: "Wherefore whosoever shall eat this bread, and drink this cup of the Lord, unworthily, shall be guilty of the body and blood of the Lord… For he that eateth and drinketh unworthily, eateth and drinketh damnation to himself, not discerning the Lord's body. For this cause many are weak and sickly among you, and many sleep" (1 Cor 11:27, 29-30). It is a historical fact that in the Orthodox Church, when communion has accidentally been spilled on the floor of the altar, the entire marble floor has been cut away and removed and given a Christian burial because it bears the body and blood of the Lord.

In the Orthodox Church the priest and the communicants partake of the body and blood (bread and wine). Hence, it is held that the communicants take the actual body and blood of Christ into their bodies. The animal sacrifice of the Temple is merely a reminder, it will not substitute for man's guilt on Judgment Day; the Lamb of God is the perfect sacrifice and those covered by His Blood will, by virtue of vicarious atonement, be found innocent on Judgment Day.

Pascal states his goals and his means of achieving them: his goals are to prove that God exists and that Christ is the Messiah and the means will be to show that an unchanging God has brought about events in the OT that are types or shadows of Christ's mission in the NT. Pascal declares, "*Proof of the two Testaments at once.*-To prove the two at one stroke, we need only see if the prophecies in one are fulfilled in the other. To examine the prophecies, we must understand them. For if we believe they have only one meaning, it is certain that the Messiah has not come; but if they have two meanings, it is certain that He has come in Jesus Christ."[6]

Pascal holds up the Jews' departure from Egypt as a type pointing to the believers' separation from the power of sin and death: "The Red Sea an image of the Redemption...God, wishing to show that He could form a people holy with an invisible holiness, and fill them with an eternal glory, made visible things..."[7] Thus Pascal establishes the connection between Exodus and freedom from sin, between the Promised Land and the Kingdom of God, and between Moses and Christ. He also declares that the Passover lamb, eaten with bitter herbs, is a type of Christ, who bought our redemption with agony and suffering: "The Old Testament contained the types of future joy, and the New contains the means of arriving at it. The types were of joy; the means of penitence; and nevertheless the Paschal Lamb was eaten with bitter herbs, *cum amaritudinibus*."[8] The bitter herbs remind us that our

Chapter Five: Typology

redemption is not free. It has been bought with a price, the finished work of the Lord on the Cross.

Hence, Pascal indicates that the Jewish feast days were types or shadows of Christ's mission of redemption. Christians regard the Jewish holidays of the OT as the blueprint of God's plan for man's redemption after Adam's fall. Messianic Jews, by following the Jewish calendar throughout the year, understand the Jewish feast days as shadows of things to come, as the map of God's intention and purpose to give eternal life to man.

There are seven major Jewish feast days that God established 3,500 years ago that constitute God's blueprint for man's salvation. Not only do the rituals that are performed in these holidays point to Christ's mission and purpose for coming to earth, but their chronological order and occurrence, either in the spring or fall, announce Christ's First and Second Coming, respectively. These major Jewish feast days, and their fulfillment in Christ, are as follows:

1. The Feast of Passover is the first feast day in the spring and it is a shadow of the Crucifixion of Christ. Ex 12:1-14; Lev 23:5; Num 9:1-14; 28:16; Deut 16:1-3a, 4b-7. It commemorates the time when the Jews were protected from the punishment that God meted out to the Egyptians; this prefigured Christ's gift of salvation on the Cross, which also offers fortification from the wrath of God. However, the difference between the two events is that Christ's pardon is eternal and everlasting. During the first Passover, the Jews killed a lamb and sprinkled its blood on the entrance to their homes. It is highly significant that God instructed them to dip a bunch of hyssop into a basin containing the blood of a sacrificial lamb and then strike the hyssop with the blood first against the lintel (top) of their doorway and then against each side of the doorway (Ex 12:22). This forms a cross and points to a time in the future when deliverance from bondage to sin for the people of God and the forgiveness of their own sins would be given by Christ on the Cross. This sign of a cross in the form of the blood of the lamb's sacrifice was ordered by God 1,500 years before Christ's Crucifixion. Moreover, it

is significant that Passover is celebrated by slaying and eating a lamb with bitter herbs and bread made without yeast. The sacrifice of the lamb foreshadows the sacrifice of Christ; the bitter herbs are a reminder that man's salvation has been bought with a price, namely, the suffering and agony of Christ. Since yeast symbolizes malice and wickedness, unleavened bread signifies a body without malice or wickedness. The unleavened bread at the Passover table is a type of Christ, in whom there was no sin. The apostle Paul exhorts us to be like Christ, typified by the unleavened bread of Passover, without malice or wickedness (1 Cor 5:6-8). Mat 26:17; Mark 14:12-16; John 2:13; 11:55; 1 Cor 5:7; Heb 11:28.

2. The Feast of Unleavened Bread is a shadow of Christ, who is without malice or wickedness. Ex 12:15-20; 13:3-10; 23:15; 34:18; Lev 23:6-8; Num 28:17-25; Deut 16:3b, 4a, 8. During this feast, bread made without yeast is eaten in remembrance of the time when God brought the Israelites out of Egypt in haste. In the Bible, leavening symbolizes sin; therefore, unleavened bread represents the absence of sin. This points to Christ, who was without sin and who bore our sins upon His shoulders. The apostle Paul exhorts the Corinthians to become "bread without yeast," that is, without malice, wickedness, boasting or immorality. He advises, "Your glorying (boasting) is not good. Know ye not that a little leaven leaveneth the whole lump? Purge out therefore the old leaven, that ye may be a new lump, as ye are unleavened. For even Christ our passover is sacrificed for us: Therefore let us keep the feast, not with old leaven, neither with the leaven of malice and wickedness; but with the unleavened bread of sincerity and truth" (1 Cor 5:6-8). Hence, believers are urged to be like Christ who was without sin. This is a calling for theosis, just as Christ has instructed, "Be ye therefore perfect, even as your Father which is in heaven is perfect" (Mat 5:48). Mark 14:1; Acts 12:3; 1 Cor 5:6-8.

3. The Feast of the First Fruits is a shadow of the Resurrection of Christ. Lev 23:9-14. The presentation of a sheaf of the first of the

barley points to Christ, the first person to enter Heaven, followed by many who are redeemed through Him: "And he is the head of the body, the church: who is the beginning, the firstborn from the dead; that in all things he might have the preeminence" (Col 1:18). Rom 8:23; 1 Cor 15:20-23. Paul also advises, "For whom he did foreknow, he also did predestinate to be conformed to the image of his Son, that he might be the firstborn among many brethren" (Rom 8:29).

4. The Feast of Weeks or the Feast of Harvest is a shadow of Pentecost. Ex 23:16a; 34:22a; Lev 23:15-21; Num 28:26-31; Deut 16:9-12. The Feast of Weeks took place 50 days after the waving of the sheaf. This feast announces the beginning of the wheat harvest. Similarly, Pentecost, which occurred 50 days after the Resurrection of Christ, announces the beginning of the harvest of Christ's work. It is the inception of the Great Commission or the carrying forth of the Good News of the Risen Lord to the ends of the earth, to all nations. On Pentecost the Holy Spirit descended upon the apostles like flames of tongues and they proceeded to speak in foreign languages telling the thousands of people who had traveled to Jerusalem about all that they had seen. The Feast of Weeks is a festival of joy, as is Pentecost, when the apostles were filled with the Holy Spirit and experienced great joy: "And suddenly there came a sound from heaven as of a rushing mighty wind, and it filled all the house where they were sitting. And there appeared unto them cloven tongues like as of fire, and it sat upon each of them. And they were all filled with the Holy Ghost, and began to speak with other tongues...every man heard them speak in his own language" (Acts 2:2-4, 6). On Pentecost Peter addressed the crowds and he spoke from personal experience: Peter had seen and conversed with the Risen Lord many times-in the Upper Room, on the road to Emmaus, on the Sea of Tiberius (when Christ instructed him to throw his net on the right side of the boat to catch many fish) and on the shore (when Christ asked him three times, "Peter, do you love me? Feed my sheep"). This same Peter, who like the

other apostles, continued to be instructed by the Lord after His Resurrection, announced to the crowds on Pentecost, "When God hath raised up, having loosed the pains of death: because it was not possible that he should be holden of it, For David speaketh concerning him…of the resurrection of Christ, that his soul was not left in hell, neither his flesh did see corruption. This Jesus hath God raised up, whereof we all are witnesses…Repent, and be baptized every one of you in the name of Jesus Christ for the remission of sins, and ye shall receive the gift of the Holy Ghost" (Acts 2:24-25, 31-32, 38)." The Bible tells us, "That day three thousand people believed and were baptized" (Acts 2:41). Peter was to be martyred in Rome, burned upside down on a cross. The fact that he was willing to die for Christ is a testimonial to the fact that he had seen the Risen Christ on many occasions and was not afraid of death. Acts 2:1-4; 20:16; 1 Cor 16:8). This is the last major feast day in the spring. The next major feast day will be in September/October. This three month interim (a full season) between the spring and fall festivals, typifies the period of time between the First and second Coming of Christ, when the calling of the Gentiles takes place (the harvest of believers).

5. Feast of the Trumpets (Rosh Hashanah or New Year's Day) is a shadow of the Second Coming of Christ, immediately followed by the resurrection of the dead in Christ. Lev 23:23-25; Num 29:1-6. The Feast of the Trumpets is characterized by an assembly on a day of rest and trumpet blasts. Its purpose is to present Israel before God for His favor. On the Feast of the Trumpets sins are symbolically cast away. After morning services, people go to a body of water, say a prayer, and shake crumbs from their pockets into the water to represent the casting off of sins. This ritual provides an iconic representation of God's forgiveness of man's sins. This feast foreshadows the Return of Christ, when believers, purified by His atonement for their sins, will stand righteous before God in His Kingdom: "For the Lord himself shall descend from heaven with a shout, with the voice of the archangel, and with the trump of God: and the dead in Christ

Chapter Five: Typology

shall rise first" (1 Thes 4:16); "Lo! I tell you a mystery. We shall not all sleep, but we shall all be change, in a moment, in the twinkling of an eye, at the last trumpet. For the trumpet will sound, and the dead will be raised imperishable, and we shall be changed" (1 Cor 15:51-52). Hence, the sounding of the trumpet prefigures not only the Second Coming of Christ, but also the resurrection of believers. The raising of the dead is always associated in Scripture with the blowing of a trumpet (1 Thes 4:13-18; 1 Cor 15:52).

6. The Day of Atonement (Yom Kippur) is a shadow of Judgment Day or the Great White Throne Judgment that will occur in the future. Lev 16; 23:26-32; Num 29:7-11. On the Day of Atonement, two goats were brought to the High Priest. The priest cast lots to decide which goat would be the sacrifice to the Lord and which would be the scapegoat. The Lord's goat was sacrificed and placed on the altar; the priest laid his hands on the other goat (the scapegoat) to indicate the transfer of Israel's sins to that animal. Then this scapegoat was led out into the wilderness and released. This symbolized the removal of sin from Israel. By analogy, Yom Kippur prefigures Judgment Day. When Christ returns, He will reign for a thousand years; after the Millennium there will occur the Great White Throne Judgment when all the unsaved dead are brought back to life to be judged according to their works. Christ told us that when He returns in glory, He will gather all of the nations of the world and separate them one from the other as a shepherd divides his sheep from his goats (Mat 25:31-32). Christ says, "Then shall he say also unto them on the left hand, Depart from me, ye cursed, into everlasting fire... And these shall go away into everlasting punishment: but the righteous into life eternal" (Mat 25:41, 46). The apostle John, in his vision on the island of Patmos, saw this: "And I saw a great white throne, and him that sat on it, from whose face the earth and the heaven fled away; and there was found no place for them. And I saw the dead, small and great, stand before God; and the books were opened: and another book was opened, which is the

book of life: and the dead were judged out of those things which were written in the books, according to their works. And the sea gave up the dead which were in it; and death and hell delivered up the dead which were in them: and they were judged every man according to their works" (Rev 20:11-15). God's books will be opened and each person will have to account for his sins. Those who have rejected Christ's vicarious atonement on the Cross when they were alive will be judged guilty and will be relegated to eternal hell.

7. Feast of Tabernacles or Feast of Booths (Ingathering, Sukkot) is a shadow of the culmination of God's plan and the event to which all of human history has been directed: the ingathering of God's people in His eternal Kingdom. Ex 23:16b; 34:22b; Lev 23:33-36a, 39-43; Num 29:12-34; Deut 16:13-15; Zech 14:16-19. This feast commemorates the period when God led the Jews through the desert into the Promised Land where they found rest and were blessed with bountiful harvests. God mandates, "Ye shall dwell in booths seven days; all that are Israelites born shall dwell in booths: That your generations may know that I made the Children of Israel to dwell in booths, when I brought them out of the land of Egypt: I am the LORD your God" (Lev 23:42-43). The key concepts here are travel from one site to a new destination and a covering or enclosure. Early Christians going back to the apostles saw the tabernacle to be a prefiguring of the human body that Christ took during His First Coming when He dwelt among us. The apostle John declares, in a literal translation of the original Greek, "And the word became flesh and tabernacled [*eskee'nosen*] among us, and we gazed upon the glory of him, glory of an only one from the Father, full of grace and truth" (John 1:14).[9] The Greek verb *skeeno'* [σκηνώ, synonymous with κατασκηνώ] means "to camp," "encamp," "pitch camp," "pitch tent," "tabernacle," "dwell in a tent." The noun *skeenee'* [σκηνή] means "tent"; the noun *skeenee'tees* [σκηνίτης], "tent-dweller"; the noun *skeenopee'ya* [σκηνοπγία], "tent-pitching"; the noun *skeenopeeyo's* [σκηνοποιός], "tent-maker." John is

Chapter Five: Typology

alluding to the Feast of Tabernacles when the Jews dwelt in temporary booths. Moreover, it is significant that Luke uses the phrase "eternal tents" to metaphorize our glorified, eternal bodies in Heaven: "they may welcome you into the eternal tents" [*aioni'ous skeena's*] (Luke 16:9).[10] Paul also compares the human body to a tabernacle: "For we know that if the earthly tent [*skee'nous*] we live in is destroyed, we have a building from God, a house not made with hands, eternal in the heavens. For in this tent [*oikeeteereeon*] we groan, longing to be clothed with our heavenly dwelling-if indeed, when we have taken it off we will not be found naked. For while we are still in this tent [*skee'nee*], we groan under our burden, because we wish not to be unclothed but to be further clothed, so that what is mortal, may be swallowed up by life...So we are always confident; even though we know that while we are at home in the body we are away from the Lord" (2 Cor 5:1-4, 6)[11] (NRSV). In the Book of Revelation, John uses "tabernacle" to metaphorize our glorified bodies in Heaven: "Rejoice then, you heavens and those who dwell [*skeenountes*] in them!" (Rev 12:12) (NRSV).[12] John also uses "tabernacle" to identify God's dwelling place and the saints' dwelling places in Heaven that the beast blasphemes: "It opened its mouth to utter blasphemies against God, blaspheming his name and his dwelling [*skeeno'n*], that is, those who dwell in heaven" (Rev 13:6) (NRSV).[13] During his vision John also experiences this: "And I heard a loud voice from the throne saying, 'See, the home [*skeenee'*] of God is among mortals. He will dwell [*skeenoh'see*] with them; they will be his peoples, and God himself with be with them'" (Rev 21:3) (NRSV).[14] Therefore, Christians understand that the Feast of Tabernacles prefigures the new glorified, incorruptible bodies that they will have in God's eternal Kingdom. St. Macarius declares, "...in the resurrection all members will rise. 'Not a hair will perish' (Luke 21:18; Mark 9:49), as it is written."[15] Paul advises that "the dead will be raised incorruptible" and "for this corruptible must put on incorruption, and this mortal must put on immortality" (1

Cor 15:52-53). The Orthodox Church teaches that in the age to come, it will not be only man who has immortality, but also the animals, trees, plants, rocks, fire and water. St. Gregory of Nyssa believed that there is growth and advancement even in the perfection of Heaven. God is infinite, and so we will always be pressing forward, learning new things and growing forever. St. Irenaeus teaches that God will always have something more to teach man, and man will always have something more to learn from God: "…God should for ever teach, and man should for ever learn the things taught him by God…while we hope ever to be receiving more and more from God, and to learn from Him, because He is good, and possesses boundless riches, a kingdom without end, and instruction that can never be exhausted."[16]

Therefore, the chronological sequence of the major Jewish feast days and the fact that they occur either in the spring or fall, bear significance and reveal God's schedule for man's spiritual and physical salvation. The spring festivals prefigure the Lord's First Coming; the three major Jewish feast days in the fall prefigure the three great events that will occur in the future, awaited by humanity since its inception: when Christ will come again in glory and when at His Second Coming, believers will be raised from the dead; when the unsaved masses will be raised from the dead to be judged; and the establishment of His new Kingdom, which will have no end (Luke 1:33). Hence, the three fall feast days point to that part of the Orthodox Creed that says, "I am waiting for the resurrection of the dead and the life of the age to come."

Because God's Word does not change and there is unity between the OT and New, the Bible speaks of the spring rain and the latter rain. The prophet Hosea specifies that God will come to earth twice: "Then shall we know, if we follow on to know the LORD: his going forth is prepared as the morning; and he shall come unto us as the rain, as the later and former rain unto the earth" (Hos 6:3). This verse is truly remarkable in its specificity: people will acquire the knowledge of God if they persevere in studying His Word; it is by this way that they will understand that He must come to earth twice. In fact, Hos 6 in its entirety can be understood to be the itinerary of

Chapter Five: Typology

Christ's mission on earth: His First Coming, Passion and Death ("torn," "smitten," "heal," "bind us up"), Resurrection on the third day, and His Second Coming. In addition, the prophet Isaiah corroborates the notion that God will come to earth twice to accomplish his mission: "And it shall come to pass in that day, that the Lord shall set his hand again the second time to recover the remnant of his people, which shall be left, from Assyria, and from Egypt, and from Pathros, and from Cush, and from Elam, and from Shinar, and from Hamath, and from the islands of the sea (Is 11:11). It is during this time, when God stretches his hand out the second time, that there will be peace and "the wolf will dwell with the lamb, the leopard shall lie down with the kid…and a little child shall lead them" (Is 11:6).

Hence, Christians view the spring festivals as types pointing to the Lord's First Coming and the fall festivals as those prefiguring His Return. It is significant that there is an interval of three months between the Feast of Weeks and the Feast of Trumpets. Three months constitute a season. There is a season between the formation of the Church at Pentecost and the Second Coming. This is the season in which all of the nations of the world come to Christ and the OT prophecies about the calling of the Gentiles are fulfilled.

In summation, Pascal uses typology to prove the unity of the Old and New Testaments. People, places, and events in the OT, indeed, even the feast days themselves (he cites the Passover lamb eaten with bitter herbs) are shadows that point towards a future reality-to the Messiah who would one day purchase salvation and eternal life for fallen humanity with His finished work on the Cross. Pascal uses typology as a tool of reason to prove the existence of God: reason demonstrates that it is beyond the realm of statistical probability that people, places, and events, transpiring over a period of 4,000 years, would all announce the same event. Hence, types indicate that a unity exists between the Old and New Testaments and therefore, they provide evidence of the will of God.

Pascal was a man of reason who knew how to appeal to skeptics who require logical proof with mathematical underpinnings that God exists. He knew how to respond to such a request-the fulfillment of hundreds of prophecies, miracles, and typology disprove coincidence and point towards the will of God. However, there was a tragic flaw in Pascal's Jansenist belief system. In the next chapter we will examine the disparity and disunity in his theology. On the surface, it appears that he was convinced that God is a God of reason and justice. However, Pascal embraced a few lies that were based on the Latin mistranslation of the original Greek NT. This is tragic, not only because his heretical belief system poisoned his view of God's goodness, mercy, and justice, but also, as we believe, because his inability to justify his theology caused him to abandon his Christian apology and leave it unfinished.

Chapter Five: Typology

Endnotes

1 "Type," *Oxford English Dictionary Online*, 1a, http://dictionary.oed.com (May 4, 2007).
2 "Typology," *Oxford English Dictionary Online*, 1, http://dictionary.oed.com (May 4, 2007).
3 John Wesley, *Explanatory Notes upon the Old Testament*, 3 vols. (Bristol: William Pine, 1765), 1:522-23.
4 Blaise Pascal, *Thoughts*, translated by W. F. Trotter, Brunschvicg numbering system (New York: P. F. Collier & Son, 1910), fragment 643. "La Mer Rouge, image de la Rédemption…Dieu, voulant faire paraître qu'il pouvait former un peuple saint d'une sainteté invisible et le remplir d'une gloire éternelle, a fait des choses visibles…

Il a donc sauvé ce peuple du déluge…

…pour n'introduire que dans une terre grasse." Blaise Pascal, *Pensées*, in *Œuvres de Blaise Pascal*, edited by Léon Brunschvicg, Pierre Boutroux, and Félix Gazier (Paris: Librairie Hachette & Cie, 1904-1914), fragment 643 (Lafuma 275; Sellier 306).
5 Ibid., fragment 646. "La synagogue ne périssait point, parce qu'elle était la figure; mais, parce qu'elle n'était que la figure, elle est tombée dans la servitude. La figure a subsisté jusqu'à la vérité, afin que l'Eglise fût toujours visible, ou dans la peinture qui la promettait, ou dans l'effet." Ibid., fragment 646 (Lafuma 573; Sellier 476).
6 Ibid., fragment 642. "*Preuve des deux Testaments à la fois.* Pour prouver d'un coup les deux, il ne faut que voir si les prophéties de l'un sont accomplies en l'autre. Pour examiner les prophéties, il faut les entendre. Car si on croit qu'elles n'ont qu'un sens, il est sûr que le Messie ne sera point venu; mais si elles ont deux sens, il est sûr qu'il sera venu en Jésus-Christ." Ibid., fragment 642 (Lafuma 274; Sellier 305).
7 Ibid., fragment 643. "La Mer Rouge image de la Rédemption…Dieu, voulant faire paraître qu'il pouvait former un peuple saint d'une sainteté invisible et le remplir d'une gloire éternelle, a fait des choses visibles…" Ibid., fragment 643 (Lafuma 275; Sellier 306).
8 Ibid., fragment 666. "L'Ancien Testament contenait les figures de la joie future, et le Nouveau contient les moyens d'y arriver.

Les figures étaient de joie; les moyens, de penitence; et néanmoins, l'agneau pascal était mangé avec des laitues sauvages, *cum amaritudinibus*." Ibid., fragment 666 (Lafuma 801; Sellier 653).
9 *The New Greek-English Interlinear New Testament*, translated by Robert K. Brown and Philip W. Comfort and edited by J. D. Douglas (Carol Stream: Tyndale House Publishers, Inc., 1993), 318.
10 Ibid., 275.
11 Ibid., 632.
12 Ibid., 882.

13 Ibid., 884.
14 Ibid., 907-08.
15 St. Macarius, *The Homilies of St. Macarius*, 15.10, in *Pseudo Macarius: The Fifty Spiritual Homilies and the Great Letter*, edited, translated, and introduced by George A. Maloney, preface by Bishop Kallistos Ware (New York: Paulist Press, 1992), 112 [Macarius, *Homiliæ spirituales*, 15.10, in Jacques-Paul Migne, ed., *Patrologiæ cursos completus...Series græca*, 161 vols. (Paris: Migne, 1857-1866), 34:581C-D].
16 St. Irenaeus, *Irenaeus against Heresies*, 2.28.3, in *The Apostolic Fathers with Justin Martyr, Irenaeus*, vol. 1 of *Ante-Nicene Fathers*, edited by Alexander Roberts and James Donaldson (New York: The Christian Literature Company, 1890-1897), 399-400 [Irenaeus, *Adversus hæreses*, 2.28.3, in Jacques-Paul Migne, ed., *Patrologiæ cursos completus...Series græca*, 161 vols. (Paris: Migne, 1857-1866), 7:805C-806C].

Predestination vs. Free Will

...every man shall receive his own reward
according to his own labour.
For we are labourers together with God...
But let every man take heed how he buildeth thereupon.
—1 Cor 3:8-10

One cannot read Pascal's *Thoughts* without getting a steady dose of the election of the damned. This Jansenist heresy that was continually before him as he wrote his apologetics must have undoubtedly been problematic, given the Christian notions of God's goodness and justice. Anthony Levi suggests that an argument can be made that his belief in double predestination may have caused him to give up on finishing his apologetic work.[1] Either he needed more time to decide whether he really embraced Jansenist theology or else perhaps he decided that it was not worth the effort of trying to save anyone. In addition, Jansenist fanaticism may have caused him to abandon science and mathematics. James A. Connor observes that Pascal had read in Saint-Cyran's book, *Reformation of the Interior Man* (*Réformation de l'homme intérieur*) that Jansenius had taught that science is synonymous with the evil of concupiscence;[2] an argument can be made that this fanaticism dictated that Blaise would live out the remainder of his Christian life renouncing his natural abilities in mathematics and science that God had given him; that he would be at continual war within himself to reconcile the injustice of the election of the damned with reason, and his natural talents with Jansenius' teaching that science is as evil as lust.

We have seen thus far that Pascal has argued that the fulfillment of prophecy, the historicity of miracles, and the unity between the OT and New, are not merely the result of random chance, but rather, that they provide evidence that the will of God is at work; that it is God, and not random chance, that has created the universe and continues to bring order out of chaos even today; that God has provided a plan for man's redemption from sin. Hence, Pascal does provide mathematical/empirical evidence of the existence of God and of Christ's divinity to intellectuals and skeptics who ask whether such evidence exists. Unfortunately, however, what Pascal has wrought with his right hand to carry out the Great Commission, he undoes with the left and negates all of his efforts: he offers an irrational, unjust, and paradoxical view of God's plan by promulgating the notion of double predestination. This Jansenist heresy concretizes the atheist's view that religion is ridiculous and inconsistent. Therefore, let us proceed by demonstrating that Scripture indicates that man does, indeed, have free will; that the future is fluid or liquid and not predetermined; that the Father's plan for man is that he become Christ-like and achieve theosis or union with Himself; that the Father's intention is that Christ be the "firstborn among many brethren" (Rom 8:29).

Let us begin, then, with a definition of terms. The *Oxford English Dictionary* defines "predestination thus: "a. The preordaining of God's elect to salvation; the fact of being so preordained. b. The action by which God is held to have immutably predetermined the course of events by an eternal decree or purpose, esp. in relation to the salvation or damnation of human beings; the fact of this having taken place; any doctrine which holds this to be true; belief in such a doctrine."[3]

The *OED* defines "free will" thus: "1. Spontaneous will, unconstrained choice (to do or elect)…left to or depending upon one's choice or election. 2a. The power of directing our own actions without constraint by necessity or fate."[4]

What the Bible teaches about predestination and free will

An examination of the NT reveals that predestination and free will both exist in God's plan for man's redemption. Both concepts are supported by Scripture, especially by the words of Christ and the writings of Paul. For example, Christ asks the apostles, "Have I not chosen you twelve" (John 6:70); He tells them, "I speak not of you all: I know whom I have chosen: but that the scripture may be fulfilled, He that eateth bread with me hath lifted up his heel against me" (John 13:18); "Ye have not chosen me, but I have chosen you, and ordained you" (John 15:16). In addition, Christ prays to the Father: "I have manifested thy name unto the men which thou gavest me out of the world: thine they were, and thou gavest them me" (John 17:6); "I pray for them: I pray not for the world, but for them which thou hast given me; for they are thine: (John 17:9); "Holy Father, keep

Chapter Six: Predestination vs. Free Will

through thine own name those whom thou hast given me" (John 17:11); "those that thou gavest me I have kept, and none of them is lost, but the son of perdition; that the scripture might be fulfilled" (John 17:12); "Father, I will that they also, whom thou hast given me, be with me where I am" (John 17:24). All of these verses reveal the Divine initiative and that God makes the first move. Also, John teaches "Herein is love, not that we loved God, but that he loved us, and sent his Son to be the propitiation for our sins" (1 John 4:10). Moreover, the following Pauline verses declare that God chose those that He would one day welcome into His kingdom from before the foundation of the world: Rom 8:28, 29, 33; Rom 9; Rom 11:5, 7, 28; Eph 1:4-5, 11; Col 3:12; 1 Th 1:4; 2 Th 2:13; 2 Tim 1:9. Paul continually reiterates God's predestination of the elect: he uses phrases such as "whom he did foreknow," "he also did predestinate," "whom he did predestinate," "them he also called," "God's elect," "touching the election," "the election of grace," "the election hath obtained it," "he hath chosen us in him before the foundation of the world," "having predestinated us," "he chose us," "he predestined us," and "we were also chosen," are a few examples.

Paul explains that God predestined believers: "For whom he did foreknow, he also did predestinate to be conformed to the image of his Son, that he might be the firstborn among many brethren" (Rom 8:29); "Moreover whom he did predestinate, them he also called: and whom he called, them he also justified: and whom he justified, them he also glorified" (Rom 8:30); "Who shall lay any thing to the charge of God's elect? It is God that justifieth" (Rom 8:33); "Even so then at this present time also there is a remnant according to the election of grace" (Rom 11:5); "What then? Israel hath not obtained that which he seeketh for; but the election hath obtained it, and the rest were blinded" (Rom 11:7); "According as he hath chosen us in him before the foundation of the world, that we should be holy and without blame before him in love: (Eph 1:4); "Having predestinated us unto the adoption of children by Jesus Christ to himself, according to the good pleasure of his will" (Eph 1:5); "To the praise of the glory of his grace, wherein he hath made us accepted in the beloved" (Eph 1:6); "In whom also we have obtained an inheritance, being predestinated according to the purpose of him who worketh all things after the counsel of his own will" (Eph 1:11); "Put on therefore, as the elect of God, holy and beloved, bowels of mercies, kindness, humbleness of mind, meekness, longsuffering" (Co. 3:12); "Knowing, brethren beloved, your election of God" (1 Th 1:4); "… God hath from the beginning chosen you to salvation through sanctification of the Spirit and belief of the truth" (2 Th 2:13); "Who hath saved us, and called us with an holy calling, not according to our works, but according to his own purpose and grace, which was given us in Jesus Christ before the world began" (2 Tim 1:9).

John also advises that God chooses us. Christ told the apostles, "Ye have not chosen me, but I have chosen you, and ordained you, that ye should go and bring forth fruit, and that your fruit should remain: that whatsoever ye shall ask of the Father in my name, he may give it to you" (John 15:16).

Peter also declares the election of God. When addressing the "strangers scattered throughout Pontus, Galatia, Cappadocia, Asia, and Bithynia," Peter says that they are "elect according to the foreknowledge of God the Father, through sanctification of the Spirit, unto obedience and sprinkling of the blood of Jesus Christ" (1 Pet 1:2). Here Peter specifies that all three persons of the Holy Trinity, the Father, the Son, and the Holy Spirit, participate in the redemption of the elect. The Father elects believers according to his foreknowledge; the Son has obeyed the Father and has fulfilled His mission of Crucifixion and Resurrection; the Holy Spirit indwells and sanctifies the believer. The Holy Spirit steers the believer towards the things that belong to God and prevents him from committing serious sin.

However, despite the proliferation of material in the NT concerning predestination, there is also ample text supporting free will. For example, Peter, in his epistle, addresses believers in a manner that indicates that they do, indeed, have free will. He advises those who will hear or read his letter, to behave "as obedient children, not fashioning yourselves according to the former lusts in your ignorance, But as he which hath called you is holy, so be ye holy in all manner of conversation" (1 Pet 14:15). The fact that Peter implores the listeners and readers of his epistle to be obedient to Christ and His commandments, to turn away from their former sins, to fashion themselves after Christ, and to be holy in their conversation, presupposes that they have free will.

Chapter Six: Predestination vs. Free Will

Furthermore, the NT indicates that not all early Christians chose to behave in a holy manner. In fact, Christ gives quite a stern warning to the original seven churches in Rev 2-3: He cautions believers in His church at Ephesus to repent of their sins or else He will remove their candlestick from its place (Rev 2:1-7); He admonishes the church at Pergamos to stop eating food sacrificed to idols and engaging in other serious sin (Rev 2:12-17); He issues stern warnings to the churches at Thyatira (Rev 2:18-29) and Sardis (Rev 3:1-6); the church at Laodicea was warned that if it did not return to its first love of Him, He would vomit it up out of His mouth (Rev 3:14-18). Christ advises that the first step down the slippery slope of idolatry is a cooling of one's original love for Him and turning towards other attractions, such as money, power, and material comforts (this was the sin of the Laodiceans).

It is precisely because Christians do have free will that Christ issued these warnings to the early churches: if they did not have free will, he would not have bothered to do so. The Bible teaches us that man has free will when Paul advises, "every man shall receive his own reward according to his own labour" (1 Cor 3:8). Paul reiterates the notion of free will when he adds that we are "coworkers with God" (1 Cor 3:9). The original Greek uses the term *synergoi* or coworkers: we are coworkers with God.

The Orthodox Church holds that the notion of free will is an essential doctrine to both the Old and New Testaments. If Adam did not have free will, then he could not have been held responsible for his choices, he could not have sinned, and a Redeemer would not have been necessary. Christians also have free will: otherwise, there would be no reward, each "according to his own labour" (1 Cor 3:8). Men have the power to accept or reject Christ (John 10:9, Rev 3:20). If they accept Him and are baptized in obedience to His command, then they have eternal life (Mark 16:16). The Father will send the Holy Spirit to indwell them, make them holy, set them apart from the world, and teach them all things (John 14:16-17, 26). When they believe in Christ, they take the first step towards theosis (union with God). Their goal is to conform their image to that of Christ (to be obedient to the Father and to conform their will to His in all things).

Death for all livings things is the result of the choice that Adam made to disobey God: "In the sweat of thy face shalt thou eat bread, till thou return unto the ground; for out of it wast thou taken: for dust thou art, and unto dust shalt thou return: (Gen 3:19); "All go unto one place; all are of the dust, and all turn to dust again" (Eccl 3:20); "For the wages of sin is death" (Rom 6:23). In addition, the Bible also teaches that once we die, we will be judged by God and held accountable for our sins unless we are justified by the Blood of Christ. We have the free will to accept or reject Christ. If we choose Christ, we are justified by the work that He did for us on the Cross: "He that believeth and is baptized shall be saved; but he that believeth not shall be damned" (Mark 16:16); "I am the door: by me if any man enter in, he shall be saved, and shall go in and out, and find pasture" (John 10:9); "He that heareth my word, and believeth on him that sent me, hath everlasting life, and shall not come into condemnation; but is passed from death unto life" (John 5:24); "If a man keep my saying, he shall never see death" (John 8:51); "For the wages of sin is death; but the gift of God is eternal life through Jesus Christ our Lord" (Rom 6:23); "And as it is appointed unto men once to die, but after this the judgment" (Heb 9:27); "For we must all appear before the judgment seat of Christ; that every one may receive the things done in his body, according to that he hath done, whether it be good or bad" (2 Cor 5:10).

    Christ makes it clear that men have the free will to either accept or reject Him. Moreover, they not only have free will, but they should also use their free will to diligently and unceasingly persevere in being a means by which God's will on earth will be realized. The believer must continuously work hard to carry out God' will: "Then saith he unto his disciples, The harvest truly is plenteous, but the labourers are few" (Mat 9:37); "Let both grow together until the harvest: and in the time of the harvest I will say to the reapers, Gather ye together first the tares, and bind them in bundles to burn them: but gather the wheat into my barn" (Mat 13:30); "…if thou wilt enter into life, keep the commandments…If thou wilt be perfect, go and sell that thou hast, and give to the poor, and thou shalt have treasure in heaven: and come and follow me" (Mat 19:17, 21); "Repent, and be baptized every one of you in the name of Jesus Christ for the remission of sins" (Acts 2:38); "But in every nation he that feareth him, and worketh righteousness, is accepted with him" (Acts 10:35); "You, my brothers, were called to be free. But do not use your freedom to indulge the sinful nature; rather, serve one another in love" (Gal 5:13, NIV); "Live as free men, but do not use

Chapter Six: Predestination vs. Free Will

your freedom as a cover-up for evil; live as servants of God" (2 Pet 2:16, NIV). All of these verses indicate that believers are commanded to perform works, to strive diligently to conform themselves to the image of Christ, and to carry out the Great Commission.

At this point it must be interjected that works do not save anyone. Paul makes that very clear: "For by grace are ye saved through faith; and that not of yourselves: it is the gift of God: Not of works, lest any man should boast" (Eph 2:8-9). Works do not save people. Belief is a gift of God and it is the first step up a ladder leading to union with God (theosis). Once we believe, then we begin a journey up the ladder in which we conform our image to that of Christ. The Desert Fathers teach that this is accomplished by cleansing our minds and hearts of vile thoughts and passions, continual prayer, and fasting. These are all works. The purpose of this effort is to turn away from the ephemeral, false attractions of the world and to turn towards the things that belong to God. The Desert Fathers and Pascal recognize the importance of cleansing the heart of passions. It is also a holy thing to take care of the poor, widows, and orphans. These are works, too. We do them because the Holy Spirit leads us to do what is right, not because works in themselves save. This was true in Pascal's case: before he died, he devised a mass transit system comprised of carriages that would stop along fixed routes in order to permit the poor to travel around Paris. Any profits were to go to charity.

The NT indicates that men may freely accept or reject Christ; they have the free will to accept Christ and thus take the first step in conforming themselves to His image, or else go their own way and determine their own values. If they choose Christ and are baptized as He commanded, they will be indwelt by the Holy Spirit who will guide them in all things. When they choose Christ, they take the first step in what will become an intimate spiritual relationship with the Living God: "And I will pray the Father, and he shall give you another Comforter, that he may abide with you for ever; Even the Spirit of truth; whom the world cannot receive, because it seeth him not, neither knoweth him: but ye know him; for he dwelleth with you, and shall be in you: (John 14:16-18); "At that day ye shall know that I am in my Father, and ye in me, and I in you" (John 14:20); "Jesus answered and said unto him, If a man love me, he will keep my words: and my Father will love him, and we will come unto him, and make our abode with him" (John 14:23); "But the Comforter, which is the Holy Ghost, whom the Father will send in my name, he shall teach you all things, and bring all things to your remembrance, whatsoever I have said unto you" (John 14:26); "Abide in me, and I in you. As the branch cannot bear fruit of itself, except it abide in the vine; no more can ye, except ye abide in me. I am the vine; no more can ye, except ye abide in me. I am the vine, ye are the branches: He that abideth in me, and I in him, the same bringeth forth much fruit: for without me ye can do nothing" (John 15:4-5). When someone accepts Christ, he enters into an intimate spiritual relationship with the Living God that both the Old and New Testaments metaphorize as a bride/groom relationship. This metaphor implies God's faithfulness, compassion, and counsel.

The question arises, then, "How do predestination and free will work concurrently, as the Bible mentions both?" The answer is in Rom 8:28-30: "And we know that all things work together for good to them that love God, to them who are the called according to his purpose" (Rom 8:28); "For whom he did foreknow, he also did predestinate to be conformed to the image of his Son, that he might be the firstborn among many brethren" (Rom 8:29); "Moreover whom he did predestinate, them he also called: and whom he called, them he also justified: and whom he justified, them he also glorified" (Rom 8:30).

In Rom 8:28 we have those who love God and these people are also those that God calls according to His purpose. Some people love God and He calls them. "Good" in "all things work together for good" means conformity to the likeness of Christ, that is, a change of heart that happens so that people become more like Christ, Himself. In Rom 8:29 God foreknows people; because He knows the future and can see into the hearts of all people, He knows everyone even before they are born. Foreknowledge is based on the future. It is not the other way around: the future is not based on foreknowledge. Men have free will and are free to make choices. It is the choices that they make that determine God's foreknowledge. This is the position of the Orthodox Church.

In Rom 8:29-30 there is an enumeration of verbs that indicates a sequence of events that happen. These events happen in this order: 1) foreknow, 2) predestinate to be conformed to the likeness of Christ, 3) call,

4) justify, 5) glorify. It is significant that the first verb in the sequence of events is foreknow. What does God foreknow? Everything about us, our future actions, and how we exercise our free will. God knows in advance whether He can use us according to His purpose. All of the verses in the NT that deal with predestination/election address step 2 in the sequence, a point that occurs after foreknowledge of the future. Again, it must be emphasized that it is the future that determines foreknowledge, not the other way around.

What the Orthodox Church teaches about predestination and free will

Our objective here is to do what Pascal was unable to do: we will give the reader the truth about the role that man's free will plays in his redemption. The source of truth will come from a tradition different from that to which Western Christianity is accustomed. Since the position of the Eastern Orthodox Church is that of Christianity's earliest belief system, based on the Bible and thinkers uninfluenced by Augustine, let us see what it has to say about the question of whether or not man has free will. Then we can compare the position of the Orthodox Church with those of the Jesuits and Jansenists, who were at odds with each other. We will get a clear understanding of why the Jesuits, who embraced the middle of the road view that predestination and free will are intertwined, take the scripturally based position, and why the Jansenists, who like Augustine, emphasized predestination to the detriment of free will because they, too, were embroiled in polemics against works, do not have a scripturally based position.

The Orthodox Church teaches that man clearly has free will. Timothy Ware, in *The Orthodox Church*, stresses that Saint Paul taught that man and God work together:

> ...the fact that the human person is in God's image means among other things that we possess free will. God wanted sons and daughters, not slaves. The Orthodox Church rejects any doctrine of grace which might seem to infringe upon human freedom. To describe the relation between the grace of God and human freedom, Orthodoxy uses the term co-operation or synergy (*synergeia*); in Paul's words: "We are fellow-workers (*synergeia*) with God" (1 Cor

3:9). If we are to achieve full fellowship with God, we cannot do so without God's help, yet we must also play our own part: we humans as well as God must make our contribution to the common work, although what God does is of immeasurably greater importance than what we do. "The incorporation of humans into Christ and our union with God require the co-operation of two unequal, but equally necessary forces: divine grace and human will."[5] The supreme example of synergy is the Mother of God... "Behold, I stand at the door and knock; if anyone hears my voice and opens the door, I will come in" (Rev 3:20). God knocks, but waits for us to open he door-He does not break it down. The grace of God invites all but compels none. In the words of John Chrysostom, "God never draws anyone to Himself by force and violence. He wishes all to be saved, but forces no one..."[6] While we cannot "merit" salvation, we must certainly work for it; since "faith without works is dead" (James 2:17)."[7]

Ware directs the reader to Rev 3:20, in which Christ says, "Behold, I stand at the door, and knock: if any man hear my voice, and open the door, I will come in to him, and will sup with him, and he with me."[8] That is the answer to the debate: man has free will and Christ indicates that that is so, time and time again. We have seen that as He was leaving the Temple, He stated that He wanted to minister unto the nation of Israel many times, but it chose to reject Him. God does not abrogate man's free will.

Ware's book is very valuable because it pinpoints the biblical verses that indicate the role that man's free will plays in his redemption. Ware points out that we know that man has free will because he has been made in God's image and God has free will;[9] Paul declares that we are coworkers [*synergoi*] with God (1 Cor 3:9);[10] "the supreme example of synergy is the Mother of God."[11] Mary was ready and willing to submit herself to God's will at any time and God knew in advance that He could rely on her to be an instrument by which He could accomplish His will. For example, when the angel informed Mary of God's plan for her, her response was, "Behold the handmaid of the Lord; be it unto me according to thy word" (Luke 1:38). Moreover, her words to Elizabeth indicate her great faith, her

Chapter Six: Predestination vs. Free Will

personal relationship with God, her willingness to submit to His will, and her humility: "My soul doth magnify the Lord, And my spirit hath rejoiced in God my Saviour. For he hath regarded the low estate of his handmaiden: for, behold, from henceforth all generations shall call me blessed. For he that is mighty hath done to me great things; and holy is his name. And his mercy is on them that fear him from generation to generation. He hath shewed strength with his arm; he hath scattered the proud in the imagination of their hearts. He hath put down the mighty from their seats, and exalted them of low degree. He hath filled the hungry with good things; and the rich he hath sent empty away. He hath helped his servant Israel, in remembrance of his mercy; As he spake to our fathers, to Abraham, and to his seed for ever" (Luke 1:46-55). These are the words of someone who would not hesitate for one moment to work together with God to accomplish His will. She was totally obedient to God.

In *The Orthodox Way*, Bishop Kallistos Ware[12] continues to support the role that man's free will plays in his redemption. Ware begins his discussion by pointing out that it is volition that distinguishes man from the animals: "Where the animals act by instinct, man is capable of making a free and conscious decision."[13] Furthermore, Ware also advises that since God has free will, and He made man in His image, so man, too, has free will and the right to exercise it.

Ware calls attention to the fact that free will and grace co-exist together and are intimately intertwined. Man must continuously exert great effort to carry out God's will; man's will is needed because God works through man's will:

> ...the active life requires on our side effort, struggle, the persistent exertion of our free will. "Strait is the gate and narrow is the way that leads to life...Not everyone that says to me, Lord, Lord, shall enter into the kingdom of heaven, but he that does the will of my Father" (Matt 7:14, 21). We are to hold in balance two complementary truths: without God's grace we *can* do nothing, but without our voluntary co-operation God *will* do nothing. "The will of man is an essential condition, for without it God does nothing"[14] (*The Homilies of St. Macarius*). Our salvation results from the convergence of two

factors, unequal in value yet both indispensable: divine initiative and human response. What God does is incomparably the more important, but man's participation is also required. ...there is also the need to fight resolutely against the deeply-rooted habits and inclinations that are the result of sin, both original and personal. One of the most important qualities needed by the traveler on the Way is faithful perseverance. The endurance required from one who climbs a mountain physically is required likewise from those who would ascent the mountain of God. "God demands everything from a man- his mind, his reason, all his actions...Do you wish to be saved when you die? Go and exhaust yourself; go and labour; go, seek and you shall find; watch and knock, and it shall be opened to you"[15] (*The Sayings of the Desert Fathers*). "The present age is not a time for rest and sleep, but it is a struggle, a combat, a market, a school, a voyage. Therefore you must exert yourself, and not be downcast and idle, but devote yourself to holy actions"[16] (*Starets* Nazarii of Valamo). "Nothing comes without effort. The help of God is always ready and always near, but is given only to those who seek and work, and only to those seekers who, after putting all their powers to the test, then cry out with their whole heart: Lord, help us"[17] (St. Theophan the Recluse). "Peace is gained through tribulation"[18] (St. Seraphim of Sarov). "To rest is the same as to retreat"[19] Yet, lest we should be too much downcast by this severity, we are also told: "The whole of a man's life is but a single day, for those who labour with eagerness"[20] (*The Sayings of the Desert Fathers*).[21]

Having seen verses that address man's free will (Rev 3:20; 1 Cor 3:9), we can better understand Rom 8:29. God calls all men. He stands at the door and knocks. Hence, God makes the first move. The moment that a person reaches towards God, God reaches towards him This is a far cry from Pascal's heresies of the election of the damned and his hidden God who veils Messianic verses so that readers of the Bible would not understand them.

Archimandrite Christoforos Stavropoulos, in *Partakers of Divine Nature*, advises that the earliest fathers of the Church have always stressed that free will and divine grace coexist together, but that faith is freely offered and man can either freely accept it or reject it:

Chapter Six: Predestination vs. Free Will

According to the tradition and teaching of the Eastern Orthodox Church, grace and human freedom are expressed concurrently and may not be understood the one without the other. There are not two separate moments. At the same time that a person freely makes the decision from within for the good and for the Christian life, at the very same moment divine grace comes and strengthens him. Just as this grace is given to the individual, the individual makes a free choice. Gregory of Nyssa says, "The grace of God is not able to visit those who flee salvation. Nor is human virtue of such power as to be adequate of itself to raise up to authentic life those souls who are untouched by grace...*But when righteousness of works and the grace of the Spirit come together at the same time* in the same soul, together they are able to fill it with blessed life..."[22] The more freely each human being receives the divine gift of grace, so much more does the Christian life become in fact grace-filled and complete; and in the same measure do the Christian's good works increase and does progress in virtue grow. What this means is that the Christian increasingly practices good works and virtues-strengthened by grace-on the way toward the realization of theosis.[23]

This background on the Eastern Orthodox point of view on man's freedom to act will come in handy as we examine the fact that Augustine was 1) working with a mistranslation of Rom 5:12 and 2) forced to move to one side of the spectrum, as often happens during modern political debates, because his opponent, Pelagius, positioned himself on the extreme other side and argued salvation through works. Fortunately, the Orthodox Church does not rely on Augustine, so it has remained unaffected by his theology.

Grace and free will are also discussed in *The Philokalia*, a compilation of writings dating from the 4th century AD to the 15th century. In this work, Makarios of Egypt, in the *Makarian Homilies*, teaches:

1. We receive salvation by grace and as a divine gift of the Spirit. But to attain the full measure of virtue we need also to possess faith and love, and to struggle to exercise our free will with integrity. In this manner we inherit eternal life as a consequence of both grace and justice. We do not reach the final stage of

spiritual maturity through divine power and grace alone, without ourselves making any effort; but neither on the other hand do we attain the final measure of freedom and purity as a result of our own intelligence and strength alone, apart from any divine assistance. If the Lord does not build the house, it is said, and protect the city, in vain does the watchman keep awake, and in vain do the labourer and the builder work (cf. Ps 127:1-4).
2. What is the will of God that St. Paul urges and invites each of us to attain (cf. 1 Thess 4:3)? It is total cleansing from sin, freedom from shameful passions and the acquisition of the highest virtue. In other words, it is the purification and the sanctification of the heart that comes about through fully experienced and conscious participation in the perfect and divine Spirit. "Blessed are the pure in heart," it is said, "for they shall see God" (Matt 5:8); and again: "Become perfect, as your heavenly Father is perfect" (Matt 5:48).[24]

Grace enters through the heart

In *The Art of Persuasion* Pascal says that God prefers for truth to enter man though his heart rather than through his mind: "I know that he wanted them to enter from the heart into the mind, and not from the mind into the heart, in order to humiliate that proud power of reasoning which claims it ought to be the judge of what is chosen by the will, and to heal that feeble will which is completely corrupted by vile attachments."[25]

Pascal's apology of the Christian faith is a marriage of faith and reason, of the heart and mind. Pascal surmised that faith is important: "If we submit everything to reason, our religion will have no mysterious and supernatural event."[26] However, we cannot disagree with reason: "Submission is the use of reason in which consists true Christianity."[27]

Pascal decided that he would bring faith to the skeptic by speaking to his heart. Now the heart is also a euphemism for intuition. People know the truth when they hear it: their intuition tells them when something it true. Marvin R. O'Connell, in *Blaise Pascal: Reasons of the Heart*, explains the importance of appealing to the heart in Pascal's apologetics: "In Pascal's vocabulary, 'the heart' is a term that means, not simply feelings or emotions,

Chapter Six: Predestination vs. Free Will

but intuition-immediate comprehension and understanding of certain things that we have without having to reason our way to them. Through 'the heart,' we immediately apprehend basic principles that reason cannot discover on its own, and that reason requires as givens for its own operation. Through the 'heart,' in fact, we apprehend truths that reason, if left to its own devices, would never touch. In one of the most famous portions of the *Pensées*, Pascal warns the lovers of reason that 'the heart has its reasons of which reason knows nothing...It is the heart which perceives God and not the reason. That is what faith is: God perceived by the heart, not by the reason.'"[28]

O'Connell also observes that Pascal describes Christianity as a religion of love whose God fills the heart of the believer with joy and peace. The Holy Spirit indwells the believer and teaches him all things; thus, the believer is never alone because the Holy Spirit lives within him. The believer has Christ, who is the Prince of Peace, and He fills his heart with peace: "The God of the Christians is not a God who is simply the author of mathematical truths, or of the order of the elements...But...is a God of love and comfort, a God who fills the soul and heart of those whom he possesses, a God...who unites Himself to their inmost soul, who fills it with humility and joy, with confidence and love, who renders them incapable of any other end than Himself."[29] Christ told His followers that He would always comfort them, give them rest, and heal their broken hearts: "Come unto me, all ye that labour and are heavy laden, and I will give you rest. Take my yoke upon you, and learn of me; for I am meek and lowly in heart: and ye shall find rest in your souls. For my yoke is easy and my burden is light" (Matt 11:28-30); "The Spirit of the Lord is upon me, because he hath anointed me to preach the gospel to the poor; he heath sent me to heal the brokenhearted, to preach deliverance to the captives, and recovering of sight to the blind, to set at liberty them that are bruised" (Luke 4:18).

The Orthodox Church agrees with Pascal that grace enters through the heart. Stavropoulos points out that "the descent of the grace of the Holy Spirit must take place in our heart."[30] He explains, "Our heart is the workshop of righteousness as well as unrighteousness. It is the vessel which contains every sin. However, at the same time 'God is found there; there the angels; there the life and the kingdom; there the light and the apostles; there the treasures of grace' (Macarius of Egypt). When grace conquers all of the springs, desires, and expressions of the heart, then it reigns in each of our members and in every thought, because the mind and thoughts of the soul are found there in the heart. When the grace of God passes through the heart, it penetrates the whole of human nature. Consequently, the descent of the grace of the Holy Spirit must take place in our heart. And the Holy Spirit must guard over our heart."[31]

What Augustine says about predestination and free will

Augustine based his theology on the Latin Vulgate, which mistranslated Rom 5:12 from the original Greek. The original Greek says, literally, "Therefore as through one man sin entered into the world and through sin death, so also to all men death came, inasmuch as all sinned."[32] This is a critical verse because it states that death came to all men because (inasmuch as) all sinned. The point is that the original Greek text indicates that Adam sinned and caused punishment, that is, death and disease, to come into the world; death came to all men because all men sinned. Each man commits his own sins. He does not inherit any of Adam's sins. This is impossible. What we have inherited from Adam is the punishment for sin, death and disease, not his sins.

The Latin Vulgate mistranslates the last clause as *in quo omnes peccaverunt*, "in whom all have sinned." This is a heretical statement and has confounded Western Christianity since it was written. The Greek text says that we have not inherited Adam's sins, we commit our own. Babies do not inherit Adam's sins. This is why the Orthodox Church rejects the notion of the damnation of unbaptized babies. It is unscriptural.

Let us see what this mistranslation has caused Augustine to posit. Kolakowski sums it up beautifully: "The doctrine of hereditary guilt, or of our unavoidable participation in the actual sin of Adam, is important insofar as it helps explain why all those damned by God are damned justly."[33] From Augustine's point of view, man is rotten to the core because he has inherited Adam's sin and without God's grace, he is incapable of doing any good on his own. He is driven by his passions, not reason. Only God's grace can turn him away from his passions and put him on the road towards denying himself and conforming to Christ's image. God decides to whom He will give His grace. These are the elected few. The road to perdition is wide, but narrow is the gate and few are those who find it. God gives His elect "irresistible efficacious grace." Those to whom it is given receive the gift of faith and the power to conform themselves to Christ's image. Those who do not receive it are incapable of belief. Hence, we have the vile, heretical concept of the election of the damned.

Below is a summary of Augustine's views on election:

- Grace (the free and unmerited favor of God) is a gift of God (Eph 2:8). God can choose to give or withhold this gift.
- God's grace is not universal. God gives it to certain individuals.
- The notion that "all have sinned in Adam" is derived from the Latin Vulgate's mistranslation of Rom 5:12 from the original Greek. This led Augustine to erroneously conclude that all men carry Adam's sin in them.
- God's grace is needed for salvation. Unless God imparts the gift of grace (faith), man cannot believe.
- Therefore, only some will be saved.
- Thus we can extrapolate predestination. From the foundation of the world, God has elected those to whom He will give grace (those He will save) and those from whom He will withhold it (those He will damn) (this is called "double predestination").
- Augustine does suggest "double predestination," but he usually discusses only the election of the saved.

Why the Orthodox Church ignores Augustine

There is a stark difference between what the Orthodox Church teaches about predestination and what Augustine/Jansenius/Pascal set forth. Let us begin by examining what the Orthodox Church teaches. Bishop Elias Minatios has written an excellent article entitled, "On Predestination," that explains the position of the Orthodox Church on the subject and how it differs from that of Augustine.[34] However, theologians do not always agree on certain issues and so, another Orthodox theologian, Father Michael Azkoul, criticizes some of the points that Minatios makes in a review of his article.[35]

Minatios begins his refutation of Augustine by reminding us that because God is just, it is His will that all be saved. He cites the following biblical verses: "He wills all men to be saved" (1 Tim 2:4); "that having granted the law to all, He excludes no one from His kingdom" (St. Ambrose); "For there is one God, and one mediator between God and men, the man Christ Jesus, Who gave Himself as ransom for all (1 Tim 2:5); "One died for all" (2 Cor 5:14); "shown forth for all, lived for all and died and is risen for all" (St. Gregory the Theologian).[36] However, Minatios goes on to explain that although God wants to save all, he does not impose His will on man: man has the free will to either draw closer to God or to go his own way. God created man in his image: God has free will and therefore, man, too, has free will. Orthodoxy teaches that it is up to men to cooperate with God.[37]

Minatios points out that there are several examples in the Bible where man was required to perform certain works in order to carry out God's will. For example, God wanted to save Noah, but first Noah had to build the ark. Similarly, God wanted to heal Nehemiah's leprosy, but Nehemiah was required to wash in the Jordan. Jesus instructed the blind man to wash in the pool of Siloam. Minatios observes that the Bible indicates that it is up to man to cooperate with God not only in the execution of His will, but also in his salvation, as well.. Hence, man has the free will to either align his will with God's or to go his own way.

In addition, Orthodoxy holds that God's foreknowledge is based on the future, it is not the other way around. The future is not based on God's foreknowledge. The future is fluid or liquid and subject to change from moment to moment. Minatios observes that Christ was not the reason of Judas' betrayal, but rather, Judas' betrayal was the cause of God's foreknowledge of the future. This is the answer to the whole issue. In contrast, it becomes apparent that the mindless, vicious cycle in Pascal's redemption is contrived, warped, and erroneous: in Pascal's theology, grace is required to understand Scripture, but one must understand Scripture in order to be saved. This circular reasoning does not exist in Orthodoxy.

Minatios gives four examples of the fluidity of the future and of the fact that God's foreknowledge is the result of future events. In the first example, the apostle Paul was held captive on a ship bound for Italy. A storm arose and the people aboard were worried about the turbulence. God

Chapter Six: Predestination vs. Free Will

sent an angel to tell Paul, "Fear not, Paul...God hath given thee all them that sail with thee" (Acts 27:24). This meant that for the crewmen to be saved, they had to choose to remain in the boat with Paul. If any of the sailors chose to jump into the water, he did not have the protection of God. Minatios advises, "Does God's destination change? Yes, it can be no other way. *Except these abide in the ship, ye cannot be saved.*"[38]

These Bible verses teach us that destiny can actually change from moment to moment because man has 100% free will 100% of the time. It is God's will to save everyone, but man must cooperate by obeying God, by being the instrument by which God's will is done. In fact, it is in the "Our Father" prayer: "Thy will be done on earth as it is in Heaven" reminds us that our purpose, as Christians, is to become the instruments by which God's will is done. This requires our choosing to align our will with God's will.

Minatios offers a second biblical example of the fluidity of the future: King Hezekiah becomes sick and the prophet Isaiah tells him, "Thus saith the Lord, Set thine house in order; for thou shalt die, and not live (2 King 20:1)." Minatios says, "The unfortunate Hezekiah turns his face to the wall, sighs, cries, pleads. What are you doing, oh hapless king?! Has not God appointed you to death? Is it not in vain that you cry and plead? Can one whom God has ordained to die, live? Does God's decision change? Yes, brothers and sisters, this determination also changed! God had pity on the tears of Hezekiah and determined that he live. He even granted him fifteen years of life. *Thus saith the Lord, I will add unto thy days fifteen years* (2 Kings 20:5, 6)."[39] This teaches us that the future is fluid, liquid, subject to change from moment to moment. While God knows the future and it is known only to him, man has free will and the power to effect changes in his life, even in the future. Again, Minatios extrapolates, "The future does not flow from foreknowledge, but foreknowledge from the future."[40]

Minatios cites a third example: Jeremiah went to a potter's house and he saw the potter drop a pot that he had been working on. The form of the pot became distorted and the pot was ruined. However, the potter picked it up and started to rework it and made it like new. God told Jeremiah, "Behold, as the clay is in the potter's hand, so are ye in mine hand" (Jer 18:6).[41] This is another example of the fact that things can change at any moment, given the fact that man has free will.

Minatios ends his article with a fourth example, this one about the Oracle of Delphi. One day a man decided to try and see whether he could make the renown Oracle out to be a liar. In order to accomplish this, the man brought the Oracle a sparrow that he was holding in his hands and that was covered with a piece of cloth. It was his intention to ask the Oracle whether the bird was alive or dead. If the Oracle were to say, "Dead," the man intended to show him that it was alive. If the Oracle were to reply, "Alive," the man intended to strangle it and show him that it was dead. When he asked the question, the Oracle responded, "It depends on you to decide, to show what you hold as living or dead." Minatios ends his article by making a brilliant analogy between the Oracle's reply and man's free will: "*It depends on you to decide*. Your predestination depends on the will of God and your will. The will of God is always ready. This means that things are determined only by your will. God desires (your salvation); if you desire this also, then you are predestined for eternal life."[42]

Theologians do not always agree with one another, and so Father Michael Azkoul criticizes Minatios for simplifying predestination as the union of God's will and man's will.[43] Azkoul points out that in order to fully understand predestination as it is expressed in the Bible, Orthodox thought, based on St. Gregory of Palamas, distinguishes among God's Uncreated Divine Energies. For example, the Will of God must be distinguished from God's foreknowledge. These are distinct and separate Energies. Hence, God foreknows that evil will occur, but He does not will it. God foreknows that some people will reject Him and go their own way, but he does not will it (*Theol. Chap* 100, PG 150 1189D).[44] It is this failure to distinguish between God's Will and His foreknowledge that led Pascal to continually reiterate the heresy of double predestination that includes the notion of the "election of the damned," and the lie that God veiled the Messianic prophecies in the OT so that the reprobate would not recognize Jesus when He came. In addition, Ware points out that St. Gregory of Palamas was able to avoid pantheism by distinguishing God's Essence from His Energies.[45]

Azkoul agrees with Augustine that man's desire for salvation is initiated by God, but he is quick to point out that this first initializing motion is based on God's purpose. Rom 8:28 says, "to them who are called according to purpose." There are many examples in the Bible in which God chooses those whose disposition is such that they would be willing to carry out His purpose. God knows what is in the hearts of men and He knows who would be willing to work for Him and with Him. For example, on His way to Galilee, Jesus finds Philip and says, "Follow me" (John 1:43). This implies that the Lord has foreknowledge of the location of Philip and searches for him. Philip follows Him and then tells Nathaniel, "We have found Him, of whom Moses in the law, and the prophets, did write, Jesus of Nazareth, the son of Joseph" (John 1:45). Jesus has foreknowledge of Nathaniel, as well, and He knows that there is no guile in him. Jesus tells Nathaniel, "Behold an Israelite indeed, in whom is not guile!" (John 1:47). Nathaniel asks Jesus, "Whence knowest thou me?" Jesus replies, "Before that Philip called thee, when thou wast under the fig tree, I saw thee" (John 1:48). When Nathaniel understands that Jesus had foreknowledge of him he declares, "Rabbi, thou are the Son of God; thou art the King of Israel" (John 1:49). Christ replies, "Because I said unto thee, I saw thee under the fig tree, believest thou? Thou shalt see greater things than these...Hereafter ye shall see heaven open, and the angels of God ascending and descending upon the son of man" (John 1:50-51). Jesus chooses Philip and Nathaniel because He has foreknowledge of their disposition and he knows that they would be willing to carry out His will.

In another example, Jesus is walking past the customs table and He says to the tax collector, Matthew, "Follow me"; Matthew arises from the customs table and follows the Lord (Matt 9:9). Christ knows beforehand that Matthew's disposition is such that He can rely on him to carry out His will.

Rom 8:28 says, "And we know that all things work together for good to them that love God, to them who are called according to his purpose." God calls (or initiates the communication between Divine Will and man's will) those whom He can use to carry out His purpose. In other words, God can look into the hearts of men and identify those whom He can use according to His purpose. One thinks of the conversion of the Pharisee Saul. Saul was a sinner who held the coats of those who stoned Stephen to death. Despite Saul's history, Christ had mercy on him and revealed Himself to him on the road to Damascus. He looked into his heart and saw that this Pharisee would be willing to carry out God's purpose, that he would be willing to become an instrument by which God's will is done. When man accepts the gift of faith that is available to all, he is on the way leading towards theosis.

Hence, Azkoul declares that Orthodoxy does teach predestination based on foreknowledge, but unlike Augustine, maintains that there is no compulsion involved. The foreknowledge is knowing the heart of someone and identifying the person who would be willing to carry out Divine Will. However, God forces no one.

Azkoul's article is valuable because he has a thorough knowledge of Augustine's many books. Azkoul cites from a diverse selection to show that not only was Augustine a proponent of the election of the damned, but that he single handedly opened the door to the Protestant Reformation by arguing predestination and the notion of the invisible and hidden Church known only to God. Azkoul does an excellent job of proving that Augustine was unwittingly responsible for the fragmentation of Western Christianity. Having cited a plethora of passages from Augustine's works, Azkoul concludes that, ironically enough, Augustine might be considered the Father of the Protestant Reformation: "As an Orthodox bishop, Augustine might have said that the 'elect' are members of the visible and historical Church; but he did not. For him, those predestined to glory belong to the hidden and 'true Church,' the invisible Church, known only to God. Augustine is thus the precursor to the Protestant reform idea of the Church. Such an ecclesiology radically alters the traditional understanding of the Church and her Mysteries. His theory of predestination surely changes the patristic teaching on God and Christ."[46]

Azkoul concludes his article by reaffirming that the Orthodox position is diametrically antithetical to that of Augustine. Man does have free will and God chooses according to His foreknowledge of whom He can use to carry out His will: "In other words, the omniscient God bases His decision of our individual destinies on the way we received Christ, obeyed His Church, and sought to make all men our brothers. Contrary to Augustine and his tradition, each person is indeed intimately responsible for whether God predestines him to eternal life…In a sense, each of us 'predetermine' his own fate by our love for Him and our quest for 'the Grace of the Spirit,' if I may quote St Seraphim of Sarov. The Mercy of God is that Christ died for the human race, since it is the Will of the Blessed Trinity (wishes?) that 'all men come to the knowledge of the Truth and be saved.' He has done all that can be done in Love (John 3:16) to rescue the creature from death and evil; by the Cross he destroyed him 'that had the power of death...'"[47]

The Orthodox Church teaches that man's purpose is theosis

The definition of theosis is divinization or union with the Living God. The Orthodox Church teaches that Scripture indicates that this is exactly what the purpose of man is: union with the Living God. *The Philokalia* declares that the way to achieve theosis may be metaphorized as a ladder to God. Christians embark on a journey. The first step on the ladder is faith. Once they believe, they begin a journey on which they become more and more like Christ.

Daniel B. Clendenin, in *Eastern Orthodox Christianity: A Western Perspective*, cites Christoforos Stavropoulos, author of *Partakers of Divine Nature*:

> In the Holy Scriptures, where God Himself speaks, we read of a unique call directed to us. God speaks to us human beings clearly and directly and He says: "I said, 'You are gods, sons of the Most High-all of you'" (Psalm 82:6 and John 10:34). Do we hear that voice? Do we understand the meaning of this calling? Do we accept that we should in fact be on a journey, a road which leads to Theosis? As human beings we each have this one, unique calling, to achieve Theosis. In other words, we are each destined to become a god; to be like God Himself, to be united with Him. The Apostle Peter describes with total clarity the purpose of life: we are to "become partakers of the divine nature" (2 Peter 1:4). This is the purpose of your life; that you be a participant, a sharer in the nature of God and in the life of Christ, a communicant of divine energy-to become just like God, a true God.[48]

Doing the things discussed in *The Philokalia* is a good way to proceed up the spiritual ladder towards theosis or union with God. *The Philokalia* is a collection of writings by monks and mystics that have been found on Mount

Athos. These writings date from the 4th century AD to the fifteenth century. The people who wrote it renounced everything for Christ and prayed and fasted continuously, many in silence, to align their will with God's will, to achieve theosis. These mystics advise "cleaning out" the intellect of anger, desire, and greed; they recommend fasting and prayer; silence; to embrace the notion of death rather than to fear it. When people put effort into doing these works, God rewards them: the mystics who practiced these works received gifts such as visions, miracles, and the Holy Spirit gave them an understanding of Holy Scripture. Orthodoxy points out, however, that theosis or union with God is achieved by grace, not by works: "...for the writers of the *Philokalia*, the gift of theosis comes by grace through faith, and not by works."[49] God gives grace, but man has to make an effort and seek to unite his will with God's will. One can say that man does not have 100% power over himself 100% of the time because man's power is tainted by sin and death. Therefore, the most that man can do is to seek to align his will with God's will, to be the instrument by which God's will is done. He can exercise his free will to do the things that are pleasing to God.

Clendenin cites St. Makarios of Egypt, who points out that salvation occurs when man exercises his free will to unite with God's will: "We receive salvation by grace and as a divine gift of the Spirit. But to attain the full measure of virtue we need also to possess faith and love, and to struggle to exercise our free will with integrity. In this manner we inherit eternal life as a consequence of both grace and justice. We do not reach the final stage of spiritual maturity through divine power and grace alone, without ourselves making any effort; but neither on the other hand do we attain the final measure of freedom and purity as a result of our own diligence and strength alone, apart from any divine assistance. If the Lord does not built the house, it is said, and protect the city, in vain does the watchman keep awake, and in vain do the labourer and builder work [Ps 127:1-4]."[50]

Clendenin concludes, "Thus, faith without works and works without faith are equally rejected (James). In Pauline language, we labor and strive, but only through the empowering grace of God working in us (Phil 2:12-13; 1 Cor 15:10-11)."[51] The techniques of achieving theosis include fasting, vigils, prostrations, tears, repentance, silence, dispassion, stillness, prayer, detachment, discrimination, participating in the sacraments, and keeping the commandments of God.

Chapter Six: Predestination vs. Free Will

The Philokalia metaphorizes the process of theosis as a ladder leading up to God. The first step is faith, which is a gift, but there are many rungs on the ladder and it requires hard work and diligent effort on the part of man to attain theosis. One of the steps, after belief, is to try to purify one's heart as Jesus proscribed: "Blessed are the pure in heart: for they shall see God" (Matt 5:8). When the heart has been purified, man will, indeed, see or experience with his spiritual eyes, God.

The early fathers stressed the importance of cleansing the intellect. They metaphorized the intellect as a well. We go to the well to draw water, but we cannot because it is full of garbage. The task, then, of the Christian is to rid his intellect of this garbage so that he can draw closer to God. One of the pieces of garbage that must be discarded is anger. Many of us walk around angry about something. Anger is spiritual poison and as long as it is present, it is blocking our spiritual eyes from seeing God. The first work in volume 3 of *The Philokalia* is *Forty Texts on Watchfulness*, by St. Philotheos of Sinai. The first line of this piece is striking: "There is within us, on the noetic plane, a warfare tougher than that on the plane of the senses. The spiritual worker has to press on with his intellect towards the goal (cf. Phil 3:14), in order to enshrine perfectly the remembrance of God in his heart like some pearl or precious stone (cf. Matt 13:44-46). He has to give up everything, including the body, and to disdain this present life, if he wishes to possess God alone in his heart. For the noetic vision of God, the divine Chrysostom has said, can by itself destroy the demonic spirits."[52] If one follows the recommendations in the *Forty Texts on Watchfulness*, one will have a pure heart and see God, and also receive many gifts from God. The monks on Mount Athos, even today, have a very close relationship with Christ and have many visions, miracles, and other gifts. The goal of the *Forty Texts* is to teach the Christian how to protect himself against principalities and powers that are always seeking to make inroads to cause him to fall. St. Philotheos has the following advice to the Christian who wants to stay pure on a noetic plane: "Keeping watch with the intellect...destroy hostile thoughts at their first appearance," remember death and meditate on it, exercise self-control in eating and drinking, try to purge the passions and attain a state of dispassion, maintain silence, and heal anger.[53]

That last one, the importance of healing anger, is especially important as anger poisons the intellect. Christ advises that if anyone is going to present a gift at the altar, but is angry with his brother, he should first go and be reconciled with him (Matt 5:23-24). Implicit in his command is honest dialogue, discussion of feelings, examination of facts and intentions, and a swift resolution or clarification so that the anger does not fester, become worse, and grow into a mountain. Also implicit is the fact that people who seek a relationship with God are embarked on a journey, they are climbing a ladder towards theosis, and this journey requires purification of the heart. Christ admonishes us to be perfect as our Father in Heaven is perfect. We are on a ladder rising towards union with God and our hearts must be made pure. This leaves no room for anger. Anger is a tool that principalities and powers use against us to hinder us on our journey towards theosis.

To date, there exists a substantial body of research that addresses the Orthodox position on theosis. We recommend the following books and articles on the subject: Panagiotes K. Chrestou, *Partakers of God*;[54] Daniel B. Clendenin's two books, *Eastern Orthodox Christianity: A Western Perspective*[55] and *Eastern Orthodox Theology: A Contemporary Reader* define and explain theosis;[56] Ben Drewery, "Deification";[57] Eleuterio Fortino, "Sanctification and Deification";[58] Jules Gross, *La divinisation du chrétien d'après les pères grecs; contribution historique à la doctrine de la grâce*;[59] Vigen Guroian, *Incarnate Love: Essays in Orthodox Ethics*;[60] Stanley S. Harakas, "Eastern Orthodox Christianity's Ultimate Reality and Meaning: Triune God and Theosis; An Ethician's View";[61] Verna Harrison, "Some Aspects of Saint Gregory the Theologian's Soteriology";[62] Maurice Fred Himmerich, *Deification in John of Damascus*;[63] Cheslyn Jones, Geoffrey Wainwright and Edward Yarnold, *The Study of Spirituality*;[64] Stephen James Juli, *The Doctrine of Theosis in the Theology of Saint Maximus the Confessor*;[65] Vladimir Lossky's two books, *In the Image and Likeness of God*[66] and *Orthodox Theology: An Introduction*;[67] Myrrha Lot-Borodine, *La déification de l'homme selon la doctrine des Pères grecs*;[68] Georgios I. Mantzaridis, *The Deification of Man: St. Gregory Palamas and the Orthodox Tradition*;[69] John Meyendorff's two books, *Byzantine Theology: Historical Trends and Doctrinal Themes*[70] and *Christ in Eastern Christian Thought*[71] and his two articles, "New Life in Christ: Salvation in Orthodox Theology"[72] and "Theosis in the Eastern Christian Tradition";[73] John Meyendorff and Robert Tobias, ed., *Salvation in Christ: A Lutheran-Orthodox Dialogue*;[74] Panayiotis Nellas, *Deification in Christ: Orthodox Perspectives on the Nature of the Human Person*;[75] Keith Edward Norman, *Deification: The Content of Athanasian Soteriology*;[76] George Papademetriou, "The Human Body According to Saint Gregory Palamas";[77] *The Philokalia: The Complete Text; Compiled by St. Nikodimos of the Holy Mountain and St. Makarios of Corinth*;[78] Symeon Rodger, "The Soteriology of Anselm of Canterbury, An Orthodox Perspective";[79] Bernard Sartorius, *La doctrine de la déification de l'homme d'après les Pères grecs en général et Grégoire Palamas en particulier*;[80] Dumitru Stăniloae, *The Experience of God*;[81] Christoforos Stavropoulos, *Partakers of Divine Nature*;[82] Gregory Telepneff and James Thornton, "Arian Transcendence and the Notion of Theosis in Saint Athanasios";[83] Nicolaos P. Vassiliades, "The Mystery of Death";[84] Bishop Kallistos Ware, *The Orthodox Way*;[85] and Timothy Ware, *The Orthodox Church*.[86]

The Jansenists vs. the Jesuits

Pascal's view that God's will subordinates man's will was greatly influenced by the heretical hermeneutics of Cornelius Jansenius, Bishop of Ypres (1585-1638) via the writings of Saint-Cyran. Jansenius, who based his theology on Augustine, posited that all men inherit Adam's sin and his instincts lead him to do evil; man is depraved at his very core. He can be saved only by the grace of God, which is given to a select few, the elect, that God has predestined and chosen to enter the Kingdom of Heaven. Jansenius was a heretic whose subtle reasoning led Pascal and many others, called Jansenists or Augustinians, to accept the notion that God forces His will on men and causes them to either accept or reject Him. Jean Duvergier de Hauranne, abbé de Saint-Cyran, had studied with Jansenius and had written prolifically on Jansenism. When he was arrested, his writings comprised 32 thick folios.

Jansenius' doctrine, which heavily influenced Pascal's thought, leads directly to a heresy that is called predestinarianism. The *Catholic Encyclopedia* describes predestinarianism as "a heresy not unfrequently met with in the course of the centuries which reduces the eternal salvation of the elect as well as the eternal damnation of the reprobate to one cause alone, namely to the sovereign will of God, and thereby excludes the free co-operation of man as a secondary factor in bringing about a happy or unhappy future in the life to come."[87] The *Catholic Encylopedia* goes on to summarize the two main heresies that predestinarianism sets forth thus:

- The absolute will of God as the sole cause of the salvation or damnation of the individual, without regard to his merits or demerits;
- As to the elect, it denies the freedom of the will under the influence of efficacious grace while it puts the reprobate under the necessity of committing sin in consequence of the absence of grace.

The *Catholic Encyclopedia* specifies that in the heresy of predestinarianism, it is mistakenly held that God saves the elect by 1) giving them efficacious grace so that their free will cannot resist Him and 2) their will, under the influence of grace, is forced to do what is right. The heresy also posits that God predestines the non-elect by 1) withholding irresistibly efficacious grace, thereby 2) causing their will to choose sin: "...if those who are predestined for eternal life are to attain this end with metaphysical necessity...God must give them during their lifetime efficacious graces of such a nature that the possibility of free resistance is systematically excluded, while, on the other hand, the will, under the influence of grace, is borne along without reluctance to do what is right and is forced to persevere in a course of righteousness to the hour of death. But from all eternity God has also made a decree not less absolute whereby he has positively predestined the non-elect to eternal torments. God can accomplish this design only by denying to the reprobate irresistibly efficacious graces and impelling their will to sin continually, thereby leading them slowly but surely to eternal damnation."[89]

The *Catholic Encyclopedia* attributes the inception and continuation of this heresy down through the centuries to a misinterpretation of Saint Augustine's work on election. It is interesting that the *Catholic Encyclopedia* points out, "...this heresy sprang up in the Church of the West, whilst that of the East was preserved in a remarkable manner from these extravagances."[90]

Chapter Six: Predestination vs. Free Will

That is because the Church of the East ignored the writings of Augustine, even though he was an Orthodox bishop.

Conversely, the Jesuits held that human nature, even though it exists in a fallen creation, still, at its core, desires to be with God. This view is set forth in Ignatius' *Spiritual Exercises*. Hence, the Jesuits' emphasis on the goodness of man's will put them in opposition to the Jansenists, who emphasized man's depravity.

The Jesuit Luis de Molina (1535-1600) taught that God decides what someone will do by foreseeing what he would do under a set of circumstances and then creates the agent and the circumstances. Generally, the Jesuits held Ockham's view that both God and man contribute to men's actions.

James A. Connor, in *Pascal's Wager: The Man Who Played Dice with God*, summarizes how the Jesuits viewed the Jansenists' notion of the election of the damned:

> The entire Society of Jesus looked askance at this. They taught that human beings have the power to do good as well as evil, and that Christ had come to save all men and women and not just the select few. For the Jesuits, otherwise known as Molinists, the human will had the power to choose good over evil, and divine grace, which was nearly ubiquitous, gave aid and comfort to those striving to achieve God's will. They recognized the impact of original sin on the lives of ordinary people, but held that Adam's sin did not utterly bestialize people but wounded them, stacking the deck toward sin.
>
> Because of the Reformers, however, Augustinian philosophy had become chic. It was perfect for times of uncertainty. If you are one of the elect, your future is assured. At that point, the spiritual life becomes less about conversion than about watching for signs of your inclusion. Just what those signs were was up to the spiritual leaders, which gave such men and women extraordinary power over their charges. Richelieu had the power of life and death, certainly, but over his followers Saint-Cyran had the power of salvation.[91]

Connor summarizes the Jesuit position on free will thus:

> While God knows what people are likely to choose, that knowledge does not determine what they do choose. Therefore, human beings share in, and in some small way limit, the power of God, for by creating humanity in his own image and likeness, God bestowed upon them the power to bring new things into the world through their freedom. God's grace does not subvert human freedom, but acts with it. It is not "efficacious," in the sense that it does not force the person who receives it to convert, but aids them in their free choice. It is therefore "sufficient" in the sense that it is enough to affect a change when working in concord with human free will.[92]

Let us return to Christ's warning in Mat 7:14, 21, that Ware uses to substantiate free will, "Strait is the gate and narrow is the way that leads to life…Not everyone that says to me, Lord, Lord, shall enter into the kingdom of heaven, but he that does the will of my Father." The point here is that men do have free will and that God wants them to align their will with His, but He is not forcing them to do so. Related to Mat 7:14, 21 are the following verses that indicate the punishment that will be meted out when men exercise their free will to go their own way: "Because Ephraim hath made many altars to sin, altars shall be unto him to sin" (Hos 8:11) (here Ephraim decided to make many altars to sin); "And why call ye me, Lord, Lord, and do not the things which I say? Whosoever cometh to me, and heareth my sayings, and doeth them, I will shew you to whom he is like: He is like a man which built an house, and digged deep, and laid the foundation on a rock: and when the flood arose, the stream beat vehemently upon that house, and could not shake it: for it was founded upon a rock. But he that heareth, and doeth not, is like a man that without a foundation built an house upon the earth; against which the stream did beat vehemently, and immediately it fell; and the ruin of that house was great" (Luke 6:46-49); "When once the master of the house is risen up, and hath shut to the door, and ye begin to stand without, and to knock at the door, saying, Lord, Lord, open unto us; and he shall answer and say unto you, I know you not whence ye are: Then shall ye begin to say, We have eaten and drunk in thy presence, and thou hast taught in our streets. But he shall say, I tell you, I know you not whence ye are; depart from me, all ye workers of iniquity. There shall be weeping and gnashing of teeth, when he shall see Abraham, and Isaac, and Jacob, and all the prophets, in the kingdom of God, and you yourselves thrust out." (Luke 13:25-28); "Who will render to every man according to his deeds: To them who by patient continuance in well doing seek for glory and honour and immortality, eternal life: but unto them that are contentious, and do not obey the truth, but obey unrighteousness, indignation and wrath, Tribulation and anguish, upon every soul of man that doeth evil" (Rom 2:6-9); "But be ye doers of the word, and not hearers only, deceiving your own selves" (Jas 1:22); "he being not a forgetful hearer, but a doer of the work, this man shall be blessed in his deed" (Jas 1:25).

Hence, it is understandable why, on May 31, 1653, the Catholic Church condemned as heretical five points that Cornelius Jansenius made in his book, *Augustinius*. Basically, Jansenius' five points denied man's free will and implied that God saves or damns people according to the will that He forces upon them or withholds from them. Connor summarizes why the Church found Jansenius to be heretical: "The gist of the five points in contention is that Augustinians denied human beings the power of full moral agency. People could commit evil on their own but not good, for doing good requires a special 'efficacious' grace from God, and, once given, that grace could not be denied. With it, one could not do evil; without it, one could not do good. The question was whether people were puppets in the hand of an all-powerful God, thereby making God's power absolute, or whether they were moral agents capable of free actions, thus in some small way limiting the power of God."[93]

Infinity, God, and Predestination

Pascal's knowledge of mathematics permitted him to see similarities between the notions of infinity/finite numbers and God/creation. Since God is infinite and exists outside of time, Pascal could apply mathematical truths about infinity to Him and use these truths to explain predestination. However, it should be pointed out that those who argue free will can also use the concept of infinity to substantiate their point of view, as well.

Pascal discusses the mathematical concept of infinity and contrasts it to its opposite, nothing: "Infinite-nothing.-Our soul is cast into a body, where it finds number, time, dimension. Thereupon it reasons, and calls this nature, necessity, and can believe nothing else. Unity joined to infinity adds nothing to it, no more than one foot to an infinite measure. The finite is annihilated in the presence of the infinite, and becomes a pure nothing. So our spirit before God, so our justice before divine justice. There is not so great a disproportion between our justice and that of God, as between unity and infinity."[94] The soul, that which does not have time or extension, is cast into the physical body, where it finds number, time, and dimension. This is not only a mathematical statement contrasting infinity to zero, it is also an amazingly prescient one regarding physics: Pascal is telling us that number, time, and dimension are characteristics of not only this physical body, but of all the created universe. The salient point here is that time is an attribute of the created universe and is therefore finite. Hence, one must necessarily extrapolate that the moment when Christ spoke and brought the universe into existence (John 1:1-3), He created space and time. Therefore, God antecedes time and He exists outside of it.

Pascal also points out that Christ is infinite and eternal: "In the same way I am not eternal or infinite; but I see plainly that there exists in nature a necessary Being, eternal and infinite."[95] Christ is the Creator who spoke and brought the universe into existence from nothing. The Apostle John declares, "In the beginning was the Word, and the Word was with God, and the Word was God. The same was in the beginning with God. All things were made by him; and without him was not any thing that was made" (John 1:1-3). God has the characteristics that are implied by the mathematical concept of infinity: He is eternal, omniscient (all knowing), omnipotent (all powerful), omnipresent (everywhere), absolutely just, sovereign, unchanging, and absolutely faithful to man. Absolute fidelity is intrinsic to the bride/groom metaphor that characterizes the relationship that Christ has with His Church.

God created number, time, and dimension when he spoke and brought the universe into existence. Therefore, number, time, and dimension are creations. Christ antecedes time: He is eternal and everlasting, as He lived before He created the universe and He created time and space at the moment when He created the universe.

Chapter Six: Predestination vs. Free Will

An infinite being cannot be compartmentalized into packets of time or parcels of space. Conversely, man is a finite creature and he can be compartmentalized into a lifespan of a certain number of years and into a physical space occupying certain dimensions.

Since God is eternal and exists outside of time, He does not have a beginning, a lifespan, or an end. Therefore, the past, the present, and the future are all the same to Him, they all exist as if they are all the past, or all the present, or all the future. This is why God knows future events before man experiences them: God can experience the future in the present. The Bible says in several places that in God's eyes, a thousand years are like a day and one day is like a thousand years: "For a thousand years in thy sight are but as yesterday when it is past, and as a watch in the night" (Psalm 90:4); "But, beloved, be not ignorant of this one thing, that one day is with the Lord as a thousand years, and a thousand years as one day" (2 Pet 3:8).

Pascal was a brilliant mathematician who was able to exploit the certainty that mathematics can bring to a problem as a tool to further his own heretical polemics. He applied infinity to theological issues and in this way, he found a way to explain foreknowledge and predestination. He took the flawed position that an eternal being, one who has no beginning or end, one who exists outside the realm of time because time is his creation, has foreknowledge of men and so one can say that He predestinates according to His foreknowledge.

However, the Orthodox Church points out that the opposite is actually true. It teaches that it is man's future choices that lead to God's foreknowledge, not the other way around. The key is in Rom 8:29, "For whom He did foreknow, he also did predestinate to be conformed to the image of his Son." Minatios advises, "This is how the wise Justin, philosopher and martyr, speaks about this: 'The cause of future events is not foreknowledge, but foreknowledge is the result of future events. The future does not flow forth from foreknowledge, but foreknowledge from the future. It is not Christ who is the cause of the betrayal of Judas. But the betrayal is the cause of the Lord's foreknowledge.'"[96] Man has free will because 1) He was made in the image of God and God has free will, 2) God wants sons and daughters conformed to the image of Christ, that is, people who choose to be obedient to the Father, and 3) without free will, man cannot be held responsible for his actions and reward and punishment would not be due; Christ's redemptive mission would have been unnecessary. Because God exists outside of time, he knows the future. It is the future (comprised of the choices that men freely make) that forms God's foreknowledge. Man has free will, as in Rev 3:20, "Behold, I stand at the door, and knock: if any man hear my voice, and open the door, I will come in to him, and will sup with him, and he with me." Christ makes the first move: He knocks on the door; now the ball is in man's side of the court-he can exercise his free will and either open the door to his heart to Christ or not. The moment that man reaches towards Christ, Christ reaches towards him. The moment one believes, God infuses him with grace. If man does choose to open the door to Christ, then the sequence of events will follow as enumerated in Rom 8:29-30: he will be given the grace to be conformed to the image of Christ (predestinated), called, justified, and glorified, in that order.

Pascal's heresies

Pascal was seduced by the lie that God's will subordinates and dominates man's will so that in the end, man has no free will. The subtleties of the heresy in Pascal's hermeneutics are sometimes so fine and so contrived, it is frequently difficult to navigate the waters and discern his orthodox statements from his heretical ones. This is because Pascal owed his thought not only to the heretics Jansenius, Saint-Cyran, and Arnaud, but also to the writings of Saint Paul, whose statements were subverted and propagandized by the Jansenists. Hence, it is not surprising that Pascal uses Paul's language regarding predestination. Pascal frequently uses the terms "elect" [*élu*], "elect ones" [*les élus*], "chosen" [*choisi*], "the chosen vine" [*la vigne élue*], "called" [*appelé*] prediction [*prediction*], to predict [*prédire*], predicted [*prédit*], to portend [*présager*].

For example, in B550/L931/S759 he declares that he is very relieved and continually grateful that God, in His mercy, has given him the gift of saving faith. This feeling is sincere and felt by all Christians who read and understand the Scripture, "For by grace are ye saved through faith; and that not of yourselves: it is the gift of God" (Eph 2:8). Pascal, breathing a sigh of relief, says, "These are my sentiments, and every day of my life I bless my Redeemer, who has implanted them in me, and who, of a man full of weaknesses, of miseries, of lust, of pride, and of ambition, has made a man free from all these evils by the power of His grace, to which all the glory of it is due, as of myself I have only misery and error."[97] This seems innocuous enough. He is merely articulating gratitude that his salvation has been sealed by Christ's very generous gift on the Cross; his statement is an orthodox one, not a heretical one.

However, in a subsequent fragment, he goes on to reiterate the heresy that God "has willed to blind some and enlighten others": "We understand nothing of the works of God, if we do not take as a principle that He has willed to blind some, and enlighten others."[98] Here Pascal is taking Scriptures out of context in order to sustain his own heretical polemics.

On the contrary, the reason that God announces all significant events in advance is that He does want people to eagerly await these happenings and recognize them when they do occur. God announces in hundreds of biblical verses that the Messiah is coming. For example, the Gentiles will see the Light. God announces this in advance precisely because He did give men free will and it was His will that they be vigilant and recognize the Messiah when he arrived. That is why God continually reiterates throughout the OT that the Messiah is coming and that people should anticipate His arrival, be vigilant for signs that he has come, and obey Him when He does arrive. These are all warnings from a God who has given men free will and who ardently desires that they choose to obey Him so that He can conform them to the image of Christ. When they believe and are baptized, they take the first step on the road towards theosis (union with God via conformity to Christ's image). God reiterates the word "blind" to warn people that that is what they should not be: "And he said, Go, and tell this people, Hear ye indeed, but understand not; and see ye indeed, but perceive not" (Is 6:9); "To open the blind eyes, to bring out the prisoner from prison, and them that sit in darkness out of the prison house" (Is 42:7); "And I will bring the blind by a way that they knew not; I will lead them in paths that they have not" (Is 42:16); "Hear, ye deaf; and look, ye blind, that ye may see" (Is 42:18); "Who is blind, but my servant: or deaf, as my messenger that I sent? Who is blind as he that is perfect, and blind as the LORD's servant?" (Is 42:19); "Seeing many things, but thou observest not; opening the ears, but he heareth not" (Is 42:20); "we wait for light, but behold obscurity; for brightness, but we walk in darkness. We grope for the wall like the blind, and we grope as if we had no eyes: we stumble at noon day as in the night" (Is 59:9-10). These are the words of a God who went out of His way to continually caution that one should not be blind, but rather, seeing; not ignorant, but rather, wise. As Orthodoxy points out, the future is not sealed; it can change from moment to moment. Therefore, God warns people to be vigilant and watch for the Messiah, precisely because they do have free will to accept or reject Him. We see that even though God repeatedly gave many prophecies warning people to remain vigilant, and not be blind or deaf, nevertheless, the future did happen exactly as prophecized. Again, man has free will and the choices that he makes in the future determines God's foreknowledge; it is not the other way around.

God has kept His promise that He announces all things before they happen. Even this fact must be reiterated, lest one forget: "Behold, the former things are come to pass, and new things do I declare: before they spring forth I tell you of them" (Is 42:9); "who hath declared this from ancient time? Who hath told it from that time? Have not I the LORD?" (Is 45:21); "Remember the former things of old...Declaring the end from the beginning, and from ancient times the things that are not yet done" (Is 46:9-10); "I have declared the former things from the beginning; and they went forth out of my mouth, and I shewed them; I did them suddenly, and they came to pass...I have even from the beginning declared it to thee... Thou hast heard, see all this; and will not ye declare it? I have shewed thee new things from this time, even hidden things, and thou didst not know them. They are created now, and not from the beginning; even before the day when thou heardest them not; lest thou shouldest say, Behold, I knew them" (Is 48:3, 5-7). These are the words of a God who is making a concerted effort to direct people; they are not the words of a God who has predestined people to disbelief and then remained aloof. It was God's will that the world have the timetable of the Messiah's arrival so that when He performed His miracles, it would know that He had arrived and it would obey Him and submit to His authority. Remember, submission to Christ's authority is the first step on a ladder leading towards theosis or union with God. God's goal is to fill Heaven with many Christ-like individuals; Christ will be the first among many brethren in His Father's Kingdom. All of these people will have already demonstrated their willingness to obey and to trust in God. God does not want any repeats of angelic rebellions.

The multitudes gathered around the Lord and He both taught them and fed them. Those who wanted to conform their will to God's and submit to His authority are metaphorized as sheep in the Bible. Jesus continually metaphorizes his followers as sheep. They are sheep because they have exercized their free will and have chosen to submit themselves to the will of the Master, to align themselves with His will: "I am the good shepherd, and know my sheep, and am known of mine" (John 10:14) (He knows who they will be in advance because He sees the future); "But ye believe not, because ye are not of my sheep, as I said unto you" (John 10:26) (He knows in advance those who will reject Him); "My sheep hear my voice, and I know them, and they follow me" (John 10:27). Who are the sheep of God? Those who seek Him and desire to be the means by which His will is done on earth and in Heaven.

The problem is that Pascal's statements do lead to predestinarianism. His heresy is that God foists His will on men and that His foreknowledge determines men's future actions. In Pascal's cosmology, all men are robots as far as their destiny goes.

In the chapter on miracles we have seen how Pascal uses continual contradiction (thesis, antithesis) as a tool to demonstrate that the power of reason is limited. He uses this same tool in his discussions on the problem of predestination vs. free will to state what on the surface appears to be a contradiction and to then resolve the conflict with his own propaganda. For example, he cites Mat 7:7, in which the Lord says, "Ask and it shall be given you."[99] In this imperative statement, Christ commands us to pray and ask for what we need. When we do, He will answer our prayers. Pascal reiterates this command by concluding, "Therefore, it is in our power to ask."[100] The issue appears to be settled.

However, then there is a surprise: Pascal then undermines the argument that he has just made, that it is in man's power to ask God for things, and begins to introduce a heresy. He adds, "On the other hand, there is God. So it is not in our power, since the obtaining of (the grace) to pray to Him is not in our power. For since salvation is not in us, and the obtaining of such grace is from Him, prayer is not in our power."[101] Unfortunately, this is a heretical statement and contrary to Christ's command in Luke 11:5-8 to pray continuously and unceasingly. Pascal articulates the lie that the elect pray because God has foisted His will on their will by giving them "efficacious grace." The elect may pray, but they do so because God's dominates theirs and they are forced to pray because it is His will; their will is subservient to His. The reader is led to conclude, having read this paragraph in B514/L969/S803, that prayer is not within man's power. This position is diametrically antithetical to Christ's command that we diligently labor in all things to carry out God's will.

But, wait, it gets worse! Pascal carries his heresy even further: he argues long and hard that God has deliberately veiled the Messianic prophecies in the OT so that those individuals that He predestined to disbelieve would never recognize the Messiah when He came and that they would therefore reject Him. This is not only heretical, it is also blasphemous: it articulates the lie that God does evil. The truth is that it was Christ's ardent will to minister unto all people, to the reprobate and to the godly, regardless of ethnicity or gender, to the freeman and to the slave. God's Divine Uncreated Energies, His will and foreknowledge, are distinct, and even though He wills obedience, He does not impose it; men's future choices based on their own free will determine His foreknowledge.

Pascal's statements are the exact opposite of the truth: God provides a panoply of Messianic prophecies that can be readily recognized by all, saint and reprobate alike, in the OT. In fact, Alfred Edersheim counts 456 Messianic prophecies that Christ has fulfilled ie: that He would be born in Bethlehem, of a virgin, of the house of David, that He would die in our place for our transgressions, that they would look up at Him whom they have pierced, that His legs would not be broken, that they would cast lots for His clothing, that His soul would not suffer corruption, that he would rise on the third day, that He would sit on the right hand of the Father, that He is ancient, from time everlasting, that He would be a stumbling block that many would fall on, that He would be the cornerstone that the builders rejected. Even before His Crucifixion, Christ made it clear that He was God: He raised Lazarus from the dead, as well as Jairus' daughter and the widow's son at Nain. Only God can raise the dead. In addition, He fed more than 4,000 and 5,000 people from a few fish and loaves of bread on

Chapter Six: Predestination vs. Free Will

two occasions; he healed the sick. Nicodemus, a member of the Sanhedrin, admitted that the miracles that Jesus performed attested to the fact that He was from God. Nothing was hidden from anyone. Pascal's "hidden God" cannot be justified. Christ knocked on everyone's door in full view, in broad daylight. Men had miracles, prophecy, and Christ's teachings by which to decide whether or not to follow Him. They had 100% free will 100% of the time.

Moreover, God continually and relentlessly reiterates in the OT that He announces all things in advance, the end from the beginning, expressly for the purpose that everyone will know what to expect, will be watchful, will be the first to know when an anticipated event transpires. Hence, Pascal's argumentation that God veils His language so that it is unintelligible is the exact opposite of Scriptural teaching and a perversion of God's goodness.

Pascal continually reiterates the heresy that God blinds people and that He hides Himself from them so that He does not have to save them: "From those who are in despair at being without faith, we see that God does not enlighten them; but as to the rest, we see there is a God who makes them blind";[102] "…He has willed to leave them in the loss of the good which they do not want. It was not then right that He should appear in a manner manifestly divine, and completely capable of convincing all men…";[103] "We understand nothing of the works of God, if we do not take as a principle that He has willed to blind some, and enlighten others";[104] "Therefore it was well that the spiritual meaning should be concealed…";[105] "*God willing to blind and to enlighten*";[106] "There is sufficient obscurity to blind the reprobate, and sufficient clearness to condemn them, and make them inexcusable";[107] "*That God willed to hide Himself*…God being thus hidden, every religion which does not affirm that God is hidden, is not true; and every religion which does not give the reason of it, is not instructive. Our religion does all this: '*Vere tu es Deus absconditus*'" [Truly you are the hidden God, Is 45:15];[108] "He is to blind the learned and the wise, Is 6, 8, 29."[109]

In response to Pascal's hidden God, a few general comments must be made about Christ's ministry. First, He had mercy on all people, regardless of ethnic origin. This is evident in the story about the Canaanite woman whose daughter He healed (Mat 15:22-28). Secondly, He clearly demonstrated that the Kingdom of Heaven was at hand: He raised the dead, healed the sick, conducted exorcisms, and fed more than 4,000 and 5,000 people on two different occasions in order to convince people to believe in Him. It was evident that this was the awaited Messiah who had the power to abolish death forever and set up an eternal kingdom on earth. Furthermore, there were no wars anywhere while He was on earth. There were wars before His birth and after His Crucifixion, but while the Prince of Peace was on earth, there were no wars. This is a significant reprieve from war on earth.

Thirdly, in Rev 10:8-10 there is a significant lesson regarding man's free will to receive the Word of God. In these verses, an angel (Christ) is holding a book. John says to the angel, "Give me the little book," but rather than hand it over, the angel replies, "Take it." John is required to reach forward and actually lift the book out of the angel's hand. This is significant: these verses are teaching us that God does not force His will on anyone. Man is commanded to take God's gifts, but God does not force them into men's hands. Man has to reach forward and grasp them: "And the voice which I heard from heaven spake unto me again, and said, Go and take the little book which is open in the hand of the angel which standeth upon the sea and upon the earth. And I went unto the angel, and said unto him, Give me the little book. And he said unto me, Take it, and eat it up…And I took the little book out of the angel's hand, and ate it up…" (Rev 10:8-10).

Christ does not thrust the book into John's hands: rather, he stretches out his hands and commands, "Take it." This is very revealing. This scene is an iconic representation of the fact that the Word exists, but God is not going to force feed it to anyone. Rather, people have free will and the choice to either obey or disobey Christ's command, "Take it." Those who are obedient will receive many more gifts, the greatest of which is eventual theosis or union with God. "Take it," therefore, is a command, but man has the option of obedience or disobedience. The Gospel is available to the whole world, but men must reach forward of their own free will and accept it.

Hence, we can now discern just how erroneous Pascal's continual reiteration that God withholds "efficacious grace" from "those he has already damned" really is. His doctrine is antithetical to Christ's words. The longer that Pascal thought about the statements that he made, the more they must have troubled him. Let us examine the following statements that contradict

Chapter Six: Predestination vs. Free Will

Christ's declaration that He came to minister unto sinners: "We understand nothing of the works of God, if we do not take as a principle that He has willed to blind some, and enlighten others";[110] "Jesus Christ does not say that He is not of Nazareth, in order to leave the wicked in their blindness; nor that He is not Joseph's son";[111] "Jesus Christ came to blind those who saw clearly, and to give sight to the blind; to heal the sick, and leave the healthy to die; to call to repentance, and to justify sinners, and to leave the righteous in their sins; to fill the needy, and leave the rich empty";[112] "There is sufficient clearness to enlighten the elect, and sufficient obscurity to humble them. There is sufficient obscurity to blind the reprobate, and sufficient clearness to condemn them, and make them inexcusable. The genealogy of Jesus Christ in the Old Testament is intermingled with so many others that are useless, that it cannot be distinguished. If Moses had kept only the record of the ancestors of Christ, that might have been too plain."[113]

These are all false assertions: quite to the contrary, Christ came to minister unto all people, regardless of ethnicity, as all have sinned and have fallen short of the glory of God. God does not force Himself on anyone. Man can willfully separate himself from God. When this happens, God does not force Himself on man.

Nicodemus, a member of the Sanhedrin, visited Jesus one night and they discussed spiritual matters. Jesus taught him that in order to enter Heaven a man must be born of water and of the Spirit; those that are born of the Spirit are like the wind, no one knows where they go (John 3:5-8). Nicodemus was incredulous and asked, "How can this be?" Christ responded, "We speak that we do know, and testify that we have seen; and ye receive not our witness. If I have told you earthly things, and ye believe not, how shall you believe, if I tell you of heavenly things?" (John 3:11-12). That answers Pascal's point "Jesus Christ does not say that He is not of Nazareth, in order to leave the wicked in their blindness; nor that he is not Joseph's son."[114] On the contrary, Christ's response to Nicodemus in John 3:11-12 indicates that there is no point in explaining spiritual matters (ie: that He was born in Bethlehem in fulfillment of Micah 5:2; that His heavenly parentage is also in fulfillment of Micah 5:2 and Prov 30:4), to a man who rejects His earthly teachings.

In addition the NT recounts an instance in which a group of people, whose hearts were hardened against Christ, entered the Temple and asked Him who had given Him the authority to do the things He did (Mark 11:28). Christ replied that He would also ask them one question, and after they answer, He would tell them by what authority He performed His miracles. Christ asked them, "The baptism of John, was it from heaven, or of men?" (Mark 11:30). They reasoned among themselves that if they replied, "From heaven," He would ask them why they did not believe him. Conversely, if they replied, "Of men," the populace would revolt against them because it regarded John as a prophet. Therefore, they answered, "We cannot tell." Jesus responded, "Neither do I tell you by what authority I do these things" (Mark 11:33).

There is a parallel here: Christ's question implies that His authority, like that of John's baptism, comes from God. When He asked them the question, He already knew, even before they entered the Temple, that they had chosen separation from Him and that they did not want to surrender to His authority. When they would not admit that John's baptism was from God, they were professing their rejection of Him. They preferred to maintain authority over themselves, rather than surrender to His. Since Christ had the ability to look into their hearts and discern their choice to remain separate from Him, He let them exercise their free will and have what they wanted. He did not press His authority on them. It was up to them to submit to His authority. Here we see free will. Christ did not force His will on theirs. They chose to reject Him even before they entered the Temple to question Him. He knew that and so He did not bother to reveal Himself any more than He had already done. Again, His words to Nicodemus are relevant here: "…ye receive not our witness. If I have told you earthly things, and ye believe not, how shall you believe, if I tell you of heavenly things?" (John 3:11-12). He already knocked on their door many, many times, by performing miracles in front of them.

In his *Writings on Grace*, Pascal expounds further on the notion that God foists his will upon man by giving "irresistible efficacious grace" to those He has selected to save and withholding it from those He has chosen to damn. Let us expose Pascal's heresies by the light of the Orthodox faith. Pascal declares, "It is also true that those who are damned certainly

Chapter Six: Predestination vs. Free Will

wished to commit the sins which merited their damnation, and that God too wished to condemn them."[115] The first clause may or may not be true, but the second is clearly false: Pascal does not know what is in men's hearts, only God does; he does not know that those who sin want to; they may be compulsive and cannot control themselves; they may have learned bad habits under the influence of bad friends; perhaps they sin from ignorance. He cannot truthfully say that everyone who sins wants to. His statement is based on Augustine's view that man is driven by his passions and that his power of reasoning is subordinate to his passions. This is based on the Latin mistranslation of Rom 5:12 that all men have inherited Adam's sin. Again, the original Greek says that men inherit Adam's punishment, which is death and disease, not his sin. The second clause, "God too wished to condemn them," is a lie. Nowhere in the Bible does it say that God wishes to condemn anyone. Rather, the contrary is true. Christ suffered a horrific death on the Cross in our place for our transgressions: "For God so loved the world, that he gave his only begotten Son, that whosoever believeth in him should not perish, but have everlasting life" (John 3:16). Grace is freely offered to everyone. However, God's Will (that all men obey) and His foreknowledge are two separate Divine Uncreated Energies, and hence, he imposes His will on no one. He wants to save the sinner, but He will not abrogate man's free will.

When men move towards God, God moves towards them. When people search for God, they find Him. God does not wish to damn anyone. It is man who chooses separation from God. Pascal's heretical statement, "God too wished to condemn them" is very clever and very nuanced. Carried to its logical conclusion, one would determine that there is no point in trying to save anyone, nullifying the Great Commission. The longer that Pascal thought about the statements that he made, the more they must have troubled him. How could a just and loving God elect people for damnation? The answer is that He does not: having been made in the image of God, men have free will. It is the choices that they make in the future that determine God's foreknowledge, not the other way around.

He goes on to introduce a Jansenist heresy: to achieve the salvation of man after the fall, God sent Jesus Christ "for the salvation of those only whom he chose and predestined amongst that body. That it was only for their salvation that Jesus Christ died, and the others, for whose salvation he did not die, have not been spared universal and just damnation."[116] Here Pascal articulates the heresy that God chooses men for salvation or damnation. He declares that amid this mass population of people worthy of eternal death, he has selected certain individuals that would stand apart from the rest: "However, it pleased God to choose, elect, and distinguish from within this equally corrupt mass, in which he saw only wickedness, a number of people...God distinguished his elect from the others for reasons unknown to men and angels through pure mercifulness and without any merit."[117]

Pascal's thesis is based on the Latin mistranslation of Rom 5:12 from the original Greek and the subsequent erroneous corollaries that have persisted for two millennia in the West: that all men inherit Adam's sin and that therefore, even unborn and newly born babies are meritorious of eternal damnation. Given his erroneous premise that "all have sinned in Adam," all subsequent suppositions must necessarily be flawed. Nowhere in the Bible does it say that God expressly wants certain men to reject Him, disobey Him, turn away from Him, to go their own way, seek material wealth, to go after idols. Nowhere in the Bible does it say that God chooses people for damnation. Pascal's heretical stance becomes more pronounced in the material that follows.

He goes on to discuss the doctrine of Saint Augustine at length. The reader is led to believe that this is a moderate, middle of the road philosophy that Pascal is promulgating. At this point Pascal declares and then continually reiterates the heresy that God arbitrarily chooses people for salvation or damnation by either giving them irresistible efficacious grace or withholding it from them. The heresy is this: "With the result that men are saved or damned according to whether it pleased God to choose them to be given His grace amongst the corrupt mass of men in which he could justly abandon them all."[118]

In order to be saved, one needs to be given the gift of grace. Thus we have a vicious cycle: man receives grace by reading Scripture, but in order to understand Scripture, he needs grace. This vicious cycle does not exist in Orthodox theology. On the contrary, the Orthodox Church teaches that grace if freely offered to all and man has the free will to accept it or reject it. Hence, man and God are coworkers (*synergoi*) together (1 Cor 3:9).

Chapter Six: Predestination vs. Free Will

What the critics say

Pierre Force, in *The Hermeneutical Problem in Pascal's Writing* (*Le Problème herméneutique chez Pascal*), points out the vicious cycle intrinsic to Augustinian grace. A person needs grace to understand the Bible, but he needs to understand the Bible in order to believe. Force summarizes the hermeneutical problem in Pascal's writing thus: a person looks for enlightenment by reading the Bible, but he will understand what he reads only when he has been already given the gift of grace by God. It is a cycle out of which there is no escape: "The hermeneutical problem lies at the heart of Pascalian apologetics. As an apologist for the Christian religion, Pascal is looking for a cause to have faith. He finds this cause in Scripture. It is in the sacred texts that God speaks to man and gives him reasons to believe. However, the divine nature of the texts becomes visible only to those who already believe. Faith refers to Scripture and Scripture refers to faith, in a circular motion that does not release the apologist from being entangled. Such is, at any rate, the way that modern interpreters of Pascal, from M.J. Lagrange up to Philippe Sellier, pose the problem of the basis of religion. Knowledge of God through scripture seems in fact not to be able to escape from the vicious circle that characterizes, according to Heidegger, the rational understanding of every text..."[119]

Force explains that Pascal's method of converting the skeptic is to place him in the position of reading the Scriptures in order to interpret them.[120] Therefore, the first step is to expose the person to the Bible. The next step is to get him to see that there is a hidden meaning beneath the surface meaning. Once the reader understands that, he will see that the prophecies in the OT were fulfilled in the NT and extrapolate that the fact that one man fulfilled hundreds of prophecies falls outside the realm of chance, coincidence or statistical probability. Pascal says: "*Proofs of the two Testaments at once.*-To prove the two at one stroke, one need only see if the prophecies in one are fulfilled in the other. To examine the prophecies, we must understand them. For if we believe that they have only one meaning, it is certain that the Messiah has not come; but if they have two meanings, it is certain that He has come in Jesus Christ. The whole problem then is to know if they have two meanings."[121] Pascal demonstrates that the most that the Christian apologist can do is to put the skeptic in the position of reading the Bible and then pray that God will do the rest.

Ben Rogers, in *Pascal*, agrees that Pascal used reason to pique the curiosity and appeal to the intellect of the skeptic until God could take the reins of his heart. Pascal believed that the heart has reasons that reason does not know. His goal then, was to appeal to the skeptic's mind until God takes control of the heart: "Pascal is sometimes describes as fideist-someone who believes that religion is a matter of blind faith rather than reasoned belief... But it should be clear that Pascal did not reject reason. On the contrary, his fragments offer arguments for believing in the truth of the Bible and putting one's trust in God; ultimately we come to religious faith through a movement of the heart, but to those who do not have it, we can only give such faith through reasoning, until God gives it by moving their heart' (110)."[122]

Pierre Force, in *Self-Interest before Adam Smith: A Genealogy of Economic Science*, points out that for both Augustine and Pascal, human beings are motivated by pleasure. After the fall, Adam's power of reason became subservient to his passions. Therefore, man will always be ruled by this quest for pleasure. Augustine extrapolated that human beings will always be motivated by pleasure and that people follow God because "His lessons are a pleasure to learn."[123] Force cites Augustine: "Lead us behind you; let us follow the sweet smell of your perfumes...being led on by one's will is not much, if one is not also led on by pleasure. What is it to be led on by pleasure? It is finding one's pleasure in God...If the poet could say, Each is led on by his own pleasure Not necessity, but pleasure, not obligation, but enjoyment; how much more strongly shall humans be led on towards Christ, in whom one enjoys truth, happiness, and justice?...Show a green branch to a sheep, and it will follow you; show walnuts to a child, and he will follow you. If it is true that everyone is led on by his own pleasure, won't they follow Christ revealed by the Father?...This is how the Father attracts us: his lessons are a pleasure to learn."[124]

Force advises that Pascal uses this quote to explain the mechanics of efficacious grace. Force states, "In his *Writings on Grace*, Pascal uses the Augustine quote to explain why God's grace never fails to move those who receive it. The power of grace is comparable, on a spiritual level, to the power a green branch exerts on a sheep, or a bunch of walnuts on a child. It is absolute, because we never fail to choose what pleases us most."[125] Force

Chapter Six: Predestination vs. Free Will

cites Pascal, who said, "Is there anything more evident than the proposition that we always do what delights us most? In other words, we always do what we like best, or we always will what pleases us, or we always will what we will, and in the current, fallen state of our soul, it is inconceivable that the soul could will something other than what it likes to will, i.e. what delights it most."[126] Force adds, "Elsewhere, Pascal claims that pleasure 'is the coin for which we will give others all they want.'"[127]

In *The Art of Persuasion*, Pascal maintains that before the fall, Adam had control over his power of reason. However, after the fall, Adam became irrational and his power of reasoning became subservient to pleasure. Pascal opines, "…we believe almost only in the things we like. Hence, our estrangement from consenting to the truths of the Christian religion which are quite contrary to our pleasures. *Tell us the things we like and we will listen to you* (Adapted, Exod. 20:19), the Jews said to Moses, as if pleasure should regulate belief! So it is to punish this disorder by an order true to himself that God sows his illumination in people's minds only after quelling the rebellion of will by a totally heavenly sweetness which delights and overwhelms it."[128]

Force also discusses Pascal's wager. Many believe that Pascal wrote the wager in order to appeal to the intellect of the skeptic and bring him to Christ. However, Force contends that the wager was not intended to convince anyone. He points out that wishing that something is true is not the same as knowing that it is."[129] The purpose of the wager is to show that it is rational to bet that God exists. If the skeptic argues that he cannot believe, Pascal would retort, "If you are unable to believe, it is because of your passions"[130] and "Since reason impels you to believe and yet you cannot do so, concentrate then not on convincing yourself by multiplying proofs of God's existence but by diminishing your passions."[131]

In other words, Pascal succeeds in proving that it is rational to bet that God exists. However, people do not want to give up the world and its pleasures for a bet. They are slaves to the flesh and worldly pursuits. These are the obstacles in their way. Pascal teaches that if the skeptic can diminish his passions, that is, bring himself to the point where the flesh and worldly pursuits will lose their hold on him, then he can be rational and bet that God exists and live the requisite lifestyle.

It is interesting that Pascal points out the importance of diminishing one's passions in order to get closer to God. There is a parallel point of view in Eastern Orthodox theology. The *Philokalia* advises that the way out of bondage to the flesh is fasting, continual prayer, and by cleaning out the rubbish from one's mind (ie: anger, doubting, greed, and jealousy). However, theosis comes through grace, not through works. The monks perform the works, God sees the works that they will do in the future, and gives grace based on foreknowledge of the future. Again, man's will and God's will are intimately intertwined.

Leszek Kolakowski deems that Pascal was a heretic in his doctrine, even though the Church never declared him to be one; that Pascal concurs with Jansenius and Arnauld on the notion of efficient grace.[132] Kolakowski concludes, "...therefore-even though Pascal does not say so in so many words-that the Jansenists differ from the Calvinists insofar as the status of Adam is concerned, but agree on the subsequent condition of mankind and on efficient grace.[133]

Kolakowski agrees with Force that Pascal puts himself in the skeptic's shoes and articulates the doubter's view of the world, his concerns: "First, to be effective, a defense of religion must examine and recognize the state of mind of the people whom it is supposed to convince. The author has to step into the shoes of his addressee, to take, at least provisionally, his standpoint, his interest."[134]

To convince the skeptic Pascal points to prophecies and miracles as the greatest proofs of Christ. However, Pascal embellishes on the fact that the OT contains hundreds of Messianic prophecies that were fulfilled in Christ. Pascal points out that not only were they fulfilled in Christ, but the prophecies themselves were announced in a veiled way so that only the elect would understand them. Again, Pascal is promulgating the heresy that God wills to hide Himself from select individuals and that He elects the damned. Kolakowski advises:

> ...the dominant theme of the *Pensées*: the hidden God. God discloses himself in part and conceals himself in part, and this is just. The prophecies, conforming to the same order of things, both enlighten and blind: they are understood

unhesitatingly by those who are pure in heart and they portent doom to obdurate sinners. This is indeed both a Jansenist and a Calvinist principle: "there is enough clarity to enlighten the elect and enough obscurity to humiliate them. There is enough obscurity to blind the reproved and enough clarity to condemn and leave them without excuse" (B578/L236/S268). Calvin said the same: however little natural light can instruct us about God, it is just sufficient for the damnation of the damned. That this is so Scripture itself proves to Pascal: "prophecies should be unintelligible to the impious [Dan. 12, Hosea Ult. 10] but intelligible to those who are well instructed" (B727/L487/S734).

No doubt there are many similar warnings in the Scriptures to the effect that God's children listen to, and understand, his words, but others do not.

This leads us back to the same perplexing question: natural light is sufficient to believe in God, but in order to see this you have first to be elected, and to believe.[135]

It is a great shame that Pascal concluded that miracles do not convince anyone, but rather they serve to condemn unbelievers. Kolakowski observes this and he points it out, advising that Pascal teaches that miracles "are not for converting people but for condemning them (B825/L379/S411). This clearly suggests what was said about prophecies: miracles are good enough to deprive the unbelievers of an excuse but not good enough to convert them. Like prophecies, miracles and other proofs are not 'absolutely convincing,' but 'one cannot say that to believe them is to be unreasonable. They have enough light to enlighten some and enough obscurity to blind others. It is not reason that might induce people not to follow what is obvious in them, therefore it must be concupiscence and viciousness of heart.' They show that 'those who follow [these obvious signs] do so by grace and not by reason, and those who run away [from them] do so by concupiscence and not by reason' (B564/L835/S423)."[136] Hence, the elect recognize miracles and the fulfillment of prophecy because they have been given grace and the non-elect are repelled by them because of their passions. This is unscriptural and pure heresy.

Pascal also discusses the importance that the heart plays in salvation: God speaks to the elect in their hearts. Until God reveals Himself in the skeptic's heart, the Christian apologist must try to appeal to his reason. Kolakowski cites Pascal: "therefore those to whom God gave religion by the feeling in their hearts are blessed and legitimately convinced, but to those who do not have it we can give it only by reasoning and wait until God gives it to them by the feeling in their hearts, without which faith in only human and useless for salvation" (B282/L110/S142).[137] Kolakowski advises, "It appears that to know God by 'feeling in one's heart' is the same as having faith in the proper sense, that is, receiving the supernatural gift of grace."[138] In addition, Pascal establishes that the heart, which one might also call "instinct," also grasps certain principles such as space, time, movement, and number. The heart grasps the notion of the dimensions of length, width and height, number and all kinds of mathematical abstractions. Since the heart and instinct are the same, if the Christian apologist can show the skeptic that the fact that Christ fulfilled hundreds of Messianic prophecies is beyond the realm of statistical probability, the instinct or intuition would be able to grasp that. Similarly, miracles such as that of the Holy Thorn, is physical proof that God exists and that He heals. Hence, when Pascal uses prophecies and miracles to appeal to the intellect, he is really striking at intuition, common sense, or the heart.

Other critics have observed and commented on the fact that it is a tragedy that the Jansenist belief system cost Pascal everything that he loved in life-he abandoned his natural talents in mathematics and science because he thought that these subjects were sinful. The harsh Jansenist theology that he continuously imbibed caused him to turn away from the greatest interests in his life, from the things that kept him occupied and distracted him from his illness and physical pain. Critics have noticed this and have commented on the tragic consequences that Jansenism had on one of its most faithful defenders.

Connor elucidates on the great price that Pascal's conversion to Jansenism cost him. By reading Saint-Cyran's *Reformation of the Interior Man* (*Réformation de l'homme intérieur*), Pascal learned all about Cornelius Jansenius' interpretation of Scripture. What struck him was that Jansenius anathematized science and mathematics, the two fields that Pascal loved the most and gave him the most pleasure in an otherwise miserable existence. Unfortunately, Pascal was led to believe that the sciences were evil and that he had to renounce them for Christ.

Connor says, "There was much that troubled Blaise in Saint-Cyran's book-as much as what excited him. In one passage, he read that Jansenius believed that scientific curiosity was nothing more than another kind of sexual indulgence, and this agonized him. Suddenly, the thing that had given Blaise his identity, his greatest joy in life of pain, had become a wickedness. How could he seek the salvation of the soul under these conditions? How much of himself would he have to give up? Everything, it seemed. A shadow fell on his spirit that would never lift."[139]

Anthony Levi also notices the tragic consequences of Pascal's conversion to Jansenism. Levi brilliantly establishes a causality between the fact that Pascal left his *Pensées* unfinished, and the futility of trying to save anyone that is intrinsic to Jansenism. Levi hypothesizes that continually focusing on and arguing on behalf of the doctrine of election, which was an essential point in *Thoughts* may have, ironically, caused Pascal to give up on trying to save the skeptic: "It now seems clear that the project to write an apologetic was not abandoned for reasons of health, as is still often assumed, and even that, on Pascal's own premises, the intended apologetic could have served no purpose, but we have no clear indication from his pen of why he gave up…Pascal believed that without Christian belief and practice the individual's fate was certainly eternal damnation, but, if salvation was God's gratuitous gift to a minority of chosen human souls, how could any moral act, and in particular any freely chosen commitment of belief or behavior, affect the individual's eternal destiny?"[140]

The futility of trying to save the non-elect may be one reason that Pascal left *Thoughts* unfinished. There is another reason that Levi also considers: perhaps Pascal, himself, questioned the rigid belief system that people are destined for non-election through no fault of their own. Levi says, "the apologetic remained unwritten, and it is perfectly possible that in late 1661 Pascal was uncertain about how far he was prepared to allow his theological commitment to go in the fact of the religious realities he had to envisage, including the unceasing pain of the damned on account of no personal choice of their own."[141]

Hence, Pascal's abandonment of *Thoughts* may have been the result of where heresy leads: he embraced the lies that man does not have free will and that God chooses people for destruction. Perhaps that is why he gave up on his goal of using the talents that God had given him to carry out the Great Commission. What a tragedy.

However, not all critics believe that Pascal deliberately abandoned his apologetic work. Some feel that Pascal was able to reconcile Augustinian election with the Great Commission. One is led to ask why, if he believed in the election of the damned, Pascal even bothered to posit a wager as a means to entice skeptics to come to Christ. If he believed that people are predestined to doubt, a wager would be pointless. One would also ask why he worked so hard on a book of considerable length in a quest to win souls for Christ. Harold Bloom, in *Pascal*, has the answer: Pascal acknowledged that the names in the Book of Life are known only to God. Therefore, it is the duty of every Christian to try to save people as long as there is a breath of life in them, and to leave the rest to God. Harold Bloom cites Pascal:

> That all men in this world are compelled, under pain of eternal damnation and of the sin against the Holy Ghost for which there is no forgiveness either in this world or the next, to believe that they belong to the small number of the elect for whose salvation Christ died; and that they should, moreover, believe the same thing about each man and every man who is now on this earth, however wicked and impious he may be; and that for as long as he still has a moment of life; and that all men should leave the distinction between the Elect and the Reprobate as part of the impenetrable secret of God.

And in a highly significant variant, Pascal adds that:

> All men are compelled to believe, but with a belief mingled with fear and not accompanied by certainty, that they belong to the small number of the Elect whom Jesus Christ wishes to save; and that they should never place any man now alive, however wicked and impious he may be, for as long as he has a moment of life, elsewhere than in the

ranks of those He destined, leaving the distinction between the Elect and the Reprobate as part of the impenetrable secret of God. And that they should therefore do for their fellows everything which can contribute to their salvation.

There is thus no contradiction at all between Pascal's complete acceptance of the Augustinian theories on Grace and Predestination and the fact that he acted as if every man could be saved, doing everything possible to contribute to his salvation (in spite of the fact that, in the final analysis, this depends solely upon the Will of God).[142]

Hence, Bloom reconciles Pascal's predeterminist theology with his effort to save souls by pointing out Pascal's belief that it is the duty of every Christian to regard all men as saved as long as they are alive. One wonders, however, how much time Pascal must have spent ruminating about the fact that Jansenism is a affront to reason, God's goodness, God's justice, God's love, and God's mercy.

In summation, we have seen that Pascal's notion of double predestination is based on many errors: on the Latin Vulgate's mistranslation of Rom 5:12 from the original Greek text and on a misinterpretation of Rom 8:29. The Augustinians mistakenly held that God's foreknowledge determines the future, that He chooses to whom He will impart saving grace and to whom He will withhold it before man has had a chance to act.

Fortunately, the Orthodox Church, uninfluenced by Augustine, is present in the world and teaches that man's purpose is to achieve theosis, or union with God. Faith is the first step on a ladder that leads to conformity to the image of Christ. Hence, it becomes evident that the notion of irresistible efficacious grace is diametrically antithetical to the fact that God wants people to be Christ-like, which means obedient to the Father of their own free will, as was Christ when He walked among us and as He is today. It is God's intention that the Kingdom of Heaven be filled with many of His children, of whom Christ is the first among many brethren. This means people who are willing to be instruments by which God's will is realized. Orthodoxy points out that imparting or withholding grace without the cooperation of man results in robots or slaves that are not made in God's image because they do not have free will

Minatios brings our attention critical biblical verses that show that the future is not sealed, but rather, is fluid.[143] His first example recounts Paul's voyage to Italy when he was held captive. A turbulent storm arose at sea, but God sent an angel to tell Paul, "Fear not, Paul...God hath given thee all them that sail with thee" (Acts 27:24). This meant that for the crewmen to be saved, they had to remain in the boat with Paul. However, they had the free will to stay or jump ship. If any of the sailors decided to jump into the water, he did not have the protection of God. Minatios says, "Does God's destination change? Yes, it can be no other way. *Except these abide in the ship, ye cannot be saved.*"[144]

In Minatios' second example, King Hezekiah becomes sick. The prophet Isaiah tells Hezekiah, "Thus saith the LORD, Set thine house in order; for thou shalt die, and not live (2 King 20:1)." When Hezekiah turns his face to the wall, sighs, cries, and pleads, God takes pity on him and decides not only that he will live, but He even grants him fifteen years of life: "I have heard thy prayer, I have seen thy tears: behold, I will heal thee... And I will add unto thy days fifteen years" (2 Ki 20:5-6). The future is fluid. Minatios extrapolates, "The future does not flow from foreknowledge, but foreknowledge from the future."

In a third example, Jeremiah goes to a potter's house and he sees the potter drop a pot that he had been working on. The form of the pot becomes distorted and the pot is ruined. However, the potter picks it up and starts to rework it and make it like new. God tells Jeremiah, "Behold, as the clay is in the potter's hand, so are ye in mine hand" (Jer 18:6). This is another example of the fact that things can change at any moment, given the fact that man has 100% free will 100% of the time.

Therefore, Orthodoxy teaches that the future determines God's foreknowledge; the future is fluid: it is based on man's free will and is subject to change from moment to moment. As soon as man takes a step towards God, God reaches out to Him.

This fits in perfectly with God's plan for man's theosis. God wants beings in Heaven who choose to be with Him, not separate from Him, who trust His judgment and want to align their will with His, not rebel against

Chapter Six: Predestination vs. Free Will

Him. The Bible says, "I have said, Ye are gods; and all of you are children of the most High" (Ps 82:6, John 10:34). Peter implores us to "become partakers of the divine nature" (2 Pet 1:4). *The Philokalia* advises that the way to do this is by continual prayer and fasting, silence, embracing the notion of death rather than fearing it, and cleaning out the heart of anger, desire, greed, jealousy, and unforgiveness. When men believe, God gives them the grace to achieve more, as they strive harder to achieve theosis.

Orthodoxy also points out the difference among God's Uncreated Divine Energies. Each of His Energies are separate and distinct from one another. God's will is separate and distinct from His foreknowledge. God wills that all obey, but He does not compel anyone to do so. He foreknows that evil will exist, but He does not will that it exist. He does not impose His will on men. His foreknowledge is based on the future: The future is fluid and subject to change; it is based on man's free will.

Endnotes

1. Anthony Levi, "Introduction," in *Pensées and Other Writings*, translated by Honor Levi and edited, introduced, and annotated by Anthony Levi (Oxford: Oxford University Press, 1999), ix, xix.
2. James A. Connor, *Pascal's Wager: The Man Who Played Dice with God* (New York: HarperCollins Publishers, 2006), 73.
3. "Predestination," *Oxford English Dictionary Online*, a and b, http://dictionary.oed.com (Apr. 4, 2007).
4. "Free will," *Oxford English Dictionary Online*, 1 and 2a, http://dictionary.oed.com (Apr. 9, 2007).
5. Archimandrite Lev Gillet, *Orthodox Spirituality: An Outline of the Orthodox Ascetical and Mystical Tradition by a Monk of the Eastern Church* 2.2, 2nd ed. (London: SPCK, 1978), 23.
6. St. John Chrysostom, *Sermon on the Words "Saul, Saul..."* 6, in Jacques-Paul Migne, ed., *Patrologiæ cursos completus...Series græca*, 161 vols. (Paris: Migne, 1857-1866), 51:144.
7. Timothy Ware, *The Orthodox Church*, revised edition (London: Penguin Books, 1997), 221-22.
8. Ibid., 222.
9. Ibid., 221.
10. Ibid.
11. Ibid., 222.
12. Bishop Kallistos Ware is Timothy Ware, author of *The Orthodox Church*. He received the name Kallistos in 1966 when he was ordained an Orthodox priest and became a monk.
13. Bishop Kallistos Ware, *The Orthodox Way* (Crestwood, NY: St Vladimir's Seminary Press, 1995), 48.
14. Macarius advises, "The will of man, therefore, is like a support inserted into his nature. When the will is lacking, God himself does nothing, because of man's free will, even though he could. The successful working of the Spirit depends on man's will." St. Macarius, *The Homilies of St. Macarius* 37.10, in *Pseudo Macarius: The Fifty Spiritual Homilies and the Great Letter*, edited, translated, and introduced by George A. Maloney, preface by Bishop Kallistos Ware (New York: Paulist Press, 1992), 210.
15. *The Sayings of the Desert Fathers*, anonymous collection, 122, ed. F. Nau, *Revue de l'orient chrétien* 12 (1907): 403. Page 403 is in Greek. The book translates the saying into French: "122.-Un vieillard dit: Dieu demande à l'homme l'esprit, la parole et l'action." *Histoires des solitaires égyptiens*, 122, ed. F. Nau, *Revue de l'orient chrétien* 12 (1907): 413.
16. Abbot Nazarius of Valaam, *Abbot Nazarius of Valaam*. Vol. 2 of *Little Russian Philokalia*, translated by Father Seraphim Rose (Platina: Saint Herman of Alaska Brotherhood, 1983), 28.
17. St. Theophan the Recluse, *The Fruits of Prayer* 2.2, in Igumen Chariton of Valamo, compiler, *The Art of Prayer: An Orthodox Anthology*, translated by E. Kadloubovsky and E.M. Palmer, edited and introduced by Timothy Ware (London: Faber and Faber Limited, 1966), 133.

Chapter Six: Predestination vs. Free Will

18 Irina Gorainoff, *Séraphim de Sarov* (Bégrolles-en-Mauges: Abbaye de Bellefontaine, 1973), 234.
19 Tito Colliander, *The Way of the Ascetics*, translated by Katharine Ferré, edited and introduced by R.M. French (London: Hodder and Stoughton, 1960), 55.
20 Gregory the Theologian, *Sayings* 2, in *The Sayings of the Desert Fathers: The Alphabetical Collection*, translated with a forward by Sister Benedicta Ward, preface by Metropolitan Anthony of Sourozh, rev. ed. (Kalamazoo: Cistercian Publications, Inc., 1984), 45.
21 Bishop Kallistos Ware, *The Orthodox Way* (Crestwood, NY: St. Vladimir's Seminary Press, 1995), 112-13.
22 Selection from Archimandrite Christoforos Stavropoulos, *Partakers of Divine Nature* (Minneapolis: Light and Life Publishing Co., 1976), in Daniel B. Clendenin, *Eastern Orthodox Theology: A Contemporary Reader*, 2nd edition (Grand Rapids: Baker Academic, 2003), 190-91. Stavropoulos cites Gregory of Nyssa, *Peri tou kata Theon skopou*, in Jacques Paul Migne, ed., *Patrologiæ cursos completus... Series græca*, 161 vols. (Paris: Migne, 1857-1866), 46:289C.
23 Ibid., 191.
24 St. Makarios of Egypt, *St. Symeon Metaphrastis Paraphrase of the Homilies of St. Makarios of Egypt* 1.1, in *The Philokalia*, edited by G.E.H. Palmer, Philip Sherrard, and Kallistos Ware, 4 vols. (London: Faber and Faber Limited, 1979-1995), 3:285.
25 Blaise Pascal, *The Art of Persuasion*, in *Pensées and Other Writings*, translated by Honor Levi and edited, introduced, and annotated by Anthony Levi (Oxford: Oxford University Press, 1999), 193, fragment 3. *The Art of Persuasion* is the second section of *Mathematical Mind* (*De l'esprit géométrique*). "Je sçay qu'il a voulu qu'elles entrent du cœur dans l'esprit, et non pas de l'esprit dans le cœur, pour humilier cette superbe puissance du raisonnement, qui pretend devoir estre juge des choses que la volonté choisit, et pour guerir cette volonté infirme, qui s'est toute corrompue par ses sales attachemens." Blaise Pascal, *De l'art de persuader*, section 2 of *De l'esprit géométrique*, in *Œuvres de Blaise Pascal*, edited by Léon Brunschvicg, Pierre Boutroux, and Félix Gazier (Paris: Librairie Hachette & Cie, 1904-1914), 9:272.
26 Blaise Pascal, *Thoughts*, translated by W. F. Trotter, Brunschvicg numbering system (New York: P. F. Collier & Son, 1910), fragment 273. "Si on soumet tout à la raison, notre religion n'aura rien de mystérieux et de surnaturel." Blaise Pascal, *Pensées*, in *Œuvres de Blaise Pascal*, edited by Léon Brunschvicg, Pierre Boutroux, and Félix Gazier (Paris: Librairie Hachette & Cie, 1904-1914), fragment 273 (Lafuma 173; Sellier 204).
27 Ibid., fragment 269. "Soumission et usage de la raison, en quoi consiste le vrai christianisme." Ibid., fragment 269 (Lafuma 167).
28 Marvin R. O'Connell, *Blaise Pascal: Reasons of the Heart* (Grand Rapids: William B. Eerdmans Publishing Company, 1997), xi. O'Connell cites fragments B277/L423/S680 and B277/L424/S680. "Le cœur a ses raisons, que la raison ne connaît point." Ibid., fragment 277 (Lafuma 423; Sellier 680); "C'est le cœur qui sent Dieu et non la raison. Voilà ce que c'est que la foi: Dieu sensible au cœur, non à la raison." Ibid., fragment 278 (Lafuma 424; Sellier 680).

29 Ibid. O'Connell cites fragment B556/L449/S690. "Le Dieu des chrétiens ne consiste pas en un Dieu simplement auteur des vérités géométriques et de l'ordre des éléments...Mais...est un Dieu d'amour et de consolation; c'est un Dieu qui remplit l'âme et le cœur de ceux qu'il possède; c'est un Dieu...qui s'unit au fond de leur âme; qui la remplit d'humilité, de joie, de confiance, d'amour; qui les rend incapables d'autre fin que de lui-même." Ibid., fragment 556 (Lafuma 449; Sellier 690).
30 Selection from Archimandrite Christoforos Stavropoulos, *Partakers of Divine Nature* (Minneapolis: Light and Life Publishing Co., 1976), in Daniel B. Clendenin, *Eastern Orthodox Theology: A Contemporary Reader*, 2nd edition (Grand Rapids: Baker Academic, 2003), 192.
31 Ibid.
32 *The New Greek-English Interlinear New Testament*, translated by Robert K. Brown and Philip W. Comfort and edited by J. D. Douglas (Carol Stream: Tyndale House Publishers, Inc., 1993), 544.
33 Leszek Kolakowski, *God Owes Us Nothing: A Brief Remark on Pascal's Religion and on the Spirit of Jansenism* (Chicago: The University of Chicago Press, 1998), 32.
34 Bishop Elias Minatios, "On Predestination," *Orthodox Life*, translated by Father Gregory Naumenko 40, no. 6 (Nov-Dec 1990), 27-36.
35 Father Michael Azkoul, "What is Predestination?" in "Book Reviews by Hieromonk Moses and Reader Nicholas Franck." http://www.orthodoxcanada.org/reviews/ (May 2, 2007).
36 Bishop Elias Minatios, "On Predestination," *Orthodox Life*, translated by Father Gregory Naumenko 40, no. 6 (Nov-Dec 1990), 29.
37 Ibid., 30.
38 Ibid., 34.
39 Ibid., 35.
40 Ibid., 34.
41 Ibid., 35.
42 Ibid., 36.
43 Father Michael Azkoul, "What is Predestination?" in "Book Reviews by Hieromonk Moses and Reader Nicholas Franck." http://www.orthodoxcanada.org/reviews/ (May 2, 2007).
44 Ibid.
45 Timothy Ware, *The Orthodox Church*, revised edition (London: Penguin Books, 1997), 69.
46 Ibid.
47 Ibid.
48 Daniel B. Clendenin, *Eastern Orthodox Christianity: A Western Perspective*, 2 ed. (Grand Rapids: Baker Academic, 2003), 120. Clendenin cites Christoforos Stavropoulos, *Partakers of Divine Nature* (Minneapolis: Light and Life, 1976), 17-18.
49 135.
50 Ibid., 135-36. St. Makarios of Egypt, *St. Symeon Metaphrastis Paraphrase of the Homilies of St. Makarios of Egypt* 1.1, in *The Philokalia*, edited by G.E.H.

Chapter Six: Predestination vs. Free Will

Palmer, Philip Sherrard, and Kallistos Ware, 4 vols. (London: Faber and Faber Limited, 1979-1995), 3:285. See also Theodoros the Great Ascetic's invocation of Chrysostom to the same effect: "God does not want us to be lying idly on our backs; therefore he does not effect everything Himself. Nor does he want us to be boastful; therefore He did not give us everything. But having taken away from each of the two alternatives what is harmful, he has left us what is for our good." Theodoros the Great Ascetic, *A Century of Spiritual Texts* 69, in *The Philokalia*, 2:28.

51 Ibid., 136.
52 St. Philotheos of Sinai, *Forty Texts on Watchfulness* 1, in *The Philokalia*, edited by G.E.H. Palmer, Philip Sherrard, and Kallistos Ware, 4 vols. (London: Faber and Faber Limited, 1979-1995), 3:16.
53 Ibid., 16-22.
54 Panagiotes K. Chrestou, *Partakers of God* (Brookline: Holy Cross Orthodox Press, 1984).
55 Daniel B. Clendenin, *Eastern Orthodox Christianity: A Western Perspective*, 2nd edition (Grand Rapids: Baker Academic, 2005), 64-65, 68-69, 117-37, 150, 157-59.
56 Daniel B. Clendenin, ed., *Eastern Orthodox Theology: A Contemporary Reader*, 2nd edition (Grand Rapids: Baker Academic, 2003), 27, 39-40, 54, 57, 60, 69, 183-92.
57 Ben Drewery, "Deification" in *Christian Spirituality: Essays in Honour of Gordon Rupp*, edited by Peter Brooks (London: SCM Press, 1975), 33-62.
58 Eleuterio Fortino, "Sanctification and Deification," *Diakonia* 17, no. 3 (1982): 192-200.
59 Jules Gross, *La divinisation du chrétien d'après les pères grecs; contribution historique à la doctrine de la grâce* (Paris: J. Gabalda et Cie, 1938).
60 Vigen Guroian, *Incarnate Love: Essays in Orthodox Ethics* (Notre Dame: University of Notre Dame Press, 1987), 14-17, 22, 27.
61 Harakas, Stanley S. "Eastern Orthodox Christianity's Ultimate Reality and Meaning: Triune God and Theosis; An Ethician's View," *Ultimate Reality and Meaning* 8, no. 3 (1985): 209-23.
62 Verna Harrison, "Some Aspects of Saint Gregory the Theologian's Soteriology," *Greek Orthodox Theological Review* 34, no. 1 (Spring 1989): 11-18.
63 Maurice Fred Himmerich, *Deification in John of Damascus*, Ph.D diss., Marquette University, 1985.
64 Cheslyn Jones, Geoffrey Wainwright and Edward Yarnold, *The Study of Spirituality* (New York: Oxford University Press, 1986), 11, 100-01, 158, 161-62, 189, 194-95, 235-36, 251-52.
65 Stephen James Juli, *The Doctrine of Theosis in the Theology of Saint Maximus the Confessor*, S.T.L. thesis, Catholic University of America, 1990.
66 Vladimir Lossky, *In the Image and Likeness of God*, introduced by A.M. Allchin (London: Mowbrays, 1974).
67 Vladimir Lossky, *Orthodox Theology: An Introduction*, translated by Ian and Ihita Kesarcodi-Watson (Crestwood: St. Vladimir's Seminary Press, 1978).
68 Myrrha Lot-Borodine, *La déification de l'homme selon la doctrine des Pères grecs* (Paris: Editions du Cerf, 1970).

69 Georgios I. Mantzaridis, *The Deification of Man: St. Gregory Palamas and the Orthodox Tradition*, translated by Liadain Sherrard, forward by Bishop Kallistos Ware (Crestwood: St. Vladimir's Seminary Press, 1984).
70 John Meyendorff, *Byzantine Theology: Historical Trends and Doctrinal Themes* (New York: Fordham University Press, 1974), 2-4, 32-33, 35, 39, 49, 67-68, 72, 77, 103, 133, 138-41, 146, 153, 163-64, 169, 171-75, 186-88, 205, 215, 219, 221, 225-26.
71 John Meyendorff, *Christ in Eastern Christian Thought* (Washington DC: Corpus Books, 1969), ix, 10, 13, 97, 109, 114-15, 129-31, 145-46, 151, 156, 159, 164.
72 John Meyendorff, "New Life in Christ: Salvation in Orthodox Theology," *Theological Studies* 50, no. 3 (September 1989): 481-99.
73 John Meyendorff, "Theosis in the Eastern Christian Tradition," *Christian Spirituality: Post-Reformation and Modern*, edited by Louis Dupré and Don E. Saliers in collaboration with John Meyendorff (New York: The Crossroad Publishing Company, 1989), 470-76.
74 John Meyendorff and Robert Tobias, ed., *Salvation in Christ: A Lutheran-Orthodox Dialogue* (Minneapolis: Augsburg Fortress Publishing House, 1992).
75 Panayiotis Nellas, *Deification in Christ: Orthodox Perspectives on the Nature of the Human Person* (Crestwood: St. Vladimir's Seminary Press, 1987).
76 Keith Edward Norman, *Deification: The Content of Athanasian Soteriology*, Ph.D diss., Duke University, 1980.
77 George Papademetriou, "The Human Body according to Saint Gregory Palamas," *Greek Orthodox Theological Review* 34, no. 1 (Spring 1989): 1-9.
78 *The Philokalia: The Complete Text; Compiled by St. Nikodimos of the Holy Mountain and St. Makarios of Corinth*, translated and edited by G.E.H. Palmer, Philip Sherrard, Kallistos Ware, 4 vols. (London: Faber and Faber Limited, 1979-1995), 1:155, 288, 349, 355; 2:38, 43, 48, 86-87, 125, 135, 143, 171, 173, 177-78, 181-82, 190, 193, 216, 218-19, 240, 243, 246, 248, 263, 267, 271, 276, 278, 282-84, 286-87, 297, 304, 312, 364, 375; 3:34, 38, 48, 76, 79, 93, 98, 124, 130, 139, 142; 4:56, 82, 134-35, 148, 153, 189, 213, 220-22, 258, 265, 291-92, 378, 381, 389-90, 392, 396-97, 419-21.
79 Symeon Rodger, "The Soteriology of Anselm of Canterbury, an Orthodox Perspective," *Greek Orthodox Theological Review* 34, no. 1 (Spring 1989): 19-43.
80 Bernard Sartorius, *La doctrine de la déification de l'homme d'après les Pères grecs en général et Grégoire Palamas en particulier* (Geneva: Cercle du Bibliophile, 1965).
81 Dumitru Stăniloae, *The Experience of God*, translated and edited by Ioan Ioniță and Robert Barringer, foreword by Bishop Kallistos Ware (Brookline: Holy Cross Orthodox Press, 1994).
82 Christoforos Stavropoulos, *Partakers of Divine Nature* (Minneapolis: Light and Life Publishing Company, 1976), 17-38.
83 Gregory Telepneff and James Thornton, "Arian Transcendence and the Notion of Theosis in Saint Athanasios," *Greek Orthodox Theological Review* 32, no. 3 (Fall 1987): 271-77.
84 Nicolaos P. Vassiliades, "The Mystery of Death," *Greek Orthodox Theological Review* 29 (Autumn 1984): 269-82.

85 Bishop Kallistos Ware, *The Orthodox Way*, revised edition (Crestwood: St. Vladimir's Seminary Press, 1995), 22, 74, 109, 125-26.
86 Timothy Ware, *The Orthodox Church* (London: Penguin Books, 1997), 21, 219, 231-38.
87 "Predestinarianism," *Catholic Encyclopedia: An International Work of Reference on the Constitution, Doctrine, Discipline, and History of the Catholic Church*, edited by Charles G. Herbermann, Edward A. Pace, et al (New York: Robert Appleton Company, 1907-1912), 12:376.
88 Ibid.
89 Ibid.
90 Ibid.
91 James A. Connor, *Pascal's Wager: The Man Who Played Dice with God* (New York: HarperCollins Publishers, 2006), 62-63.
92 Ibid., 160.
93 Ibid., 163.
94 Blaise Pascal, *Thoughts*, translated by W. F. Trotter, Brunschvicg numbering system (New York: P. F. Collier & Son, 1910), fragment 233. "*Infini. Rien.-* Notre âme est jetée dans le corps, où elle trouve nombre, temps, dimensions. Elle raisonne là-dessus, et appelle cela nature, nécessité, et ne peut croire autre chose.

L'unité jointe à l'infini ne l'augmente de rien, non plus qu'un pied à une mesure infinie. Le fini s'anéantit en presence de l'infini, et devient un pur néant. Ainsi notre esprit devant Dieu; ainsi notre justice devant la justice divine. Il n'y a pas si grande disproportion entre notre justice et celle de Dieu, qu'entre l'unité et l'infini." Blaise Pascal, *Pensées*, in *Œuvres de Blaise Pascal*, edited by Léon Brunschvicg, Pierre Boutroux, and Félix Gazier (Paris: Librairie Hachette & Cie, 1904-1914), fragment 233 (Lafuma 418; Sellier 680).
95 Ibid., fragment 469. "Je ne suis pas aussi eternal, ni infini; mais je vois bien qu'il y a dans la nature un être nécessaire, éternel et infini" Ibid., fragment 469 (Lafuma 135; Sellier 167).
96 Bishop Elias Minatios, "On Predestination." http://www.orthodoxinfo.com/inquirers/predestination.aspx (May 2, 2007).
97 Blaise Pascal, *Thoughts*, translated by W. F. Trotter, Brunschvicg numbering system (New York: P. F. Collier & Son, 1910), fragment 550. "Voilà quels sont mes sentiments, et je bénis tous les jours de ma vie mon Rédempteur qui les a mis en moi, et qui, d'un homme plein de faiblesse, de misère, de concupiscence, d'orgueil et d'ambition, a fait un homme exempt de tous ces maux par la force de sa grâce, à laquelle toute la gloire en est due, n'ayant de moi que la misère et l'erreur." Blaise Pascal, *Pensées*, in *Œuvres de Blaise Pascal*, edited by Léon Brunschvicg, Pierre Boutroux, and Félix Gazier (Paris: Librairie Hachette & Cie, 1904-1914), fragment 550 (Lafuma 931; Sellier 759).
98 Ibid., fragment 566. ""On n'entend rien aux ouvrages de Dieu, si on ne prend pour principe qu'il a voulu aveugler les uns, et éclairer les autres." Ibid., fragment 566 (Lafuma 232; Sellier 264).
99 Ibid., fragment 514. "...*Petenti dabitur*." Ibid., fragment 514 (Lafuma 969; Sellier 803).

100 Ibid. "Donc, il est en notre pouvoir de demander." Ibid.
101 Ibid. "Au contraire du…Il n'y est pas, puisque l'obtention qui le prierait n'y est pas. Car puisque le salut n'y est pas, et que l'obtention y est, la prière n'y est pas." Ibid.
102 Ibid., fragment 202. "Par ceux qui sont dans le déplaisir de se voir sans foi, on voit que Dieu ne les éclaire pas; mais les autres, on voit qu'il y a un Dieu qui les aveugle." Ibid., fragment 202 (Lafuma 596; Sellier 493).
103 Ibid., fragment 430. "…il a voulu les laisser dans la privation du bien qu'ils ne veulent pas. Il n'était donc pas juste qu'il parût d'une manière manifestement divine, et absolument capable de convaincre tous les homes…" Ibid., fragment 430 (Lafuma 149; Sellier 182).
104 Ibid., fragment 566. "On n'entend rien aux ouvrages de Dieu, si on ne prend pour principe qu'il a voulu aveugler les uns, et éclairer les autres." Ibid., fragment 566 (Lafuma 232; Sellier 264).
105 Ibid., fragment 571. "Si le sens spiritual eût été découvert, ils n'étaient pas capables de l'aimer; et, ne pouvant le porter, ils n'eussent point eu le zèle pour la conservation de leurs livres et de leurs ceremonies…

Voilà pourquoi il était bon que le sens spiritual fût couvert…" Ibid., fragment 571 (Lafuma 502; Sellier 738).
106 Ibid., fragment 576. "*Dieu voulant aveugler et éclairer.*" Ibid., fragment 576 (Lafuma 594; Sellier 491).
107 Ibid., fragment 578. "Il y a assez d'obscurité pour aveugler les réprouvés et assez de clarté pour les condemner et les rendre inexcusables." Ibid., fragment 578 (Lafuma 236; Sellier 268).
108 Ibid., fragment 585. "*Que Dieu s'est voulu cacher…*

Dieu étant ainsi caché, toute religion qui ne dit pas que Dieu est caché n'est pas veritable; et toute religion qui n'en rend pas la raison n'est pas instruisante. La nôtre fait tout cela: *Vere tu es Deus absconditus.*" Ibid., fragment 585 (Lafuma 242; Sellier 275).
109 Ibid., fragment 727. "Il doit aveugler les sages et les savants. Is., VI, VIII, XXIX…" Ibid., fragment 727 (Lafuma 487; Sellier 734).
110 Ibid., fragment 566. "On n'entend rien aux ouvrages de Dieu, si on ne prend pour principe qu'il a voulu aveugler les uns, et éclairer les autres." Ibid., fragment 566 (Lafuma 232; Sellier 264).
111 Ibid., fragment 796. "Jésus-Christ ne dit pas qu'il n'est pas de Nazareth, pour laisser les méchants dans l'aveuglement, ni qu'il n'est pas fils de Joseph." Ibid., fragment 796 (Lafuma 233; Sellier 265).
112 Ibid., fragment 771. "Jésus-Christ est venu aveugler ceux qui voyaient clair, et damner la vue aux aveugles; guérir les malades, et laisser mourir les sains; appeler à penitence et justifier les pécheurs, et laisser les justes dans leurs péchés; remplir les indigents, et laisser les riches vides." Ibid., fragment 771 (Lafuma 235; Sellier 267).
113 Ibid., fragment 578. "-Il y a assez de clarté pour éclairer les élus et assez d'obscurité pour les humilier. Il y a assez d'obscurité pour aveugler les réprouvés et assez de

clarté pour les condamner et les rendre inexcusables…

La généalogie de Jésus-Christ dans l'Ancien Testament est mêlée parmi tant d'autres inutiles, qu'elle ne peut être discernée. Si Moïse n'eût tenu registre que des ancêtres de Jésus-Christ, cela eût été trop visible." Ibid., fragment 578 (Lafuma 236; Sellier 268).

114 Ibid., fragment 796. "Jésus-Christ ne dit pas qu'il n'est pas de Nazareth, pour laisser les méchants dans l'aveuglement, ni qu'il n'est pas fils de Joseph." Ibid., fragment 796 (Lafuma 233; Sellier 265).

115 Blaise Pascal, *Writings on Grace*, in *Pensées and Other Writings*, translated by Honor Levi and edited, introduced, and annotated by Anthony Levi (Oxford: Oxford University Press, 1999), 213. "Il est constant qu'il y a plusieurs des hommes damnez et plusieurs sauvez." Blaise Pascal, *Ecrits sur la Grâce*, in *Œuvres de Blaise Pascal*, edited by Léon Brunschvicg, Pierre Boutroux, and Félix Gazier (Paris: Librairie Hachette & Cie, 1904-1914), 11:128.

116 Ibid., 218. "Que pour cet effet Dieu a envoyé J.-C. pour sauver absolument et par des moyens tres efficaces ceux qu'il a choisis et predestinez de cette masse, qu'il n'y a que ceux là à qui il ait voulu absolument meriter le salut par sa mort, et qu'il n'a point eu cette mesme volonté pour le salut des autres qui n'ont pas esté delivrez de cette perdition universelle et juste." Ibid., 11:136.

117 Ibid., 222. "Et néanmoins il plaist à Dieu de choisir, elire et discerner de cette masse egalement corrompuë, et où il ne voyoit que de mauvaises merites, un nombre d'hommes de tout sexe, ages, conditions, complexions, de tous les païs, de tous les tems, et enfin de toutes sortes.

Que Dieu a discerné ses Elûs d'avec les autres, par des raisons inconnües aux hommes et aux anges et par une pure misericorde sans aucun merite." Ibid., 11:148.

118 Ibid., 223. "De sorte que les hommes sont sauvés ou damnés, suivant qu'il a plu à Dieu de les choisir pour leur donner cette grace dans la masse corrompuë des hommes, dans laquelle il pouvait avec justice les abandonner tous." Ibid., 11:150.

119 "Le problème herméneutique est au cœur de l'apologétique pascalienne. En tant qu'apologiste de la religion chrétienne, Pascal cherche un fondement à la foi. Il trouve ce fondement dans l'Ecriture. C'est dans les texts sacrés que Dieu parle à l'homme et lui donne des raisons de croire. Cependant, le caractère divin de ces texts n'apparaît qu'à ceux qui ont déjà la foi. La foi renvoie à l'Ecriture et l'Ecriture à la foi, dans un mouvement circulaire qui ne laisse pas d'embarrasser l'apologiste. Telle est du moins la façon dont les interprètes modernes de Pascal, de M. J. Lagrange jusqu'à Philippe Sellier, posent le problème des fondements de la religion. La connaissance de Dieu par l'Ecriture semble en effet ne pas pouvoir échapper au cercle vicieux qui caractérise, selon Heidegger, la comprehension rationnelle de tout texte…" Pierre Force, *Le Problème herméneutique chez Pascal* (Paris: Librairie philosophique J. Vrin, 1989), 15.

120 Ibid, 16.

121 Ibid., 17. "Preuve des deux testaments à la fois. Pour prouver tout d'un coup tous les deux, il ne faut voir que si les prophéties de l'un sont accomplies en l'autre. Pour examiner les prophéties il faut les entendre. Car si on croit qu'elles n'ont qu'un sens, il est sûr que le Messie ne sera point venu, mais si elles ont deux sens, il est sûr qu'il sera venu en J.-C. Toute la question est donc de savoir si elles ont deux sens." Force cites Blaise Pascal, *Pensées*, fragment B642/L274/S305.
122 Ben Rogers, *Pascal* (New York: Routledge, 1999), 12-13.
123 Pierre Force, *Self-Interest before Adam Smith: A Genealogy of Economic Science* (Cambridge: Cambridge University Press, 2004), 51.
124 Ibid., 50-51. "Trahe nos post te; curremus in odorem unguentorum tuorum… Parum est, inquit, voluntate trahi, etiam voluptate traheris. Quid est trahi voluptate? Delectari in Domino…si Poeta licuit dicere: Trahit sua quemque voluptas non necessitas, sed voluptas, non obligatio, sed delectatio, quanto fortius dicere debemus trahi hominem ad Christum, qui delectatur veritate, beatitudine, justitia? Et postea: Ramum viridem ostendis ovi, et trahis illam; nuces puero, et trahitur. Si ergo trahit sua quemque voluptas, non trahit revelatus Christus a Patre?...Ecce quomodo trahit pater: docendo delectate, etc." Augustine, *Tractatus in Joannem*, 26.30.
125 Ibid., 51.
126 Ibid. "Car qu'y a-t-il de plus clair que cette proposition qu'on fait toujours ce qui délecte le plus? Puisque ce n'est autre chose que de dire que l'on fait toujours ce qui plaît le mieux, c'est-à-dire que l'on veut toujours ce qui plait, c'est-à-dire qu'on veut toujours ce que l'on veut, et que dans l'état où est aujourd'hui notre âme réduite, il est inconcevable qu'elle veuille autre chose que ce qu'il lui plaît de vouloir, c'est-à-dire ce qui la délecte le plus." Force cites Blaise Pascal, *Ecrits sur la grace*, in *Œuvres complètes*, edited by Jean Mesnard (Paris: Desclée de Brouwer, 1991), 3:704.
127 Ibid. "La monnaie pour laquelle nous donnons tout ce qu'on veut." This is Force's translation of Blaise Pascal, *Pensées*, edited by Louis Lafuma (Paris: Seuil, 1963), fragment 710 (Brunschvicg 24; Sellier 588).
128 Blaise Pascal, *The Art of Persuasion*, in *Pensées and Other Writings*, translated by Honor Levi and edited, introduced, and annotated by Anthony Levi (Oxford: Oxford University Press, 1999), 193-94, fragment 4. "…en effet nous ne croyons presque que ce qui nous plaist. Et de là vient l'esloignement où nous sommes de consentir aux véritez de la religion chrestienne, tout opposée à nos plaisirs. *Dites nous des choses agreables et nous vous ecouterons*, disoient les Juifs à Moïse; comme si l'agrement devoit regler la creance! Et c'est pour punir ce desordre par un ordre qui luy est conforme, que Dieu ne verse ses lumieres dans les esprits qu'apres avoir dompté la rebellion de la volonté par une douceur toute celeste qui la charme et qui l'entraisne." Blaise Pascal, *De l'art de persuader*, section 2 of *De l'esprit géométrique*, in *Œuvres de Blaise Pascal*, edited by Léon Brunschvicg, Pierre Boutroux, and Félix Gazier (Paris: Librairie Hachette & Cie, 1904-1914), 9:272-73.
129 Pierre Force, *Self-Interest before Adam Smith: A Genealogy of Economic Science* (Cambridge: Cambridge University Press, 2004), 116.

130 Ibid., 117. "Votre impuissance à croire vient de vos passions." Pascal, *Pensées*, B233/L418/S680.
131 Ibid. "Puisque la raison vous y porte et que néanmoins vous ne le pouvez, travaillez donc non pas à vous convaincre par l'augmentation des preuves de Dieu, mais par la diminution de vos passions." Ibid.
132 Leszek Kolakowski, *God Owes Us Nothing: A Brief Remark on Pascal's Religion and on the Spirit of Jansenism* (Chicago: University of Chicago Press, 1998), 113.
133 Ibid., 115.
134 Ibid., 121.
135 Ibid., 142-43.
136 Ibid., 144.
137 Ibid., 146.
138 Ibid.
139 James A. Connor, *Pascal's Wager: The Man Who Played Dice with God* (New York: HarperCollins Publishers, 2006), 73.
140 Anthony Levi, "Introduction," in *Pensées and Other Writings*, translated by Honor Levi and edited, introduced, and annotated by Anthony Levi (Oxford: Oxford University Press, 1999), ix.
141 Ibid., xix.
142 Harold Bloom, *Blaise Pascal* (New York: Chelsea House Publishers, 1989), 61-62.
143 Bishop Elias Minatios, "On Predestination," *Orthodox Life*, translated by Father Gregory Naumenko 40, no. 6 (Nov-Dec 1990), 34-35.
144 Ibid., 34. Minatios cites Acts 27:31.

Conclusion

Whereby are given unto us
exceeding great and precious promises:
that by these ye might be
partakers of the divine nature...
—2 Pet 1:4

Pascal's legacy

Pascal's genius resided in his ability to provide mathematical/empirical evidence of the existence of God and of Christ's divinity. He did this by demonstrating the following:

1. The statistical probability that hundreds of Messianic prophecies would be fulfilled by one man is infinitesimally remote and therefore, evidence of the Will of God.
2. The historicity of miracles is certain. Credible witnesses have attested to miracles throughout Church history, as well as in modern times. The Port Royal community witnessed some 80 miracles performed by the Holy Thorn. The cure of Pascal's niece was declared to be a miracle by the doctors and surgeons of Paris as well as the Archbishop of Paris in 1656.
3. The unity between the OT and New (ie: evidence of the Holy Trinity in the OT; types; the fact that a single race of people, despite persecution, predicted the same event over the course of 4,000 years) provides a blueprint of God's plan for man's redemption and eventual theosis.

First, Pascal employs the tool of statistical probability to show that Christ's fulfillment of prophecy is no coincidence. He uses the word "chance" [*hasard*] a number of times: "And what crowns all this is prediction, so that it should not be said that it is chance which has done it";[1] "And in order that this agreement might not be taken for an effect of chance, it was necessary that this should be foretold."[2] Also, he reminds the reader that God announces things in advance so that people would know that it is He who had done them: "I foretold it long since that they might know that it

Conclusion

is I."³ Pascal painstakingly counted and recorded hundreds of Messianic prophecies that Christ fulfilled and proved that the statistical probability that one man would fulfill so many is astronomically miniscule; therefore, it must be the Will of God.

Secondly, there are miracles that provide evidence that Christ was the long awaited Messiah. Pascal enumerates miracles performed by Christ, as well as some that occurred later in Church history ie: Helena's discovery and identification of the True Cross from three by the raising of a dead man that was placed over it.

In addition, mention should be made of some acts of God that Pascal does not mention, but which strongly support his thesis. For example, both Talmuds, the Jerusalem and Babylonian Talmud, recount five miracles that occurred in the Temple during the years 30 AD-70AD. These are the Miracle of the Lots, the Miracle of the Crimson Cloth, the Miracle of the Crimson Thread, the Miracle of the Temple Doors, and the Miracle of the Temple Menorah. These miracles indicate that something significant had changed in the sacrifice of Yom Kippur and in the Jews' relationship with the Living God.

It is significant that while the Miracle of the Crimson Cloth ceased, another miracle commenced that continues to this very day. The most stunning evidence of the Resurrection of Christ in modern times occurs every year in the Church of the Resurrection in Jerusalem on Holy Saturday. When the Patriarch of Jerusalem passes his unlit candle over the Tomb of Christ, it miraculously lights. This miracle has been documented as far back as 870 by the French monk Bernard. On many years the candles in the hands of the pilgrims also miraculously light. People travel to Jerusalem from all over the world to be present when the miracle occurs and many return home with the news that their own candle miraculously lit. Moreover, the historicity of miracles is attested to by the early Christians who had seen the Risen Christ, believed, lost their fear of death, and were willing to be martyred for what they had seen and knew to be true.

Third, the absolute unity of the OT and New concretizes the existence of God. It has been said that the OT provides candlelight on the nature of the Godhead, while the NT sheds full blown daylight on it. In the Schema, "Hear, O Israel: The LORD our God is one LORD," the Hebrew word for "one" is *echad*, meaning unity or cluster, not a numeric one. *Echad* is used again in Gen 2:24 to mean the unity of a marital couple and in Num 13:23 to mean a cluster of grapes. The Father is speaking to the Son in Ps 110:1 and in Is 49:7-9; Christ is relating what the Father has said to Him in Ps 2:7-9. The Son is mentioned again in Ps 2:12. Prov 30:4 clearly describes God ("who hath gathered the wind in his fists? who hath bound the waters in a garment? who hath established all the ends of the earth?") and ends by asking, "What is his son's name, if thou canst tell?" We have a high definition color print of Christ's Passion and Crucifixion in Is 50:5-6; Is 52:14; all of Is 53. Christ is walking in the fire with Shadrach, Meshach, and Abednego in Dan 3: Nebuchadnezzar says, "I see four men loose, walking in the midst of the fire, and they have no hurt; and the form of the fourth is like the Son of God" (Dan 3:25). Moses put some of the Holy Spirit on the 70 elders and they begin to prophecize (Num 11:25-26) (a type of Pentecost, Acts 2:2-4). Furthermore, people, places, events, even the Jewish Feast Days themselves, are types (shadows that point to a future reality) of the redemptive mission of Jesus Christ.

However, it must be pointed out that what Pascal accomplished with the one hand, he undermined with the other. Although he used logic and reason to prove the veracity of the NT, he negated his efforts by promulgating the intrinsically flawed theology of double predestination. Because Pascal embraced tenets that were antithetical to Scripture, we chose to expose his heresies by the truth of the Eastern Orthodox Church. Bishop Minatios points out that because God is just, it is His will that all be saved. He cites the following biblical verses: "He wills all men to be saved" (1 Tim 2:4); "that having granted the law to all, He excludes no one from His kingdom" (St. Ambrose); "For there is one God, and one mediator between God and men, the man Christ Jesus, Who gave Himself as ransom for all (1 Tim 2:5); "One died for all" (2 Cor 5:14); "shown forth for all, lived for all and died and is risen for all" (St. Gregory the Theologian).[4] Man has free will to accept or reject Christ. Timothy Ware reminds us that in Rev 3:20, Christ says, "Behold, I stand at the door, and knock: if any man hear my voice, and open the door, I will come in to him, and will sup with him, and he with me."[5] When man reaches towards God, God reaches towards him. The moment that man believes, God infuses him with grace. Hence, salvation is the intertwining of God's grace and man's free will. The moment that man believes, he takes the first step on a ladder leading towards theosis. That is God's ultimate plan for humanity. The Bible says, "I have said, ye are gods; and all of you are children of the most High" (Is 82:6 and John 10:34). In addition, the Apostle Peter instructs us that this is the purpose of life: we are to "become partakers of the divine nature" (2 Pet 1:4). Christ implores us, "Become perfect, as your heavenly Father is perfect" (Mat 5:48). Paul advises that we are to "be conformed to the image of his Son, that he might be the firstborn among many brethren" (Rom 8:29).

Regarding predestination, the future is fluid or liquid. Man has free will to make whatever choices he wants. God's foreknowledge is based on the future, it is not the other way around. The future is not based on God's foreknowledge.

Those who have followed in Pascal's footsteps

Many Christian apologists who succeeded Pascal also set out to provide skeptics with mathematical/empirical proof of God's existence and Christ's divinity. Three scholars are notable and stand out among the rest. First, in 1883 Alfred Edersheim, in *The Life and Times of Jesus the Messiah*, appendix 9, identified and enumerated 456 Messianic prophecies that Christ fulfilled. Edersheim's work is the result of having carefully scrutinized over 8,000 verses of Bible prophecy.[6]

Secondly, Peter W. Stoner, in *Science Speaks*, has calculated the statistical probability that one man would fulfill just eight Messianic prophecies.[7] The 8 prophecies that Stoner used to perform his calculations were that the Messiah would:

4. be born in Bethlehem (Mic 5:2)
5. be preceded by a messenger (Is 40:3, Mal 3:1)
6. enter Jerusalem on a donkey (Zech 9:9)
7. be betrayed by a friend (Ps 41:9, 55:12-14, Zech 13:6)
8. be sold for 30 pieces of silver (Zech 11:12)
9. that this blood money would be thrown to the potter in God's house (Zech 11:13)
10. be silent before His accusers (Is 53:7)
11. be crucified as a thief (Ps 22:16, Zech 12:10, Is 53:5, 12).

In order to accomplish this task, Stoner recruited 12 college classes comprised of 600 students. The students exercised great care in gauging the fine points of each prophecy before factoring. For example, they calculated that the chances that one man would be born in Bethlehem was 1:280,000. They arrived at this figure by estimating the average population of Bethlehem from Micah to the present time and dividing it by the average population of the earth during the same period. Stoner concluded that the statistical probability that one man would fulfill all eight of these prophecies is $1:10^{17}$ (that is, 1 in 1 followed by 17 zeroes).

In a subsequent exercise, Stoner calculated that the statistical probability that one man would fulfill 48 prophecies is $1:10^{157}$.[8]

Grant R. Jeffrey, as mentioned in chapter 1, has been able to use Daniel's books of sevens in Dan 9:25 to calculate that the first Palm Sunday, when the Lord entered Jerusalem triumphantly on the back of a donkey, is April 6, 32 AD.[9]

Endnotes

1. Blaise Pascal, *Thoughts*, translated by W.F. Trotter, Brunschvicg numbering system (New York: P.F. Collier & Son, 1910), fragment 694. "Et ce qui couronne tout cela est la prédiction, afin qu'on ne dît point que c'est le hasard qui l'a faite." Blaise Pascal, *Pensées*, in *Œuvres de Blaise Pascal*, edited by Léon Brunschvicg, Pierre Boutroux, and Félix Gazier (Paris: Librairie Hachette & Cie, 1904-1914), fragment 694 (Lafuma 326; Sellier 358).
2. Ibid., fragment 707. "Et afin qu'on ne prît point ce concert pour un effet du hasard, il fallait que cela fût prédit." Ibid., fragment 707 (Lafuma 385; Sellier 4).
3. Ibid., fragment 716. "Je l'ai prédit depuis longtemps afin qu'on sût que c'est moi." Ibid., fragment 716 (Lafuma 334; Sellier 366). The aforementioned quote is Pascal's paraphrase of the biblical verse, "I have even from the beginning declared it to thee; before it came to pass I showed it thee" (Is 48:5).
4. Bishop Elias Minatios, "On Predestination," *Orthodox Life*, translated by Father Gregory Naumenko 40, no. 6 (Nov-Dec 1990), 29.
5. Timothy Ware, *The Orthodox Church*, revised edition (London: Penguin Books, 1997), 222.
6. Alfred Edersheim, *The Life and Times of Jesus the Messiah* (New York: Anson D.F. Randolph, 1883), appendix 9, 707-38.
7. Peter W. Stoner, *Science Speaks* (Chicago: Moody Press, 1958). This book is available online at http://www.geocities.com/stonerdon/science_speaks.html (February 14, 2007).
8. Ibid.
9. Grant R. Jeffrey, *Armageddon: Appointment with Destiny* (New York: Bantam Books, 1990), 26-33.

Bibliography

Primary Sources on Pascal

Arnauld, Antoine. *Œuvres de messire Antoine Arnauld*. 43 vols. Paris; Lausanne: Sigismond d'Arnay & Co., 1775-1783.

Arnauld, Antoine and Pierre Nicole. *La Logique, ou l'art de penser: Contenant outre les regles communes, plusieurs observations nouvelles, propres à former le jugement*. Paris: Charles Savreux, 1662.

_____. *La Perpétuité de la foy de l'Eglise catholique touchant l'Eucharistie: Défendu contre le livre du Sieur Claude, Ministre de Charenton*. Paris: la veuve Charles Savreux, 1669.

Filleau de la Chaise, Jean. *Discours sur les Pensées de m. Pascal, Ou l'on essaye de faire voir quel estoit son dessein avec un autre discours sur les preuves des livres de Moyse*. Paris: Guillaume Desprez, 1672.

Fontaine, Nicolas. *L'Histoire du Vieux et du Nouveau Testament, avec des explications édifiantes, tirées des Saints Peres pour regler les mœurs dans toutes sortes de conditions, dédiée à Monseigneur le Dauphin, par le Sieur de Royaumond Prieur de Sombreval*. Paris: Pierre le Petit, 1670.

Garasse, François. *La Doctrine curieuse des Beaux esprits de ce temps ou prétendus tels, contenant plusieurs maximes pernicieuses à la religion, à l'estat et aux bonnes mœurs, combattue et renversée par le Père François Garassus*. Paris: S. Chappelet, 1623.

Holy Bible. KJV. Grand Rapids: Zondervan, 2000.

Jansenius, Cornelius. *Augustinus, seu doctrina S. Augustini de humanæ naturæ sanitate, ægritudine, medicina, adversus Pelagianos et Massilienses*. 3 vols. Louvain: Typis I. Zegeri, 1640.

Lemaistre de Sacy, Isaac-Louis. *La Génèse traduite en françois avec l'explication du sens littéral et du sens spirituel, tirée des Saints Peres des auteurs ecclesiastiques*. Paris: Guillaume Desprez, 1683.

_____. *La Sainte Bible traduite en françois, la latine de la vulgate à côté, avec de courtes notes tirées des Saints Peres et des meilleurs interpretes, pour l'intelligence des endroits les plus difficiles; et la concorde des quatre evangelistes en latin and en françois*. Liège: Jean-François Broncart, 1702.

Lucretius Carus, Titus. *De rerum natura*, edited by H.A.J. Munro. London: George Bell and Sons; Cambridge: Deighton Bell and Company, 1905.

Bibliography

———. *On the Nature of the Things*. Translated by Cyril Bailey. Oxford: Clarendon Press, 1910.

Nicole, Pierre. *De l'education d'un prince.*. Paris: la veuve Charles Savreux, 1670.

———. *De la foy humaine* in *Les Imaginaires, et les visionnaires, Traité de la foy humaine, Jugement equitable, tirés des œuvres de S. Augustin, Lettre de Messire Nicolas Pauillon, evêque d'Alet, à Messire Hardouyn Perefixe, archevêque de Paris*. Cologne: Pierre Marteau, 1683.

———. *Essais de morale*. Paris: Guillaume Desprez, 1671.

NIV Study Bible. Grand Rapids: Zondervan, 2002.

Oxford English Dictionary Online. http://dictionary.oed.com (Jan. 24, 2007).

Pascal, Blaise. *Œuvres de Blaise Pascal*. Edited by Léon Brunschvicg, Pierre Boutroux, and Félix Gazier. Paris: Librairie Hachette & Cie, 1904-1914.

———. *Œuvres complètes*. Edited by Louis Lafuma. Paris: Seuil, 1963.

———. *Œuvres completes*. Edited by Philippe Sellier. Paris: Desclée de Brouwer, 1964-1992.

———. *Pensées*. Introduced and translated by A. J. Krailsheimer. Lafuma numbering system. London: Penguin Books, 1995.

———. *Pensées*. Edited and translated by Roger Ariew. Sellier numbering system. Indianapolis: Hackett Publishing Company, 2005.

———. *Pensées and Other Writings*. Translated by Honor Levi. Edited, introduced, and annotated by Anthony Levi. Oxford: Oxford University Press, 1999.

———. *Thoughts*. Translated by W. F. Trotter. Brunschvicg numbering system. New York: P. F. Collier & Son, 1910.

Plutarch. *Moralia, Book V*. Translated by Frank Cole Babbitt. Cambridge, MA: Harvard University Press, 2003.

Richelieu, Armand Jean du Plessis, duc de. *Testament politique d'Armand du Plessis, cardinal, duc de Richelieu*. Amsterdam: Henri Desbordes, 1689.

Saint-Cyran, Jean Duvergier de Hauranne, abbé de. *La Somme des fautes et faussetés capitales continues en la Somme théologique du P. fr. Garasse*. Paris: Joseph Bouillerot, 1626.

Strabo. *Geography*, translated by Horace Leonard Jones. Cambridge, MA: Harvard University Press, 1924.

Yoma, in *Seder Mo'ed*, in *The Babylonian Talmud, Translated into English with Notes, Glossary and Indices under the Editorship of Rabbi Dr I. Epstein*. London: The Soncino Press, 1938.

Yoma in *The Talmud of the Land of Israel: A Preliminary Translation and Explanation*. Translated by Jacob Neusner. Chicago: The University of Chicago Press, 1990.

Primary Sources on Eastern Orthodox Theology

Ambrose, Saint. *On the Death of Theodosius* in *Ambrose of Milan: Political Letters and Speeches*. Translated, introduced, and annotated by J.H.W.G. Liebeschuetz. Liverpool: Liverpool University Press, 2005, 196-201.

Bernard. *The Voyage of Bernard the Wise, A.D. 867* in *Early Travels in Palestine, comprising the Narratives of Arculf, Willibald, Bernard, Sæwulf, Sigurd, Benjamin of Tudela, Sir John Maundeville, De La Brocquière, and Maundrell*. Edited and annotated by Thomas Wright. London: Henry G. Bohn, 1848.

Chariton of Valamo, Igumen, compiler. *The Art of Prayer: An Orthodox Anthology*. Translated by E. Kadloubovsky and E.M. Palmer. Edited and introduced by Timothy Ware. London: Faber and Faber Limited, 1966.

Cyril of Jerusalem, Saint. *The Catechetical Lectures* in *Cyril of Jerusalem, Gregory Nazianzen*. Vol. 7 of *Nicene and Post-Nicene Fathers of the Christian Church. 2nd series*. Edited by Philip Schaff and Henry Wace. New York: Christian Literature Company, 1890-1893.

_____. *Letter to Constantinus* in Edward Yarnold, *Cyril of Jerusalem*. London and New York: Routledge, 2000.

Daniel of Tchernigov, Abbot. *The Pilgrimage of the Russian Abbot Daniel in the Holy Land 1106-1107 AD*. Translated from the French by Madame Sophie de Khitrowo. Edited by C.W. Wilson. London: Palestine Pilgrims' Text Society, 1895.

Eusebius Pamphilus. *Life of Constantine* in *Eusebius Pamphilus: Church History, Life of Constantine, Oration in Praise of Constantine*. Vol. 1 of *Nicene and Post-Nicene Fathers of the Christian Church. 2nd series*. Edited by Philip Schaff and Henry Wace. New York: Christian Literature Publishing Company, 1890.

_____. *Oration in Praise of Constantine* in *Eusebius Pamphilus: Church History, Life of Constantine, Oration in Praise of Constantine*. Vol. 1 of *Nicene and Post-Nicene Fathers of the Christian Church. 2nd series*. Edited by Philip Schaff and Henry Wace. New York: Christian Literature Publishing Company, 1890.

Bibliography

A Greek-English Lexicon. Edited by Henry George Liddell and Robert Scott. Revised and unabridged. Oxford: Clarendon Press, 1958.

Gregory of Nyssa, Saint. *From Glory to Glory: Texts from Gregory of Nyssa's Mystical Writings*. Edited by Jean Danielou and Herbert Musurillo. London: Scribner, 1961.

Gregory Palamas, Saint. *The Triads*. Edited and introduced by John Meyendorff. Translated by Nicholas Gendle. Preface by Jaroslav Pelikan. New York: Paulist Press, 1983.

Ireneaus, Saint. *Ireneaus against Heresies* in *The Apostolic Fathers with Justin Martyr, Irenaeus*. Vol. 1 of *Ante-Nicene Fathers*. Edited by Alexander Roberts and James Donaldson. New York: The Christian Literature Company, 1890-1897.

Julian, Emperor of Rome. *Against the Galileans* in *The Works of the Emperor Julian*. Vol. 3. Translated by Wilmer Cave Wright. London: William Heinemann, 1913-1923.

Lactantius. *Of the Manner in which the Persecutions Died* in *Fathers of the Third and Fourth Centuries: Lactantius, Venantius, Asterius, Victorinus, Dionysius, Apostolic Teaching and Constitutions, Homily, and Liturgies*. Vol. 7 of *Ante-Nicene Fathers*. Edited by Alexander Roberts and James Donaldson. New York: The Christian Literature Company, 1890-1897.

Macarius of Egypt, Saint. *Pseudo Macarius: The Fifty Spiritual Homilies and the Great Letter*. Edited, translated, and introduced by George A. Maloney. Preface by Bishop Kallistos Ware. New York: Paulist Press, 1992.

Migne, Jacques-Paul, ed. *Patrologiæ cursus completus...Series græca*. 161 vols. Paris: Migne, 1857-1866.

_____. *Patrologiæ cursus completus...Series latina*. 221 vols. Paris: Migne, 1844-1879.

Nazarius of Valaam, Abbot. *Abbot Nazarius of Valaam*. Vol. 2 of *Little Russian Philokalia*. Translated by Father Seraphim Rose. Platina: Saint Herman of Alaska Brotherhood, 1983.

The New Greek-English Interlinear New Testament. Translated by Robert K. Brown and Philip W. Comfort. Edited by J.D. Douglas. Carol Stream: Tyndale House Publishers, Inc., 1993).

Oxford Greek-English Learner's Dictionary. Edited by G. N. Stavropoulos. Oxford: Oxford University Press, 2005.

Paulinus of Nola, Saint. *Letters of St. Paulinus of Nola*. Translated and annotated by P.G. Walsh. 2 vols. Westminster, MD: The Newmann Press, 1966-1967.

The Philokalia: The Complete Text; Compiled by St. Nikodemus of the Holy Mountain and St. Makarius of Corinth. Translated and edited by G.E.H. Palmer, Philip Sherrard, and Kallistos Ware. 4 vols. London: Faber and Faber Limited, 1979-1995.

Rufinus of Aquileia. *The Church History of Rufinus of Aquileia: Books 10 and 11*. Translated by Philip R. Amidon. New York: Oxford University Press, 1997.

The Sayings of the Desert Fathers. Anonymous series in Greek. Edited by F. Nau. *Revue de l'orient Chrétien* 10 (1905): 409-14; 12 (1907): 48-68 (even numbered pages only), 171-81, 393-404; 13 (1908): 47-57, 266-83; 14 (1909): 357-79; 17 (1912): 204-11, 294-301; 18 (1913): 137-46. Some sayings, but not all, are translated into French: *Apophtegmes des saints vieillards* 12 (1907): 49-69 (odd numbered pages only); *Histoires des solitaires égyptiens* 12 (1907): 181-89, 404-13; 13 (1908): 57-66, 283-97.

The Sayings of the Desert Fathers: The Alphabetical Collection. Translated with a forward by Sister Benedicta Ward. Preface by Metropolitan Anthony of Sourozh. Rev. ed. Kalamazoo: Cistercian Publications, Inc., 1984.

Socrates Scholasticus. *The Ecclesiastical History of Socrates Scholasticus*. Vol. 2 of *Nicene and Post-Nicene Fathers of the Christian Church*. 2nd series. Edited by Philip Schaff and Henry Wace. New York: Christian Literature Publishing Company, 1893.

Sozomen. *The Ecclesiastical History of Sozomen, comprising a History of the Church, from A.D. 323 to A.D. 425*. Vol. 2 of *Nicene and Post-Nicene Fathers of the Christian Church*. 2nd series. Edited by Philip Schaff and Henry Wace. New York: Christian Literature Publishing Company, 1893.

Sulpitius Severus. *The Sacred History of Sulpitius Severus* in *Sulpitius Severus, Vincent of Lerins, John Cassian*. Vol. 11 of *Nicene and Post-Nicene Fathers of the Christian Church*. 2nd series. Edited by Philip Schaff and Henry Wace. New York: Christian Literature Publishing Company, 1890-1900.

Symeon the New Theologian, Saint. *Hymns of Divine Love*. Introduced and translated by George A. Maloney. Denville: Dimension Books, 1976.

———. *The Practical and Theological Chapters and the Three Theological Discourses*. Translated and introduced by Paul McGuckin. Kalamazoo: Cistercian Publications, 1982.

———. *St. Symeon the New Theologian: The Discourses*. Translated by C.J. de Catanzaro. Introduced by George Maloney. Preface by Basile Krivocheine. New York: Paulist Press, 1980.

Theodoretus. *Ecclesiastical History* in *The Ecclesiastical History, Dialogues, and Letters of Theodoret*. Vol. 3 of *Nicene and Post-Nicene Fathers of the Christian Church*. 2nd series. Edited by Philip Schaff and Henry Wace. New York: Christian Literature Publishing Company, 1892.

Secondary Sources on Pascal

Abercrombie, Nigel. *The Origins of Jansenism*. Oxford: Clarendon Press, 1936.

Adam, Antoine. *Du mysticisme à la révolte: Les jansénistes du XVIIe siècle*. Paris: Fayard, 1968.

Alexandrescu, Vlad. *Le Paradoxe chez Blaise Pascal*. Bern: Peter Lang, 1997.

Armour, Leslie. *"Infini rien": Pascal's Wager and the Human Paradox*. Carbondale: Southern Illinois University Press, 1993.

Attali, Jacques. *Blaise Pascal ou le génie français*. Paris: Fayard, 2000.

Barnett, Richard. "Maxim-al Codes of Minimal Closure: Pascal's Sequestered Schema." *L'Esprit créateur* 22 (Fall 1982):28-38.

Baudin, Emile. *Etudes historiques et critiques sur la philosophe de Pascal*. Neuchâtel: Editions de la Baconnière, 1948.

Béguin, Albert. *Pascal*. Paris: Seuil, 1952.

Bennett, Deborah J. *Randomness*. Cambridge, MA: Harvard University Press, 1998.

Bernstein, Peter L. *Against the Gods: The Remarkable Story of Risk*. New York: John Wiley & Sons, 1996.

Birault, Henri. "Science et métaphysique chez Descartes et chez Pascal/" *Archives de philosophie* 27 (1964): 483-526.

Bishop, Morris. *Pascal: The Life of Genius*. New York: Reynal & Hitchcock, 1936.

Blanchet, Léon. "L'attitude religieuse des jésuites et les sources du pari de Pascal." *Revue de métaphysique et de morale* 26 (1919): 477-516, 617-47.

Bloom, Harold, ed. *Blaise Pascal*. New York: Chelsea House, 1989.

Bold, Stephen C. *Pascal Geometer: Discovery and Invention in Seventeenth-Century France*. Geneva: Droz, 1996.

Bonsirven, Joseph. "Exégèse juive" in "Interprétation (Histoire de l')," *Dictionnaire de la Bible; Supplément*. Paris: Librairie Letouzey et Ané, 1949, 4:562-70.

_____. *Exégèse rabbinique et exégèse paulinienne*. Paris: Beauchesne, 1939.

Borne, Etienne. *De Pascal à Teilhard de Chardin, précédé d'un homage à Pascal*. Clermont-Ferrand: G. de Bussac, 1963.

Bouveresse, Jacques. "Herméneutique et linguistique," in *Meaning and Understanding*. Edited by Herman Parret and Jacques Bouveresse. Berlin: Walter de Gruyter & Co., 1981, 112-53.

Bremond, Henri. *Histoire littéraire du sentiment religieux en France*. 11 vols. Paris: Bloud et Gay, 1916-1933.

Briggs, Robin. "The Catholic Puritans: Jansenists and Rigorists in France." In Donald Pennington and Keith Thomas, ed., *Puritans and Revolutionaries: Essays in Seventeenth-Century History Presented to Christopher Hill*. Oxford: Clarendon Press, 1978, 333-81.

Broome, Jack Howard. *Pascal*. New York: Barnes & Noble, 1965.

Brunet, Georges. *Le Génie de Pascal*. Paris: Hachette, 1924.

_____. *Le Pari de Pascal*. Paris: Desclée de Brouwer, 1956.

Brunschvicg, Léon. *Descartes et Pascal lecteurs de Montaigne*. Neuchâtel: Editions de la Baconnière, 1945.

Bugnion-Secrétan, Perle. *Mère Agnès: abbesse de Port-Royal*. Paris: Editions du Cerf, 1996.

_____. *La mère Angélique Arnauld, 1591-1661, d'après ses écrits: abbesse et réformatricede Port-Royal*. Paris: Editions du Cerf, 1991.

Busson, Henri. *La pensée religieuse française de Charron à Pascal*. Paris: J. Vrin, 1933.

Carraud, Vincent. *Pascal et la philosophie*. Paris: Presses Universitaires de France, 1992.

Catholic Encyclopedia: An International Work of Reference on the Constitution, Doctrine, Discipline, and History of the Catholic Church. 15 vols. Edited by Charles G. Herbermann, Edward A. Pace, et al. New York: Robert Appleton Company, 1907-1912.

Chambers, Frank M. "Pascal's Montaigne." *PMLA* 65 (1950):790-804.

Chevalier, Jacques. *Pascal*. Paris: Plon, 1938.

Clark, William. *Pascal and the Port-Royalists*. New York: Scribner's, 1902.

Cognet, Louis. *Le Jansénisme*. Paris: Presses Universitaires de France, 1961.

Cole, John Richard. *Pascal: The Man and His Two Loves*. New York: New York University Press, 1995.

Connor, James A. *Pascal's Wager: The Man Who Played Dice with God*. New York: HarperCollins Publishers, 2006.

Coppens, Joseph. "L'argument des prophéties messianiques dans les *Pensées*." *Ephemerides theologicæ lovanienses* 21 (1946):337-61.

Costabel, Pierre. "La Physique de Pascal et son analyse structurale." *Revue d'histoire des sciences* 29, no. 4 (1976):309-24.

Croquette, Bernard. *Pascal et Montaigne: Etudes des reminiscences des Essais dans l'œuvre de Pascal*. Geneva: Droz, 1974.

David, Florence Nightingale. *Gods, Games and Gambling*. New York: Hafner Publishing Company, 1962.

David, Madeleine V. *Le débat sur les écritures et l'hiéroglyphie aux XVIIe et XVIIIe siècles, et l'application de la notion de déchiffrement aux écritures mortes*. Paris: Service d'Edition et de Vente des Publications de l'Education Nationale, 1965.

Davidson, Hugh McCullough. *The Origins of Certainty: Means and Meaning in Pascal's Pensées*. Chicago: University of Chicago Press, 1979.

_____. *Pascal and the Arts of the Mind*. Cambridge: Cambridge University Press, 1993.

_____. "Pascal's Arts of Persuasion," in *Renaissance Eloquence: Studies in the Theory and Practice of Renaissance Rhetoric*. Edited by James J. Murphy. Berkeley: University of California Press, 1983, 292-300.

Dear, Peter Robert. *Discipline and Experience: The Mathematical Way in the Scientific Revolution*. Chicago: University of Chicago Press, 1995.

Demorest, Jean-Jacques. *Dans Pascal; Essai en partant de son style*. Paris: Editions de Minuit, 1953.

Descotes, Dominique. *L'Argumentation chez Pascal*. Paris: Presses Universitaires de France, 1993.

Devlin, Keith J. *Goodbye, Descartes: The End of Logic and the Search for a New Cosmology of the Mind*. New York: John Wiley & Sons, 1997.

Dionne, J. Robert. *Pascal et Nietzsche: Etude historique et comparé*. New York: B. Franklin, 1974.

Doyle, William. *Jansenism: Catholic Resistance to Authority from the*

Reformation to the French Revolution. New York: St. Martin's Press, 2000.

Dubarle, André Marie. "Pascal et l'interprétation de l'Ecriture," *Revue des sciences philosophiques et théologiques*, 30, no. 2 (1941-1942):346-79.

———. "Quelques allusions Scripturaires des *Pensées* de Pascal." *Revue des sciences philosophiques et théologiques*, 30, no. 1 (1941-1942):84-95.

———. "La Science humaine du Christ selon saint Augustin." *Revue des sciences philosophiques et théologiques*, 29, no. 2-4 (1940):244-63.

Duchêne, Roger. *L'Imposture littéraire dans les Provinciales de Pascal; Suivi des actes du colloque tenu à Marseille, le 10 mars 1984*. 2 ed. Aix-en-Provence: Université de Provence, 1985.

Dugas, René and Pierre Costabel. "Pascal et la statique des fluides" in *La Science moderne (de 1450 à 1800)*. Vol. 2 of *Histoire générale des sciences*. Edited by René Taton. Paris: Presses Universitaires de France, 1957-1964, 2:256-60.

Eden, Kathy. *Hermeneutics and the Rhetorical Tradition: Chapters in the Ancient Legacy and its Humanist Reception*. New Haven: Yale University Press, 1997.

Edersheim, Alfred. *The Life and Times of Jesus the Messiah*. New York: Anson D.F. Randolph, 1883, appendix, 707-78.

Edwards, Anthony William Fairbank. "Pascal and the Problem of Points." *International Statistical Review* 50 (1982):259-66.

———. *Pascal's Arithmetical Triangle*. New York: Oxford University Press, 1987.

———. "Pascal's Problem: The 'Gambler's Ruin.'" *International Statistical Review* 51 (1983):73-79.

———. "Pascal's Work on Probability" in *The Cambridge Companion to Pascal*. Edited by Nicholas Hammond. Cambridge: Cambridge University Press, 2003, 40-52.

Eliot, T.S. "Introduction" in Pascal, Blaise, *Pensées*. Translated by W.F. Trotter. London: J.M. Dent & Sons Ltd, 1931, vii-xix.

Ernst, Pol. *Approches pascaliennes: L'unité et le mouvement, le sens et la fonction de chacune des vingt-sept liasses titrées*. Preface by Jean Mesnard. Gembloux: J. Ducolot, 1970.

———. *La Trajectoire pascalienne de "l'Apologie."* Paris: Lettres Modernes, 1967.

Fanton d'Andon, Jean Pierre. *L'horreur du vide: Expérience et raison dans la physique pascalienne*. Paris: Editions du Centre Nationale de la Recherche Scientifique, 1978.

Ferreyrolles, Gérard. *Blaise Pascal: Les provinciales*. Paris: Presses Universitaires de France, 1984.

_____. *Pascal et la raison du politique*. Paris: Presses Universitaires de France, 1984.

_____. *Les Reines du monde: L'imagination et la coutume chez Pascal*. Preface by Jean Mesnard. Paris: Champion, 1995.

Fletcher, Frank Thomas Herbert. *Pascal and the Mystical Tradition*. Oxford: Blackwell, 1954.

Force, Pierre. "Innovation as Spiritual Exercise: Montaigne and Pascal." *Journal of the History of Ideas* 66, no. 1 (Jan. 2005): 17-35.

_____. "Invention, disposition et mémoire dans les *Pensées* de Pascal." *Dix-septième siècle* no. 181 (1993): 757-72.

_____. *Le Problème herméneutique chez Pascal*. Paris: J. Vrin, 1989.

_____. *Self-Interest before Adam Smith*. Cambridge: Cambridge University Press, 2003.

Franklin, James. *The Science of Conjecture: Evidence and Probability before Pascal*. Baltimore: John's Hopkins University Press, 2001.

Frieden, Pierre. "Pascal et Newman: Le drame de l'homme libre." *Newman Studien* 3 (1951):170

Gazier, Augustin. *Histoire générale du mouvement janséniste depuis ses origines jusqu'à nos jours*. Paris: E. Champion, 1922.

Gilberte et Jacqueline Pascal. Vol. 31 of *Chroniques de Port-Royal*. Paris: J. Vrin, 1982.

Gilby, Emma. "Reflexivity in the *Pensées*: Pascal's Discourse on Discourse." *French Studies* 55, no. 3 (2001): 315-26.

Goldmann, Lucien. *Le Dieu caché: Etude sur la vision tragique dans les Pensées de Pascal et dans le théâtre de Racine*. Paris: Gallimard, 1959.

Gouhier, Henri Gaston. *Blaise Pascal: Commentaires*. Paris: J. Vrin, 1966.

_____. *Blaise Pascal: Conversion et apologétique*. Paris: J. Vrin, 1986.

_____. *Cartésianisme et augustinisme au XVIIe siècle*. Paris: J. Vrin, 1978.

_____. *Pascal et les humanistes chrétiens: L'affaire Saint-Ange*. Paris: J. Vrin, 1974.

Grant, Edward. *Much Ado about Nothing: Theories of Space and Vacuum from the Middle Ages to the Scientific Revolution.* Cambridge: Cambridge University Press, 1981.

Groothius, Douglas.R. *On Pascal.* Belmont, CA: Wadsworth, 2001.

Guardini, Romano. *Pascal for Our Time.* Translated by Brian Thompson. New York: Herder and Herder, 1966 [*Christliches Bewussein: Versuche über Pascal.* Munich: Kösel Verlag, 1956].

Guenancia, Pierre. *Du vide à Dieu: Essai sur la physique de Pascal.* Paris: F. Maspero, 1976.

———. "Pascal et la méthode expérimentale" in *Méthodes chez Pascal: Actes du colloque tenu à Clermont-Ferrand, 10-13 juin 1976.* Paris: Presses Universitaires de France, 1979, 121-37.

Guitton, Jean. *Génie de Pascal.* Paris: Aubier, 1962.

———. *Pascal et Leibniz: Etude sur deux types de penseurs.* Paris: Aubier, 1951.

Hacking, Ian. *The Emergence of Probability.* London: Cambridge University Press, 1975.

Hald, Anders. *A History of Probability and Statistics and their Applications before 1750.* New York: Wiley, 1990.

Hammond, Nicholas, ed. *The Cambridge Companion to Pascal.* Cambridge: Cambridge University Press, 2003.

———. "L'illusion de la parole chez Pascal." *Littératures classiques* 44 (Winter 2002): 305-11.

———. *Playing with the Truth: Language and the Human Condition in Pascal's Pensées.* Oxford: Clarendon Press, 1994.

Harl, Marguerite. "Origène et les interprétations patristiques grecques de 'l'obscurité' biblique." *Vigiliæ christianæ* 36, no. 4 (Dec. 1982):334-71.

Harrington, Thomas More. *Pascal philosophe: Une étude unitaire de la pensée de Pascal.* Paris: Société d'Edition d'Enseignement Supérieur, 1982.

Hildesheimer, Françoise. *Le jansénisme en France aux XVIIe et XVIIIe siècles.* Paris: Publisud, 1991.

Howe, Virginia K. "Les *Pensées*: Paradoxe and Signification." *Yale French Studies* 49 (1974):120-31.

Hubert, Sister Marie-Louise. *Pascal's Unfinished Apology: A Study of His Plan.* New Haven: Yale University Press, 1952.

Irwin, W.R. "The Survival of Pan." *PMLA* 76, no. 3 (June 1961): 159-67.

Jeffrey, Grant. *Armageddon: Appointment with Destiny*. New York: Bantam Books, 1990.
Jones, Matthew L. "Writing and Sentiment: Blaise Pascal, the Vacuum and the *Pensées*." *Studies in History and Philosophy of Science* 32 (2001): 139-81.
Kennedy, George Alexander. *Classical Rhetoric and its Christian and Secular Tradition from Ancient to Modern Times*. Chapel Hill: University of North Carolina Press, 1980.
Kim, Hyung-Kil. *De l'art de persuader dans les Pensées de Pascal*. Preface by Antony McKenna. Paris: Nizet, 1992.
Koch, Erec R. *Pascal and Rhetoric: Figural and Persuasive Language in the Scientific Treatises, the Provinciales, and the Pensées*. Charlottesville, VA: Rookwood Press, 1997.
Kolakowski, Leszek. *God Owes Us Nothing: A Brief Remark on Pascal's Religion and on the Spirit of Jansenism*. Chicago: University of Chicago Press, 1998.
Koyré, M. Alexandre. "Pascal savant" in *Blaise Pascal: L'homme et l'œuvre*. Paris: Les Editions de Minuit, 1956, 259-95.
Krailscheimer, Albin J. *Pascal*. New York: Hill and Wang, 1980.
Lacombe, Roger Etienne. *L'apologétique de Pascal: Etude critique*. Paris: Presses Universitaires de France, 1958.
Laporte, Jean Marie Frédéric. *Le cœur et la raison selon Pascal*. Paris: Elzévir, 1950.
_____. *La doctrine de la grâce chez Arnauld*. Paris: Press Universitaires de France, 1922.
Lazzeri, Christian. *Force et justice dans la politique de Pascal*. Paris: Presses Universitaires de France, 1993.

Le Guern, Michel. *L'image dans l'œuvre de Pascal*. Paris: Armand Colin, 1969.
_____. *Pascal et Descartes*. Paris: Nizet, 1971.
Un Lieu de mémoire: Port-Royal de Paris. Vol. 40 of *Chroniques de Port-Royal*. Paris: Bibliothèque Mazarine, 1991.
Loeffel, von Hans. *Blaise Pascal: 1623-1662*. Basel: Birkhäuser, 1987.
Lønning, Per. *Cet effrayant pari: Une "Pensée" pascalienne et ses critiques*. Paris: J. Vrin, 1980.

Lycan, William and George Schlesinger. "You Bet Your Life: Pascal's Wager Defended" in *Reasons and Responsibility: Readings in Some Basic Problems of Philosophy*. Edited by Joel Feinberg. Belmont, CA: Wadsworth Publishing Company, 1989.

MacKenzie, Louis A., Jr. *Pascal's "Lettres provinciales": The Motif and Practice of Fragmentation*. Birmingham, AL: Summa Publications, 1988.

Manson, Neil A. "The Precautionary Principle, the Catastrophic Argument, and Pascal's Wager." *Ends and Means* 4, no. 1 (Autumn 1999): 412-16.

Marin, Louis. *La critique du discours: Sur la 'Logique de Port-Royal' et les 'Pensées' de Pascal*. Paris: Les Editions de Minuit, 1975.

_____. "Le lieu du point? Pascal." *Etudes de lettres* 2 (1982):17-38.

_____. "Secret, dissimulation et art de persuader chez Pascal." *Versants, Revue suisse des littératures romaines* 11 (Winter 1981):53-74.

Martin, Michael. "Pascal's Wager as an Argument for not Believing in God." *Religious Studies* 19, no. 1 (March 1983): 57-64.

McGarvey, J.W. and Philip Y. Pendleton. *The Fourfold Gospel or A Harmony of the Four Gospels*. Cincinnati: The Standard Publishing Company, 1914.

McKenna, Antony. *De Pascal à Voltaire: Le role des Pensées de Pascal dans l'histoire des idées entre 1670 et 1734*. Vols. 276-277 in *Studies on Voltaire and the Eighteenth Century*. Oxford: The Voltaire Foundation at the Taylor Institution, 1990.

La Mère Angélique Arnauld (1591-1661): Relation-Colloque. Vol. 41 of *Chroniques de Port-Royal*. Paris: Bibliothèque Mazarine, 1992.

Melzer, Sara. *Discourses of the Fall: A Study of Pascal's "Pensées."* Berkeley: University of California Press, 1986.

Mesnard, Jean. "Jansénisme et literature," in *Le Statut de la littérature: Mélanges offerts à Paul Bénichou*. Edited by Marc Fumaroli. Geneva: Droz, 1982, 117-35.

_____, ed. *Méthodes chez Pascal: Actes du colloque tenu à Clermont-Ferrand, 10-13 juin 1976*. Paris: Presses Universitaires de France, 1979.

_____. *Pascal*. Translated by Claude and Marcia Abraham. University, AL: University of Alabama Press, 1969 [Jean Mesnard. *Pascal*. Bruges: Desclée de Brouwer et Cie, 1965].

_____. *Pascal, l'homme et l'œuvre*. Paris: Boivin, 1951.

_____. *Pascal et les Roannez*. Paris: Desclée de Brouwer et Cie., 1965.

_____. *Les Pensées de Pascal*. Paris: Société d'Edition d'Enseignement Supérieur, 1976.

———. *La Science et son ordre."* Communio 8, no. 4 (July-August 1984):77-84.
Miel, Jan. *Pascal and Theology*. Baltimore: Johns Hopkins Press, 1969.
Moles, Elizabeth. "Pascal's Theory of the Heart." *Modern Language Notes* 84, no. 4 (May 1969):548-64.
Morris, Thomas V. "Pascalian Wagering." *Canadian Journal of Philosophy* 16, no. 3 (1986): 437-53.
Mortimer, Ernest. *Blaise Pascal: The Life and Work of a Realist*. New York: Harper, 1959.
Nadler, Steven M. *Arnauld and the Cartesian Philosophy of Ideas*. Manchester: Manchester University Press, 1989.
Natoli, Charles M. *Nietzsche and Pascal on Christianity*. New York: Peter Lang, 1985.
Nelson, Robert J. *Pascal: Adversary and Advocate*. Cambridge, MA: Harvard University Press, 1981.
Neveu, Bruno. "Le Statut théologique de saint Augustin au XVIIe siècle" in *Troisième centenaire de l'édition mauriste de saint Augustin: Communications présentées au colloque des 19 et 20 avril 1990*. Paris: Institut d'Etudes Augustiniennes, 1990, 15-28.
Norman, Buford. *Portraits of Thought: Knowledge, Methods, and Styles in Pascal*. Columbus: Ohio State University Press, 1988.
O'Connell, Marvin Richard. *Blaise Pascal: Reasons of the Heart*. Grand Rapids: William B. Eerdmans Publishing Company, 1997.
———. *The Counter Reformation, 1559-1610*. New York: Harper & Row, 1974.
Orcibal, Jean. *Jansénius d'Ypres (1585-1638)*. Paris: Centre National des Lettres, 1989.
———. *Jean Duvergier de Hauranne, abbé de Saint-Cyran, et son temps, 1581-1638*. Louvain: Bureaux de la Revue, 1947.
———. *Origines du jansénisme*. Louvain, Bureaux de la Revue; Paris, J. Vrin, 1947-1962.
———. *Saint-Cyran et le jansénisme*. Paris: Editions du Seuil, 1961.
———. *La Spiritualité de Saint-Cyran: Avec ses écrits de piété inédits*. Paris: J. Vrin, 1962.
Ore, Oystein. "Pascal and the Invention of Probability Theory." *American Mathematical Monthly* 67 (1960): 409-19.

Parish, Richard. *Pascal's Lettres provinciales: A Study in Polemic*. Oxford: Clarendon Press, 1989.
Pasqua, Hervé. *Blaise Pascal: Penseur de la grâce*. Preface by Philippe Sellier. Paris: Pierre Téqui, 2000.
Patrick, Denzil G.M. *Pascal and Kierkegaard: A Study in the Strategy of Evangelism*. 2 vols. London: Lutterworth Press, 1948.
Périer, Gilberte. *La Vie de Monsieur Pascal* in *Les moralistes français: Pensées de Pascal; Maximes et réflexions de La Rochefoucauld; Caractères de La Bruyère; Œuvres de Vauvenargues*. Paris: Garnier, 1875.
Pintard, René. *Le Libertinage érudit dans la première moitié du XVIIe siècle*. Geneva: Slatkine, 1983.
Plainemaison, Jacques. *Blaise Pascal polémiste*. Clermont-Ferrand: Presses Universitaires Blaise Pascal, 2003.
Pour ou contre Sainte-Beuve: Le "Port-Royal": Actes du colloque de Lausanne, septembre 1992. Vol. 42 of *Chroniques de Port-Royal*. Geneva: Labor et Fides, 1993.
Pugh, Anthony R. *The Composition of Pascal's Apologia*. Toronto: The University of Toronto Press, 1984.
Reisler, Marsha. "'Persuasion through Antithesis': An Analysis of the Dominant Rhetorical Structure of Pascal's *Lettres provinciales*." *Romanic Review* 69 (1978): 172-85.
Rescher, Nicholas. *Pascal's Wager: A Study of Practical Reasoning in Philosophical Theology*. Notre Dame: University of Notre Dame Press, 1985.
Rideau, Emile. *Descartes, Pascal, Bergson*. Paris: Boivin, 1937.
Robertson, Archibald Thomas, ed. *A Harmony of the Gospels for Students of the Life of Christ: Based on the Broadus Harmony in the Revised Version*. New York: George H. Doran Company, 1922.
Rogers, Ben. *Pascal*. New York and London: Routledge, 1999.
Russier, Jeanne. *La Foi selon Pascal*. Paris: Presses Universitaires de France, 1949.
Sainte-Beuve, Charles-Augustin. *Port-Royal*. 3rd Ed. 7 vols. Paris: Hachette, 1867.
Saka, Paul. "Pascal's Wager and the Many Gods Objection." *Religious Studies* 37, no. 3 (2001): 321-41.
Schmitz du Moulin, Henri. *Blaise Pascal: Une Biographie spirituelle*. Assen, Pays-bas: Van Gorcum, 1982.

Sedgwick, Alexander. *Jansenism in Seventeenth Century France: Voices in the Wilderness*. Charlottesville: University Press of Virginia, 1977.

Sellier, Philippe. *Pascal et la liturgie*. Paris: Presses Universitaires de France, 1966.

_____. *Pascal et saint Augustin*. Second edition. Paris: Albin Michel, 1995.

_____. *Port-Royal et la littérature*. Paris: Honoré Champion, 1999.

Serfes, Demetrios, Father. "St. Lazarus the Friend of Christ and First Bishop of Kition, Cyprus." http://www.serfes.org/lives/stlazarus.htm (Mar. 7, 2007).

Shea, William R. *Designing Experiments and Games of Chance: The Unconventional Science of Blaise Pascal*. Canton, MA: Science History Publications, 2003.

Stoner, Peter W. *Science Speaks*. Chicago: Moody Press, 1958. Also, http://www.geocities.com/stonerdon/science_speaks.html (February 14, 2007).

Strong, James, ed. *The New Strong's Exhaustive Concordance of the Bible*. Nashville: Thomas Nelson Publishers, 1990.

Strowski, Fortunat. *Pascal et son temps*. 3 vols. Paris: Plon-Nourrit, 1922.

Tapié, Victor Lucien. *La France de Louis XIII et de Richelieu*. Paris: Flammarion, 1952.

Thirouin, Laurent. "Le défaut d'une droite méthode." *Littératures classiques* 20 Suppl. (1994): 7-21.

_____. *Le hasard et les règles: Le modèle du jeu dans la pensée de Pascal*. Paris: J. Vrin, 1991.

_____. "Pascal et l'art de conférer." *Cahiers de l'Association internationale des études françaises* 40 (1988): 199-218.

Tillman, Mary Katherine. "The Two-Fold Logos of Newman and Pascal: L"Esprit géométrique." *Louvain Studies* 15 (1990):233-55.

Todhunter, Isaac. *A History of the Mathematical Theory of Probability from the Time of Pascal to that of Laplace*. Cambridge: Macmillan and Company, 1865.

Topliss, Patricia. *The Rhetoric of Pascal: A Study of His Art of Persuasion in the Provinciales and the Pensées*. Leicester: Leicester University Press, 1966.

Weaver, Warren. *Lady Luck: The Theory of Probability*. Garden City: Anchor Books, 1963.

Wesley, John. *Explanatory Notes upon the Old Testament*. 3 vols. Bristol: William Pine, 1765.
Wetsel, David. *L'Ecriture et le reste: The Pensées of Pascal in the Exegetical Tradition of Port-Royal*. Columbus: Ohio State University Press, 1981.
_____. *Pascal and Disbelief: Catechesis and Conversion in the Pensées*. Washington, DC: Catholic University of America Press, 1994.
Williams, Bernard Arthur Owen. "Deciding to Believe," chapter 9, in *Problems of the Self: Philosophical Papers 1956-1972*. Cambridge: Cambridge University Press, 1973, 136-51.
Woshinsky, Barbara R. "Biblical Discourse: Reading the Unreadable." *L'Esprit créateur* 21, no. 2 (Summer 1981): 13-24.

Secondary Sources on Eastern Orthodox Theology

Andia, Ysabel de, ed. *Denys l'Aréopagite et sa posterité en orient et en occident: Actes du colloque international, Paris, 21-24 septembre 1994*. Paris: Institute d'Etudes Augustiniennes, 1997.
_____. *Denys l'Aréopagite: Tradition et métamorphoses*. Preface by Maurice de Gandillac. Paris: J. Vrin, 2006.
_____. *Henosis: L'union à Dieu chez Denys l'Aréopagite*. Ledin: E.J. Brill, 1996.
_____. *Homo vivens: Incorruptibilité et divinisation de l'homme selon Irénée de Lyons*. Paris: Etudes Augustiniennes, 1986.
Arseniew, Nicholas. *Mysticism and the Eastern Church*. Translated by Arthur Chambers. Preface by Friedrich Heiler. Introduced by Evelyn Underhill. London: Student Christian Movement, 1926.
Azkoul, Michael, Father. *God, Immortality, and Freedom of the Will according to the Church Fathers: A Philosophy of Spiritual Cognition*. Lewiston: Edwin Mellen Press, 2006.
_____. *Influence of Augustine of Hippo on the Orthodox Church*. Lewiston: Edwin Mellen Press, 1990.
_____. *St. Gregory of Nyssa and the Tradition of the Fathers*. Lewiston: Edwin Mellen Press, 1995.
_____. *Teachings of the Holy Orthodox Church*. Edited by Hieromonk Gregory. Vol. 1. Buena Vista: Dormition Skete, 1986.

Bibliography

———. "What is Predestination?" in "Book Reviews by Hieromonk Moses and Reader Nicholas Franck." http://www.orthodoxcanada.org/reviews/ (May 2, 2007).

Balás, David L. *Metousia Theou: Man's Participation in God's Perfection according to St. Gregory of Nyssa*. Rome: I.B.C. Herder, 1966.

Benz, Ernst. *The Eastern Orthodox Church, its Thought and Life*. Translated by Richard and Clara Winston. Garden City: Anchor Books, 1963.

Breck, John. *Scripture in Tradition: The Bible and its Interpretation in the Orthodox Church*. Crestwood: St. Vladimir's Seminary Press, 2001.

———. *Spirit of Truth: The Holy Spirit in Johannine Tradition*. Vol. 1. Crestwood: St. Vladimir's Seminary Press, 1991- .

Calian, Carnegie Samuel. *Icon and Pulpit: The Protestant-Orthodox Encounter*. Philadelphia: Westminster Press, 1968.

———. *Theology without Boundaries: Encounters of Eastern Orthodxy and Western Tradition*. Louisville: Westminster/John Knox Press, 1992.

Chrestou, Panagiotes K. *Partakers of God*. Brookline: Holy Cross Orthodox Press, 1984.

Clendenin, Daniel B. *Eastern Orthodox Christianity: A Western Perspective*. 2nd ed. Grand Rapids: Baker Academic, 2003.

———. *Eastern Orthodox Theology: A Contemporary Reader*. 2nd ed. Grand Rapids: Baker Academic, 2003.

Colliander, Tito. *The Way of the Ascetics*. Translated by Katharine Ferré. Edited and introduced by R.M. French. London: Hodder and Stoughton, 1960.

Collins, Carr. "Theosis: Deification of Man." *Diakronia* 15, no. 3 (1980): 229-35.

Coniaris, Anthony M. *Introducing the Orthodox Church, its Faith and Life*. Minneapolis: Light and Life Publishing Co., 1982.

Dawkins, Richard McGillivray. *The Monks of Athos*. London: G. Allen & Unwin, Ltd, 1936.

Drewery, Ben. "Deification" in *Christian Spirituality: Essays in Honour of Gordon Rupp*. Edited by Peter Brooks. London: SCM Press, 1975, 33-62.

Florovsky, Georges, Father. *Bible, Church, Tradition: An Eastern Orthodox View*. Vol. 1 of *Collected Works of Georges Florovsky*. 14 vols. Belmont: Nordland Publishing Co., 1972-1989.

———. *The Byzantine Fathers of the Fifth Century*. Vol. 8 of *Collected Works of Georges Florovsky*. 14 vols. Belmont: Nordland Publishing Co., 1972-1989.

_____. *The Byzantine Fathers of the Sixth to Eighth Centuries*. Vol. 9 of *Collected Works of Georges Florovsky*. 14 vols. Belmont: Nordland Publishing Co., 1972-1989.

_____. *The Eastern Fathers of the Fourth Century*. Vol. 7 of *Collected Works of Georges Florovsky*. 14 vols. Belmont: Nordland Publishing Co., 1972-1989.

Fortino, Eleuterio. "Sanctification and Deification." *Diakonia* 17, no. 3 (1982): 192-200.

Gillet, Lev, Archimandrite. *Orthodox Spirituality: An Outline of the Orthodox Ascetical and Mystical Tradition by a Monk of the Eastern Church*. 2nd ed. London: SPCK, 1978.

_____. *The Year of the Grace of the Lord: A Scriptural and Liturgical Commentary on the Calendar of the Orthodox Church*. Translated by Deborah Cowan. Crestwood: St. Vladimir's Seminary Press, 1980.

Gorainoff, Irina. *Séraphim de Sarov*. Bégrolles-en-Mauges: Abbaye de Bellefontaine, 1976.

Gross, Jules. *La divinisation du chrétien d'après les pères grecs; contribution historique à la doctrine de la grâce*. Paris: J. Gabalda et Cie, 1938.

Guroian, Vigen. *Incarnate Love: Essays in Orthodox Ethics*. Notre Dame: University of Notre Dame Press, 1987.

Harakas, Stanley S. "Eastern Orthodox Christianity's Ultimate Reality and Meaning: Triune God and Theosis; An Ethician's View." *Ultimate Reality and Meaning* 8, no. 3 (1985): 209-23.

Harrison, Verna. "Some Aspects of Saint Gregory the Theologian's Soteriology." *Greek Orthodox Theological Review* 34, no. 1 (Spring 1989): 11-18.

Himmerich, Maurice Fred. *Deification in John of Damascus*. Ph.D diss., Marquette University, 1985.

Jones, Cheslyn, Geoffrey Wainwright and Edward Yarnold. *The Study of Spirituality*. New York: Oxford University Press, 1986.

Juli, Stephen James. *The Doctrine of Theosis in the Theology of Saint Maximus the Confessor*. S.T.L. thesis, Catholic University of America, 1990.

Karmiris, John. *A Synopsis of the Dogmatic Theology of the Orthodox Catholic Church* Translated by George Dimopoulos. Scranton: Christian Orthodox Edition, 1973.

Kesich, Veselin. *The Gospel Image of Christ: The Church and Modern Criticism*. Crestwood: St. Vladimir's Seminary Press, 1992.

Krivocheine, Basil. *In the Light of Christ: St. Symeon the New Theologian (949-1022), Life, Spirituality and Doctrine*. Translated by Anthony P. Gythiel. Crestwood: St. Vladimir's Seminary Press, 1986 [*Dans la lumière du Christ: Saint Syméon le Nouveau Théologien, 949-1022, vie, spiritualité, doctrine*. Chevetogne: Editions de Chevetogne, 1980].

Lossky, Vladimir. *In the Image and Likeness of God*. Introduced by A.M. Allchin. London: Mowbrays, 1974.

————. *The Mystical Theology of the Eastern Church*. Translated by members of the Fellowship of St. Albans and St. Sergius. London: J. Clarke, 1957 [*Essai sur la théologie mystique de l'Eglise d'Orient*. Paris: Aubier, 1944].

————. *Orthodox Theology: An Introduction*. Translated by Ian and Ihita Kesarcodi-Watson. Crestwood: St. Vladimir's Seminary Press, 1978.

————. *The Vision of God*. Translated by Asheleigh Moorhouse. Preface by John Meyendorff. London: Faith Press, 1963 [*Vision de Dieu*. Preface by John Meyendorff. Neuchâtel: Delachaux & Niestlé, 1962].

Lot-Borodine, Myrrha. *La déification de l'homme selon la doctrine des Pères grecs*. Paris: Editions du Cerf, 1970.

Louth, Andrew. *Denys, the Areopagite*. Wilton: Morehouse, 1989.

————. *Maximus the Confessor*. London and New York: Routledge, 1996.

————. *The Origins of Christian Mystical Tradition: From Plato to Denys*. Oxford: Clarendon Press, 1981.

Makrakis, Apostolos. *An Orthodox-Protestant Dialogue*. Translated by Denver Cummings. Chicago: Orthodox Christian Educational Society, 1966.

Maloney, George A. *The Mystic of Fire and Light: St. Symeon the New Theologian*. Denville, Dimension Books, 1975.

Mantzaridis, Georgios I. *The Deification of Man: St. Gregory Palamas and the Orthodox Tradition*. Translated by Liadain Sherrard. Forward by Bishop Kallistos Ware. Crestwood: St. Vladimir's Seminary Press, 1984.

Meyendorff, John. *The Byzantine Legacy in the Orthodox Church*. Crestwood: St. Vladimir's Seminary Press, 1982.

————. *Byzantine Theology: Historical Trends and Doctrinal Themes*. New York: Fordham University Press, 1974.

————. *Christ in Eastern Christian Thought*. Washington, DC: Corpus Books, 1969 [*Le Christ dans la théologie byzantine*. Paris: Editions du Cerf, 1969].

_____. *Living Tradition: Orthodox Witness in the Contemporary World.* Crestwood: St. Vladimir's Seminary Press, 1978.

_____. "New Life in Christ: Salvation in Orthodox Theology." *Theological Studies* 50, no. 3 (September 1989): 481-99.

_____. *The Orthodox Church: Its Past and Its Role in the World Today.* Translated by John Chapin. New York: Pantheon Boos, 1962 [*L'Eglise orthodoxe, hier et aujourd'hui.* Paris: Editions du Seuil, 1960].

_____. *Orthodoxy and Catholicity.* New York: Sheed & Ward, 1966 [*Orthodoxie et catholicité.* Paris: Editions du Seuil, 1965].

_____. *St. Gregory Palamas and Orthodox Spirituality.* Translated by Adele Fiske.Crestwood: St. Vladimir's Seminary Press, 1974 [*St. Grégoire Palamas et la mystique orthodoxe.* Paris: Editions du Seuil, 1959].

_____. *A Study of Gregory Palamas.* Translated by George Lawrence. London: Faith Press, 1964 [*Introduction a l'étude de Grégoire Palamas.* Paris: Edition du Seuil, 1959].

_____. "Theosis in the Eastern Christian Tradition." *Christian Spirituality: Post-Reformation and Modern.* Edited by Louis Dupré and Don E. Saliers in collaboration with John Meyendorff. New York: The Crossroad Publishing Company, 1989, 470-76.

_____. *The Vision of Unity.* Crestwood: St. Vladimir's Seminary Press, 1987.

Meyendorff, John and Bernard McGinn, ed. *Christian Spirituality: Origins to the Twelfth Century.* New York: Crossroad, 1985.

Meyendorff, John and Robert Tobias, ed. *Salvation in Christ: A Lutheran-Orthodox Dialogue.* Minneapolis: Augsburg Fortress Publishing House, 1992.

Minatios, Elias, Bishop. "On Predestination." *Orthodox Life.* Translated by Father Gregory Naumenko 40, no. 6 (Nov-Dec 1990), 27-36.

Nassif, Bradley, ed. *New Perspectives on Historical Theology: Essays in Memory of John Meyendorff.* Grand Rapids: William B. Eerdmans, 1996.

Nellas, Panayiotis. *Deification in Christ: Orthodox Perspectives on the Nature of the Human Person.* Crestwood: St. Vladimir's Seminary Press, 1987.

Niesel, Wilhelm. *Reformed Symbolics: A Comparison of Catholicism, Orthodoxy and Protestantism.* Translated by David Lewis. Edinburgh: Oliver and Boyd, 1962.

Nissiotis, Nikos A. "The Unity of Scripture and Tradition: An Eastern Orthodox Contribution to the Prolegomena of Hermeneutics." *The Greek Orthodox Theological Review* 11, no. 2 (Winter 1965-1966): 183-208.

Norman, Keith Edward. *Deification: The Content of Athanasian Soteriology.* Ph.D diss., Duke University, 1980.

O'Callaghan, Paul. *An Eastern Orthodox Response to Evangelical Claims.* Minneapolis: Light and Life Publishing Co., 1984.

The Orthodox Church and the Churches of the Reformation: A Survey of Orthodox-Protestant Dialogues. Faith and Order Paper 76. Geneva: Faith and Order Commission, World Council of Churches, 1975.

Papademetriou, George. "The Human Body according to Saint Gregory Palamas." *Greek Orthodox Theological Review* 34, no. 1 (Spring 1989): 1-9.

Pelikan, Jaroslav. *The Christian Tradition: A History of the Development of Doctrine.* Vols. 1-Chicago: University of Chicago Press, 1971-1989.

————. "Fundamentalism and/or Orthodoxy" in *The Fundamentalist Phenomenon: A View from Within, A Response from Without.* Edited by Norman J. Cohen. Grand Rapids: W.B. Eerdmans Publishing Co., 1990, 3-21.

————. *The Spirit of Eastern Christendom (600-1700).* Chicago: University of Chicago Press, 1974.

Places, Edouard des, et al. "Divinisation." *Dictionnaire de spiritualité ascétique et mystique, doctrine et histoire.* Paris: G. Beauchesne et ses fils, 1957, 3:1370-1459.

Rodger, Symeon. "The Soteriology of Anselm of Canterbury, an Orthodox Perspective." *Greek Orthodox Theological Review* 34, no. 1 (Spring 1989): 19-43.

Russell, Norman. *The Doctrine of Deification in the Greek Patristic Tradition.* Oxford: Oxford University Press, 2004.

Sartorius, Bernard. *La doctrine de la déification de l'homme d'après les Pères grecs en général et Grégoire Palamas en particulier.* Geneva: Cercle du Bibliophile, 1965.

————. *L'Eglise Orthodoxe.* Geneva: Cercle du Bibliophile, 1968.

Sherrard, Philip. *Athos, the Holy Mountain.* London: Sidgwick & Jackson, 1982.

Stăniloae, Dumitru. *The Experience of God*. Translated and edited by Ioan Ioniță and Robert Barringer. Foreward by Bishop Kallistos Ware. Brookline: Holy Cross Orthodox Press, 1994.

⎯⎯⎯⎯. "Image, Likeness, and Deification in the Human Person." *Communio: International Catholic Review* 13 (Spring 1986): 64-83.

Stavropoulos, Christoforos. *Partakers of Divine Nature*. Minneapolis: Light and Life Publishing Company, 1976.

Telepneff, Gregory and James Thornton. "Arian Transcendence and the Notion of Theosis in Saint Athanasios." *Greek Orthodox Theological Review* 32, no. 3 (Fall 1987): 271-77.

Thunberg, Lars. *Man and Cosmos: The Vision of St. Maximus the Confessor*. Forward by A.M. Allchin. Crestwood: St. Vladimir's Seminary Press, 1985.

⎯⎯⎯⎯. *Microcosm and Mediator: The Theological Anthropology of Maximus the Confessor*. Forward by A.M. Allchin. Chicago: Open Court, 1995.

Turner, H.J.M. *St. Symeon the New Theologian and Spiritual Fatherhood*. Leiden: E.J. Brill, 1990.

Vassiliades, Nicolaos P. "The Mystery of Death." *Greek Orthodox Theological Review* 29 (Autumn 1984): 269-82.

Ware, Kallistos, Bishop. *The Orthodox Way*. Crestwood: St. Vladimir's Seminary Press, 1995.

Ware, Timothy. *The Orthodox Church*. London: Penguin Books, 1997.

Williams, Anna Ngaire. *The Ground of Union: Deification in Aquinas and Palamas*. New York: Oxford University Press, 1999.

Winslow, Donald F. *The Dynamics of Salvation: A Study in Gregory of Nazianzus*. Cambridge, MA: Philadelphia Patristic Foundation, 1979.

Index

A

Aaron 93, 96, 161-62, 196
Abednego 31, 192, 281
Acceptance of Christ ...28, 56-57, 115, 159-160, 216, 218-21, 225, 235-36, 240, 249, 253, 257, 266, 281
Adam 12, 17, 33-34, 120, 140, 173, 200, 202, 218, 229-30, 240, 242, 256-57, 259-61
Adam, Antoine 37
Advent of Christ 31, 51, 68, 82-83, 93, 111, 117-18, 153, 182
    calculation of 22, 78, 282-83
Aemilianus 62-63
Age of the earth 72-73
Ambrose, Saint 28, 159, 231, 281
Ananias 129, 135
Angels 19, 53, 65, 69, 133-34, 141, 205, 223, 228, 232, 234, 250, 253, 257, 267
Anselm of Canterbury 240
Antoninus of Piacenza 12
Arnauld, Agnes, Mother 37
Arnauld, Antoine 37-38, 261
Artaxerxes Longanimus,
    decree of 78-79
Athelstan, King of England 13
Augustine, Saint 6, 28, 33-35, 38, 42, 166, 222, 226, 229-31, 233, 235, 240-42, 256-57, 259, 266
Augustine's mistranslation of
    Rom 5:12 ....7, 33-35, 165, 211, 226, 229-30, 256-57, 266
Augustinians .. 6-7, 38, 165, 240, 244, 266

Augustus Caesar 19, 66, 111
Azkoul, Father Michael .. 230, 233-35

B

Babylonian Talmud .76, 135, 139, 280
Baldwin II, Latin Emperor
    of Constantinople 13
Bartimaeus, blind 72, 132
Bernard the Monk 12, 29, 77, 141-42, 280
Bethlehem prophecy 18-19, 23, 25, 52, 61, 65-66, 113, 154, 251, 254, 282-83
Blindness
    Christ's healing of physical 53, 72, 98, 123, 131-32, 141, 164, 228, 231
    Christ's healing of spiritual 20, 53, 98-99, 141, 192, 228, 248, 254
    Pascalian metaphor 57-58
    Paul's 151
Bloom, Harold 38, 265-66
Boaz 21
Booths, Feast of 207-09
Bremond, Henri 37
Bride metaphor for the Church 29, 120, 159, 221, 245

C

Calvinists 38-39, 261-62
Cassiodorus 12
Cephas 26, 35, 53, 126, 128-35, 189, 199, 204-05, 217, 236, 268, 282

Chance, random ... 6, 8, 15-16, 18, 20, 48-49, 54, 61, 77, 82-84, 136, 171, 214, 258, 279-80, 283
Charlemagne 13
Charles the Bald, Emperor 13
Chosen 186, 215-17, 240, 247, 250, 255-56, 264
Chrestou, Panagiotes K. 239
Chrysostom, Saint John ..34, 223, 238
Church of the Resurrection 28-29, 77, 141-49, 158, 280
Clair-obscure 59-60
Clement of Alexandria, Saint 12
Clendenin, Daniel B. 236-37, 239
Cleopas, Saint 26, 128
Complete career prophecies 56
Conformity of man
    to Christ's image 221, 248, 266
    to the will of God 21
Coniah 69-71
Connor, James A. 214, 242-44, 263-64
Consciousness 14-15, 49, 58-59, 150, 155-56
Constantine I 28, 157-58
Contradictions (*contrariétés*) .. 159-60
Conversion
    of the Gentiles 74, 94, 97, 101, 103-05, 108-10, 113-14, 173, 185, 188
    Pascal's 9, 42, 263-64
    Paul's 234
Cooperation with God 36, 218, 222-23, 231-32, 257, 266-67
Crown of Thorns 10-13, 35, 60
Crucifixion of Christ 11-12, 18, 22, 24-25, 27, 32, 68, 74, 94-95, 99, 103-07, 111, 114, 118, 120, 126-27, 132-34, 138, 157-58, 183-84, 187-89, 198, 202, 217, 251, 253, 281-82
Cyril of Jerusalem, Saint 28, 158, 176-77n40
Cyrus, decree of 78

D

Daniel of Tchernigov, Abbot ... 142-46
Daniel's book of weeks 22, 61, 68, 77-79, 84, 112, 283
Darius, decree of 78
David, Florence Nightingale 37
David, King ... 9, 18, 21-22, 56-57, 61, 66, 68-72, 83, 117, 182, 184, 205, 251
Davidson, Hugh McCullough . 169-73
Day of Atonement 136, 206-07
Deafness
    Christ's healing of physical ...123, 131
    Christ's healing of spiritual 99, 248
    Pascalian metaphor 59
Deification of man 15, 40-41, 120, 139, 152, 173, 196, 203, 215, 218, 226, 235-40, 248-50, 261, 266-68
Democritus 48
Desert Fathers 41, 152, 220, 225
Deus absconditus 39, 225, 252, 261-62
Diodorus I, Patriarch of
    Jerusalem 147-48
Divinization of man ... 15, 40-41, 120, 139, 152, 173, 196, 203, 215, 218, 226, 235-40, 248-50, 261, 266-68
Double predestination ..11, 15, 34, 37, 165, 214-15, 230, 233, 266, 281

Index

D'rash (*drash* or *drosh*) 53
Drewery, Ben 239

E

Echad vs. *yachid* 29-30, 54, 94, 180-82, 280
Edersheim, Alfred 51, 84, 251, 282
Edwards, Anthony William Fairbank 37
Efficacious grace 6, 11, 34-36, 38-39, 240-41, 244, 250-51, 253, 255, 257, 259, 261, 266
Election ... 7, 10-11, 15, 33-39, 42, 56, 74, 81, 110, 115, 159, 169, 171, 214-17, 222, 225, 229-30, 233, 235, 240-43, 247, 251, 254-57, 261-66
Epicurus 48
Epitherses 62-64
Er 22
Eusebius Pamphilus 28, 157-58

F

Factoring 49-50, 283
Faith is a gift 6-7, 14, 34, 60, 155-56, 159-60, 169, 184, 189, 219-20, 226, 230, 235, 237-38, 247, 253, 257-58, 263-64
First Fruits, Feast of ... 26, 32, 65, 118, 203-04
Fermat, Pierre 8, 37
Force, Pierre 6, 35, 38-40, 258-60
Fortino, Eleuterio 239
Free will 6, 16, 33, 35-36, 56, 119, 160, 166, 173, 214-68
Future, liquidity of the 36, 215, 231-33, 282

G

Gabriel, the angel 112, 133
Galilee 66, 127, 129, 131-32, 234
Gazier, Augustin 37
Germanus, Bishop of Paris, Saint ...13
Geyer, Paul 12
Gillet, Archimandrite Lev 71
God's
    Essence 57, 233
    foreknowledge 35-36, 78, 217, 221-22, 231-35, 246-47, 249-51, 256, 261, 266-68, 282
    Uncreated Divine Energies 233, 251, 256, 268
    will 6, 14-15, 18-21, 26, 37, 49-50, 54, 61, 77, 83, 104, 166, 169, 210, 214, 227, 233-35, 241, 266, 279-80
Grace
    Augustine and 6, 34, 229-30
    efficacious 6, 11, 14, 34-36, 38-39, 240-41, 244, 250-51, 253, 255, 257, 259, 261, 266
    the Holy Fire and 143-46
    Jansenists and 6, 14, 240-41
    Jesuits and 242-43
    Molinists and 38, 242-43
    Orthodox Church and 36, 222-40, 243, 246-47, 266-68
    Pascal and 6, 14, 35-39, 42, 164-67, 227, 247, 250-52, 255-66
    Paul and 216-17, 220
    Semi-Pelagians and 36, 38
Great Pan is dead 19, 61-65
Gregory of Nazianzus, Saint 34
Gregory of Nyssa, Saint ..34, 209, 226

Gregory Palamas, Saint 34, 233, 239-40
Gross, Jules 239
Guroian, Vigen 239

H

Hacking, Ian 37
Hald, Anders 37
Harakas, Stanley S. 239
Harrison, Verna 239
Harvest, Feast of 204-05
Helena, Saint 27-28, 151, 157-59, 280
Heli 71
Hermes 63
Herod, King 19, 53, 65-66
Hezekiah, King 36, 232, 267
Hidden God 39, 225, 252, 261-62
Hillel 134, 188
Himmerich, Maurice Fred 239
Holy Sepulcher 28-29, 77, 141-49, 158, 280
Hoshama 69
Hugh the Great 13
Hvidt, Niels Christian 147-49

I

Ingathering 68, 132, 207-09
Irenaeus, Saint 70-71, 209
Irene, Empress 13
Iscariot, Judas 133, 231, 246

J

Jacob 9, 24, 56, 67-68, 74, 81, 83, 110, 130, 150-53, 184-85, 244
Jairus' daughter 26, 99, 103, 116, 118, 122, 131, 251
James, the apostle 123, 126
Jansenism 6, 16, 37-39, 42, 171, 240-41, 263-66
Jansenius, Cornelius 38, 214, 230, 240, 244, 247, 261, 263-64
Jecamiah 69
Jeconiah 69-71
Jeffrey, Grant R. 22, 78-79, 283
Jehoiachin 69-71
Jehoiakim 69-70
Jerome 33
Jerusalem Talmud 76, 135, 138-39
Jesuits 11, 33, 38, 152, 160, 222, 240-43
Jewish Feast Days 31-33, 195, 202-11, 281
Joachim 69-70
Joanna 128
Jonah 196
Jones, Cheslyn 239
Joseph of Arimathea 125, 166
Josiah 69
Judah, Tamar's father-in-law 22
Judas' betrayal 133, 231, 246
Juli, Stephen James 239
Julian, Emperor 158
Justinian I, Emperor 13

K

Kolakowski, Leszek 37-39, 229, 261-63

Index

L

Lactantius 157
Laporte, Jean Marie Fréderic 37
Latin Vulgate's mistranslation of Rom 5:12 .... 33-34, 165, 229-30, 266
Lazarus 26, 99, 103, 116, 123-25, 132, 251
Leo III, Pope 13
Leucippus 48
Levels of biblical interpretation 51-57, 76, 83, 117, 140, 163
Levi, Anthony 42, 214, 264
Lightfoot, John 73-74
Lossky, Vladimir 239
Lot-Borodine, Myrrha 239
Louis IX, King of France, Saint 13
Lucretius 48-49

M

Macarius, Bishop of Jerusalem 158
Macarius of Egypt, Saint 208, 224, 228, 269n14
Magi, three 121, 133
Magic 27, 160-63, 167-68
Maimonides, Moses 19, 50-51, 181-82
Makarios of Corinth, Saint 240
Malchiram 69
Mantzaridis, Georgios I. 239
Martha, sister of Lazarus 123-24
Mary, Mother of Christ 19, 53, 65-66, 69, 71-72, 121, 125, 133, 223-24
Mary, mother of James 128
Mary, sister of Lazarus 123-24
Mary Magdalene 128, 151
Maximus the Confessor, Saint 34, 239

Melchizedek 30-31, 93, 96, 183
Mély, Fernand de 12
Memorial 9, 149-56
Meshach 31, 192, 281
Mesnard, Jean 165, 171-73
Meyendorff, John 239-40
Minatios, Elias, Bishop 36, 230-33, 246, 267, 281
Miracle of the Holy Flame . 27-29, 77, 141-149
Miracle of the Holy Thorn 10-14, 26-27, 35, 39, 60, 149, 160, 165, 263, 279
Miracles in the Temple 76-77, 135-39, 280
Miracles vs. magic 27, 160-63, 167-68
Mistranslation of Rom 5:12 in the Latin Vulgate 7, 33-35, 165, 211, 226, 229-30, 256-57
Molina, Luis de 242
Molinists 38, 242-43
Moriarty, Michael 38
Mosaic Law 21, 32, 196, 199
Moses vs. Pharaoh 27, 160-64, 198
Mount Athos 236-38

N

Naomi 150
Nathan 71-72
Nathaniel, the apostle 129, 234
Nazarii of Valamo 225
Nebuchadnezzar ..31, 69, 111, 192-93, 281
Nedabiah 69
Nellas, Panayiotis 240
Neusner, Jacob 76
New Year's Day 205-06, 210

Nicodemus 107, 155, 162, 166-67, 190, 252, 254-55
Night of fire, Pascal's 9, 149-57
Nobility of man 15
Norman, Keith Edward 240

O

Obed 21
O'Connell, Marvin R. .40-41, 150-51, 227-28
Onan 22
Opposites 57-61
Oracle of Delphi 233
Ore, Oystein 37
Origen 12
Orthodox Church
    and free will 33-37, 217-27, 230-37, 243, 246-49, 251-53, 255-57, 266-68, 281-82
    and grace 36, 222-40, 243, 246-47, 266-68
    and Lazarus 26, 116, 125
    and the liquidity of the future ..36, 215, 231-33, 282
    and the Miracle of the Holy Flame 27-29, 77, 141-49
    and theosis 15, 40-41, 120, 139, 152, 173, 196, 203, 215, 218, 226, 235-40, 248-50, 261, 266-68

P

Palestinian Talmud 76, 135, 138-39
Pan 19, 61-65
Pantheism 14-15, 233
Papademetriou, George 240

Pascal
    The Art of Persuasion 227, 260
    Essay on Conics 7
    heresies .15-16, 34-35, 37, 39, 42, 159-60, 225, 240-44, 247-57
    inventions 7-8
        Law of Pressure 8
    night of fire 9, 149-56
    Thoughts 6, 11, 23, 34, 39, 115, 214, 264
    Writings on Grace 34, 42, 255-57, 259
Pascaline 7-8
Passions 40-42, 220, 227, 229, 238, 256, 259-62
Passover 32, 134, 188, 201-03, 210
Paul, Saint 26, 32-35, 71, 117-18, 122, 125, 135, 140, 151, 198-201, 203-04, 208-09, 215-23, 227, 231-32, 237, 247, 267, 282
Paulinus of Nola, Saint 12, 28, 159
Peddaiah 69
Pelagians 36, 38
Penelope 63
Perez 22
Périer, Gilberte 9-10
Périer, Louis 149
Périer, Marguerite 11
Personal God .. 7, 10, 60, 149-51, 153, 204, 223-24
Peter, Saint .... 26, 35, 53, 123, 126, 128-35, 189, 199, 204 -05, 217, 236, 268, 282
Pharaoh 27, 160-64, 198
Philip, the apostle 154, 234
Philokalia 41-42, 226-27, 236-40, 261, 268

Index

Philotheos of Sinai, Saint 238
Photius, Saint 34
Plato's cave 59
Plutarch 19, 61-65
Port Royal 9, 11, 13, 27, 37, 149, 160, 165, 279
Predestinarianism 240-41, 250
Predestination 10-11, 14-16, 27, 33-38, 160, 165, 214-68
Probability . 6-8, 15-16, 19, 26, 37, 39, 49-51, 54, 60-61, 77, 84, 136, 152 155, 169, 210, 258, 263, 279-80, 282-83
Prophecies fulfilled by Christ ... 6-7, 9, 15-16, 18-20, 23-26, 30, 37, 39, 48-84, 93-114, 120-21, 140, 169-70, 173, 180, 193, 201, 210, 233, 249, 251, 258, 261-63, 279-83
    as a sheep before her shearers is dumb 17, 23, 106, 190
    Bethlehem will be birthplace of one whose goings forth have been from old, from everlasting 19, 25, 52, 65-66, 113, 126, 154, 191
    betrayed by a friend . 18, 127, 133, 231, 246, 282
    blood money thrown to the potter in God's house 18, 282
    bore our sins 12, 96, 203
    born in Bethlehem . 18-19, 23, 25, 52, 61, 65-66, 113, 154, 251, 254, 282-83
    borne our griefs ... 17, 23, 48, 105, 189
    bring light to the blind . 20, 39, 53, 72, 98-99, 123, 131-32, 141, 164, 192, 228, 231, 248
    brought as a lamb to the slaughter 17, 23, 32, 74, 76, 84, 104, 106, 136, 189-90, 199, 201-03, 210
    bruised for our iniquities ... 17, 23, 48, 106-07, 189-90
    carried our sorrows 17, 23, 48, 105, 189
    cast lots for His clothing 23-24, 95, 251
    conversion of the Gentiles 18-24, 51, 64, 73, 75, 79-82, 94, 98, 101-05, 108-10, 113-14, 125, 127, 130, 155, 183-88, 205, 210, 248
    Crucifixion scene ... 18, 24-25, 82, 94-95, 104-07, 114, 186-90
    darken the earth on a clear day 24, 82, 104, 111, 134, 187
    despised and abhorred 23, 48, 103, 105, 186, 189
    encompassed by enemies 24-25, 94-95
    enter Jerusalem on a donkey ... 18, 22, 79, 114, 282-83
    exalted 18, 183, 188
    forgiveness of sin 16-17, 50, 103-04, 116, 118-19, 121, 130, 139-40, 155, 172, 188-89, 191-92, 197, 202, 205
    give back to smiters ... 23, 80, 104, 188
    given gall and vinegar to drink 23, 95
    hair plucked off cheeks 23, 104, 188
    hands and feet pierced . 18, 23-26, 74, 95, 114, 129, 181, 188, 251

heart melted like wax ..18, 24, 48, 95
King comes having salvation 20, 24, 79, 102, 104, 108, 114, 184-89, 200-10 passim,............... 217, 219, 226-27
kings and princes will worship Him .. 20, 24, 79-82, 103, 105, 109, 185-88
lowly and riding an ass, and upon a colt the foal of an ass .24, 114
made his grave with the wicked and with the rich in his death ...23, 107, 190
man of sorrows 17, 23, 48, 105, 189
mourning of an only son 18, 24, 80, 114, 181
New Covenant .. 16-17, 20, 74-75, 110, 113, 120, 137, 153, 155, 192
pierced 18, 23-26, 74, 95, 114, 129, 181, 188, 251
preceded by a messenger.....18, 24, 114, 282
rejected 23, 48, 96-99, 102-05 108, 110, 127, 187, 189, 207, 251
Resurrection on third day ..18, 23, 54, 94-95, 113, 126-28, 132, 210, 251
sent to bind up the brokenhearted 24, 109, 140-41, 191-92, 228
silent before accusers 18, 104, 106, 282
sold for thirty pieces of silver ..18, 24, 114
spat at 23, 80, 82, 104, 128, 188

sprinkle many nations 20, 23, 105, 188
sun will go down at noon ..24, 82, 111
taken from prison and from judgment 23, 107, 190
virgin birth 23, 61, 69-70, 251
visage marred 23, 105, 188
will be Mighty God,
Everlasting Father 23, 97, 126
will sit on the right hand of the Father 24, 30-31, 54, 56-57, 96, 182-83, 193, 198, 251
wounded for our transgressions 17, 23, 48, 106, 189
P'shat (pashat, peshat) 52-56, 76, 140

Q

Quirinius 66

R

Red heifer, sacrifice of the . 17, 31-32, 82, 106-07, 187, 189, 196-99
Remez 53, 55
Resurrection
of Christ 9, 23, 26, 28-29, 31-32, 54, 63, 77, 82-83, 95, 109, 116-18, 123-29, 132-35, 183, 189-91, 196, 199, 203-06, 208-10, 217, 280
of Jairus' daughter 26, 99, 103, 116, 118, 122, 131, 251
of Lazarus 26, 99, 103, 116, 123-25, 132, 251
of OT saints 26, 82, 116-17

Index

of widow's son at Nain 26, 116, 130, 251
Rodger, Symeon 240
Rogers, Ben 259
Rosh Hashanah 205-06
Rufinus 28, 158
Ruth 21-22, 150

S

Saint-Corneille of Compiègne, Abbey 13
Saint-Cyran, Jean Duvergier de Hauranne, the Abbot of . 37-38, 214, 240, 242, 247, 263-64
Sainte-Beuve, Charles-Augustin 37
Salathiel 69
Salome 128
Sartorius, Bernard 240
Sea of Galilee 131
Sea of Tiberius 26, 129, 204
Second Coming of Christ . 55-56, 101, 183-85, 187, 202, 205-10
Sellier, Philippe 23, 38, 165, 258
Semi-Pelagians 36, 38
Seraphim of Sarov, Saint 225, 235
Shadrach 31, 192, 281
Shelah 22
Shema 29, 54, 180-81
Shenazar 69
Sheol 117-18
Shiloh prophecy 67-68, 77, 80, 83, 93
Simon Peter 26, 35, 53, 123, 126, 128-35, 189, 199, 204-05, 217, 236, 268, 282
Skeptic, persuading the 6-7, 9, 14, 28, 30, 36, 38-42, 48-51, 60-61, 159, 210, 214, 227, 258-65, 282

Society of Jesus ..11, 33, 38, 152, 160, 222, 240-43
Socrates Scholasticus 28, 158
Sod 53-54, 83, 140
Son of God 31, 56-57, 81, 96-97, 124, 134, 154, 156, 192-93, 234, 281
Sorcery 27, 160-63, 167-68
Sozomen 28, 158
Spinoza, Benedict de 14
Stăniloae, Dumitru 240
Statistical probability ..6-8, 15-16, 19, 26, 37, 39, 49-51, 54, 60-61, 77, 84, 136, 152, 155, 169, 210, 258, 263, 279-80, 282-838
Stavropoulos, Archimandrite Christoforos 225-26, 228-29, 236, 240
Stephen, stoning of 135, 234
Stoner, Peter W. 51, 84, 282-83
Strabo 64
Sukkot 68, 132, 207-09
Sulpicius Severus 28, 159
Symeon the New Theologian, Saint 34
Synagogue as a type of the Church 36, 218, 222-23, 231-32, 257, 266-67

T

Tabernacles, Feast of . 68, 132, 207-09
Talmud
    Babylonian 76, 135, 139, 280
    Palestinian (Jerusalem) 76, 135, 138-39
Tamar 21-22
Telepneff, Gregory 240
Thales 48
Thamus 62-63
Theodocretus 28

Theophan the Recluse, Saint 225
Theosis 15, 40-41, 120, 139, 152, 173, 196, 203, 215, 218, 226, 235-40, 248-50, 261, 266-68
Thirouin, Laurent 37
Thomas, the apostle 26, 115, 129
Thornton, James 240
Three magi 121, 133
Tiberius Caesar 63
Tobias, Robert 240
Todhunter, Isaac 37
Trumpets, Feast of 205-06, 210
Types 6, 15-16, 31-32, 68, 170, 173, 196-211, 279, 281

U

Unity of the OT and NT 6-7, 15-16, 26, 31-33, 37, 196-211, 214, 279-81
Universe, inanimate and insensate 14-15
Ussher, James 73

V

Vassiliades, Nicolaos P. 240
Vicious cycle 6, 35-37, 231, 257-58

W

Wager 39-41, 260, 265
Wainwright, Geoffrey 239
Ware, Timothy (Bishop Kallistos Ware) 77, 142, 222-25, 233, 240, 243, 281
Weeks, Feast of 204-05
Wesley, John 83, 182, 197-98

Will of God 6, 14-15, 18-21, 26, 37, 49-50, 54, 61, 77, 83, 104, 166, 169, 210, 214, 227, 233-35, 241, 266, 279-80
Wirth, Nicklaus 8
Worship of Christ 17, 20, 24, 57, 74, 79, 81, 84, 96, 99, 102-04, 108, 114, 121 22, 185-88
Wretchedness of man 57-58, 153, 165

Y

Yarnold, Edward 176-77n40, 239
Yom Kippur . 17, 136-37, 183, 206-07, 280

Z

Zakkai, Rabban Yohanan ben 138
Zebedee, sons of 129
Zedekiah 69
Zerah 22